THE SEAGULL READER

Poems

Third Edition

W. W. Norton & Company, Inc., also publishes

THE SEAGULL READER: STORIES, Third Edition

THE SEAGULL READER: ESSAYS, Second Edition

THE SEAGULL READER: PLAYS, Third Edition

THE SEAGULL READER: LITERATURE, Third Edition

THE SEAGULL READER

Poems

Third Edition

edited by Joseph Kelly

College of Charleston

W. W. Norton & Company, Inc. · New York · London

To Hannah Kelly

Copyright © 2015, 2008, 2001 by W. W. Norton & Company, Inc.

All rights reserved.

Printed in the United States of America.

The text of this book is composed in Adobe Garamond
with the display set in Bernhard Modern.
Composition by Cenveo, Inc.
Manufacturing by Courier-Westford.
Book design by Chris Welch.
Production manager: Ashley Horna.

Library of Congress Cataloging-in-Publication Data

The Seagull reader. Poems / edited by Joseph Kelly, College of Charleston.—Third edition.

pages cm

Includes index.

ISBN **978-0-393-93822-7** (pbk.)

1. English poetry. 2. American poetry. 3. College readers. I. Kelly, Joseph, 1962– editor.

PR1175.S388   2015

821.008—dc23   2014044156

W. W. Norton & Company, Inc., 500 Fifth Avenue, New York, N.Y. 10110
www.wwnorton.com

W. W. Norton & Company Ltd., Castle House, 75/76 Wells Street,
London W1T 3QT

1 2 3 4 5 6 7 8 9 0

Contents

✳

Acknowledgments

I owe a great debt to John Ruszkiewicz, which this acknowledgment barely begins to discharge. I want to thank Susan Farrell for her help and kindness. And I must mention also Scott Dupree, who first taught me much of what I have contributed to this book.

Along with the publisher, I am happy to thank the following for their assistance during various stages of this project:

For the third edition: Troy Appling (Florida Gateway College), Jason Brown (Herkimer Community College), Patrick Callan (Monroe Community College), William Bedford Clark (Texas A&M University), Paul Cockeram (Harrisburg Area Community College), Linda DeFelice (Glouster Community College), James Donahue (SUNY Potsdam), Michael Given (Stephan F. Austin State University), Anthony Holsten (Pitt Community College), Laura Howes (University of Tennessee), Betty LaFace (Bainbridge College), Alison Langdon (Western Kentucky University), Luke Leonard (Brevard Community College), Mary McKinlay (University of Dubuque), John Morillo (North Carolina State University), Roxanna Pisiak (SUNY Morrisville), Keri Sanburn Behr (Marylhurst University), Ritu Sharma (Lake Erie College), Amie Siedman (Bainbridge College), Kenneth Untiedt (Stephen F. Austin State University), and Deborah Zeringue (Florida Gateway college).

For the first and second editions: Cieltia Adams (Nicholls State University), Lori Alfe (Rock Valley College), Bruce Beasley (Western Washington University), Mary Behrman (Emory University), David Bergman (Towson University), Michael Bibby (Shippensburg University), John Bienz (Mount Union College), Darl Biniaz

(Dixie State College of Utah), Margaret Boerner (Villanova University), Sr. Brigid Brady (Caldwell College), James Brewbaker (Columbus State University), Nick Carbó (Florida International University), Anne Caston (University of Alaska, Anchorage), Michael Cherry (Bowling Green State University), Howell Chickering (Amherst College), T. Coakley (Mount Aloysius College), Linda Coblentz (University of Houston Downtown), David Craig (Franciscan University of Steubenville), Ashley Cross (Manhattan College), Ashley Crump (Nicholls State University), Steven Daniels (Southern Methodist University), Mark Defoe (West Virginia Wesleyan College), Erika Deiters (Moraine Valley Community College), Sandra M. Doe (Metropolitan State College of Denver), Ellen Dolgin (Dominican College of Blauvelt), Daniel Donaghy (Elizabeth City State University), Ronald L. Dotterer (Salisbury University), Theresa Dougal (Moravian College), Jeremy Downes (Auburn University), Scott Dransfield (Southern Virginia University), Bart Edelman (Glendale College), Gregory Eiselein (Kansas State University), B. Elfert (Nicholls State University), Edmund L. Epstein (Queens College, CUNY), Darlene Erickson (Ohio Dominican University), Logan Esdale (Chapman University), Deirdre Fagan (Quincy University), Sascha Feinstein (Lycoming College), Jessica Feldman (University of Virginia), Norman Finkelstein (Xavier University), Johanna Fisher (Buffalo State College, SUNY), Dennis Flynn (Bentley College), Ernest Fontana (Xavier University), Mark K. Fulk (Buffalo State College, SUNY), Melissa Garner (Nicholls State University), Lara Gary (Sacramento City College), Rebecca K. Gibson (Tufts University), Melissa Girard (University of Illinois at Urbana-Champaign), Nancy K. Gish (University of Southern Maine), Alexander G. Gonzalez (Cortland College, SUNY), Hugh R. Goodheart (Westminster Choir College of Rider University), Paul Grady (Los Angeles Harbor College), Kate Gray (Clackamas Community College), Joseph Green (Lower Columbia College), Sayre Greenfield (University of Pittsburgh, Greensburg), Debora Greger (University of Florida), R. S. Gwynn (Lamar University), Hannah Haas (Indiana University–Purdue University, Indianapolis), Rachel Hadas (Rutgers University, Newark), Corrinne Hales (California State University, Fresno), Kathy Heininge (George Fox University), Phil Hey (Briar Cliff University), Lisa Higgins

(College of DuPage), Scott Hightower (New York University), Perry Higman (Eastern Washington University), John Hildebidle (M.I.T.), Rick Hilles (Vanderbilt University), Janet Holmes (Boise State University), Arthur Homer (University of Nebraska, Omaha), Ann Hostetler (Goshen College), Sherry Howard (Northwest State Community College), George Hudson (Colgate University), Luisa Igloria (Old Dominion University), Claudia Ingram (University of Redlands), James Irons (College of Southern Idaho), Kristen Isabelle (Columbia-Greene Community College), Tammy Jabin (Chemeketa Community College), Jackie W. Jackson (Nicholls State University), Kathleen Jacquette (Farmingdale State University of New York), Barbara L. Janoff (Fashion Institute of Technology), Frank Jordan (University of Scranton), Pierre Joris (SUNY, Albany), Jeannie Judge (University of Massachusetts, Lowell), Philip H. Kelly (Gannon University), George Killough (College of St. Scholastica), Peter E. Knox (University of Colorado), Virginia Kouidis (Auburn University), Joseph Kronick (Louisiana State University), Martin Lammon (Georgia College & State University), Marjory Lange (Western Oregon University), Joseph Lemrow (Southwestern Michigan College), Wallis Leslie (De Anza College), Mark Levine (University of Iowa), Ellen Levy (Vanderbilt University), John Lewis (Southern Methodist University), Stephen E. Lewis (Franciscan University of Steubenville), Paul Lindholdt (Eastern Washington University), James Loucks (Ohio State University, Newark), Helen Marlborough (Depaul University), Charles J. Marr (Edinboro University of Pennsylvania), Carlos Martinez (Western Washington University), John Mason (SUNY, Albany), Johnnie Clemens May (Glendale Community College), Rosemary McNeil (Carl Sandburg College), Lewis Meyers (Hunter College), Feisal Mohamed (Texas Tech University), James J. Mooney (Immaculata University), Berwyn Moore (Gannon University), Drew Morse (John Carroll University), Jonathan Morse (University of Hawaii at Manoa), Nicholas Moschovakis (Reed College), Laura Mullen (Louisiana State University), Stephen Myers (Desales University), James Najarian (Boston College), Amy Nawrocki (University of Bridgeport), Beth Newman (Southern Methodist University), Mel Nichols (George Mason University), Teddy Norris (St. Charles Community College), Onno Oerlemans (Hamilton College), Catherine O'Neil (United States

Naval Academy), Jacqueline Osherow (University of Utah), James Papworth (Brigham Young University, Idaho), Kathleen Peirce (Texas State University), Bob Perelman (University of Pennsylvania), Jim Sanderson (Lamar University), June Sylvester Saraceno (Sierra Nevada College), Jeff Schiff (Columbia College, Chicago), Louis Schwartz (University of Richmond), Maureen Seaton (University of Miami), Eric Selinger (Depaul University), John N. Serio (Clarkson University), Diane Seuss (Kalamazoo College), Nicholas Sharp (Virginia Commonwealth University), Stephen Shepherd (Loyola Marymount University), Loretta Shpunt (Trinity University DC), Maurya Simon (University of California, Riverside), Zak Sitter (Xavier University), Stanley Solomon (Fashion Institute of Technology), Renee Soto (Roger Williams University), James Soular (Flathead Valley Community College), Michael Stuprich (Ithaca College), Ernest Suarez (Catholic University of America), Marianne Taylor (Kirkwood Community College), R. S. Tomlinson (Richland Community College), Jeremy Trabue (Chemeketa Community College), Hugh Tribbey (East Central University), Terry Tricomi (Berkeley City College), Tony Trigilio (Columbia College, Chicago), Jane Vandervelde (University of Kansas), Lawrence Venuti (Temple University), Anthony Vital (Transylvania University), Jennifer Wagner (West Valley College), Beth Wallace (Boston College), William Wallis (Los Angeles Valley College), Kathleene West (New Mexico State University), Patrick Whitfill (Texas Tech University), Lucette Wood (Linnbenton Community College), Robert Wrigley (University of Idaho), Andrea Zemgulys (University of Michigan), and Sander Zulauf (County College of Morris).

Note on Dates

After each poem, we cite the date of first book publication on the right, in some instances, this date is followed by the date of a revised version for which the author was responsible. In a few instances (when the information may be relevant to the reading of a poem), we cite the date of composition on the left.

✶

What Is Poetry?

When we listen to most music, we hear poetry's most popular form: song. In fact, lyrics that are set to music might be considered the most *poetic* of all **poems**, because anything written in meter is poetry, and we can best define meter as music. In the lines of poetry, stressed and unstressed syllables rise and fall with a musical lilt. These rhythms are most obvious in songs: we've all sometimes felt the spell, the almost physical power, in the music of our favorite lyrics. When we replay the lyrics of a favorite song in our heads, we often remember the band's music and the singer's voice. And if we say the lines aloud, we often even mimic the rhythms given to them by the band and singer. If you're familiar with Bruce Springsteen's "The River," when you read his lyrics on page 295, the music of the recording probably will invade your mind. The song's power will reach you through the tones of the harmonica or through your memory of Springsteen's unique singing style.

Literary poems, including those printed here, have this disadvantage: no instruments play the rhythm and no singer conveys the phrasing. The music can come to you through your own voice only. Try reading aloud these lines from the end of Alfred Tennyson's "Ulysses":

> *Though much is taken, much abides; and though*
> *We are not now that strength which in old days*
> *Moved earth and heaven; that which we are, we are,*
> *One equal temper of heroic hearts,*

Made weak by time and fate, but strong in will
To strive, to seek, to find, and not to yield.

Read it two or three more times, slowly, letting the rhythms settle themselves in your speech. Leaving aside any consideration of the words' meaning, their sound has a pleasure and a musical power. The meter directs you to say the lines a certain way. We can hear the difference from prose, even literary prose. Consider this passage for comparison:

> The *Nellie*, a cruising yawl, swung to her anchor without a flutter of the sails and was at rest. The flood had made, the wind was nearly calm, and being bound down the river the only thing for it was to come to and wait for the turn of the tide.

These lines, from the opening of Joseph Conrad's *Heart of Darkness*, capture the elegance and pleasure of natural speech at its best. But they are not musical, not in the way Tennyson's are.

If ever you've been moved to tears by a song, if you have a favorite track you blast in the car with the windows rolled down in the sun, or if listening to a good song can change your mood, then you have a talent for poetry. And who does not? No matter how educated or unsophisticated, we all know the pleasure of listening to song. The root of that pleasure may be a mystery, but we all know it's true: that words wrestled into music have a charm and power ordinary language does not.

Like most descriptions of literary genres, this definition is fuzzy. Some prose writers do write in an almost musical style, while some poets consciously suppress the music in their poems. But roughly speaking, the definition will serve our needs: poetry is writing that sounds musical. A **lyric poem** is a short poem. There's no specific length requirement. We call a poem a lyric if it's about the size of a song. Of course, some songs are longer than others, so the division between lyrics and narratives can blur. And we can divide lyric poetry into more genres, like the **sonnet**, **dramatic monologue**, **elegy**, **ode**, and **ballad**. These special genres are defined in the section devoted to the structure of poetry.

How Do You Read Poems?

The literary forms that you know well, whether they're movies or TV shows or novels or popular songs, have laid the groundwork for reading poems. Songs, whose conventions you probably have been internalizing your whole life, are especially close to the poems in this volume. When you learn to interpret poems, you are not learning new skills so much as becoming more aware of what you already do pretty well. But as you become more aware, you'll find yourself able to handle these analytical tools with more precision and confidence.

Speaker

Every lyric poem has a **speaker**. You should imagine that every poem is a little speech by a real person: the speaker. Sometimes, the speaker's identity is a total mystery, but usually a poem will give you some clues. More often than not, it will tell you a lot about the speaker. The first thing to do when you analyze a poem is define the speaker as precisely as you can. For example, take this poem by William Wordsworth:

> She dwelt among the untrodden ways
>   Beside the springs of Dove,
> A Maid whom there were none to praise
>   And very few to love;
>
> A violet by a mossy stone
>   Half hidden from the eye!
> —Fair as a star, when only one
>   Is shining in the sky.
>
> She lived unknown, and few could know
>   When Lucy ceased to be;
> But she is in her grave, and, oh,
>   The difference to me.

The speaker tells very little about himself, but we can speculate about him. In fact, it's really speculation to say the speaker is male. He sounds like he was in love with Lucy and perhaps was courting her. From the way he describes Lucy we might further guess that he was a little older than she was, perhaps he is a bit cosmopolitan, probably he has seen some of the world. But even if he's seen some of the world, we also might assume that he's lived near the Dove River or that he's had a reason to spend some time on the "untrodden ways," or he never would have discovered Lucy himself.

We are often tempted to associate the speaker with the singer or poet, and sometimes this works. Some poems are obviously autobiographical. Poems from the Romantic era especially often invite us to equate the speaker with the poet. But it is good practice to assume that the speaker is a fictional persona unless you have evidence to prove otherwise. In other words, don't say, "William Wordsworth loved a girl named Lucy, but she died before he ever married her." In this case, though Wordsworth is a Romantic poet and did write many autobiographical poems, "She Dwelt Among the Untrodden Ways" does not tell a "true" story. We should always begin by assuming the poet is playing a role.

Audience and Rhetorical Situation

If every poem has a speaker, you might logically assume that every poem also has a listener or **audience**. Ultimately, of course, anyone who reads the poem is the audience, just as anyone who hears a song in concert or streamed online is the singer's audience. But as a literary term, *audience* has a specialized meaning. It is the character(s) or persona(e) whom the speaker is addressing.

In Wordsworth's poem, we have a much tougher time defining the audience than the speaker. This is not always the case. Most love poems, for example, are addressed to the speaker's lover. Turn to page 12 and look at Matthew Arnold's "Dover Beach." From clues in the poem we can guess that the audience is the speaker's beloved.

We can also determine the **rhetorical situation** of "Dover Beach," what occasions the speaker to address the audience in these words. We might guess that the speaker and his audience are newlyweds, because many English couples in the nineteenth century spent their wedding night at Dover and then took the ferry to the Continent for their honeymoon. Whether the speaker and his lover are embarking on a honeymoon or not, they seem to be on a vacation, because the speaker marvels at the seascape in a way that a local probably wouldn't. He and his lover may be in a cottage or house or a hotel room. We can't be sure, but we know they are inside some building, because they are looking out a window at the ocean.

In Wordsworth's poem, we don't have many clues about the rhetorical situation. The speaker's audience doesn't know Lucy, but he or she seems to be on fairly intimate terms with the speaker because the speaker is unburdening his grief. Perhaps the audience is the speaker's close friend, someone from the city far from Lucy's home near Dove River. But where are they? Are they talking late at night before a hearth fire? Are they old men recounting their youth and their regrets? We don't really know.

The first couple of times you read a poem, you should focus on these three elements: speaker, audience, and rhetorical situation. Try to figure out the story of the poem, who is speaking to whom on what occasion. If you read a poem that confuses you, guess who the speaker is. Then try out your hypothesis by rereading the poem. You'll probably have to adjust your idea. That's normal. Even professional critics have to reread poems to understand them. Keep rereading until you're confident you know who the speaker is and to whom he or she is talking.

Paraphrase

The next thing you should do is make sure you understand the literal level of the poem: the basic meaning of the speaker's words. Some poems, like Wordsworth's, are so clear that you don't have to **paraphrase** at all. But most poems have at least a few lines that are challenging to figure out even on the literal level. Let's look again at Matthew Arnold's "Dover Beach," for example. The first eight lines are straightforward. If you read them slowly and carefully, you will probably understand the literal level. The following lines are a little more difficult:

Listen! you hear the grating roar
Of pebbles which the waves draw back, and fling,
At their return, up the high strand,
Begin, and cease, and then again begin,
With tremulous cadence slow, and bring
The eternal note of sadness in.

Arnold is taxing our sense of grammar to its limits. It helps, of course, to know that *strand* is an English word for "beach." A good dictionary would tell you that, and a good dictionary is an indispensable tool for reading poetry. But even knowing the meaning of *strand* doesn't clear things up totally. Where does that "Begin, and cease" belong, for example? Does the "you" in the first line begin and cease and then again begin?

By translating these lines into your own language, you can usually clear up those grammatical confusions. Here's one paraphrase of Arnold's lines:

> Listen to the loud noise of the pebbles. When the waves go out they drag the pebbles out to sea, and when the waves come crashing back they throw the pebbles up on the beach. You can hear the noise of the pebbles begin and stop and begin again, almost like they are beating out a slow rhythm. The sound they make makes me feel sad.

A paraphrase should be as straightforward as this. You should be able to read it aloud to your roommate, and your roommate should understand perfectly, without the slightest confusion, everything you say. If something in your paraphrase sounds a little unclear, then you should try again.

Note that this paraphrase used sixty-six words to express in prose what Arnold said in forty-one words of poetry. That's typical. Poetry is economical. In a paraphrase, you should expect to use at least one and a half times as many words as the poet, and you should suspect you've omitted some important details if you use fewer. Notice also that this paraphrase broke Arnold's single sentence into four sentences. This technique of separating out the details can help you see the big picture. For instance, after paraphrasing the second and third lines of the selection from Arnold's poem you may be able to see that "you" did not "Begin, and cease." Those verbs simply complete the thought that begins with these words: "you hear the grating roar / Of pebbles." Everything in between is an interruption. When you skip the interruption, the sentence makes more sense: "Listen! you can hear the grating roar / Of pebbles . . . / Begin, and cease, and then again begin."

You don't need to paraphrase every line of a poem. When you read through a poem, you should mark the parts that don't seem to make sense to you grammatically. Then go back and spend some time paraphrasing those lines. Be sure to trace the confusing lines back to the start of a sentence, and begin paraphrasing the lines there. You don't have to actually write the words down, but you should work them out in your head. When verbs seem to dangle by themselves, hunt down their subjects. When you see descriptive phrases, find out what thing they describe. Fill the margins of your book with the results, so you'll remember them.

Sometimes you'll find that you do have to write down the paraphrase. Sometimes, only by taking a pen to a blank piece of paper can you unravel the **syntax** of unclear lines. You should do this for any poem that you're writing a paper about, just to make sure that you understand the literal level perfectly, because the success of your interpretation hinges on accurately reading the poem's literal level. For example, to say that the speaker in "Dover Beach" is standing on the beach along the *French* coast rather than the *English* coast is just dead wrong. It would set your interpretation off in the wrong direction, and you would never get back on the right track.

After you've mastered the literal level of a poem, you should begin examining the **figurative levels**. As you read the poem over and over again, you'll begin to recognize how it communicates much more than what is conveyed literally. Through metaphors and patterns of images and symbols, even through the physical sound of the words, a poem conveys meanings that deepen and amplify the literal level. What might have seemed a flat piece of writing suddenly explodes into a third dimension, and you'll find your emotions and your intellect caught up in the complexities. The following sections should help you see, understand, and feel this dimension.

Tone

Tone in a poem is the same as tone in speech. When someone is talking to you, you unconsciously determine the tone of her voice. By visual clues, like facial expression, you determine her emotion, and that information helps you fully appreciate the meaning of her words. Take this dialogue, for example:

"How are you doing?"
"I'm doing all right, I guess."

Compare it to this version, which includes tonal clues:

"How are you doing?" he asked lightly.
"I'm doing all right," she said slowly, with a resigned look on her face. "I guess."

Sometimes, tone does not just contribute to the meaning of the words: it reverses the literal meaning. Someone asks you how you are doing, and you answer sarcastically, "I'm doing all right," and he knows that you are *not* doing all right. You convey the sarcasm through tonal qualities in your voice and maybe by rolling your eyes.

The text of a poem, of course, can use neither facial expression nor voice. Therefore, the tone of a poem is harder to detect than the tone of someone speaking to you. Nevertheless, with some careful attention, you should be able to determine the tone of the speaker in a poem, even though you cannot hear him or her.

Sometimes you might notice a difference between the speaker's tone and the poet's tone. In a poem like Gwendolyn Brooks's "We Real Cool," for example, we get a strong sense that the poet does not entirely approve of the speakers' swagger, especially when they nonchalantly conclude, "We / Die soon." Brooks's attitude is more knowing and more critical than the speakers'. When you recognize such a difference, you have detected **irony**. What the poet means is different from what the speaker means. Often the degree of irony in a poem is a matter of interpretation and debate. Does Ulysses speak for Tennyson in that dramatic monologue? Is Poe critical of the hypersensitive speaker in "The Raven"? These are matters that cannot be decided with finality, but it is nearly always useful to entertain the possibility that the speaker is ironized.

Imagery

An **image** is anything you see, hear, smell, touch, or taste in a poem. Anything concrete (to use a familiar metaphor) as opposed to abstract is an image. Images are the basic building blocks of just about any poem.

Consider these two poems, the first by A. E. Housman and the second by W. B. Yeats:

When I Was One-and-Twenty

When I was one-and-twenty
  I heard a wise man say
"Give crowns and pounds and guineas
  But not your heart away;
Give pearls away and rubies
  But keep your fancy free."
But I was one-and-twenty,
  No use to talk to me.

When I was one-and-twenty
  I heard him say again,
"The heart out of the bosom
  Was never given in vain;
'Tis paid with sighs a plenty
  And sold for endless rue."
And I am two-and-twenty,
  And oh, 'tis true, 'tis true.

Down by the Salley Gardens

Down by the salley gardens my love and I did meet;
She passed the salley gardens with little snow-white feet.
She bid me take love easy, as the leaves grow on the tree;
But I, being young and foolish, with her would not agree.

In a field by the river my love and I did stand,
And on my leaning shoulder she laid her snow-white hand.
She bid me take life easy, as the grass grows on the weirs;
But I was young and foolish, and now am full of tears.

The first poem doesn't give us many vivid images. Some vague pictures might come to your mind when you read them. You might picture a wise man speaking to a young man, though even that rhetorical situation is hardly described. There are some concrete nouns (currency and coins, hearts and bosoms) but for the most part the poem functions in the abstract. The lines do convey information (love leads to heartache), but they don't engage our imagination.

The second poem delivers the same information, but it conveys it through a series of evocative images: two young lovers meeting under willow trees; the woman is small, perhaps even frail in stature, with very white skin; we see the two argue, perhaps playfully; we see them by a river; we see the girl leaning her head on the speaker's shoulder; we see the speaker weeping. The final lines of the two poems will drive this point home: " 'The heart . . . / [is] sold for endless rue.' / And I am two-and-twenty, / And oh, 'tis true, 'tis true," compared to "But I was young and foolish, and now am full of tears." *Rue* is an abstraction; *tears* are an image.

If you read the two poems over and over again, you'll probably find yourself more attracted to the second. Housman's poem is pithy and witty, and, though it's light verse, perhaps it is laced with serious undertones. Yeats's poem conveys the same information about young lovers, but it interests us more. It excites our imagination and draws out our emotions. That's why poets use images more than abstractions.

Most poems lay out their images in a pattern. Take this poem by Robert Browning:

Home-Thoughts, from Abroad

I

Oh, to be in England
Now that April's there,
And whoever wakes in England

Sees, some morning, unaware,
That the lowest boughs and the brushwood sheaf
Round the elm-tree bole are in tiny leaf,
While the chaffinch sings on the orchard bough
In England—now!

2

And after April, when May follows,
And the whitethroat builds, and all the swallows!
Hark, where my blossomed peartree in the hedge
Leans to the field and scatters on the clover
Blossoms and dewdrops—at the bent spray's edge—
That's the wise thrush; he sings each song twice over,
Lest you should think he never could recapture
The first fine careless rapture!
And though the fields look rough with hoary dew,
All will be gay when noontide wakes anew
The buttercups, the little children's dower
—Far brighter than this gaudy melon flower!

The speaker, living or vacationing abroad, feels nostalgia for the springtime sights and sounds of his native country. It is a sentiment *anyone* from *anywhere* might feel when abroad for a long time, and it could be summed up by this short sentence: I miss home. But if we examine the images in this poem—the details the speaker chooses to mention—we can begin to see that the poem communicates much more than this universal statement of homesickness. We can detect a moral judgment about England.

Here are the images:

low branches with tiny new leaves
dense underbrush with tiny leaves surrounding the trunk of an
    elm
a chaffinch singing from the branch of a tree in a (pear?)
    orchard
a whitethroat building a nest
many swallows
the little white blossoms of a pear tree

a hedge
clover, sprinkled with pear blossoms
dewdrops on clover
a thrush singing
fields all white with dew
buttercups in a yard reserved for children

When we list these images, we can begin to see some commonalities among them. All of the images are natural, and nearly all are small. Buttercups, pear blossoms, and clover blossoms are all tiny flowers, yellow and white. We see small young leaves. The animals—a chaffinch, a whitethroat, swallows, and a thrush—are small songbirds. The only big image is an elm tree, and all we see of this is its trunk surrounded by bushes and its branches that hang down low. The combination of these images makes us feel that England is a place where everything is on a small scale, unthreatening, and comfortable. The only humans mentioned are children, and they along with the white flowers and young leaves and the little birds suggest an innocence, as if life in England were free of the complexities that plague grown-up life.

Contrasted to all of these images is the "gaudy melon flower" that concludes the poem. From what we know of Robert Browning's life, that flower is probably in Italy, but even without that knowledge we could guess that the speaker is in a semitropical locale where colors are brilliant, noises are loud, and the sun is blazing hot. If we think of the small, white pear blossom next to the colorful, big melon flower, we might even detect some sexual connotations. If England is the place of childhood's prepubescent innocence, the semitropical place abroad is associated in the speaker's mind with sexual knowledge, perhaps even promiscuity. The tropics themselves tend to have these connotations to people in colder climes, and Italy has long figured in the English imagination as a place where the staid, respectable English citizen can enjoy sensual pleasures. So the pattern of these concrete images—the generalizations that tie the specific images to each other—reveals an otherwise obscured theme in the poem.

It is especially important that you learn to track such patterns, because they're working on your unconscious mind whether you know it or not. Even if you had not recognized the qualities that the images in "Home-Thoughts, from Abroad" have in common, on some level you would have been *feeling* England's innocence and youthful wholesomeness, and you would have sensed the corruption of the locale abroad. It is good to be able to recognize consciously these manipulations of your unconscious mind. Certainly if you want to articulate how a poem affects you, you need to trace these patterns.

If you analyze the imagery of almost any poem, you're bound to find patterns like this. Obviously, you don't want to write out a column of images for every poem you read, nor should you. That would ruin the pleasure. But you should foster the habit of looking for these patterns. And for any poem you write about in an English class, you probably should actually write the images down.

Metaphors

A **metaphor** is a comparison. For example, *the ship plowed through the water* is a metaphor: a ship does not literally plow through water. The expression is a **figure of speech** that compares the way the ship's prow moves through water to the way a plow moves through soil. To interpret the metaphor, we imagine to ourselves the work a plow does: it throws the earth up to the side in long ridges as it digs a straight shallow furrow. The prow of the ship, then, must have been rolling up the water on either side in ridges higher than the level sea. And it must have left behind a shallow trough like a furrow in a plowed field.

Without even knowing it, your mind went through a short-hand version of this process when you first read the words *plowed through the water*. In an instant you pictured the water spurting up on either side of the ship's nose. More than likely, you skipped the step of picturing the plow in the earth. We've seen this metaphor so often in our lives that it has lost its ability to conjure up any comparison. The verb *plow* seems to have taken on a second literal meaning, so that it refers not only to what plows do but also to what prows do.

When a metaphor becomes so overused that it brings to our mind only one image rather than two, we call it a "dead metaphor" or a "cliché." You could hardly utter a dozen words without using one. *The Yankees got slaughtered last night* and *I was just cruising home when out of nowhere this ambulance flies through a red light* and *I'm dying to get those tickets* all use metaphors. A baseball team's loss is compared to the butchering of cattle or swine; a car is compared to a boat; an ambulance is compared to an airplane; and a person's eagerness is compared to a fatal illness. But these metaphors might as well be literal because they don't conjure up any figurative images anymore. To be slaughtered now literally means to be beaten badly in a game. To beat someone is itself a dead metaphor: no one pictures one team punching or clubbing the other team into submission.

But new, fresh metaphors will conjure up *two* images in your mind. Take these famous lines from T. S. Eliot's "The Love Song of J. Alfred Prufrock":

> *Let us go then, you and I,*
> *When the evening is spread out against the sky*
> *Like a patient etherized upon a table.*

We see two images here. One is the evening sky (which is *literally* there in the poem). The other is a body anesthetized and awaiting surgery (which is there in the poem *figuratively* but not literally). You might wonder how these two things could be compared. How can an evening be like a surgery patient? They seem to have nothing in common. By answering that question you interpret the metaphor. Remember to ask the correct question: we're not interested in how a patient can be like a sky, but in how a sky can be like a patient. The metaphor is about the literal term in the comparison, not about the figurative term.

So the first step is to think about the figurative image. What is an etherized patient like? An etherized patient is senseless, dulled to pain, horizontal, apparently lifeless though living, completely still though slightly breathing. Many of these ideas might apply to the evening sky. Perhaps the air is so still that there is only the slightest breath of wind, or no wind at all. The clouds and the colors of twilight might stretch horizontally just above the horizon. There might not be any motion, not even a single bird, to suggest life.

We could develop the comparison even further by thinking about our associative responses to the image of the patient, even the emotions it arouses in us. We might recoil slightly from the image of the etherized patient as if it were something creepy. If we imagine the patient's cool, clammy, bloodless skin that's hardly more animate than a corpse's, we may get a difficult-to-define, unsavory feeling. Those are the feelings that the evening sky arouses in the speaker.

Some metaphors are easy to spot. Eliot's comparison is a **simile**, which is a metaphor that announces itself with the word *like* or *as* and is hard to miss. But some metaphors are so subtle that half the work of interpreting them is recognizing them in the first place. Take these lines from Eliot's poem: "And I have known the eyes already, known them all— / The eyes that fix you in a formulated phrase[.]" The speaker is remembering the way women look at him at tea parties: they "fix" him, which we know cannot be literally true. Even so, we might forget to ask, *To what, exactly, are the eyes being compared?* Have the eyes *repaired* the speaker? Have they *put him in a fix?* Or have they *fastened* him to something? In this case, the following lines leave no doubt: "And when I am formulated, sprawling on a pin, / When I am pinned and wriggling on the wall . . ." The eyes, then, are like a scientist fixing an insect specimen to a display with a needle. The woman's clever, withering phrase is the pin. And Prufrock, the speaker, is the not-yet-dead insect under scrutiny. This particular example is an **extended metaphor**, because Eliot draws out the comparison over a few lines.

Symbols

A **symbol** is an object that represents something else, sometimes another object but more often an abstraction. For example, consider General Robert E. Lee's surrender to Ulysses S. Grant at Appomattox. One object represented another: Lee stood for the defeated Army of Northern Virginia, and by surrendering himself to Grant he surrendered his entire command. So he dressed in his last clean uniform and belted on his sword in order to present his ragtag army in the best possible light. Grant might have taken Lee prisoner, but he didn't. He refused, even, to confiscate Lee's sword. In this context, the sword represented a number of abstractions, not the least of which was Lee's honor. Grant's refusal to take the sword communicated his esteem for Lee and for the soldiers who had until that minute been his enemies.

Some things seem to carry the same symbolic meaning in just about any culture. The sunrise will probably call to mind birth or new beginnings no matter where you go, just as the sunset seems to naturally represent death or ending. They are the same in Bali as they are in Belgium. Ferocious predators might represent evil in many different cultures. A dense forest might symbolize the unknown. These are **universal symbols**, and typically they are drawn from the natural world that every culture experiences.

Poets use universal symbols. Look at Yeats's "The Lake Isle of Innisfree," for example. The island represents isolation, but Yeats did not invent this symbol himself. Whether you are in Ireland or in Argentina, an island seems to naturally represent isolation and seclusion. Other objects carry meaning only in the context of a particular culture. The rose is a good example. In North America and Great Britain, a red rose symbolizes love. But if you went to a town whose inhabitants never read Western literature, saw Hollywood movies, or heard of Valentine's Day, the citizens might look at a rose as they do a daffodil or tulip. The symbol is not universal: it is a convention contrived by a particular population of people. The rose, then, is a **conventional symbol**.

Sometimes, it is obvious that the symbolic meanings of conventional symbols are contrived. Consider the regalia of clubs and political organizations: the mascot of a sports team is chosen by the team's owner or by a committee of professional marketers, and thereafter the Major League baseball team in Arizona is symbolized by a rattlesnake. A flag is sewn by Betsy Ross and adopted by a committee, and instantly it symbolizes a nation.

But most conventional symbols have a mysterious pedigree. It is impossible to say who invented them, as if they arose anonymously out of the culture itself. Who can say when apple pie came to symbolize the values of middle America? Did anyone decide that the Midwest would represent wholesomeness and näiveté? Or that the American West would symbolize rugged individualism? Show a picture of John Wayne on a horse in a Western landscape to people raised in North America, and they will understand the symbolism.

In fact, most people in Europe would recognize it too, for the icon of the American cowboy, and the notions of self-reliance and freedom and violence that he represents, is one of America's cultural exports. But show the picture of John Wayne to farmers in China, and they would see just a man on a horse. No one person or committee decided that these objects would convey symbolic meaning in our culture; nevertheless, they do. And outside our culture they are often meaningless.

William Blake's "The Sick Rose" provides a good example. Most of us probably would jump to the conclusion that the flower represents love, and this connection does yield a coherent interpretation of the whole poem. In our post-Freudian culture, we might even guess the worm in the poem represents a penis. The rose, then, would symbolize not only love but also a woman's virginity. Both of these interpretations are provided by our culture. (Some might argue that the symbols Freud interpreted are *universal*, not *conventional*, and perhaps they'd be right.) But most North Americans would miss something obvious to most British: the rose is a symbol of England.

Your ability to recognize conventional symbols is exactly proportional to your familiarity with a culture. You are probably adept at recognizing symbols that arise out of general North American culture, but the symbols of particular subcultures in America might escape your notice. And many of the poems in this book come from outside North America—many from England, a few from South America, Africa, Wales, and Ireland. Certainly North Americans share a lot of culture with these continents and countries, but there might be some things that are symbols in, say, England that are not symbols in North America. For example, Dover means something to the English, as discussed earlier. It brings to mind newlyweds the way Niagara Falls might for Americans, and its tall chalk cliffs symbolize England the way the Statue of Liberty, which greets people arriving in New York harbor, symbolizes the United States. Dover may not mean anything to you. Likewise, quite a few of these poems were written generations ago, and objects that might have carried symbolic meaning three hundred years ago no longer do. In this case, only familiarity with the culture will help you recognize conventional symbols and their meanings. If you haven't lived in a culture, you might have seen enough movies or TV programs or read enough books or listened to enough music to recognize its symbols. Or you might study the culture, or learn about it in a footnote. Otherwise, you'll need to treat these conventional symbols as if they were literary symbols.

A **literary symbol** is an object that represents something else only within the very narrow context of a particular work of literature. Outside the poem the object does not mean what it does inside the poem. A literary symbol, then, is authored neither by nature nor by a culture but by a writer. As with a conventional symbol, when you take a literary symbol out of its original context, it stops being a symbol.

You need a good deal of ingenuity to recognize that an object in a poem not only is its literal self but also represents something else. There are a few clues you can count on to help you. If the title of a poem is a literal object in the poem, you can assume it also symbolizes something. That was the case in "Dover Beach" (Dover represented something), and it's true in most poems. For instance, the title to Elizabeth Bishop's poem "The Fish" tips us off to the fish's importance. We should expect the fish to carry meaning beyond the literal level of the poem. Right away you should be asking yourself, *what could the fish represent?* William Blake's "The Tyger" and "The Lamb" also call attention to important symbols.

For the most part, it is impossible to teach someone how to recognize which objects are symbolic and which are not. You have to trust your own gut feelings. If you find your attention drawn to an object, if you suspect that something might have more than literal significance, you're probably right. The text itself will call attention to its literary symbols: Listen to what the poem tells you. For example, "Dover Beach" tells us that the sea is a symbol. It appears in the first line of the poem ("The sea is calm tonight"), we hear its sound throughout the first stanza, and it figures again in the second stanza. The poem calls so much attention to the sea that, in a second or third read through the poem, we should guess that the sea is there to represent something other than its literal self. But what?

The second task in interpreting a literary symbol is to figure out what the object represents. Again, you have to trust your instincts.

Read the poem a few times and an idea will more than likely come to you: the object represents the speaker's love, it represents death, it represents the American dream, it represents hope. Usually, a symbol represents abstractions: love, death, dreams, hopes. And often it represents a range of things, not just one.

To come back to the "Dover Beach" example: we wonder, *What could the sea represent?* The speaker makes it easy for us when he says, "The Sea of Faith / Was once, too, at the full, and round earth's shore[.]" We know that it represents "faith." But we might further ask, *Faith in what?* Some possibilities: faith in God, faith in political institutions, faith in traditional mores and values, perhaps all of these. We'll have to see if any or all of these abstractions work in the poem.

Be prepared to revise your hypotheses. If you try to interpret an object symbolically and it just does not seem to work, maybe you were wrong. To paraphrase Sigmund Freud, sometimes a cigar is just a cigar. Or maybe you were wrong about what the object represents. Keep revising and refining your ideas always until you think you get it exactly right.

You can tell if you got it right by interpreting the **symbolic action**. Look at what happens to the symbol in the poem; the same thing happens to what the symbol represents. Think of the symbol of the rose again. The morning after two college sophomores' first date, the young man gets up at dawn to bring a dozen roses to the apartment door of the woman. He knocks on the door and runs downstairs and around to the parking lot where he can see without being seen. The young woman opens the door, finds the roses at her feet, picks them up, smells them. She knows that roses symbolize love, so she can interpret the symbolic action: the guy likes her a lot. By leaving these flowers at her door, he is offering his esteem, his affection, even his love. In short, he has given her his heart. Now the young man, from the parking lot, watches her pick up the flowers, smell them, think for a moment about what they mean. He sees her toss them on the ground. He watches in horror as she stomps them. She grinds the petals with her heel. She's grinding more than the flowers: she's stomping his love into the ground. And we know that he won't be calling her for a second date.

So interpreting a literary symbol takes three steps (the first two steps are automatic with universal and conventional symbols):

1. Identify which object(s) you think might be symbols.
2. Establish what the object(s) represent(s).
3. Interpret the symbolic action.

For example, let's consider the symbolic action of the sea in "Dover Beach." The tide is going out, and the speaker hears a note of sadness in its "long withdrawing roar." Similarly, then, faith is withdrawing from Europe, and its departure leaves people in misery. All of the earlier possibilities—faith in God, in political institutions, in traditional values—work in this context. According to Arnold, periods of faith and faithlessness go in cycles, like the tides, and the mid-nineteenth century was a low point in the cycle.

Structure

Prosody

Prosody is the study of poetry's **rhythms**. We can describe the rhythms of a poem by scanning its **meter**. To **scan** a poem, first read it aloud two or three times, until you can feel yourself using the rhythm dictated by the words. Then mark the stressed syllables by putting an ictus (´) above them. Mark the unstressed syllables with a mora (˘). A scanned line might look like this one from Shakespeare's Sonnet 73:

˘ ´ ˘ ´ ˘ ´ ˘ ´ ˘ ´

That time of year thou mayst in me behold

Once you've identified where the stresses fall, you should see a pattern. In this case, the pattern is unstressed/stressed. This repeated unit of unstressed/stressed syllables is called a **foot**. Feet are marked with slashes (/):

˘ ´ /˘ ´ /˘ ´ /˘ ´ /˘ ´

That time / of year / thou mayst / in me / behold

You can scan just about any line of poetry in English if you know six different kinds of feet:

iamb:	(˘ ´)	as in "the book"
trochee:	(´ ˘)	as in "printer"
anapest:	(˘ ˘ ´)	as in "intercede"
dactyl:	(´ ˘ ˘)	as in "willowy"
spondee:	(´ ´)	as in "big truck"
pyrrhic:	(˘ ˘)	as in "of the"

So the line from Sonnet 73 has five **iambs**. Our shorthand designation for lines of five iambs is "iambic pentameter." If the stresses had been reversed, the line would have been "trochaic pentameter." The names for the line lengths are

one foot:	monometer
two feet:	dimeter
three feet:	trimeter
four feet:	tetrameter
five feet:	pentameter
six feet:	hexameter
seven feet:	heptameter

By combining the names of the feet and the line lengths, you can describe the rhythm—the meter—of just about any line of poetry.

But don't get the idea that poets are thinking about spondees and iambs and heptameter when they compose their poems. Nearly all good poets know how to measure their own lines, just as carpenters know how to measure the wood they work with. Yet poetry is unlike carpentry in this way: you do not measure the lines before you put them together. You do not work from a plan. Poets don't sit down and say to themselves, "All right, to complete this line I need three more iambs." Poets trust their own ears to get the line to sound right. In revision, they might scan their lines and tinker with the stresses with some conscious purpose. But for the most part, they just listen to the music. Prosody is a way of measuring lines *after* they have been composed.

Further, poetry violates regular rhythm all the time. For example, you will never find a poem written entirely in iambic pentameter.

If you ever came across such a poem, say a sonnet, with fourteen lines of iambic pentameter, you'd be reading a hundred and forty straight syllables with the unstressed/stressed rhythm. It would sound like a metronome. Its music would be the unrelenting, steady beat of a drum, which is fine if you're marching, but otherwise it's pretty boring. Instead, the poet will substitute a spondee or a trochee or a pyrrhic here and there, or maybe an anapest, for a few iambs. For example, here is how we might scan the first four lines of Shakespeare's sonnet:

˘ ′ ˘ ′ ˘ ′ ˘ ′ ˘ ′

That time / of year / thou mayst / in me / behold

˘ ′ ˘ ′ ˘ ′ ˘ ′ ˘ ′

When yel / low leaves, / or none, / or few, / do hang

˘ ′ ˘ ′ ˘ ′ ˘ ′ ˘ ′

Upon / those boughs / which shake / against / the cold,

′ ′ ˘ ′ ˘ ′ ˘ ′ ′ ′

Bare ru / ined choirs, / where late / the sweet / birds sang.

Depending on how you read the poem, some of these lines could be scanned differently. Does "those boughs" have two stressed syllables? Is "which shake" a spondee? It's not certain. But the first and last feet of the fourth line are definitely spondees. It is completely unnatural to say "bare" without stressing it, just as it is impossible to say "birds" without a stress. By the fourth line of the poem, Shakespeare has disrupted the rhythm he laid down in the first two lines. Usually, the disruptions happen much sooner. Sometimes a poet disrupts the rhythm so often that it's hard to find a single line with a string of perfectly regular feet.

With so many disruptions to the rhythm, you might at first find it hard to scan poetry. Consider this tip. Most monosyllabic nouns will take a stress, just as most articles ("a," "an," "the") and one syllable prepositions ("of," "in," "on," etc.) will be unstressed. After scanning a few poems, you'll begin to get a feel for such shortcuts. But the best advice is to read the poem aloud again and again, and mark where you find yourself giving stresses. Listen for the rhythm. Mark where the stresses are trying to fall, even if it doesn't quite work. More than likely, you'll find a lot of iambs. At least four out of five poems written in English use iambs as the basic foot. But whether you discover that the underlying rhythm is iambs or trochees or anapests, mark the whole poem as if it were perfectly regular. (Note: some poems might combine types of feet. The basic rhythm of a poem might begin each line with three iambs and conclude with an anapest.) Your goal at this stage is to recognize such regularities.

Then go back and find the spots that disrupt the rhythmic pattern. Properly mark those feet. The point to scanning a poem is not to figure out what the underlying rhythm is. Knowing that a poem is written in iambic pentameter doesn't help us understand it at all. We analyze a poem's regular rhythm only so we can figure out where it breaks the rhythm. In other words, we scan Shakespeare's sonnet not to see the iambs, which are all over the place, but to find the spondees.

What's the point of finding those irregularities? That's the toughest question to answer. It is not always possible to link such rhythmic irregularities to the meaning of a poem. Who can say with any confidence what is the effect on a reader of the spondee opening line 4 of Shakespeare's Sonnet 73?

Bare ru / ined choirs, / where late / the sweet / birds sang.

All we can say for sure is that such irregularities call attention to themselves. They add a bit of "umph" to the feet that contain them. The barrenness of those choirs might stick in our mind a little more emphatically than if we heard about them in another iamb.

Surely the rhythms of a poem contribute to its tone, but, again, it is a delicate business to claim something like this: *the two spondees of line 4, following as they do on three lines of regular iambic pentameter, give us a sense of the echoing hollowness of the silent church ruins described in the line.* The images convey this melancholic tone more ably than the rhythm. As you begin your study of poetry, then, you should make only the slightest claims about how the meter of a poem contributes to its meaning. Probably the best use of prosody is to help you compose your own poetry. It is the basic tools of the art—the brushstrokes and paints, if you will, of poetry. It is the most physical part of poetry.

Rhyme and Stanzas

Rhyme is the repetition of sound in different words. Usually, the repeated sound is in the end of the word. *Round, sound, ground,* and *profound* all rhyme. If a rhyme is in the middle of a line, it's called an **internal rhyme.**

Poets often use **end rhymes** to group the lines of their poems. We use a simple system of letters to describe the rhymes. The last sound of the first line is assigned the letter *a,* as are all subsequent lines ending with the same sound. Each line that introduces a new end-sound is assigned the next letter of the alphabet. So the rhyme scheme for the opening of Emily Dickinson's "Because I could not stop for Death—" looks like this:

Because I could not stop for Death—	a
He kindly stopped for me—	b
The Carriage held but just Ourselves—	c
And Immortality. b	
We slowly drove—He knew no haste	d
And I had put away	e
My labor and my leisure too,	f
For His Civility—	e

Away is not an exact rhyme for *civility,* so it's called an **off rhyme.** A **feminine rhyme** is a two-syllable rhyme with the stress falling on the next-to-last syllable, as in these lines from Anne Bradstreet's "A Letter to Her Husband":

So many steps, head from the heart to sever,
If but a neck, soon should we be together.

The end rhymes give a poem structure by dividing it into groups of lines, which are typically called **stanzas**. Notice in Dickinson's poem that the rhymes gather the lines into groups of four. Poets usually indicate the divisions between stanzas with a blank line on the page, but even if you don't see the text of a poem, when you hear it read aloud, the rhymes will tell you where each stanza ends. Like meter, rhymes establish a rhythm in our minds.

Often, the literal meaning of the poem will divide into sections just as the stanzas do. It is not surprising, for example, that each of the stanzas in Dickinson's poem ends by finishing a sentence. In this way, the rhyme scheme will help you analyze a poem because it divides the poem into smaller coherent parts. Each stanza usually develops a single thought. Likewise, the rhyming end of each line usually mirrors a strong grammatical pause, as the ends do in Bradstreet's poems.

Just as with meter, you should be especially interested in rhyme irregularities. In Dickinson's poem, for example, the rhyme suggests that we ought to pause after "away" in the sixth line, but the grammar of the sentence compels us to hurry on to line 7. Poets often do this, using our natural sense of syntax to work against the rhythm of the rhyme. When one line seems to launch you without pause into the next, we call it **enjambment**.

You can use rhymes to find irregularities in a poem. For example, if you look at Bruce Springsteen's "The River" (on page 295), you'll quickly see that it is a ballad. The stanzas follow the rhyme scheme *abcb defe*, etc. But in the ninth stanza the rhyme changes to *aabb*. The lyrics are calling your attention to these lines, and if you listen to a recording of the song, you will hear that the music changes at this point also. This stanza is what is often called a *bridge* in songwriting: a sudden shift in tempo and melody that leads to the song's conclusion, which goes back to the musical patterns established earlier in the song. Often, the bridge provides a sort of climax to the song, and also in the case of "The River" that climax is conveyed not only by a change in music but also by this change in rhyme scheme.

Some subgenres of lyric poetry have fairly strict rules about rhyme schemes. By convention, certain rhyme schemes and certain stanzaic patterns have come to be associated with particular subjects.

So stanzaic forms are linked to a poem's meaning by convention. Ballads, sonnets, and odes, each of which has a set of standard subjects, are defined by their stanzaic form.

Subgenres

Some poems have so many elements in common that they have created their own genres within the larger **genre** of lyric poems. Each of these **subgenres** calls up in the reader's mind certain expectations, just as the opening scene of a TV show will usually indicate if you're watching a sitcom or a drama. When you recognize the subgenre, you expect certain things. The ballad, for example, has its own grammar, its own conventions. Following are descriptions of the subgenres that appear in this anthology, accompanied by some of the elements you should expect when you encounter each one.

Ballads
Ballads are the most popular form of lyric poetry. They were first sung in the city streets, at folk gatherings in the country, and at the fire's side. Now, most popular styles of music use ballads: rock, blues, pop, and particularly country. Ballads tell stories in short, terse narratives. The classic **ballad stanza** is four lines long with a rhyme scheme of *abab*; the *a* lines are tetrameter, and the *b* lines are trimeter. But just about any narrative lyric with four-line stanzas would be called a ballad today.

Dramatic Monologues
A dramatic monologue is a poem that seems as if it were a speech lifted right out of a play. These generally have one or a few long stanzas, usually unrhymed or in couplets, though the rhyme schemes can vary. Almost always, the poet's beliefs do not exactly correspond to the speaker's beliefs in a dramatic monologue. Robert Browning's "My Last Duchess" is a dramatic monologue, as is Alfred, Lord Tennyson's "Ulysses."

Elegies
Elegy used to designate poems written in alternating lines of hexameter and pentameter, usually on the theme of love. But a few

hundred years ago the genre began to deal exclusively with death. Sometimes an elegy might be a lament for a particular dead person, sometimes a complaint about mortality in general, often both. Though today elegies have no particular meter or rhyme, typically they are longish, meditative poems. Thomas Gray's "Elegy Written in a Country Churchyard" fits this description, as does W. H. Auden's "In Memory of W. B. Yeats," though that poem's stanzaic form suggests that it is an irregular ode. Ben Jonson's poems "On My First Daughter," which is short enough to be engraved on tombstones, is an epitaph rather than an elegy.

Odes

John Keats's odes in this volume are modeled on the odes of the Roman poet Horace. These Horatian odes usually meditate on fairly abstract concepts or on objects that symbolize something abstract. They use **colloquial diction**, and typically, they are calm statements of praise or judgment. The stanzas can follow any invention of the poet, but every stanza must have the same meter and rhyme scheme.

Sonnets

Traditionally, the sonnet has been used to express the feelings that a beloved arouses in the speaker. Often, sonnets come in sequences or "cycles" that chronicle the speaker's varying emotions. The sentiment expressed in one poem might be contradicted in the very next poem, just as the moods of love can change quickly. Often the speaker's love is unrequited. William Shakespeare's, Elizabeth Barrett Browning's, and Edna St. Vincent Millay's sonnets in this anthology are from cycles of love poems.

In the Romantic era especially, but also in other ages, the sonnet has been used for different purposes, such as political commentary. Sonnets on such themes are usually not part of a sequence but stand alone.

There are two types of sonnets: the **Italian** (or **Petrarchan**) **sonnet**, and the **English** (or **Shakespearean**) **sonnet**. They each have fourteen lines, but the rhyme schemes divide the lines differently. An English sonnet has this rhyme scheme: *ababcdcdefefgg*. As a result, the poem is divided into four sections: three **quatrains** (four lines) and a concluding **couplet** (two lines). An Italian sonnet has this rhyme scheme: *abbaabbacdecde*. As a result, the poem divides into an **octave** (eight lines) and a **sestet** (six lines). Sometimes the rhyme scheme of the sestet will vary, but an Italian sonnet always divides in two between the eighth and ninth lines. Recognizing these divisions, whether in an English or in an Italian sonnet, will help you interpret the poem: analyze it section by section.

How Do You Write About Poems?

Your instructor might ask you to write one of several different types of paper—for instance, a response paper, an explication, a research paper—but this section guides you through only one of those: an interpretive essay. In an interpretive essay, you tell your readers what you think a particular poem means, and then using evidence from the text of the poem, you construct an argument to support your opinion. This mode of writing is the foundation for all critical essays, so even if your instructor gives you a more complex assignment, such as a research paper, you'll find the advice about interpretation helpful.

In the beginning of this book, I said that you already interpret poems intuitively. You've grown up listening to songs on the radio or via online streaming, and you've probably pored over the lyrics to your favorite tune or memorized the complex lines of a rap song. And so you've internalized the conventions of poetry, its grammar so to speak, just as you've learned to understand sentences by growing up in your native language. You already get the meaning of most poems, at least on a gut level. We all do.

Even so, you should not be tempted to think that all interpretations are equally valid. I once had a student who insisted that the speaker in Robert Frost's "Stopping by Woods on a Snowy Evening" was Santa Claus. It was a good hypothesis—after all, the harness bells sound like the reindeer on Santa's sleigh, and the concluding refrain is, "But I have promises to keep, / And miles to go before I sleep." I had to admit, Santa Claus does have miles to go to deliver all those toys. Nevertheless, several details just did not add up: there are no reindeer, for instance, just a horse. Given what the legends say about Santa Claus, what business would he have driving a horse sleigh through an unpeopled woods? I asked her to explain why she thought the poem meant what she asserted it did, and she replied, "That's just how I read the poem." I hear that kind of reasoning often, and on one hand I can't really argue with it—she was the highest authority on what something meant *to her.*

But on the other hand, when you write an interpretive paper you're adding a dimension to that claim. Not only are you asserting what the poems means to you but also that your reader ought to agree with you. In other words, you're trying to persuade people that the meaning you get from a poem is probably the meaning that the poem intended you to get. When you think of interpretation that way, it becomes clear that some interpretations are more plausible than others, and some are so implausible that we might as well say they're wrong[1].

This section explains how to develop your own interpretations and, once you've done that, how to best persuade others to agree with you.

Theme, Meaning, and Interpretation

One of the first things you want to do is determine what you think the poem is about. I do not mean what it's about in a literal sense but in a figurative sense. For example, it is pretty obvious that "Stopping by Woods on a Snowy Evening" is about a tired traveler in winter on a lonely road. But the poem is also about things that are more abstract: work and social obligations, the lure of nature, the lure of death, one's relation to God. These and possibly several other abstractions are its themes. The poem could be about any of these things. This multiplicity of themes is characteristic of poetry. Six readers of the same poem might be interested in six

---

1. In fairness to my student, I should admit that at least one critic, using the very techniques of close analysis I'm advocating here, *has* argued that the speaker in the poem is St. Nick. I just don't think his use of evidence is very convincing. For example, he deals with the issue of the horse by speculating "that the animal is really a reindeer disguised as a horse by the poet's desire for obscurity" (Herbert R. Coursen Jr. "The Ghost of Christmas Past: 'Stopping by Woods on a Snowy Evening'" *College English* 24.3 [December 1962]: 237).

different themes. As a matter of fact, various literary critics have explored each of those themes I listed.[2]

In most theories of poetry, **theme** is what the poem is about on an abstract level, those generalized issues invoked or embodied in the literal level of the poem. Theme distinguishes a poem from a mere description or observation of a scene or event. If someone you know happened to tell you about stopping by the woods on a snowy evening, he might mean nothing more by it than to paint a picture of the scene in your mind or even convey to you the feeling he had at the time. These are certainly important and part of a poem's meaning, but theme deepens the particular scene or event, giving it significance beyond the literal. A poem's theme indicates how it might concern not only the life of the speaker but also the life of the reader. If some of us have never stopped by a woods on a snowy evening, we have all felt the press of obligations when we'd rather tarry, or we've looked on a scene of nature and been attracted by its peacefulness and beauty.

A poem's **meaning** is what it has to say about its theme. For example, you might ask yourself the question, *What does "Stopping by Woods" have to say about obligations and duties?* or *What does the poem say about how nature appeals to people?* You can almost think of poems as pieces of rhetoric, as if they were little arguments trying to persuade readers to think something, believe something, or feel something in a different or deeper way. I say "almost" because, of course, poems do not use argument in the conventional sense; they don't trot out before readers orderly parades of inductive or deductive reasoning. Logical arguments touch you more superficially, like wind on the surface of a lake. Imaginative literature moves you like deep ocean currents, where your heart swims. Poems engage our senses vicariously and stimulate real emotions. You *see* the snow falling in the woods, you *hear* the quiet broken only by the harness bells, you *feel* the stillness, and the stillness tempts you to rest. This is not to say that poetry is never rational or that every poem triggers powerful emotions. Some do appeal more to the intellect than to the heart. But generally speaking, poetry conveys its meaning

2. See Brian D. Doyle, "Enhancing Perspective, Inviting Response: Multiple Interpretations of a Frost Poem," *The English Journal* 81.7 (November 1992): 68–72.

in a different language from conventional argument. The language poems use is the subject of the "How Do You Read Poems?" section. Speaker, audience, image, metaphor, symbol: these constitute the grammar of poetry. These are the conventions you need to master if you want to persuade someone to agree with your opinion about a poem.

Because it is so tied up in imagination, the meaning of poems can be hard to pin down, almost as hard as interpreting the meaning of life itself. We don't read poems to extract some moral, as we would read a fable. Poems do not offer some universally applicable lesson that can be easily paraphrased, such as "Slow and steady wins the race," which is the meaning of Aesop's fable of the tortoise and the hare. It's pretty hard work to put into your own, clear prose what a poem does to you on a deep level. Meaning involves how a poem makes readers *feel,* what it makes them *think* about, where it *directs* their sympathies, all sorts of things you don't expect from expository prose.

Your **interpretation** is your statement of what you think the poem means. Your thesis sums up that interpretation. It's a sentence or two that tells your readers what you think the poem means. Just as a poem might have several different themes, it can also support several different, sometimes even contradictory, interpretations. And while meaning might be tough to pin down, you can follow some simple steps that will help you do it. I'll give you practical advice about that later. The following sections will help you develop your interpretation and give you strategies for persuading other people to agree with you.

The Writing Process

No one, not even the cleverest of literary critics, can write an effective interpretive essay completely off the top of their head. *Thinking* takes you only so far. It is by *writing* that we generate ideas, test those ideas with evidence, try out arguments, rethink our initial notions, revise our strategies of persuasion.

Rhetoricians describe the writing process as **recursive**. In other words, writing a paper rarely follows step-by-step instructions like a recipe in a cookbook, even if it sometimes is represented that way in textbooks like this one. When you're cooking, you might have to melt the butter before you toss the onions in the pan, and you might have to sauté the onions before you put them in the soup. Steps go in a necessary order.

Writing doesn't work that way. You'll find yourself constantly circling back to earlier steps. Don't worry if it seems more natural for you to do step 4 before you've finished step 2, and don't worry if you want to go back to step 3 after you've finished step 5. Follow your instincts. The writing process is not linear. It spirals back on itself all the time.

Nor should you worry about completing each and every step in the first place. Writing is a lot messier than cooking, and you should violate these instructions whenever you're more productive by going your own way, skipping a step, adding your own. Writing is very individual: no two people go through the process exactly the same way. One of the most important things you can do in a writing class is to figure out what's the most productive writing process *for you*. You might find that you can't generate your ideas unless you're already writing a rough draft of your paper, so you might begin with drafting rather than discovery. Or you might find that you can't think of anything to say when you're at the keyboard: that you need a cup of coffee, a pen, and your literature book open to the story. Everybody does it a little differently, and you've got to figure out what's your own most productive process.

But the one universal is this: writing is a *process*. It takes several stages to produce an effective paper, and each of those stages takes time and energy. Your hard work will be rewarded with several intellectual pleasures, but you must remember that writing an interpretive essay is hard work.

1. Paraphrase

Earlier, I suggested that you should completely paraphrase any poem you're going to write about. Be thorough. Translate every line and every phrase into your own words. Don't leave anything out. Even if the literal level of the poem is pretty clear and straightforward, force yourself to write this paraphrase: you'll probably discover a subtlety of syntax you didn't notice before. And if the parts of the poem are unclear at the literal level, writing your paraphrase will clarify those confusions. If you're to have any chance of persuading people to agree with your interpretation, you must master the literal level of the poem—it is the foundation of your analysis.

Your paraphrase will help you "chunk" the poem into grammatical units of thought. Often, these units will correspond to sentences, though poets are so creative with punctuation that you cannot always rely on stops like periods and semicolons to identify these units. You're looking for units of meaning here: on the literal level, where does the speaker finish one thought before moving on to the next? Sometimes the end rhymes will delineate these units (for instance, you'll often find that each quatrain in a Shakespearean sonnet is not only a self-contained rhyming unit (*abab–cdcd–efef–gg*) but also a grammatical unit. Take the first quatrain of Sonnet 73:

> *That time of year though mayst in me behold*
> *When yellow leaves, or none, or few, do hang*
> *Upon those boughs which shake against the cold,*
> *Bare ruined choirs, where late the sweet birds sang.*

The rhyme scheme forms a unit that corresponds to the grammar: in this case, we have one complete unit of thought (in which the speaker compares himself to an autumn tree). The next unit of rhyme (the second quatrain) consists of a second complete grammatical thought. Ballads tend to be as easy to chunk into parts as sonnets. Often, each four-line stanza will be one complete grammatical unit on the literal level of the poem. Stanzas tend to function that way—they contain one unit of literal meaning.

But sometimes one thought will run over the stanzaic break. And many poems, especially more contemporary poems, have no rhyme scheme or their rhymes don't help you divide the poem into grammatically complete units. Those poems will be harder to paraphrase; you'll have to rely entirely on your understanding of syntax.

Use paragraph breaks in your paraphrase to delineate these units. You'll find that it's very helpful to have divided the poem into these smaller parts for the next stage.

2. Discovery

Discovery simply means finding things to say: you discover ideas and evidence. Discovery is a collaboration between you and the poem.

You bring to the poem all sorts of things—your knowledge of how the world works and how people behave, your sense of right and wrong, your own personal set of things that you tend to notice and things you tend to overlook—that individualize your experience of the text. In discovery, you explore your own interaction with the poem. You slow it down and observe it.

This is what English teachers call **close reading**. You're reading the text with a more specific purpose than the general reader. You're not just letting it do things to you: you're trying to figure out *how* it does things to you. *How* does it get you to sympathize with the speaker? *How* does its pattern of images affect you? You're looking more closely, looking for specific things, using examination tools almost the way a scientist will use some specialized instrument, such as a microscope or a spectrometer or stethoscope.

Write in your book! Fill up the margins of the poem with your notes. Record your reactions. Mark where you see a pattern of images. Circle striking metaphors. Put question marks where you don't understand something. Mark anything and everything. Get into dialogue with the poem. Are the white spaces surrounding the poem cluttered by your own handwriting? If not, you probably haven't analyzed it enough. You need to do some more close reading.

Explication

An **explication** is a careful, sequential analysis of each of those parts of the poem that you discovered when you paraphrased it. Reconsider the poem section by section, according to those divisions, only this time you should get beyond the literal level of the poem. Analyze the various elements of poetry: tone, images, metaphors, and symbols. Explore everything you notice, even if the different things you come up with seem unrelated to each other. You're still trying ideas out here. Be creative in your reading process: there's no need to reject anything yet. You should be attuned to any progression that might manifest itself in the poem. Does the first section of the poem lead into the next? Does the second section prepare readers psychologically, emotionally, intellectually for the third section?

In an explication, you write your ideas down in paragraph format, essentially rewriting your paraphrase: summarizing the literal level of the poem while adding into the discussion these other levels of meaning. This discovery exercise serves your interpretation in two ways. First of all, when you've finished analyzing each section of the poem, you should be able to identify what you think is the most important or the most interesting theme, and you should be able to assert what you think the poem says about that theme, which is your first stab at a thesis. Second, your explication will supply you with a treasure trove of text-based arguments that you can draw on for your interpretive paper.

Heuristics

Explication is not the only way to generate ideas and evidence. Some tried-and-true methods go back to Aristotle and the ancient Greeks. You'll see that most of them involve asking and answering questions. The technical term for using questions this way is **heuristics**.

Talk. Find someone who will talk about the poem with you: argue, agree, explore your thoughts together. Ask each other why you think the poem says one thing or why it says another. Do any themes concern your own personal life? You might begin with some basic questions: do you sympathize with the speaker? Why? Take Yeats's "Down by the Salley Gardens," for instance. Ask yourself what it felt like the first time you fell in love. Did you ever get your heart broken? Was that similar or dissimilar to the emotion evoked in the poem? Let the conversation go where your interests take it.

Class discussion. Classroom analysis is talk extraordinaire. What did people have to say about the poem in class? Did you discover any angles to the poem that did not occur to you before? Did anyone react differently from you? Which passages did you discuss? What was said about those passages?

Brainstorm. Brainstorming is just talking with a little more direction or formality. With pen and paper in hand, talk with a classmate about the poem, jotting down everything that you think might be useful to you. Let one idea lead you to the next, and write everything down, both promising and unpromising ideas. You can sort them out later.

Free writing. I've found that free writing can be the best way for college students to develop ideas and arguments. Give yourself a small stretch of time—say fifteen or twenty minutes—and write down everything you can think of about the poem. What attracts you to it? What do you find interesting? Don't police your thoughts. Write it all down. You'll mine all of those sentences later, finding the nuggets among the dross.

The proverbial shower. You might have that eureka moment of discovery in the shower, where so many brilliant ideas have hatched. Or is it a cup of coffee and a blank computer screen that helps you think? Does your mind grow fruit sitting on the bus? Listening to classical music? Figure out for yourself what makes *your* intellect productive, and *do it.*

Whatever heuristics you used, review all of those notes, whether they're in the margins of your book or in a notebook or in a computer document or on sticky notes stuck on edges of your desk. Try to identify a theme that emerges. What is it you most want to talk about? What issue raised in the poem interests you the most? Remember, themes tend to be abstractions, like "friendship" or "war" or "gender roles." Perhaps there's a cluster of ideas that are all related to each other. Try to identify them. Write them down. Even if it's only one or two words, write the theme down. That cements it in your mind. Now ask yourself, *What is the poem saying about this theme?* Another way to ask it is: *What do I want my readers to believe about this poem?* Your answer to that question will be your first draft of a thesis. You want to come away from these exercises with a theme, a thesis, and lots of notes about the poem's elements, which will provide you with textual evidence.

3. Planning

Take out a blank piece of paper or a new text document and write your thesis at the top. A **thesis** is a short statement, usually one or two sentences, that encapsulates your interpretation. The purpose of your paper is to persuade readers to agree with the thesis, so this is the most important part of your paper. That's your essay's destination. It will guide you as you construct your arguments: every paragraph should play some role in getting readers to arrive eventually at that thesis.

Sift through your discovery notes and identify the ideas that emerged. Discard those that seem unrelated to your theme; hold onto those that are. Arrange those ideas in an order. Which idea needs to come first? What seems to come logically after that? What's the third thing you want to talk about? What idea does that point logically set up? It should seem to you that *X* logically precedes *Y*; that you have to dispense with *Y* before you can proceed to *Z*. Each of these ideas must push your audience closer to their ultimate destination: your thesis. This is not an amble, like an explication, where the organization is dictated by the order of the poem. In fact, if you find your paper's organization following that of the poem, that should be a warning to you that you're not really creating an argument in support of a thesis. What do you need to do to get readers to agree with your thesis? What steps must they follow? The answers to those questions will probably dictate a sequence of main points that bears no relation to the order of the parts in the poem itself.

You might be able to keep your arrangement in your head, but I recommend that at the very least you jot down a sketchy outline. Probably, you don't want to get more detailed than that. But at this stage, you should be thinking that each of the items in your outline is a potential paragraph. The paragraph is your main unit of organization, and you'll use paragraphing to help your reader recognize the stages in your argument.

Don't forget that writing is recursive. As you are arranging your thoughts, you might discover new ideas; and almost surely, as you begin drafting your paper, you'll realize you need to rearrange your paragraphs.

4. Drafting

In the **drafting** stage, you actually write what resembles a paper. Consequently, students often find this part of the writing process the most challenging: the words don't come; you stare at a blank screen; the fingers on the keyboard are uninspired. If you're prone to this kind of writer's block, the advice here should help.

Don't worry about writing an introduction. Most writers find that to write an effective introduction, they have to wait to the very last stage of the process. Fretting about an introduction at this early stage is probably wasted energy. All you need at the head of your paper right now is your first version of your thesis.

Then use your outline. You don't have to write from beginning to end. Pick a section that you feel most confident about. Maybe it's your third point, and you already have a couple of passages in the text that you know support that idea. Begin where you're most sure of yourself. Then, once the ball is rolling, go back to the other parts.

Many writers try too hard on their first draft. They'll work on one paragraph, realize that it's not quite right, and so they'll tinker with it, rewrite it, improve it, revise it again. Resist the temptation to perfect one paragraph before you move on to the next. Your main goal in drafting is to get all of your ideas and evidence down in paragraph format. You're in conversation with yourself, so there's no need for perfection. No one else is going to see what you've written. If you tend toward this kind of perfectionism, you should train yourself to be comfortable with a poorly argued train of thought or an awkwardly stated complex idea. You'll have plenty of time to improve things later, so just keep moving on from one point in your outline to another.

You might even time yourself: allow ten minutes to write your second paragraph. After ten minutes, move on to paragraph three, no matter what stage paragraph two is in—even if you've nothing on paper but a couple of broken sentences. When I assign a rough draft for homework, I tell my students to give themselves a time limit: maybe an hour; no more than two. Don't waste time polishing anything: just write.

When you're done writing your arguments, you should draft a full conclusion. Sum up your arguments and restate your thesis, probably in different words. If you're successful, your readers are going to agree with your interpretation. Now that you've drafted your first version of your arguments, ask yourself again, *What is it that I want my readers to believe about the poem?* You might discover that your answer to that question is different—perhaps even very different—from what it was in the discovery stage. That's OK. In fact, it's a good sign, as you'll see in the next section below.

5. Revising

Revising is a lot more important than many writers realize. This stage will probably require most of your effort and time. If writing the entire paper, from discovery to proofreading, takes you ten hours, you could easily spend five or more hours on this stage.

Take a hard look at your rough draft. It's best to take a day off after writing your rough draft, so you can come to it cold, so to speak, reading it with a more objective eye. "Rough" draft is probably the wrong metaphor, because it implies that your draft is a gemstone that just needs a little judicious cutting and polish before you turn it in. Instead, think of drafts like mountains that you're going to mine to find veins or seams of argument imbedded in the paragraphs. I really think of that first draft almost as a type of discovery: by writing it, you discover your arguments.

Finding your thesis

The first thing you want to dig out is your thesis. What is it that you really want to prove about the poem? What do you think the poem means? Take some real care here. This statement must be an opinion, something debatable. For example, let's consider again Robert Frost's poem, "Stopping by Woods on a Snowy Evening." Here's a statement that is *not* a thesis:

> In Frost's poem, the speaker is on a long journey, and he pauses to watch the snow peacefully falling in the woods. He is tempted to give up the journey, but he ends up deciding to continue. The poem gives us insight into social obligations and duties, and how they burden people.

This statement names one of the poem's themes: the poem is about duty and obligations. Very few if anyone who's read the poem would disagree with that statement, so it's not really an opinion. If it's not an opinion, there's no point to writing a paper about it because the purpose of an interpretive paper is to persuade skeptical readers to agree with your interpretation.

This writer would need to take her interpretation one step further by asking and answering the question, *What is that insight that the poem gives us?* One answer to that question might read like this:

> According to Frost's poem, though social obligations and duties prevent us from pursuing things that benefit our own well-being, submitting to them is the right thing to do.

Some readers might disagree with that interpretation. They might think the poem tells us it's wrong to chose duty at the expense of our well-being. Other readers might have yet a third interpretation: Submitting to public duties protects us from temptations that look like they're good for us, but really are self-destructive. As she writes her interpretive essay, our student-critic should imagine that her readers are those who disagree with her. Her job in writing the paper would be to convince them to change their minds.

Usually, you'll find your best articulation of your interpretation in that concluding paragraph of your rough draft. That's because it is often in the act of writing that first draft that you figure out what it is you want to prove to readers. Look at that conclusion. Is it an opinion? Is it something that some people will disagree with? Is it worth writing a whole paper to prove that point? If not, then you need to work on it some more. At this stage, you *must* have a solid thesis statement. Put that thesis statement at the head of a new outline.

Outlining

Now ask yourself, *What do I need to do to prove that I'm probably right?* You're trying to map out the steps in your argument. Remember that the thesis governs all. For example, let's consider again that thesis about "Stopping by Woods": *According to Frost's poem, though social obligations and duties prevent us from pursuing things that benefit our own well-being, submitting to them is the right thing to do.* Our writer's outline might look like this:

- prove the falling snow and the speaker's attraction to it represent an impulse to rest
- demonstrate that rest and relaxation would be restorative (remembering that some people might think the snow represents a self-destructive impulse, a surrender)
- show how the impulse to continue the journey represents doing things that benefit others (rather than the self)
- prove that, according to the poem, continuing the journey is the right choice

Each of those bullet points relates back to that thesis.

Redrafting

Now you're ready to write your second draft. Open an entirely new word processing document: a completely blank page. This will prevent you from merely tinkering with that first draft, adding a few sentences, moving paragraphs around, editing for grammar and usage, polishing the style. Though the work you put into the rough draft was absolutely essential—only through *writing* that draft could you discover what you have to say—the purpose of that first draft was to help you develop your ideas. *You* were the audience. You wrote it in order to communicate something to yourself. Your second draft is a public document. Your audience is someone else, perhaps your fellow classmates; the general public; your teacher; an imaginary, thoughtful literary critic; above all, imagine that your readers are people who disagree with your thesis. In revision, you start making rhetorical decisions based on how you want to affect that audience, which calls for a fresh start.

Using your new outline, write the second draft of your paper on this blank page. Each of those bullet points might serve as the main points of the body paragraphs. You might end up cutting and pasting significant portions of your rough draft. That's perfectly fine. But I think you'll probably find that, while you're using ideas from the first draft, there are very few complete sentences and practically no paragraphs that can be cut and pasted into the second draft. The second draft is a true *rewriting*: you're writing the paper a second time. All the while, you need to be thinking about your audience: will this idea be clear to my reader or do I need to explain it a little more fully? Is my argument convincing to a skeptical reader? What do I need to do to improve it?

You need to gather evidence to support each one of those main points. Your evidence will come from your rough draft. Let's imagine you're thinking about how to prove the first bullet point: how the snow represents rest. To prove that point, you would draw on your close reading of the poem. Probably, you'll find in your notes or in your explication and then in your rough draft an analysis of the snow as a symbol, based not only on the first stanza of the poem but also the last stanza, which describes the woods as ("lovely, dark and deep"). Perhaps those descriptors make you think of a deep sleep, and the softness of the snow banks seem a natural representation of a bed's mattress. This is a good example of how your interpretive paper differs from an explication: in a simple explication, you would not discuss the "lovely, dark and deep" image until your fourth paragraph, because it occurs in the fourth stanza. In your interpretive paper, your analysis of the symbolism constitutes the evidence proving your main point in this paragraph, drawing its evidence from wherever it occurs in the poem. Similarly, an explication might make observations unrelated to the main point of this paragraph. The first paragraph of the explication might discuss at some length the neighbor and his indifference to the speaker's visit to his woods, which all occur in the first stanza. But those elements are irrelevant to the point in this interpretive essay. Everything in this paragraph must be devoted only to that one goal: proving to readers that the snow and the speaker's reaction to the snow represent an impulse to rest.

6. Editing

Editing means polishing your arguments. Read through your revision, trying to imagine you're someone who disagrees with the thesis. Go from beginning to end, marking up the revision. Don't stop to fix anything yet, just identify all of the problems. Look for places in your logic that are weak or unconvincing. Do you need more evidence someplace? Does it seem odd that paragraph three leads into paragraph four? Do several sentences within one paragraph seem to be unrelated to that paragraph's main purpose?

After you've marked the entire paper, correct the problems.

Don't be afraid to change things pretty significantly in the editing phase. You might find yourself moving several sentences from one paragraph to another. You might cut out chunks of the paper that are unrelated to proving your thesis. You might even tweak your thesis, in which case you need to reassess everything to make sure the paper still relates to it. Maybe you'll realize that before you get to point X you have write a whole new paragraph. Editing can be pretty labor intensive, even if it does not rise to the level of a full revision.

7. Quotation and Citation

You need to cite your references to the poem, whether you're paraphrasing, summarizing, or quoting. That's so your readers can go back to the source of your evidence and check things out for themselves. Don't forget also that precision in **citations** has its own rhetorical effect. You look like an expert when you cite with perfect competence, and readers, including the teachers grading your essay, are more likely to believe your arguments.

You'll find a few references to on-line citation guides later, which will give you more detail. But I'll give you a short passage here that will model proper MLA in-text citations of evidence in an interpretive essay:

> The speaker in Robert Frost's "Stopping by Woods on a Snowy Evening" is tempted to stay on the road and continue watching the snowfall. In the first two stanzas, this choice might seem to be uncomfortable, anything but restful, and perhaps even threatening. After all, he stops "[b]etween the woods and frozen lake / The darkest evening of the year" (7–8). Even the horse knows that it is strange to tarry on the road exposed to dangerous elements (5–6). However, in this context, the snow does not threaten frostbite but instead offers something like a soft and comfortable bed:
>
> > The only other sound's the sweep
> > Of easy wind and downy flake.
> > The woods are lovely, dark and deep,
> > But I have promises to keep,
> > And miles to go before I sleep. (11–15)

Citing poetry has several formatting conventions you need to keep in mind:

- Cite the poem's line numbers, not the page on which it appears.
- Line breaks are indicated with a slash with a space on either side (/).
- Quotations of more than three lines are set off with special margins, not quotation marks.
- If you don't reference the poem or poet before your quotation, note the title and author as well as the line numbers, as in (Frost, "Stopping by Woods on a Snowy Evening, 7–8).

Your general rule of thumb should follow this piece of practical advice: *Have I told my readers where to find each piece of evidence I take from the poem?* If you have, then you'll be in good shape.

Often the texts you use for your poems are anthologies, such as this book. You must remember that your Works Cited items must be alphabetized by the poet, not by the editor:

Frost, Robert. "Stopping by Woods on a Snowy Evening." *Seagull Reader: Poems.* Ed. Joseph Kelly. 3rd ed. New York: Norton, 2015: 125. Print.

Different types of sources have their own formulations on a Works Cited page. If you cite a news article, a journal entry, or even a tweet in your essay, you need to format each citation in its own correct way. There are too many variations to list here, but you can see a complete overview of different sources and their proper citations, as well as more advice on MLA formatting (among others) in general, at this book's supporting website, www.wwnorton .com/write.

8. Proofreading

Read your edited revision. At this stage, **proofreading**, you're fine-tuning your sentences rather than working on your arguments. Read through the entire paper. I often tell my students to read the paper backward, sentence by sentence. That way, you get out of the flow of your argument and can see each sentence as a sentence. You're looking for sentences that sound confusing or even ungrammatical. You're looking for spelling and punctuation errors. Have you documented your quotations and paraphrases correctly? Mark anything that's suspicious. If it sounds slightly unclear to you, you can be sure the sentence is very unclear to your readers. Go through the entire paper, pausing only long enough to mark where there's a problem.

Fix the problems.

Some of those problems will be easy to fix because they're mere typos, either mistyped words or simple errors that derive from haste or inattention, like an *it's* for an *its*. But some problems might take more work, especially those sentences that sound confusing to you.

If you've got a sentence that seems tangled, whose sense is not clear and you're not quite sure why, try this easy trick of the trade: ask yourself, *What was I trying to say here?* Then write down the answer as it comes to you. Probably, your answer to that question will be clearer, the grammar will be correct, and you can just plug it into your paper, replacing the problem sentence. Usually, your correction will be longer than the original, and sometimes you might find that you use two or three sentences to explain what you were trying to say. That's not surprising because often the problem with tangled sentences is that you're trying to do too much all at once.

Once all of the problems you noted in your proofreading have been corrected, you're ready to turn in your essay.

Conclusion

After this long discussion of the parts of poems, of stanzaic forms and feminine rhymes and iambs, you may find yourself wondering if the pleasure of poetry has been ruined for you. Does analyzing and writing essays about poetry mean you can't enjoy it anymore? In a sense Wordsworth *was* right: we do murder to dissect. The casual fan enjoys a figure skater's grace and agility with a simplicity and awe that the afficionado can only remember. The unlearned ear listens to a jazz ensemble with an innocence that the trained ear can never recapture. It is the same with poetry. As you discover how poems work, as you grow more adept at analysis, as you master the art of interpretation, something is lost.

But the loss is more than recovered by a different pleasure. The afficionado recognizes a thousand subtleties the casual observer can never notice, and each of those subtleties might occasion some analysis. The casual fan views a skater's jump, and her appreciation amounts to the awestruck phrase: *How can they do that?* The afficionado, who *knows* how the skater can do that, who knows the names of particular jumps, who knows the strength each requires and the technique, who can recognize the slight defect in the landing and notice the skater's smooth recovery, can appreciate and explain to others each subtlety in the performance and the sum of them all. The learned observer's reaction is less pure, perhaps, but also more profound.

But the most ardent claims on this regard cannot convince you of anything. Study, analyze, write about, reread, recite like an aficionado of poetry and confirm it for yourself.

THE SEAGULL READER

Poems

Third Edition

Anonymous

"Western Wind" and "Sir Patrick Spens," two anonymous poems, were written in the early sixteenth and mid-seventeenth centuries, respectively. "Western Wind," a short lyric, was originally set to music and was later incorporated into Mass services, despite its seemingly secular subject matter. "Sir Patrick Spens" is a ballad, a subgenre of lyric poetry that tells a story in a compact, yet detailed narrative. It recounts what may be the true experience of Spens, a Scottish nobleman sent against his will by the king to deliver a princess to her bridegroom in Norway. All members of the escort party drowned on the way home.

Western Wind

Western wind, when will thou blow,
   The small rain down can rain?
Christ, if my love were in my arms
   And I in my bed again!

Sir Patrick Spens

I

The king sits in Dumferling town,[1]
   Drinking the blude-reid wine:
"O whar will I get guid sailor,
   To sail this ship of mine?"

2

Up and spak an eldern knicht,   5
   Sat at the king's richt knee:
"Sir Patrick Spens is the best sailor
   That sails upon the sea."

---

1. Now the city of Dunfermline, an ancient capital of the kingdom of Fife in Scotland.

3

The king has written a braid[2] letter
   And signed it wi' his hand,
And sent it to Sir Patrick Spens,
   Was walking on the sand.

10

4

The first line that Sir Patrick read,
   A loud lauch lauched he;
The next line that Sir Patrick read,
   The tear blinded his ee.

15

5

"O wha is this has done this deed,
   This ill deed done to me,
To send me out this time o' the year,
   To sail upon the sea?

20

6

"Mak haste, mak haste, my mirry men all,
   Our guid ship sails the morn."
"O say na sae, my master dear,
   For I fear a deadly storm.

7

"Late, late yestre'en I saw the new moon
   Wi' the auld moon in hir arm,
And I fear, I fear, my dear master,
   That we will come to harm."

25

2. Broad, i.e., long.

8

O our Scots nobles were richt laith
   To weet their cork-heeled shoon,
But lang or a' the play were played   30
   Their hats they swam aboon.[3]

9

O lang, lang may their ladies sit,
   Wi' their fans into their hand,
Or ere they see Sir Patrick Spens   35
   Come sailing to the land.

10

O lang, lang may the ladies stand
   Wi' their gold kems in their hair,
Waiting for their ain dear lords,
   For they'll see them na mair.   40

11

Half o'er, half o'er to Aberdour[4]
   It's fifty fadom deep,
And there lies guid Sir Patrick Spens
   Wi' the Scots lords at his feet.

1765

3. I.e., their hats swam above (them).
4. A coastal town near Dumferling.

Diane Ackerman
b. 1948

"School Prayer" is the first poem in Ackerman's book I Praise My Destroyer. *It functions as a sort of "invocation of the muse" for that volume. Traditionally in such invocations, the poet prays for inspiration at the start of a long work. The title of this poem and the rhetorical attitude of its speaker also suggest we might contrast it with the Pledge of Allegiance, which, alongside a moment of prayerful silence, starts the day for many American schoolchildren, or with other such ritual pledges, like the Boy Scouts'.*

School Prayer

In the name of the daybreak
and the eyelids of morning
and the wayfaring moon
and the night when it departs,

I swear I will not dishonor   5
my soul with hatred,
but offer myself humbly
as a guardian of nature,
as a healer of misery,
as a messenger of wonder,   10
as an architect of peace.

In the name of the sun and its mirrors
and the day that embraces it
and the cloud veils drawn over it
and the uttermost night   15
and the male and the female
and the plants bursting with seed
and the crowning seasons
of the firefly and the apple,

I will honor all life   20
—wherever and in whatever form
it may dwell—on Earth my home,
and in the mansions of the stars.

2000

Kim Addonizio
b. 1954

> *The sonnenizio is a parody Addonizio invented, combining* sonnet
> *with her own last name. Her note to the poem is a playful fiction,*
> *though the description of the form is accurate, and now so many*
> *other poets have written their own sonnenizios that it has become*
> *a legitimate subgenre among lyric poems. Acknowledging influences*
> *from Edna St. Vincent Millay, Dorothy Parker, and Sharon Olds,*
> *Addonizio is as much admired for her lyrical wit as her unblink-*
> *ing frankness. No matter if you might offend someone close to you*
> *or if your poem seems too personal, Addonizio advises young poets*
> *to "write it."*

Sonnenizio on a Line from Drayton

Since there's no help, come let us kiss and part;
or kiss anyway, let's start with that, with the kissing part,
because it's better than the parting part, isn't it—
we're good at kissing, we like how that part goes:
we part our lips, our mouths get near and nearer,   5
then we're close, my breasts, your chest, our bodies partway
to making love, so we might as well, part of me thinks—
the wrong part, I know, the bad part, but still
let's pretend we're at that party where we met
and scandalized everyone, remember that part? Hold me   10
like that again, unbutton my shirt, part of you
wants to I can tell, I'm touching that part and it says
yes, the ardent partisan, let it win you over,
it's hopeless, come, we'll kiss and part forever.

2004

Note: The sonnenizio was invented in Florence in the thirteenth century by Vanni Fucci as an irreverent form whose subject was usually the impossibility of everlasting love. Dante retaliated by putting Fucci into the seventh chasm of the Inferno as a thief.[1] Originally composed in hendecasyllabics, the sonnenizio gradually moved away from metrical constraints and began to tackle a wider variety of subject matter. The sonnenizio is fourteen lines long. It opens with a line from someone else's sonnet, repeats a word from that line in each succeeding line of the poem, and closes with a rhymed couplet.

Paul Allen
b. 1945

  "The Man with the Hardest Belly" is a narrative poem, so we read it with some of the same tools we use to read a story, looking for a conflict and resolution. It is also a study in irony. Readers, as well as the characters in the poem, view the preacher and his sermon differently from the way he expects to be viewed. But in the last three lines of the poem we discover a possible conflict and the role the preacher played in resolving the conflict. With these last three lines in mind, you might reread the poem and consider the irony once again.

The Man with the Hardest Belly

I

THE MAN WITH THE HARDEST BELLY knows God
compensates his loss of limbs—legs
to knee, nub arms—with a gift
to titillate the congregations when he is delivered
from Ocala in his motor home to call us to Christ.   5
This handsome chunk of what was left
after he'd been shucked, he says, at 14
found God by serving himself on our tables
if we had canned corn at all in 19 and 55.

---

  1. In Canto XXIV of his *Inferno*, Date Alighieri (1256–1321) relegates Vanni Fucci, a real-life contaporary, to the eighth circle of hell.

We are not members here. As Dad said, we   10
have our own faith. But someone spirit-filled
made Mother promise. So we're here cross-legged
on the cool ground at the river,
and my father is chosen. The Youth Director
is chosen. The man high up in Amway   15
is chosen. The three of them hang
THE MAN WITH THE HARDEST BELLY over the first branch
of the maple like a sandbag on the levee.
He pops his torso, flips, chins
to the next branch, flips, grabs a limb   20
with his thighs. Left nub for leverage,
he hooks another V with the back
of his head, walks on stumps up the trunk
to the next limb, flips to his belly, bends,
flips, holds with his teeth. He maneuvers   25
like something stained and mating
toward the top of our slide in godless biology,
or like the little dots we see inside our own eyes
on days we're morose. The thing
we've come to watch we can't watch   30
directly as he works toward the sun. The higher
he goes, the more we must look down to save
our eyes. We pull grass, look up and squint
to check his progress, kill an ant climbing our shoe.
Some stand to change the angle,   35
to keep him closer to the shaded cars.
Settling high, balanced and swaying, he preaches
from the texts painted on his motor home
under the faded "DOUBT AND DELIVERY."

II

. . . so look with me now at Genesis, whole people, Genesis 15:1–6.   40
Abram. Abram was a cripple in bed, had no standing among

men. Listen to me, had no standing among men, praise God, and
Moses, who said no, not me, not me, God gave Moses what he
needed. And Joshua at their first real trial? Joshua didn't think he
could do nothing. Joshua 7:1–10. I thank God my arms and legs 45
went to your soft tummies in '55. I was born again in that
shucking machine, look at my belly, my hard and strong belly, you
could park a truck on my belly praise God, God gives you what
you need. I need a strong belly and a lithe neck to climb trees and
show you the Holy Spirit at work, and show you the 50
compensations of our precious Lord. Praise you, Lord. The Holy
Spirit turns my pages for me. Look at Joshua splashing dirt up in
his face. I'm here to tell you people there's no dirt in my face, no
Lord. And Gideon. It's right there in your book. Judges 6:1–14.
What does God say to that worthless garment of feces? (Excuse me, 55
ladies, but the compensations of God is nothing to be delicate
about.) Says to Gideon, go in your power. Go in your power.
Listen to me now: Go in your power and save my people. Read it.
Isn't that what it says? Your power. Don't look at me, I know I'm
pretty. Look at your book, look at your own Holy Word. Now 60
examine, if you will, First Corinthians 10:13. See? God won't give
you nothing wrong without a correlational power to get out of it.
. . . Jesus himself, his wonderment self, take this cup from my lips,
listen now, take this cup from my lips, take this cup. . . .

III

We pull off the road to let the other cars by. 65
The Youth Director finds a wide place.
And the man high up in Amway finds a wide place.
The three of us wait, our hazard lights blinking,
while the born again wave and the kids shout
from their windows that Jesus is the One 70
and fathers honk (Honk If You Love Jesus).
My father nods occasionally. My sister starts
it. We are arguing about whether
THE MAN WITH THE HARDEST BELLY crawls on all
four nubs around the rooms of his scriptural 75
motor home, or slithers like something run over.

Crawls. Slithers. My father hushes us. My sister hits
me, says, "For unto you is born *a child*." I hit
my sister: "Let the women keep silent
in the Chevrolet." My mother has had enough.   80
She separates us. We aren't to speak. We aren't
to utter a peep. Each of us must look out our own window.

IV

The cars are thinning. We can hear the hazards now.
The road is dark and the dust is settling.
"I told her we'd go, and we went," my mother says.   85
"I told you we'd come, and we came," my father says.
"I thought it a bit much, though," she says, "when
he stood on his perch, spread those arms
and screamed, 'Nail me. Nail me.' "
"Me too," my father says, "nails wouldn't work."   90
My mother is looking at him. He says,
"Toggle bolts might work."
"Go help him down," my mother says, "and let's go home."

My father joins the other two on the road. They walk
back toward the river. My mother tells us it will   95
turn cool; we don't need to bathe when we get home,
but we do need to wash our feet. My father appears.
He eases us between the Youth Director and the man
high up in Amway. When we're on the main road
and the others have turned off, my mother says,   100
"I thought we'd have your mother over tomorrow.
Remind me to get a ham out when we get home."
"And corn?" my father says. "Whatever," she says.

V

Tonight down the cold upstairs hall we hear
them laughing, my mother and father.   105
Tonight we hear them making love again.
                1997

Matthew Arnold
1822–1888

> *Because Dover is the spot on the English coast closest to France, newlyweds would often spend their wedding night there before sailing for the Continent, and some evidence indicates that Arnold first drafted this poem on his honeymoon in 1851. The poem was not published until 1867, so it made its debut in the midst of the religious doubts fomented by Darwin's* On Origin of Species *(1859). In the wake of what he considered religion's failure, Arnold imagined that poetry would do the work religion no longer could.*

Dover Beach

The sea is calm tonight.
The tide is full, the moon lies fair
Upon the straits; on the French coast the light
Gleams and is gone; the cliffs of England stand,
Glimmering and vast, out in the tranquil bay.   5
Come to the window, sweet is the night-air!
Only, from the long line of spray
Where the sea meets the moon-blanched land,
Listen! you hear the grating roar
Of pebbles which the waves draw back, and fling,   10
At their return, up the high strand,
Begin, and cease, and then again begin,
With tremulous cadence slow, and bring
The eternal note of sadness in.

Sophocles[1] long ago   15
Heard it on the Aegean,[2] and it brought
Into his mind the turbid ebb and flow
Of human misery; we

---

1. The best of the Greek tragedians (495–406 B.C.E.). In his play *Antigone*, he compares the fortunes of humankind to the rising and falling tides.

2. The eastern part of the Mediterranean that surrounds Greece.

Find also in the sound a thought,
Hearing it by this distant northern sea.   20

The Sea of Faith
Was once, too, at the full, and round earth's shore
Lay like the folds of a bright girdle furled.
But now I only hear
Its melancholy, long withdrawing roar,   25
Retreating, to the breath
Of the night-wind, down the vast edges drear
And naked shingles[3] of the world.

Ah, love, let us be true
To one another! for the world, which seems   30
To lie before us like a land of dreams,
So various, so beautiful, so new,
Hath really neither joy, nor love, nor light,
Nor certitude, nor peace, nor help for pain;
And we are here as on a darkling plain   35
Swept with confused alarms of struggle and flight,
Where ignorant armies clash by night.

                                        1867

John Ashbery
b. 1927

Ashbery is one of the first generation of the New York School of poetry, which is known for mixing a philosophical tone with a concern for a careful, even loving attention to the little events of life. Ashbery wrote "The Painter" early in his career, publishing it in his 1956 collection, Some Trees. *It might be compared to other poems about art's relation to the world, to its audience, and to the artist, such as Auden's "Musée des Beaux Arts." "North Farm" was first published in the 1987 collection* A Wave. *Ashbery is notoriously hard to understand. It is especially difficult*

---

3. Beaches of smooth pebbles.

to keep personalities distinct, even the personality of the speaker.
In Ashbery's poems, what we think of as "character" is often fluid
and unfixed.

The Painter

Sitting between the sea and the buildings
He enjoyed painting the sea's portrait.
But just as children imagine a prayer
Is merely silence, he expected his subject
To rush up the sand, and, seizing a brush,   5
Plaster its own portrait on the canvas.

So there was never any paint on his canvas
Until the people who lived in the buildings
Put him to work: "Try using the brush
As a means to an end. Select, for a portrait,   10
Something less angry and large, and more subject
To a painter's moods, or, perhaps, to a prayer."

How could he explain to them his prayer
That nature, not art, might usurp the canvas?
He chose his wife for a new subject,   15
Making her vast, like ruined buildings,
As if, forgetting itself, the portrait
Had expressed itself without a brush.

Slightly encouraged, he dipped his brush
In the sea, murmuring a heartfelt prayer: 20
"My soul, when I paint this next portrait
Let it be you who wrecks the canvas."
The news spread like wildfire through the buildings:
He had gone back to the sea for his subject.

Imagine a painter crucified by his subject!   25
Too exhausted even to lift his brush,

He provoked some artists leaning from the buildings
To malicious mirth: "We haven't a prayer
Now, of putting ourselves on canvas,
Or getting the sea to sit for a portrait!"   30

Others declared it a self-portrait.
Finally all indications of a subject
Began to fade, leaving the canvas
Perfectly white. He put down the brush.
At once a howl, that was also a prayer,   35
Arose from the overcrowded buildings.

They tossed him, the portrait, from the tallest of the buildings;
And the sea devoured the canvas and the brush
As though his subject had decided to remain a prayer.

                                                    1956

At North Farm

Somewhere someone is traveling furiously toward you,
At incredible speed, traveling day and night,
Through blizzards and desert heat, across torrents, through
    narrow passes
But will he know where to find you,
Recognize you when he sees you,   5
Give you the thing he has for you?

Hardly anything grows here,
Yet the granaries are bursting with meal,
The sacks of meal piled to the rafters.
The streams run with sweetness, fattening fish;   10
Birds darken the sky. Is it enough
That the dish of milk is set out at night,
That we think of him sometimes,
Sometimes and always, with mixed feelings?

                                                    1987

Margaret Atwood

b. 1939

"You Fit into Me" is the first poem in Atwood's Power Politics *(1971). This book tells the story of a relationship between a female speaker and her male lover, who is the audience. As it follows the pair going to the movies, going out to dinner, doing all the things courting couples do,* Power Politics *demythologizes the romance of domestic love. The book's title echoes that of Kate Millett's* Sexual Politics *(1970), a landmark volume demonstrating that political power is exercised through domestic and romantic relations between men and women.*

You Fit into Me

you fit into me
like a hook into an eye

a fish hook
an open eye

1971

W. H. (Wystan Hugh) Auden

1907–1973

Auden, a political liberal and a homosexual, was the leading figure in a group of disillusioned 1930s British poets (Stephen Spender was in Auden's circle). "As I Walked Out One Evening" represents the sentiments of these writers well. They are also marked by a high degree of political awareness. Auden wrote "Musée des Beaux Arts" (Museum of Fine Arts) while staying in Paris in December 1938. He believed that Western democracies were doing nothing as fascists in Spain, Germany, and Italy violently oppressed communists, homosexuals, Jews, and others. The first stanza describes Pieter Brueghel's painting The Massacre of the Innocents, *which depicts Herod's attempt to kill the infant Jesus by slaughtering all young Jewish children. The second stanza refers to Brueghel's* The Fall of Icarus, *in which that mythical figure, who flew too near the sun wearing wings of feathers and wax, falls from the sky in a corner of the painting, almost unnoticed.*

As I Walked Out One Evening

As I walked out one evening,
  Walking down Bristol Street,
The crowds upon the pavement
  Were fields of harvest wheat.

And down by the brimming river   5
  I heard a lover sing
Under an arch of the railway:
  "Love has no ending.

"I'll love you, dear, I'll love you
  Till China and Africa meet,   10
And the river jumps over the mountain
  And the salmon sing in the street,

"I'll love you till the ocean
  Is folded and hung up to dry
And the seven stars[1] go squawking   15
  Like geese about the sky.

"The years shall run like rabbits,
  For in my arms I hold
The Flower of the Ages,
  And the first love of the world."   20

But all the clocks in the city
  Began to whirr and chime:
"O let not Time deceive you,
  You cannot conquer Time.

---

1. Probably the Seven Sisters, or the Pleiades, of Greek mythology, who were pursued by Orion for seven years until, in answer to their prayers, Zeus transformed them into doves and placed them in a cluster in the night sky. When Orion was transformed into a constellation, he was put behind the Pleiades, whom he pursues forever.

"In the burrows of the Nightmare   25
    Where Justice naked is,
Time watches from the shadow
    And coughs when you would kiss.

"In headaches and in worry
    Vaguely life leaks away,   30
And Time will have his fancy
    To-morrow or to-day.

"Into many a green valley
    Drifts the appalling snow;
Time breaks the threaded dances   35
    And the diver's brilliant bow.

"O plunge your hands in water,
    Plunge them in up to the wrist;
Stare, stare in the basin
    And wonder what you've missed.   40

"The glacier knocks in the cupboard,
    The desert sighs in the bed,
And the crack in the tea-cup opens
    A lane to the land of the dead.

"Where the beggars raffle the banknotes   45
    And the Giant is enchanting to Jack,
And the Lily-white Boy is a Roarer,
    And Jill goes down on her back.²

"O look, look in the mirror,
    O look in your distress;   50
Life remains a blessing
    Although you cannot bless.

2. All of these references are to fairy tales or children's rhymes: "Jack and the Bean Stalk,"
"Green Grow the Rushes, O," and "Jack and Jill." Jack and the giant are enemies in the orig-
inal story. Roarer: a partier, in contrast with the purity suggested by "lily white." In Auden's
line, the innocent child Jill is offering herself to a lover.

"O stand, stand at the window
    As the tears scald and start;
You shall love your crooked neighbour   55
    With your crooked heart."

It was late, late in the evening,
    The lovers they were gone;
The clocks had ceased their chiming,
    And the deep river ran on.   60
1937   *1940*

Musée des Beaux Arts

About suffering they were never wrong,
The Old Masters: how well they understood
Its human position; how it takes place
While someone else is eating or opening a window or just
    walking dully along;
How, when the aged are reverently, passionately waiting   5
For the miraculous birth, there always must be
Children who did not specially want it to happen, skating
On a pond at the edge of the wood:
They never forgot
That even the dreadful martyrdom must run its course   10
Anyhow in a corner, some untidy spot
Where the dogs go on with their doggy life and the torturer's
    horse
Scratches its innocent behind on a tree.

In Brueghel's *Icarus*, for instance: how everything turns away
Quite leisurely from the disaster; the ploughman may   15
Have heard the splash, the forsaken cry,
But for him it was not an important failure; the sun shone
As it had to on the white legs disappearing into the green
Water; and the expensive delicate ship that must have seen
Something amazing, a boy falling out of the sky,   20
Had somewhere to get to and sailed calmly on.
                    1938

Jimmy Santiago Baca
b. 1952

Born in New Mexico and abandoned by his parents, Baca lived with his grandmother, then in an orphanage, and by the age of thirteen he ran away and lived on the streets. By twenty-one, he was in a maximum security prison serving time for drugs. Behind bars, he learned to read and write, discovered poetry, and began composing his own poems. The magazine Mother Jones *published several while he was still in jail, and the same year he was released, he published his first book,* Immigrants in Our Own Land *(1979). Every poem in that collection, including this one, explores the lives of the dispossessed, downtrodden, and imprisoned.*

I Am Offering This Poem

I am offering this poem to you,
since I have nothing else to give.
Keep it like a warm coat
when winter comes to cover you,
or like a pair of thick socks   5
the cold cannot bite through,

        I love you,

I have nothing else to give you,
so it is a pot full of yellow corn
to warm your belly in winter,   10
it is a scarf for your head, to wear
over your hair, to tie up around your face,

        I love you,

Keep it, treasure this as you would
if you were lost, needing direction,   15
in the wilderness life becomes when mature;
and in the corner of your drawer,
tucked away like a cabin or hogan
in dense trees, come knocking,
and I will answer, give you directions,   20

and let you warm yourself by this fire,
rest by this fire, and make you feel safe,

　　　I love you,

It's all I have to give,
and all anyone needs to live,　　　　　　　　　　　　　25
and to go on living inside,
when the world outside
no longer cares if you live or die;
remember,

　　　I love you.　　　　　　　　　　　　　　　　　30

　　　　　1979

Anna Letitia Barbauld
1743–1825

When the French Revolution of 1789 seemed to free men from the yoke of aristocratic and church privilege, Mary Wollestonecraft wrote A Vindication of the Rights of Woman *to argue that women deserved the same liberty and opportunity for growth as men. She deplored the means of indirect influence—the "feminine" wiles—that were typically taught to middle- and upper-class women, criticizing in particular another poem by Anna Letitia Barbauld. This poem is Barbauld's reply to Wollestonecraft's criticism—a somewhat ironic call for women to use what weapons they have to defeat men. Pay careful attention to Barbauld's tone, especially to any changes.*

The Rights of Woman

Yes, injured Woman! rise, assert thy right!
Woman! too long degraded, scorned, opprest;
O born to rule in partial Law's despite,
Resume thy native empire o'er the breast!

Go forth arrayed in panoply divine;   5
That angel pureness which admits no stain;
Go, bid proud Man his boasted rule resign,
And kiss the golden sceptre of thy reign.

Go, gird thyself with grace; collect thy store
Of bright artillery glancing from afar;   10
Soft melting tones thy thundering cannon's roar,
Blushes and fears thy magazine of war.

Thy rights are empire: urge no meaner claim,—
Felt, not defined, and if debated, lost;
Like sacred mysteries, which withheld from fame,   15
Shunning discussion, are revered the most.

Try all that wit and art suggest to bend
Of thy imperial foe the stubborn knee;
Make treacherous Man thy subject, not thy friend;
Thou mayst command, but never canst be free.   20

Awe the licentious, and restrain the rude;
Soften the sullen, clear the cloudy brow;
Be, more than princes' gifts, thy favours sued;—
She hazards all, who will the least allow.

But hope not, courted idol of mankind,   25
On this proud eminence secure to stay;
Subduing and subdued, thou soon shalt find
Thy coldness soften, and thy pride give way.

Then, then, abandon each ambitious thought,
Conquest or rule thy heart shall feebly move,   30
In Nature's school, by her soft maxims taught,
That separate rights are lost in mutual love.

                            1825

Aphra Behn
1640–1689

Behn wrote during the English Restoration, an era famous for its witty and explicit treatment of the relations between the sexes. Nevertheless, in poems like this one, Behn challenged the prevalent sexual mores of her society. Even in the Restoration, her utopian vision of a world of frank and shameless sexual relations was provocative. In her influential feminist treatise, A Room of One's Own, Virginia Woolf declared that "[a]ll women together ought to let flowers fall upon the tomb of Aphra Behn, for it was she who earned them the right to speak their minds." But it was not until the twentieth century that this tribute was paid: from shortly after her death until the early 1900s, Behn's work was generally ignored or vilified for being too frank and bawdy, especially for a woman writer.

To the Fair Clarinda,[1] Who Made Love to Me, Imagined More Than Woman

Fair lovely maid, or if that title be
Too weak, too feminine for nobler thee,
Permit a name that more approaches truth,
And let me call thee, lovely charming youth.
This last will justify my soft complaint,   5
While that may serve to lessen my constraint;
And without blushes I the youth pursue,
When so much beauteous woman is in view.
Against thy charms we struggle but in vain
With thy deluding form thou giv'st us pain,   10
While the bright nymph betrays us to the swain.
In pity to our sex sure thou wert sent,
That we might love, and yet be innocent:
For sure no crime with thee we can commit;

---

1. Critics have not identified a real person who might be Clarinda, nor has anyone identified Cloris and Alexis (line 19), who are, presumably, Clarinda's parents.

Or if we should—thy form excuses it.   15
For who, that gathers fairest flowers believes
A snake lies hid beneath the fragrant leaves.

Thou beauteous wonder of a different kind,
Soft Cloris with the dear Alexis joined;
When e'er the manly part of thee, would plead   20
Thou tempts us with the image of the maid,
While we the noblest passions do extend
The love to Hermes, Aphrodite[2] the friend.

1688

John Berryman
1914–1972

> *Berryman's magnum opus was the two-volume* The Dream Songs, *the first 77 of which appeared in 1964. In response to readers' misunderstandings of those poems, he later wrote that* The Dream Songs, *"whatever [their] wide cast of characters, is essentially about an imaginary character (not the poet, not me) named Henry, a white American in early middle age, sometimes in black-face, who has suffered an irreversible loss and talks about himself sometimes in the first person, sometimes in the third, sometimes even in the second; he has a friend, never named, who addresses him as Mr Bones and variants thereof."*

from The Dream Songs

14

Life, friends, is boring. We must not say so.
After all, the sky flashes, the great sea yearns,
we ourselves flash and yearn,

---

2. The Greek god Hermes and goddess Aphrodite had a child Hermaphroditus, who was fused to the nymph Salmacis. Hermaphroditus and Salmacis became one body, both man and woman.

and moreover my mother told me as a boy
(repeatedly) 'Ever to confess you're bored   5
means you have no

Inner Resources.' I conclude now I have no
inner resources, because I am heavy bored.
Peoples bore me,
literature bores me, especially great literature,   10
Henry bores me, with his plights & gripes
as bad as achilles,[1]

who loves people and valiant art, which bores me.
And the tranquil hills, & gin, look like a drag
and somehow a dog   15
has taken itself & its tail considerably away
into mountains or sea or sky, leaving
behind: me, wag.

1964

Elizabeth Bishop
1911–1979
> Bishop spent most of 1940 in Key West, where she caught a giant
> Caribbean jewfish, the subject of "The Fish." Partisan Review
> published the poem in March 1940 and launched Bishop's career.
> Readers often take the speakers in Bishop's poems to be the poet her-
> self. In "Sestina" Bishop writes about her own childhood, just as
> "One Art," a villanelle written in 1975, was inspired by her battle
> with alcohol. When reading Bishop, consider whether the strict for-
> mal requirements of the sestina and villanelle increase or diminish
> the emotions expressed in her poems.

---

1. In Homer's *Iliad*, Achilles was the greatest Greek soldier of the Trojan War but was also a complainer who exaggerated slights against his honor.

The Fish

I caught a tremendous fish
and held him beside the boat
half out of water, with my hook
fast in a corner of his mouth.
He didn't fight.   5
He hadn't fought at all.
He hung a grunting weight,
battered and venerable
and homely. Here and there
his brown skin hung in strips   10
like ancient wallpaper,
and its pattern of darker brown
was like wallpaper:
shapes like full-blown roses
stained and lost through age.   15
He was speckled with barnacles,
fine rosettes of lime,
and infested
with tiny white sea-lice,
and underneath two or three   20
rags of green weed hung down.
While his gills were breathing in
the terrible oxygen
—the frightening gills,
fresh and crisp with blood,   25
that can cut so badly—
I thought of the coarse white flesh
packed in like feathers,
the big bones and the little bones,
the dramatic reds and blacks   30
of his shiny entrails,
and the pink swim-bladder
like a big peony.
I looked into his eyes
which were far larger than mine   35
but shallower, and yellowed,

the irises backed and packed
with tarnished tinfoil
seen through the lenses
of old scratched isinglass.[1]   40
They shifted a little, but not
to return my stare.
—It was more like the tipping
of an object toward the light.
I admired his sullen face,   45
the mechanism of his jaw,
and then I saw
that from his lower lip
—if you could call it a lip—
grim, wet, and weaponlike,   50
hung five old pieces of fish-line,
or four and a wire leader
with the swivel still attached,
with all their five big hooks
grown firmly in his mouth.   55
A green line, frayed at the end
where he broke it, two heavier lines,
and a fine black thread
still crimped from the strain and snap
when it broke and he got away.   60
Like medals with their ribbons
frayed and wavering,
a five-haired beard of wisdom
trailing from his aching jaw.
I stared and stared   65
and victory filled up
the little rented boat,
from the pool of bilge
where oil had spread a rainbow
around the rusted engine   70
to the bailer rusted orange,

1. A transparent gelatin made from the air bladders of some fish.

the sun-cracked thwarts,
the oarlocks on their strings,
the gunnels—until everything
was rainbow, rainbow, rainbow!   75
And I let the fish go.

                    1946

Sestina

September rain falls on the house.
In the failing light, the old grandmother
sits in the kitchen with the child
beside the Little Marvel Stove,
reading the jokes from the almanac,   5
laughing and talking to hide her tears.

She thinks that her equinoctial tears
and the rain that beats on the roof of the house
were both foretold by the almanac,
but only known to a grandmother.   10
The iron kettle sings on the stove.
She cuts some bread and says to the child,

It's time for tea now; but the child
is watching the teakettle's small hard tears
dance like mad on the hot black stove,   15
the way the rain must dance on the house.
Tidying up, the old grandmother
hangs up the clever almanac

on its string. Birdlike, the almanac
hovers half open above the child,   20
hovers above the old grandmother
and her teacup full of dark brown tears.
She shivers and says she thinks the house
feels chilly, and puts more wood in the stove.

It was to be, says the Marvel Stove.　　　　　　　　25
I know what I know, says the almanac.
With crayons the child draws a rigid house
and a winding pathway. Then the child
puts in a man with buttons like tears
and shows it proudly to the grandmother.　　　　　30

But secretly, while the grandmother
busies herself about the stove,
the little moons fall down like tears
from between the pages of the almanac
into the flower bed the child　　　　　　　　　　35
has carefully placed in the front of the house.

Time to plant tears, says the almanac.
The grandmother sings to the marvelous stove
and the child draws another inscrutable house.

　　　　　　　　　　　　　　　　　1965

One Art

The art of losing isn't hard to master;
so many things seem filled with the intent
to be lost that their loss is no disaster.

Lose something every day. Accept the fluster
of lost door keys, the hour badly spent.　　　　　5
The art of losing isn't hard to master.

Then practice losing farther, losing faster:
places, and names, and where it was you meant
to travel. None of these will bring disaster.

I lost my mother's watch. And look! my last, or　　10
next-to-last, of three loved houses went.
The art of losing isn't hard to master.

I lost two cities, lovely ones. And, vaster,
some realms I owned, two rivers, a continent.
I miss them, but it wasn't a disaster.   15

—Even losing you (the joking voice, a gesture
I love) I shan't have lied. It's evident
the art of losing's not too hard to master
though it may look like (*Write* it!) like disaster.

1976

Sonnet

Caught—the bubble
in the spirit-level,
a creature divided;
and the compass needle
wobbling and wavering,   5
undecided.
Freed—the broken
thermometer's mercury
running away;
and the rainbow-bird   10
from the narrow bevel
of the empty mirror,
flying wherever
it feels like, gay!

1979

William Blake

1757–1827

> Blake, an Englishman sympathetic to political and social revolution, was an engraver, and his books included his own illustrations. In 1789, the year of the French Revolution, Blake published Songs of Innocence, which he expanded five years later to include his Songs of Experience. The two sections of this book were meant to display "the two Contrary States of the Human Soul," as his title page announces. The "innocent" poems are prefaced by a picture of an angelic child and a rustic musician. The child asks the musician to "Pipe a song about a Lamb," and the musician sings the "songs of innocence" in response. Of the five poems here, only "The Lamb" comes from Songs of Innocence. The poems of "experience" include its counterpart, "The Tyger," as well as "The Sick Rose" and "London."

To Autumn

O Autumn, laden with fruit, and stained
With the blood of the grape, pass not, but sit
Beneath my shady roof, there thou may'st rest,
And tune thy jolly voice to my fresh pipe;
And all the daughters of the year shall dance!   5
Sing now the lusty song of fruits and flowers.

'The narrow bud opens her beauties to
'The sun, and love runs in her thrilling veins;
'Blossoms hang round the brows of morning, and
'Flourish down the bright cheek of modest eve,   10
'Till clust'ring Summer breaks forth into singing,
'And feather'd clouds strew flowers round her head.

'The spirits of the air live on the smells
'Of fruit; and joy, with pinions[1] light, roves round
'The gardens, or sits singing in the trees.'   15
Thus sang the jolly Autumn as he sat,

---

1. Birds' wings or the end feathers of wings.

Then rose, girded himself, and o'er the bleak
Hills fled from our sight; but left his golden load.

1783

The Lamb

   Little Lamb, who made thee?
   Dost thou know who made thee?
Gave thee life & bid thee feed,
By the stream & o'er the mead;
Gave thee clothing of delight,   5
Softest clothing wooly bright;
Gave thee such a tender voice,
Making all the vales rejoice!
   Little Lamb who made thee?
   Dost thou know who made thee?   10

   Little Lamb I'll tell thee,
   Little Lamb I'll tell thee!
He is calléd by thy name,
For he calls himself a Lamb:
He is meek & he is mild,   15
He became a little child:
I a child & thou a lamb,
We are calléd by his name.
   Little Lamb God bless thee.
   Little Lamb God bless thee.   20

1789

The Sick Rose

O Rose, thou art sick.
The invisible worm
That flies in the night
In the howling storm

Has found out thy bed   5
Of crimson joy,

And his dark secret love
Does thy life destroy.
1794

The Tyger

Tyger! Tyger! burning bright
In the forests of the night,
What immortal hand or eye
Could frame thy fearful symmetry?

In what distant deeps or skies   5
Burnt the fire of thine eyes?
On what wings dare he aspire?
What the hand, dare seize the fire?

And what shoulder, & what art,
Could twist the sinews of thy heart?   10
And when thy heart began to beat,
What dread hand? & what dread feet?

What the hammer? what the chain?
In what furnace was thy brain?
What the anvil? what dread grasp   15
Dare its deadly terrors clasp?

When the stars threw down their spears,
And water'd heaven with their tears,
Did he smile his work to see?
Did he who made the Lamb make thee?   20

Tyger! Tyger! burning bright
In the forests of the night,
What immortal hand or eye
Dare frame thy fearful symmetry?
1794

London

I wander thro' each charter'd[1] street,
Near where the charter'd Thames does flow,
And mark in every face I meet
Marks of weakness, marks of woe.

In every cry of every man,   5
In every Infant's cry of fear,
In every voice, in every ban,[2]
The mind-forg'd manacles I hear.

How the Chimney-sweeper's cry
Every blackning Church appalls;   10
And the hapless Soldier's sigh
Runs in blood down Palace walls.

But most thro' midnight streets I hear
How the youthful Harlot's curse
Blasts the new-born Infant's tear,   15
And blights with plagues the Marriage hearse.

1794

Anne Bradstreet
1612 or 1613–1672

The primitive conditions of colonial America contrasted with the delicacy of Bradstreet's former life in England, but she prospered and raised eight children, all the while writing poetry. "The Author to Her Book" is an example of apostrophe, which is when the poet speaks to someone who's not present or to some personified thing. In this case, her comparing her poems to her children is a common poetic trope. "To My Dear and Loving Husband" is a love poem to

1. Within the city limits of London.   2. A law or notice commanding or forbidding; a published penalty.

Simon Bradstreet, who was once governor of the colony and ambassador to the court of England. She wrote it after they settled in Andover in a comfortable, three-story house, the privations of their pioneering behind them, but it was not published until after her death, in the 1678 edition of The Tenth Muse. *In many interesting ways, Bradstreet contradicts the stereotype we have of the Puritan ethic of fleshly denial.*

The Author to Her Book

Thou ill-formed offspring of my feeble brain,
Who after birth didst by my side remain,
Till snatched from thence by friends, less wise than true,
Who thee abroad, exposed to public view,
Made thee in rags, halting to th' press to trudge,   5
Where errors were not lessened (all may judge).
At thy return my blushing was not small,
My rambling brat (in print) should mother call,
I cast thee by as one unfit for light,
Thy visage was so irksome in my sight;   10
Yet being mine own, at length affection would
Thy blemishes amend, if so I could;
I washed thy face, but more defects I saw,
And rubbing off a spot still made a flaw.
I stretched thy joints to make thee even feet,   15
Yet still thou run'st more hobbling than is meet;
In better dress to trim thee was my mind,
But nought save homespun cloth i' th' house I find.
In this array 'mongst vulgars may'st thou roam.
In critic's hands beware thou dost not come,   20
And take thy way where yet thou art not known;
If for thy father asked, say thou hadst none;
And for thy mother, she alas is poor,
Which caused her thus to send thee out of door.

                                        1678

To My Dear and Loving Husband

If ever two were one, then surely we.
If ever man were loved by wife, then thee;
If ever wife was happy in a man,
Compare with me, ye women, if you can.
I prize thy love more than whole mines of gold   5
Or all the riches that the East doth hold.
My love is such that rivers cannot quench,
Nor ought but love from thee, give recompense.
Thy love is such I can no way repay,
The heavens reward thee manifold, I pray.   10
Then while we live, in love let's so persevere
That when we live no more, we may live ever.

1678

Emily Brontë

1818–1848

> *Most of Brontë's poems came out of a fantasy world she shared with her sister Charlotte; together they invented (and wrote stories about) an elaborate, fantastic world populated by an encyclopedic panoply of characters. Nearly all that remains of this byzantine world are her poems, so we know very little about the speakers, only what the poems themselves reveal.*

I'm Happiest When Most Away

I'm happiest when most away
   I can bear my soul from its home of clay
On a windy night when the moon is bright
And the eye can wander through worlds of light—

When I am not and none beside—   5
No earth nor sea nor cloudless sky—

But only spirit wandering wide
Through infinite immensity.
1838   *1910*

Gwendolyn Brooks
1917–2000

Though Brooks's early poems dealt with racial injustice, her work was initially recognized more for its fine craftmanship. "the mother" is from her first book of poems, A Street in Bronzeville *(1945), which recorded in realistic detail some of the experiences of Chicago's African American community. Brooks won the Pulitzer Prize in 1950, the first African American to do so, which expanded her audience considerably. "We Real Cool" and "The Bean Eaters" were published in* The Bean Eaters *(1960), which overtly criticized racial discrimination in America. Some critics attacked Brooks for abandoning the lyricism of her earlier work in favor of political rhetoric. The dropouts in "We Real Cool," she explained, "are people who are essentially saying, 'Kilroy is here. We are.' But they're a little uncertain of the strength of their identity. . . . I want to represent their basic uncertainty."*

the mother

Abortions will not let you forget.
You remember the children you got that you did not get,
The damp small pulps with a little or with no hair,
The singers and workers that never handled the air.
You will never neglect or beat   5
Them, or silence or buy with a sweet.
You will never wind up the sucking-thumb
Or scuttle off ghosts that come.
You will never leave them, controlling your luscious sigh,
Return for a snack of them, with gobbling mother-eye.   10

I have heard in the voices of the wind the voices of my dim
    killed children.

I have contracted. I have eased
My dim dears at the breasts they could never suck.
I have said, Sweets, if I sinned, if I seized
Your luck   15
And your lives from your unfinished reach,
If I stole your births and your names,

Your straight baby tears and your games,
Your stilted or lovely loves, your tumults, your marriages,
      aches, and your deaths,
If I poisoned the beginnings of your breaths,   20
Believe that even in my deliberateness I was not deliberate.
Though why should I whine,
Whine that the crime was other than mine?—
Since anyhow you are dead.
Or rather, or instead,   25
You were never made.
But that too, I am afraid,
Is faulty: oh, what shall I say, how is the truth to be said?
You were born, you had body, you died.
It is just that you never giggled or planned or cried.   30

Believe me, I loved you all.
Believe me, I knew you, though faintly, and I loved, I loved
      you
All.

                                                       1945

We Real Cool

THE POOL PLAYERS.
SEVEN AT THE GOLDEN SHOVEL.

We real cool. We
Left school. We

Lurk late. We   5
Strike straight. We

Sing sin. We
Thin gin. We

Jazz June. We
Die soon.   10
    1960

The Bean Eaters

They eat beans mostly, this old yellow pair.
Dinner is a casual affair.
Plain chipware on a plain and creaking wood,
Tin flatware.

Two who are Mostly Good.   5
Two who have lived their day,
But keep on putting on their clothes
And putting things away.

And remembering . . .
Remembering, with twinklings and twinges,   10
As they lean over the beans in their rented back room that is
    full of beads and receipts and dolls and clothes, tobacco
    crumbs, vases and fringes.
                                         1960

Elizabeth Barrett Browning
1806–1861

> *Elizabeth Barrett was a famous poet and an invalid when, in
> 1846, the young playwright Robert Browning secretly courted her.
> Barrett recorded her feelings of excitement, doubt, and ecstasy in
> a series of forty-four sonnets. The curious title,* Sonnets from the
> Portuguese, *was meant to disguise the autobiographical nature of
> the poems, but today they are considered an accurate portrait of
> Barrett's feelings for Browning. As suggested in "The first time,"
> Barrett was older than Robert Browning and in ill health, nearly a*

*recluse, when he courted her. "How do I love thee?" was the second
to last poem in the sequence. Though it is tempting to dismiss this
poem as sentimental, in the context of the great religious doubts of
the nineteenth century, assigning one's lover the role of savior was
provocative rather than conventional.*

Sonnets from the Portuguese

32

The first time that the sun rose on thine oath
To love me, I looked forward to the moon
To slacken all those bonds which seemed too soon
And quickly tied to make a lasting troth.
Quick-loving hearts, I thought, may quickly loathe;   5
And, looking on myself, I seemed not one
For such man's love!—more like an out-of-tune
Worn viol, a good singer would be wroth
To spoil his song with, and which, snatched in haste,
Is laid down at the first ill-sounding note.   10
I did not wrong myself so, but I placed
A wrong on *thee*. For perfect strains may float
'Neath master-hands, from instruments defaced,—
And great souls, at one stroke, may do and doat.

1850

43

How do I love thee? Let me count the ways.
I love thee to the depth and breadth and height
My soul can reach, when feeling out of sight
For the ends of Being and ideal Grace.
I love thee to the level of everyday's   5
Most quiet need, by sun and candle-light.
I love thee freely, as men strive for Right;
I love thee purely, as they turn from Praise.
I love thee with the passion put to use
In my old griefs, and with my childhood's faith.   10

I love thee with a love I seemed to lose
With my lost saints—I love thee with the breath,
Smiles, tears, of all my life!—and, if God choose,
I shall but love thee better after death.

1850

Robert Browning
1812–1889

"My Last Duchess" was first published in the collection Dramatic
Lyrics *in 1842. As that title suggests, the poem is a dramatic mono-
logue: the speaker in the poem (as well as his audience) is a charac-
ter, as if in a play. Though the Duke was suggested to Browning by
a real, historical figure, this poem has as much to say about gender
relations in Victorian England as in sixteenth-century Italy. "Love
among the Ruins," published in 1855 in* Men and Women, *is a sort
of dramatic monologue also. In the manuscript, Browning subtitled
the poem "Sicilian Pastoral." The reference to Sicily suggests that the
ruins are Roman or Greek; a "pastoral" is an older poetic conven-
tion (not much in vogue in the 1800s) in which the speaker, though
often philosophizing with some sophistication, is a shepherd.*

My Last Duchess

Ferrara[1]

That's my last duchess painted on the wall,
Looking as if she were alive. I call
That piece a wonder, now: Frà Pandolf's hands
Worked busily a day, and there she stands.
Will't please you sit and look at her? I said   5
"Frà Pandolf" by design, for never read
Strangers like you that pictured countenance,

---

1. Alfonso II d'Este, the duke of Ferrara in the sixteenth century, married the fourteen-
year-old daughter of the duke of Florence in 1558. Three years later she died suspiciously, and
Alfonso soon began negotiating for the daughter of the count of Tyrol.

The depth and passion of its earnest glance,
But to myself they turned (since none puts by
The curtain I have drawn for you, but I)   10
And seemed as they would ask me, if they durst,
How such a glance came there; so, not the first
Are you to turn and ask thus. Sir, 'twas not
Her husband's presence only, called that spot
Of joy into the Duchess' cheek: perhaps   15
Frà Pandolf chanced to say "Her mantle laps
Over my lady's wrist too much," or "Paint
Must never hope to reproduce the faint
Half-flush that dies along her throat": such stuff
Was courtesy, she thought, and cause enough   20
For calling up that spot of joy. She had
A heart—how shall I say?—too soon made glad,
Too easily impressed; she liked whate'er
She looked on, and her looks went everywhere.
Sir, 'twas all one! My favor at her breast,   25
The dropping of the daylight in the West,
The bough of cherries some officious fool
Broke in the orchard for her, the white mule
She rode with round the terrace—all and each
Would draw from her alike the approving speech,   30
Or blush, at least. She thanked men—good! but thanked
Somehow—I know not how—as if she ranked
My gift of a nine-hundred-years-old name
With anybody's gift. Who'd stoop to blame
This sort of trifling? Even had you skill   35
In speech—(which I have not)—to make your will
Quite clear to such an one, and say, "Just this
Or that in you disgusts me; here you miss,
Or there exceed the mark"—and if she let
Herself be lessoned so, nor plainly set   40
Her wits to yours, forsooth, and made excuse,
—E'en then would be some stooping; and I choose
Never to stoop. Oh sir, she smiled, no doubt,
Whene'er I passed her; but who passed without
Much the same smile? This grew; I gave commands;   45

Then all smiles stopped together. There she stands
As if alive. Will't please you rise? We'll meet
The company below, then. I repeat,
The Count your master's known munificence
Is ample warrant that no just pretense   50
Of mine for dowry will be disallowed;
Though his fair daughter's self, as I avowed
At starting, is my object. Nay, we'll go
Together down, sir. Notice Neptune,[2] though,
Taming a sea-horse, thought a rarity,   55
Which Claus of Innsbruck[3] cast in bronze for me!
                                                        1842

Love among the Ruins

I

Where the quiet-colored end of evening smiles,
    Miles and miles
On the solitary pastures where our sheep
    Half-asleep
Tinkle homeward through the twilight, stray or stop   5
    As they crop—
Was the site once of a city great and gay
    (So they say),
Of our country's very capital, its prince
    Ages since   10
Held his court in, gathered councils, wielding far
    Peace or war.

2

Now—the country does not even boast a tree,
    As you see,

2. The Roman god of the sea, corre-   3. Probably a fictional sculptor.
sponding to the Greek Poseidon.

To distinguish slopes of verdure, certain rills   15
     From the hills
Intersect and give a name to (else they run
     Into one),
Where the domed and daring palace shot its spires
     Up like fires   20
O'er the hundred-gated circuit of a wall
     Bounding all,
Made of marble, men might march on nor be pressed,
     Twelve abreast.

3

And such plenty and perfection, see, of grass   25
     Never was!
Such a carpet as, this summertime, o'erspreads
     And embeds
Every vestige of the city, guessed alone,
     Stock or stone—   30
Where a multitude of men breathed joy and woe
     Long ago;
Lust of glory pricked their hearts up, dread of shame
     Struck them tame;
And that glory and that shame alike, the gold   35
     Bought and sold.

4

Now—the single little turret that remains
     On the plains,
By the caper overrooted, by the gourd
     Overscored,   40
While the patching houseleek's[1] head of blossom winks
     Through the chinks—

---

1. Common European plant, with petals shaped like rosettes.

Marks the basement whence a tower in ancient time
    Sprang sublime,
And a burning ring, all round, the chariots traced   45
    As they raced,
And the monarch and his minions and his dames
    Viewed the games.

5

And I know, while thus the quiet-colored eve
    Smiles to leave   50
To their folding, all our many-tinkling fleece
    In such peace,
And the slopes and rills in undistinguished gray
    Melt away—
That a girl with eager eyes and yellow hair   55
    Waits me there
In the turret whence the charioteers caught soul
    For the goal,
When the king looked, where she looks now, breathless, dumb
    Till I come.   60

6

But he looked upon the city, every side,
    Far and wide,
All the mountains topped with temples, all the glades'
    Colonnades,
All the causeys,[2] bridges, aqueducts—and then,   65
    All the men!
When I do come, she will speak not, she will stand,
    Either hand
On my shoulder, give her eyes the first embrace
    Of my face,   70

2. Causeways.

Ere we rush, ere we extinguish sight and speech
    Each on each.

7

In one year they sent a million fighters forth
    South and north,
And they built their gods a brazen pillar high   75
    As the sky,
Yet reserved a thousand chariots in full force—
    Gold, of course.
Oh heart! oh blood that freezes, blood that burns!
    Earth's returns   80
For whole centuries of folly, noise, and sin!
    Shut them in,
With their triumphs and their glories and the rest!
    Love is best.

1855

Robert Burns

1759–1796

> *Burns did not exactly write "A Red, Red Rose." As he put it, he picked up this old Scots song from rustics in the country, and then he first published it in a Scots singer's book of songs. It's a fine example of a type of literature made popular among the urban educated classes in the late eighteenth and early nineteenth centuries: folk tales and songs that gave a nation (in this case, Scotland) an almost tribal sense of community. By writing in dialect and collecting folk literature, Burns hoped to help Scotland preserve its cultural independence in the face of threats from the politically dominant England. This poem is also an early example of the Romantic movement's celebration of the simple emotions, often found among low, rural people, in contrast to the urbane, artificial manners of higher society.*

A Red, Red Rose

O my luve's like a red, red rose,
  That's newly sprung in June;
O my luve's like the melodie
  That's sweetly played in tune.

As fair art thou, my bonie lass,   5
  So deep in luve am I;
And I will luve thee still, my dear,
  Till a' the seas gang dry.

Till a' the seas gang dry, my dear,
  And the rocks melt wi' the sun: 10
O I will love thee still, my dear,
  While the sands o' life shall run.

And fare thee weel, my only luve!
  And fare thee weel a while!
And I will come again, my luve,   15
  Tho' it were ten thousand mile!
                    1796

George Gordon, Lord Byron
1788–1824

> *The most famous poet of his age, Lord Byron was the embodiment of the Romantic hero—young, brilliant, rakish, iconoclastic, sexually attractive and promiscuous, moody, unconventional, self-destructive, and plagued by a dark sense of foreboding. "She Walks in Beauty" departed from the narrative poetry for which he was best known; it was the first poem in an 1815 series called* Hebrew Melodies, *which were set to music that Isaac Nathan had supposedly adapted from ancient Jewish songs. These melodies exploited the vogue for the cultures that the English supposed were less modern and closer to nature than their own: for example, Byron's friend Thomas Moore was circulating his very popular* Irish Melodies *at*

the time. "*So We'll Go No More A-Roving*" *was included in a letter Byron wrote to Moore in 1817. It reflects the world-weary sentiments he himself felt and expressed in the largely autobiographical third Canto of* Childe Harold's Pilgrimage, *which he wrote about the same time.*

She Walks in Beauty

I

She walks in beauty, like the night
   Of cloudless climes and starry skies:
And all that's best of dark and bright
   Meet in her aspect and her eyes:
Thus mellowed to that tender light   5
   Which heaven to gaudy day denies.

2

One shade the more, one ray the less,
   Had half impaired the nameless grace
Which waves in every raven tress,
   Or softly lightens o'er her face;   10
Where thoughts serenely sweet express
   How pure, how dear their dwelling place.

3

And on that cheek, and o'er that brow,
   So soft, so calm, yet eloquent,
The smiles that win, the tints that glow,   15
   But tell of days in goodness spent,
A mind at peace with all below,
   A heart whose love is innocent!

1815

So We'll Go No More A-Roving

1

So we'll go no more a-roving
  So late into the night,
Though the heart be still as loving,
And the moon be still as bright.

2

For the sword outwears its sheath,   5
  And the soul wears out the breast,
And the heart must pause to breathe,
  And Love itself have rest.

3

Though the night was made for loving,
  And the day returns too soon,   10
Yet we'll go no more a-roving
  By the light of the moon.
1817   *1830*

Thomas Campion
1527–1620
*"There is a garden in her face" is a fine example of an extended meta-
phor typical of love poetry in the age of Shakespeare, and it might be
compared to Shakespeare's Sonnet 130, which was written for an audi-
ence used to poetry like Campion's. The poem is an "ayre" or "air," meant
to be sung, and was accompanied by Campion's musical composition.
It is still popular today and is often recorded. According to Campion,
the "chief perfection" of an air is to be "short and well-seasoned." Such
poems are meant to be virtuoso performances by the poet—compact,
artificial, skillfully produced miniatures. Their pleasure is intellectual
rather than emotional.*

There is a garden in her face

There is a garden in her face,
Where roses and white lilies grow
A heavenly paradise is that place,
Wherein all pleasant fruits do flow.
There cherries grow, which none may buy   5
Till 'Cherry ripe' themselves do cry.

Those cherries fairly do enclose
Of orient pearl a double row;
Which when her lovely laughter shows,
They look like rosebuds filled with snow.   10
Yet them nor peer nor prince can buy
Till 'Cherry ripe' themselves do cry.

Her eyes like angels watch them still;
Her brows like bended bows do stand,
Threatening with piercing frowns to kill   15
All that attempt, with eye or hand,
Those sacred cherries to come nigh
Till 'Cherry ripe' themselves do cry.

1617

Nick Carbó
b. 1964

Most of Carbó's poetry is informed by his experience of American colonialism in the Philippines and uses a hodgepodge of cross-cultural references. Carbó is an experimenter, and he often displays the self-referentiality and the mixture of genres that is typical of postmodern fiction. Orpheus in this poem recurs in Carbó's work, especially the narrative Secret Asian Man. Orpheus's self-awareness here, according to Carbó, derives from techniques the poet discovered in French New Wave Cinema.

I Found Orpheus[1] Levitating

above the hood of an illegally parked red Toyota Corolla
on Mabini Street.[2] He was tired of all that descending
into and ascending from those pretentious
New Yorker and *Atlantic Monthly* poems.
He asked me to give him new clothes so I dressed him   5
in an old barong tagalog[3] and some black pants.
Because he wanted new friends in a new land, I introduced
him to Kapitan Kidlat,[4] our local comic book hero.
But after a few whips of that lightning bolt, Orpheus
recognized Kidlat as Zeus in another clever disguise.   10
So, I took him to Mt. Makiling where Malakas & Maganda
(the mythical first Filipino man and woman) live
in a mansion with an Olympic-size swimming pool.
He said Maganda's aquiline features remind him
of Eurydice[5] and Malakas has the solid torso   15
of a younger Apollo.[6] He asked me to translate
the word, *threesome* into Tagalog.
Malakas & Maganda agreed and they stripped
Orpheus of his clothes as they led him
to their giant bamboo bed.   20
I waited outside in the car all afternoon before he emerged
from the mansion smelling of Sampaguitas and Ylang-Ylang.[7]
He was hungry so we drove to the nearest
Kamayan[8] restaurant where he learned
how to eat rice and pork abobo with his bare hands.   25

1. This character has appeared in other poems by Carbó. See the reference in line 4.
2. Manila street popular among tourists for its nightclubs and strip clubs.
3. A shirt characteristic of the Philippines; it has a squarish cut and is worn untucked. Literally, the phrase means "clothes of the Tagalog," who come from one of the regions of Luzon, the main island in the archipelago.
4. A popular superhero in the Philippines; his powers were granted to him by Zeus.
5. A nymph, the wife of Orpheus in Greek mythology.
6. Greek god associated with many things, including poetry.
7. A flower indigenous to the Philippines or the perfume made from that flower. *Sampaguitas*: jasmine.
8. A Filipino cuisine eaten with the hands.

"It's wonderful! This was the way it used to be.
When the industrial revolution happened, all of us on Mt.
Olympus
suddenly had forks and knives appear in our hands. We used
them as garden tools at first." Afterwards, he wanted to drink
and go dancing. I paid the hundred-peso cover charge   30
for both of us at the Hobbit House in Ermita. The first
thing he did in the dark, smoky bar was trip over
one of the dwarf waiters, all the waiters were dwarfs. *"I'm sorry,*
I couldn't see. It feels as if I had just walked into a Fellini film."
He placed his hands in front of him as if he were pushing   35
back a glass wall. *"No, No, I'm not in a movie,*
I'm inside a fucking poem!
I can see the poet's scrunched-up face on the other side
of the computer screen!" I told Orpheus to shut up
or the bouncers, who were not the same size as the waiters,   40
would throw us out of the bar. We sat
in a booth across from each other and ordered double
shots of Tanduay Rum. I asked him if he understood
the concept of "the willing suspension of disbelief."
I asked him to look me straight   45
in the face before he ran out into the street.

                                                                    2000

Lewis Carroll
1832–1898

Carroll is remembered today for his pair of challenging children's books, Alice's Adventures in Wonderland *(1865) and* Through the Looking-Glass *(1871). Alice reads "Jabberwocky" in the first chapter of the second book, but Carroll began writing the poem much earlier and even published the first stanza, with his own glosses, in 1855. Humpty Dumpty explains to Alice that "slithy" is a combination of "slimy" and "lithe," and thus the "toves" have slick, limber, nimble bodies. But what is a "tove"? According to Humpty Dumpty, a tove is a type of badger with long back legs and horns and a hunger for cheese. And "bryllyg," Humpty explains, comes from the verb "broiling" and means late afternoon, that time of day when dinner is broiled. Obviously, we cannot even guess the meaning of some words—they exist only in Carroll's imagination. Nevertheless, as this poem demonstrates, even nonsense syllables have connotations for readers and listeners.*

Jabberwocky

'Twas brillig, and the slithy toves
    Did gyre and gimble in the wabe:
All mimsy were the borogoves,
    And the mome raths outgrabe.

"Beware the Jabberwock, my son!   5
    The jaws that bite, the claws that catch!
Beware the Jubjub bird, and shun
    The frumious Bandersnatch!"

He took his vorpal sword in hand:
    Long time the manxome foe he sought—   10
So rested he by the Tumtum tree,
    And stood awhile in thought.

And, as in uffish thought he stood,
    The Jabberwock, with eyes of flame,
Came whiffling through the tulgey wood,   15
    And burbled as it came!

One, two! One, two! And through and through
    The vorpal blade went snicker-snack!
He left it dead, and with its head
    He went galumphing back.   20

"And hast thou slain the Jabberwock?
    Come to my arms, my beamish boy!
O frabjous day! Callooh! Callay!"
    He chortled in his joy.

'Twas brillig, and the slithy toves   25
  Did gyre and gimble in the wabe:
All mimsy were the borogoves,
  And the mome raths outgrabe.

1871

Geoffrey Chaucer
1340?–1400

  *These poems are both in their original Middle English, the precursor to
the Modern English we speak today. The strange vocabulary is glossed
for you, but by reading the poems aloud you might find yourself under-
standing more than you expect. "To Rosemounde" expresses a typical
situation in courtly love poetry of the time—the lover addressing a
hesitant or inaccessible beloved. "Lak of Stedfastnesse" is addressed to
Richard II, who became king of England at age ten in 1377.*

To Rosemounde

Madame, ye been of al beautee shryne
As fer as cercled is the mapamounde;[1]
For as the cristal glorious ye shyne,
And lyke ruby been your chekes rounde.
Therwith ye been so mery and so jocounde   5
That at a revel whan that I see yow daunce,
It is an oynement unto my wounde,
Though ye to me ne do no daliaunce.

For though I wepe of teres ful a tyne.[2]
Yet may that wo myn herte nat confounder;   10
Your semy vois that ye so small out twyne
Maketh my thought in joye and blis habounde.
So curteisly I go, with love bounde,
That to myself I sey, in my penaunce,
Suffyseth me to love you, Rosemounde,   15
Though ye to me ne do no daliaunce.

---

  1. A map of the world.   2. A tub.

Nas never pyk walwed in galauntyne[3]
As I in love am walwed and y-wounde;
For which ful ofte I of myself devyne
That I am trewe Tristam the secounde.   20
My love may nat refreyde nor affounde;[4]
I brenne ay in an amorous plesaunce.
Do what yow list, I wil your thral be founde,
Though ye to me ne do no daliaunce.

ca. 14th century

Lak of Stedfastnesse

Somtyme this world was so stedfast and stable
That mannes word was obligacioun,
And now it is so fals and deceivable,
That word and deed, as in conclusioun,
Ben nothing lyk, for turned up so doun   5
Is al this world for mede and wilfulnesses.[1]
That al is lost for lak of stedfastnesse.

What maketh this world to be so variable
But lust that folk have in dissensioun?
Among us now a man is holde unable,   10
But if he can, by som collusioun,
Don his neighbour wrong or oppressioun.
What causeth this, but wilful wrecchednesse,
That al is lost, for lak of stedfastnesse?

Trouthe is put doun, resoun is holden fable: 15
Vertu hath now no dominacioun,
Pitee exyled, no man is merciable.
Thurgh covetyse is blent discrecioun:
The world hath made a permutacioun

---

3. Tasty wine sauce. *Walwed*: a wallowed.   1. Bribery.
4. Founder; as a ship on rocks. *Refreyde*:
get colder.

Fro right to wrong, fro trouthe to fikelnesse,   20
That al is lost, for lak of stedfastnesse.

Envoy [to King Richard]

O prince, desyre to be honourable,
Cherish thy folk and hate extorcioun!
Suffre nothing that may be reprevable
To thyn estate. don in thy regioun.   25
Shew forth thy swerd of castigacioun,
Dred God, do law, love trouthe and worthinesse,
And wed thy folk ageyn to stedfastnesse.

                                        ca. 14ᵗʰ century

Lucille Clifton

1936–2010

> *The poem "homage to my hips" appeared in Clifton's 1980 collection* two-headed woman *and it plays off the conventional love poem, in which a speaker, typically a male, praises parts of his beloved's body. (See, for example, Thomas Campion's "There is a garden in her face.") "Lorena" is an unusual example of an "occasional" poem, which is a poem written about some particular event or occasion. In this case, the poem refers to Lorena Bobbitt, who, in 1993, cut off her husband's penis while he was sleeping. Having suffered physical abuse from her husband, Bobbitt was judged to have been temporarily insane and was acquitted of the crime.*

homage to my hips

these hips are big hips
they need space to
move around in.
they don't fit into little
petty places. these hips   5
are free hips.
they don't like to be held back.
these hips have never been enslaved,

they go where they want to go
they do what they want to do.   10
these hips are mighty hips.
these hips are magic hips.
i have known them
to put a spell on a man and
spin him like a top!   15
                          1980

Lorena

> *Woman cuts off husband's penis, later throws it from car window.*
>   —News Report

it lay in my palm soft and trembled
as a new bird and i thought about
authority and how it always insisted
on itself, how it was master
of the man, how it measured him, never   5
was ignored or denied and how it promised
there would be sweetness if it was obeyed
just like the saints do, like the angels,
and i opened the window and held out my
uncupped hand. i swear to god,   10
i thought it could fly
                          1995

Samuel Taylor Coleridge
1772–1834

Coleridge claimed that he had composed two or three hundred lines of "Kubla Khan" in an opium reverie, writing them down upon waking until he was interrupted. This claim about his method of composition is almost certainly a fiction, a pose that is characteristic of Romantic poets, who abhorred artifice and believed poetry should flow naturally from the artist. Coleridge probably labored long over the poem, and even if he dreamed the images in 1797, most likely he did not write the poem until much later. He did not publish it until 1816. Likewise, his claim to have no special understanding of the symbolism in the poem, as if it originated in something other than his own consciousness, is Romantic. In modern terms, we might say that Coleridge's subconscious authored the symbols. The "dejection" that he discusses in the ode probably was brought on by his opium addiction, which eventually sapped his poetic powers. The "lady" addressed in the poem might be Sara Hutchinson, sister of Wordsworth's wife, with whom the married Coleridge was in love. The poet in the seventh stanza is William Wordsworth.

Dejection: An Ode

Late, late yestreen I saw the new Moon,
With the old Moon in her arms;
And I fear, I fear, my Master dear!
We shall have a deadly storm.
   Ballad of Sir Patrick Spence

I

Well! If the Bard was weather-wise, who made
 The grand old ballad of Sir Patrick Spence,
 This night, so tranquil now, will not go hence
Unroused by winds, that ply a busier trade
Than those which mould yon cloud in lazy flakes,   5
Or the dull sobbing draft, that moans and rakes
  Upon the strings of this Eolian lute,[1]
  Which better far were mute.
For lo! the New-moon winter-bright!
And overspread with phantom light,   10
 (With swimming phantom light o'erspread
 But rimmed and circled by a silver thread)
I see the old Moon in her lap, foretelling
 The coming on of rain and squally blast.
And oh! that even now the gust were swelling,   15
 And the slant night-shower driving loud and fast!

1. A stringed instrument hung like wind-chimes to be played by the wind.

Those sounds which oft have raised me, whilst they awed,
  And sent my soul abroad,
Might now perhaps their wonted impulse give,
Might startle this dull pain, and make it move and live!   20

2

A grief without a pang, void, dark, and drear,
  A stifled, drowsy, unimpassioned grief,
  Which finds no natural outlet, no relief,
    In word, or sigh, or tear—
O Lady! In this wan and heartless mood,   25
To other thoughts by yonder throstle woo'd,
  All this long eve, so balmy and serene,
Have I been gazing on the western sky,
  And its peculiar tint of yellow green:
And still I gaze—and with how blank an eye!   30
And those thin clouds above, in flakes and bars,
That give away their motion to the stars;
Those stars, that glide behind them or between,
Now sparkling, now bedimmed, but always seen:
Yon crescent Moon as fixed as if it grew   35
In its own cloudless, starless lake of blue;
I see them all so excellently fair,
I see, not feel, how beautiful they are!

3

  My genial[2] spirits fail;
  And what can these avail   40
To lift the smothering weight from off my breast?
  It were a vain endeavour,
  Though I should gaze for ever
On that green light that lingers in the west:
I may not hope from outward forms to win   45
The passion and the life, whose fountains are within.

2. Natural or birth-given (archaic usage).

4

O Lady! we receive but what we give,
And in our life alone does nature live:
Ours is her wedding-garment, ours her shroud!
   And would we aught behold, of higher worth,   50
Than that inanimate cold world allowed
To the poor loveless ever-anxious crowd,
   Ah! from the soul itself must issue forth,
A light, a glory, a fair luminous cloud
    Enveloping the Earth—   55
And from the soul itself must there be sent
   A sweet and potent voice, of its own birth,
Of all sweet sounds the life and element!

5

O pure of heart! thou need'st not ask of me
What this strong music in the soul may be!   60
What, and wherein it doth exist,
This light, this glory, this fair luminous mist,
This beautiful and beauty-making power.
   Joy, virtuous Lady! Joy that ne'er was given,
Save to the pure, and in their purest hour,   65
Life, and Life's effluence, cloud at once and shower,
Joy, Lady! is the spirit and the power,
Which, wedding Nature to us, gives in dower,
   A new Earth and new Heaven,
Undreamt of by the sensual and the proud—   70
Joy is the sweet voice, Joy the luminous cloud—
    We in ourselves rejoice!
And thence flows all that charms or ear or sight,
   All melodies the echoes of that voice,
All colours a suffusion from that light.   75

6

There was a time when, though my path was rough,
   This joy within me dallied with distress,

And all misfortunes were but as the stuff
   Whence Fancy made me dreams of happiness:
For hope grew round me, like the twining vine,   80
And fruits, and foliage, not my own, seemed mine.
But now afflictions bow me down to earth:
Nor care I that they rob me of my mirth,
   But oh! each visitation
Suspends what nature gave me at my birth,   85
   My shaping spirit of Imagination.
For not to think of what I needs must feel,
   But to be still and patient, all I can;
And haply by abstruse research to steal
   From my own nature all the natural man—   90
   This was my sole resource, my only plan:
Till that which suits a part infects the whole,
And now is almost grown the habit of my soul.

7

Hence, viper thoughts, that coil around my mind,
   Reality's dark dream!   95
I turn from you, and listen to the wind,
   Which long has raved unnoticed. What a scream
Of agony by torture lengthened out
That lute sent forth! Thou Wind, that ravest without,
   Bare crag, or mountain-tairn,[3] or blasted tree,   100
Or pine-grove whither woodman never clomb,
Or lonely house, long held the witches' home,
   Methinks were fitter instruments for thee,
Mad Lutanist! who in this month of showers,
Of dark brown gardens, and of peeping flowers,   105
Mak'st Devils' yule with worse than wintry song,
The blossoms, buds, and timorous leaves among.
   Thou Actor, perfect in all tragic sounds!
Thou mighty Poet, e'en to frenzy bold!
   What tell'st thou now about?   110

3. Pond or pool.

'Tis of the rushing of a host in rout,
  With groans of trampled men, with smarting wounds—
At once they groan with pain, and shudder with the cold!
But hush! there is a pause of deepest silence!
  And all that noise, as of a rushing crowd,   115
With groans, and tremulous shudderings—all is over—
  It tells another tale, with sounds less deep and loud!
    A tale of less affright,
    And tempered with delight,
As Otway's self had framed the tender lay,[4]   120
    'Tis of a little child
    Upon a lonesome wild,
Not far from home, but she hath lost her way:
And now moans low in bitter grief and fear,
And now screams loud, and hopes to make her mother hear.   125

8

'Tis midnight, but small thoughts have I of sleep:
Full seldom may my friend such vigils keep!
Visit her, gentle Sleep! with wings of healing,
  And may this storm be but a mountain-birth[5]
May all the stars hang bright above her dwelling,   130
  Silent as though they watched the sleeping Earth!
    With light heart may she rise,
    Gay fancy, cheerful eyes,
  Joy lift her spirit, joy attune her voice;
To her may all things live, from pole to pole,   135
Their life the eddying of her living soul!
  O simple spirit, guided from above,
Dear Lady! friend devoutest of my choice,
Thus mayest thou ever, evermore rejoice.
                    1802

---

4. Or song, similar to Wordsworth's "Lucy Gray." Thomas Otway (1652–1685), a British playwright famous for his melodramatic or tragic scenes.

5. I.e., a violent but short-lived storm, as often forms in the mountains.

Kubla Khan

In Xanadu did Kubla Khan
A stately pleasure-dome decree:
Where Alph, the sacred river, ran
Through caverns measureless to man
  Down to a sunless sea.   5
So twice five miles of fertile ground
With walls and towers were girdled round:
And there were gardens bright with sinuous rills
Where blossomed many an incense-bearing tree;
And here were forests ancient as the hills,   10
Enfolding sunny spots of greenery.

But oh! that deep romantic chasm which slanted
Down the green hill athwart a cedarn cover!
A savage place! as holy and enchanted
As e'er beneath a waning moon was haunted   15
By woman wailing for her demon-lover!
And from this chasm, with ceaseless turmoil seething,
As if this earth in fast thick pants were breathing,
A mighty fountain momently was forced:
Amid whose swift half-intermitted burst   20
Huge fragments vaulted like rebounding hail,
Or chaffy grain beneath the thresher's flail:
And 'mid these dancing rocks at once and ever
It flung up momently the sacred river.
Five miles meandering with a mazy motion   25
Through wood and dale the sacred river ran,
Then reached the caverns measureless to man,
And sank in tumult to a lifeless ocean:
And 'mid this tumult Kubla heard from far
Ancestral voices prophesying war!   30

  The shadow of the dome of pleasure
  Floated midway on the waves;
  Where was heard the mingled measure
  From the fountain and the caves.

It was a miracle of rare device,   35
A sunny pleasure-dome with caves of ice!
  A damsel with a dulcimer
  In a vision once I saw:
  It was an Abyssinian maid,
  And on her dulcimer she played,   40
  Singing of Mount Abora.
  Could I revive within me
  Her symphony and song,
    To such a deep delight 'twould win me,
That with music loud and long,   45
I would build that dome in air,
That sunny dome! those caves of ice!
And all who heard should see them there,
And all should cry, Beware! Beware!
His flashing eyes, his floating hair!   50
Weave a circle round him thrice,[1]
And close your eyes with holy dread,
For he on honey-dew hath fed,
And drunk the milk of Paradise.

                                 1816

Billy Collins
b. 1941

    "Introduction to Poetry" was published in Collins's first book of poems, The Apple That Astonished Paris *(1988), and established his unique, self-reflexive style. You might compare this poem to William Wordsworth's "The Tables Turned." "On Turning Ten" comically alludes to Shelley's "Ode to the West Wind" in its last lines (Shelley's statement, meant to be taken quite seriously, reads "I fall upon the thorns of life! I bleed!"). Collins's meditation on growing up, then, gently satirizes poems like Dylan Thomas's "Fern Hill," which regrets what is lost when we take on the knowledge of maturity. Collins is famous for these deceptively funny parodies. "Sonnet," for example, pokes fun at the formula of the Petrarchan*

---

1. A magic ritual, to protect the inspired poet from intrusion.

sonnet. But by the end of the poem Collins turns the parody into a genuine love poem, and he comments on the idealized, Platonic love relations typical of sonnet cycles. Similarly, "Man Listening to Disc" proceeds as a pleasant, comical fantasy until the last two stanzas indicate that the speaker is discussing something very important, "the only true point of view."

Introduction to Poetry

I ask them to take a poem
and hold it up to the light
like a color slide

or press an ear against its hive.

I say drop a mouse into a poem   5
and watch him probe his way out,

or walk inside the poem's room
and feel the walls for a light switch.

I want them to water-ski
across the surface of a poem   10
waving at the author's name on the shore.

But all they want to do
is tie the poem to a chair with rope
and torture a confession out of it.

They begin beating it with a hose   15
to find out what it really means.

1988

On Turning Ten

The whole idea of it makes me feel
like I'm coming down with something,
something worse than any stomach ache

or the headaches I get from reading in bad light—   5
a kind of measles of the spirit,
a mumps of the psyche,
a disfiguring chicken pox of the soul.

You tell me it is too early to be looking back,
but that is because you have forgotten   10
the perfect simplicity of being one
and the beautiful complexity introduced by two.
But I can lie on my bed and remember every digit.
At four I was an Arabian wizard.
I could make myself invisible   15
by drinking a glass of milk a certain way.
At seven I was a soldier, at nine a prince.

But now I am mostly at the window
watching the late afternoon light.
Back then it never fell so solemnly   20
against the side of my tree house,
and my bicycle never leaned against the garage
as it does today,
all the dark blue speed drained out of it.

This is the beginning of sadness, I say to myself,   25
as I walk through the universe in my sneakers.
It is time to say good-bye to my imaginary friends,
time to turn the first big number.
It seems only yesterday I used to believe
there was nothing under my skin but light.   30
If you cut me I would shine.
But now when I fall upon the sidewalks of life,
I skin my knees. I bleed.

1998

Sonnet

All we need is fourteen lines, well, thirteen now,
and after this next one just a dozen

to launch a little ship on love's storm-tossed seas,
then only ten more left like rows of beans.
How easily it goes unless you get Elizabethan   5
and insist the iambic bongos must be played
and rhymes positioned at the ends of lines,
one for every station of the cross.
But hang on here while we make the turn
into the final six where all will be resolved,   10
where longing and heartache will find an end,
where Laura will tell Petrarch[1] to put down his pen,
take off those crazy medieval tights,
blow out the lights, and come at last to bed.

1999

Man Listening to Disc

This is not bad—
ambling along 44th Street[1]
with Sonny Rollins[2] for company,
his music flowing through the soft calipers
of these earphones,   5

as if he were right beside me
on this clear day in March,
the pavement sparkling with sunlight,
pigeons fluttering off the curb,
nodding over a profusion of bread crumbs.   10

In fact, I would say
my delight at being suffused
with phrases from his saxophone—
some like honey, some like vinegar—
is surpassed only by my gratitude   15

1. Laura was the unattainable, beloved subject of Petrarch's sonnet cycle.
1. In New York City's Midtown. The speaker is walking through the Theater District, not far from Times Square, and plans to turn south on Sixth Avenue toward the downtown area of the city.
2. An influential jazz saxophonist (b. 1930).

to Tommy Potter[3] for taking the time
to join us on this breezy afternoon
with his most unwieldy bass
and to the esteemed Arthur Taylor[4]
who is somehow managing to navigate   20

this crowd with his cumbersome drums.
And I bow deeply to Thelonious Monk[5]
for figuring out a way
to motorize—-or whatever—his huge piano
so he could be with us today.   25

The music is loud yet so confidential
I cannot help feeling even more
like the center of the universe
than usual as I walk along to a rapid
little version of "The Way You Look Tonight,"   30

and all I can say to my fellow pedestrians,
to the woman in the white sweater,
the man in the tan raincoat and the heavy glasses,
who mistake themselves for the center of the universe—
all I can say is watch your step   35

because the five of us, instruments and all,
are about to angle over
to the south side of the street
and then, in our own tightly knit way,
turn the corner at Sixth Avenue.   40

And if any of you are curious
about where this aggregation,
this whole battery-powered crew,
is headed, let us just say
that the real center of the universe,   45

3. A jazz double bass player (1918–1988).   5. A jazz composer and pianist (1917–
4. A jazz drummer (1929–1995).   1982).

the only true point of view,
is full of the hope that he,
the hub of the cosmos
with his hair blown sideways,
will eventually make it all the way downtown.   50
                                        1999

Countee Cullen
1903–1946

> *This poem was published in Cullen's first collection,* Color, *in 1925, when he was just twenty-two years old—already a rising figure in the vibrant black arts movement called the Harlem Renaissance and a graduate student at Harvard. Critics note the allusion to William Blake's "The Tyger" in the third quatrain of this Shakespearean sonnet, and it might be fruitful to think about that poem's central question,* Why is there evil or cruelty in the world? *Cullen himself claimed that the poems of Edna St. Vincent Millay influenced him, which is certainly evident in the studied format of this selection. The apparent irony of the concluding couplet refers to the black experience in Jim Crow America, which at least superficially seemed hardly the stuff of poetry—at least as poetry might be conceived conventionally. In the words of one contemporary critic, "herein lies the crux of Cullen's philosophy. . . . This expression becomes symbolic of the whole problem of American democracy and of the pathetic tragedy of a poor solution."*

Yet Do I Marvel

I doubt not God is good, well-meaning, kind,
And did He stoop to quibble could tell why
The little buried mole continues blind,
Why flesh that mirrors Him must some day die,
Make plain the reason tortured Tantalus[1]   5
Is baited by the fickle fruit, declare

---

1. In Greek mythology, he is condemned to stand in a pool of water; whenever he stoops to drink, the water disappears. A tree branch overhangs him, but whenever he reaches for its fruit it recedes.

If merely brute caprice dooms Sisyphus[2]
To struggle up a never-ending stair.
Inscrutable His ways are, and immune
To catechism by a mind too strewn   10
With petty cares to slightly understand
What awful brain compels His awful hand.
Yet do I marvel at this curious thing:
To make a poet black, and bid him sing!

1925

E. E. (Edward Estlin) Cummings
1894–1962

"Buffalo Bill's" and "in Just-" appeared in Cummings's first book,
Tulips & Chimneys *(1923). They are both among the "tulips," or
organic poems, in contrast to the sonnets that make up the "chimneys" section. "Buffalo Bill's" appeared in a subsection called
"Portraits," while "in Just-" was the first of three "Chansons Innocentes," or songs of innocence. The title calls to mind Blake's* Songs
of Innocence and Experience. *Immediately reviewers fixed on the
unique typography of Cummings's poems, which garnered him considerable criticism and recognition. "anyone lived in a pretty how
town" might at first seem nonsense, but if you consider "anyone"
and "noone" as characters in a story, you'll begin to understand the
poem.*

Buffalo Bill's

Buffalo Bill's
defunct
     who used to
     ride a watersmooth-silver
                   stallion   5
and break onetwothreefourfive pigeonsjustlikethat
                            Jesus

---

2. In Greek mythology, he must roll a boulder up a mountain; just before it reaches the
top, it escapes him and rolls to the bottom, forcing him to start again in a never-ending cycle.

he was a handsome man
                and what i want to know is
how do you like your blueeyed boy   10
Mister Death

                      1920, 1923

in Just-

          in Just-
spring   when the world is mud-
luscious the little
lame balloonman

whistles far   and wee   5

and eddieandbill come
running from marbles and
piracies and it's
spring
when the world is puddle-wonderful   10

the queer
old balloonman whistles
far   and   wee
and bettyandisbel come dancing

from hop-scotch and jump-rope and   15

it's
spring
and
   the

          goat-footed[1]   20

balloonMan   whistles
far
and
wee
              1920, 1923

1. An allusion to satyrs, the lewd forest gods of Greek mythology.

anyone lived in a pretty how town

anyone lived in a pretty how town
(with up so floating many bells down)
spring summer autumn winter
he sang his didn't he danced his did.

Women and men(both little and small)   5
cared for anyone not at all
they sowed their isn't they reaped their same
sun moon stars rain

children guessed(but only a few
and down they forgot as up they grew   10
autumn winter spring summer)
that noone loved him more by more

when by now and tree by leaf
she laughed his joy she cried his grief
bird by snow and stir by still   15
anyone's any was all to her

someones married their everyones
laughed their cryings and did their dance
(sleep wake hope and then)they
said their nevers they slept their dream   20

stars rain sun moon
(and only the snow can begin to explain
how children are apt to forget to remember
with up so floating many bells down)

one day anyone died i guess   25
(and noone stooped to kiss his face)
busy folk buried them side by side
little by little and was by was

all by all and deep by deep
and more by more they dream their sleep   30
noone and anyone earth by april
wish by spirit and if by yes.

Women and men(both dong and ding)
summer autumn winter spring
reaped their sowing and went their came   35
sun moon stars rain

                    1940

Carol Ann Davis
b. 1970

> *"Tips from My Father" is one of Davis's earliest published poems.
> It appeared in the* Gettysburgh Review *in 1993. The poem is auto-
> biographical, in the American confessional tradition. Davis's father
> worked for the space program. To help interpret this poem, you
> might read it alongside Li-Young Lee's "The Gift."*

Tips from My Father

"Come out here," he'd call from the yard.
"I want to show you Mars." I'd stand
just in front of him, follow his finger up into the sky,
the house spinning away from us till
nothing mattered but my father's hand   5
and his hundred planets. And his voice a pause before he
    found it, then:
"There it is." And maybe I saw it. This is how
he taught me—in case I was ever lost at sea,
or in the desert—how to navigate my way back home.
With each new season a new sky to learn, a serious   10
business, like reading a map. "Look here,"
he'd say, "this is something you might need."

                    1993

Natalie Diaz
b. 1978

Note the elementary school textbook-type lesson that this poem mimics: every letter of the alphabet is in the title, and the first letter of each line follows the sequence of the alphabet, as if the poem were an alternative or response to a classroom lesson on English. Consider the misspellings: are they a sign of ignorance or defiance? Language conveys culture and also symbolizes it, helping us form our self-identities, a truth especially evident to marginal cultures. The loss of Native American languages and the compulsion to speak and write English are the cultural corollary to the violence of colonization, Indian removals, and confinement to reservations. The angel in this poem might refer to the visions of Joseph Smith, founder of the Mormons, who were the first white settlers in the Mojave Desert. Diaz, whose mother is Mojave and whose father is a Catholic Mexican, grew up on the Fort Mojave Indian Reservation, which spans parts of Arizona, California, and Nevada. She writes autobiographically, in the tradition of American confessional poets. In her own words, her poems reveal all of her "truths, even the Judas-truths that make [her] feel like the betrayer whose dirty hands are resting on the table for everyone to see, including God." Her writing, she says, is an "uncovering" of "darkness." Many poems painfully expose her own family, illustrating the disease, drug-addiction, poverty, and racism that plague Native American communities.

Abecedarian Requiring Further Examination of Anglikan Seraphym Subjugation of a Wild Indian Rezervation

Angels don't come to the reservation.
Bats, maybe, or owls, boxy mottled things.
Coyotes, too. They all mean the same thing—
death. And death
eats angels, I guess, because I haven't seen an angel   5
fly through this valley ever.

Gabriel?[1] Never heard of him. Know a guy named Gabe though—
he came through here one powwow and stayed, typical
Indian. Sure he had wings,
jailbird that he was. He flies around in stolen cars. Wherever he
   stops,   10
kids grow like gourds from women's bellies.
Like I said, no Indian I've ever heard of has ever been or seen an
   angel.
Maybe in a Christmas pageant or something—
Nazarene church holds one every December,
organized by Pastor John's wife. It's no wonder—   15
Pastor John's son is the angel—everyone knows angels are white.
Quit bothering with angels, I say. They're no good for Indians.
Remember what happened last time
some white god came floating across the ocean?[2]
Truth is, there may be angels, but if there are angels   20
up there, living on clouds or sitting on thrones across the sea
   wearing
velvet robes and golden rings, drinking whiskey from silver cups,
we're better off if they stay rich and fat and ugly and
'xactly where they are—in their own distant heavens.
You better hope you never see angels on the rez. If you do, they'll
   be marching you off to   25
Zion or Oklahoma, or some other hell they've mapped out for
   us.

2012

---

1. In Judaism, Christianity, and Islam, an angel who often acts as the messenger of God.
2. Perhaps a reference to the widely held belief, promoted by the Spanish, that in 1519 the Aztec ruler Montezuma II mistook the conquistador Hernán Cortés for Quetzalcoatl, an Aztec god depicted as a feathered serpent or dragon. Most scholars today dismiss the story as inaccurate.

James Dickey
1923–1997

> *Dickey said about poetry, "I like the thing that comes like a light-ning flash, that is vivid and momentarily there and intense and unmistakable and doesn't require a great deal of ratiocination." His poems are known for their concreteness and vividness of physical detail, and he credited Ezra Pound for his influence in this regard. Dickey was almost violently opposed to the kind of clever interpre-tations one often encounters in universities. This poem is one of the few examples of narrative poetry in this volume—poetry that tells a story—and it reflects Dickey's other great concern, which was the dramatic effect of his poems.*

Cherrylog Road

Off Highway 106
At Cherrylog Road I entered
The '34 Ford without wheels,
Smothered in kudzu,
With a seat pulled out to run   5
Corn whiskey down from the hills,

And then from the other side
Crept into an Essex[1]
With a rumble seat of red leather
And then out again, aboard   10
A blue Chevrolet, releasing
The rust from its other color,

Reared up on three building blocks.
None had the same body heat;
I changed with them inward, toward   15
The weedy heart of the junkyard,

For I knew that Doris Holbrook
Would escape from her father at noon

---

1. The first affordable enclosed automobile, produced between 1922 and 1932 by the Hudson Motor Company.

And would come from the farm
To seek parts owned by the sun   20
Among the abandoned chassis,
Sitting in each in turn
As I did, leaning forward
As in a wild stock-car race

In the parking lot of the dead.   25
Time after time, I climbed in
And out the other side, like
An envoy or movie star
Met at the station by crickets.
A radiator cap raised its head,   30

Become a real toad or a kingsnake
As I neared the hub of the yard,
Passing through many states,
Many lives, to reach
Some grandmother's long Pierce-Arrow[2]   35
Sending platters of blindness forth

From its nickel hubcaps
And spilling its tender upholstery
On sleepy roaches,
The glass panel in between   40
Lady and colored driver
Not all the way broken out,

The back-seat phone
Still on its hook.
I got in as though to exclaim,   45
"Let us go to the orphan asylum,
John; I have some old toys
For children who say their prayers."

I popped with sweat as I thought
I heard Doris Holbrook scrape   50

2. A luxury automobile manufactured between 1901 and 1932.

Like a mouse in the southern-state sun
That was eating the paint in blisters
From a hundred car tops and hoods.
She was tapping like code,

Loosening the screws,   55
Carrying off headlights,
Sparkplugs, bumpers,
Cracked mirrors and gear-knobs,
Getting ready, already,
To go back with something to show   60

Other than her lips' new trembling
I would hold to me soon, soon,
Where I sat in the ripped back seat
Talking over the interphone,
Praying for Doris Holbrook   65
To come from her father's farm

And to get back there
With no trace of me on her face
To be seen by her red-haired father
Who would change, in the squalling barn,   70
Her back's pale skin with a strop,
Then lay for me

In a bootlegger's roasting car
With a string-triggered 12-gauge shotgun
To blast the breath from the air.   75
Not cut by the jagged windshields,
Through the acres of wrecks she came
With a wrench in her hand,

Through dust where the blacksnake dies
Of boredom, and the beetle knows   80
The compost has no more life.
Someone outside would have seen

The oldest car's door inexplicably
Close from within:

I held her and held her and held her,   85
Convoyed at terrific speed
By the stalled, dreaming traffic around us,
So the blacksnake, stiff
With inaction, curved back
Into life, and hunted the mouse   90

With deadly overexcitement,
The beetles reclaimed their field
As we clung, glued together,
With the hooks of the seat springs
Working through to catch us red-handed   95
Amidst the gray breathless batting

That burst from the seat at our backs.
We left by separate doors
Into the changed, other bodies
Of cars, she down Cherrylog Road   100
And I to my motorcycle
Parked like the soul of the junkyard

Restored, a bicycle fleshed
With power, and tore off
Up Highway 106, continually   105
Drunk on the wind in my mouth,
Wringing the handlebar for speed,
Wild to be wreckage forever.

1964

Emily Dickinson
1830–1886

> Only a handful of Dickinson's poems were published in her lifetime. "Because I could not stop for Death—," "The Soul Selects Her Own Society—," and "I heard a Fly buzz—when I died—" were written during the Civil War, but they were not published until the 1890s. "After great pain" was first published in 1929. Four years after Dickinson died, an editor for the Atlantic Monthly smoothed and regularized some of her poems and published them in a book, which critics instantly praised. Editors did not restore her idiosyncratic punctuation and expressions until the twentieth century. Written in 1861, "Wild Nights—Wild Nights!" worried Dickinson's literary executor, who feared that readers would see in the poem more than the "virgin recluse" intended. Most readers today do not so easily dismiss the sexual suggestiveness of her poems. Similarly, the poems are ambiguous about religious beliefs, including the immortality of the soul. Dickinson is notoriously difficult to pin down: her poems often support entirely contradictory interpretations.

249

Wild Nights—Wild Nights!
Were I with thee
Wild Nights should be
Our luxury!

Futile—the Winds—   5
To a Heart in port—
Done with the Compass—
Done with the Chart!

Rowing in Eden—
Ah, the Sea!   10
Might I but moor—Tonight—
In Thee!

ca. 1861

254

"Hope" is the thing with feathers—
That perches in the soul—
And sings the tune without the words—
And never stops—at all—

And sweetest—in the Gale—is heard—   5
And sore must be the storm—
That could abash the little Bird
That kept so many warm—

I've heard it in the chillest land—
And on the strangest Sea—   10
Yet, never, in Extremity,
It asked a crumb—of Me.
                            1861

303

The Soul selects her own Society—
Then—shuts the Door—
To her divine Majority—
Present no more—

Unmoved—she notes the Chariots—pausing—   5
At her low Gate—
Unmoved—an Emperor be kneeling
Upon her Mat—

I've known her—from an ample nation—
Choose One—   10
Then—close the Valves of her attention—
Like Stone—
                            ca. 1862

341

After great pain, a formal feeling comes—
The Nerves sit ceremonious, like Tombs—
The stiff Heart questions was it He, that bore,
And Yesterday, or Centuries before?

The Feet, mechanical, go round—   5
Of Ground, or Air, or Ought[1]—
A Wooden way
Regardless grown,
A Quartz contentment, like a stone—

This is the Hour of Lead—   10
Remembered, if outlived,
As Freezing persons, recollect the Snow—
First—Chill—then Stupor—then the letting go—

                                        ca. 1862

419

We grow accustomed to the Dark—
When Light is put away—
As when the Neighbor holds the Lamp
To witness her Goodbye—

A Moment—We uncertain step   5
For newness of the night—
Then—fit our Vision to the Dark—
And meet the Road—erect—

And so of larger—Darknesses—
Those Evenings of the Brain—   10
When not a Moon disclose a sign—
Or Star—come out—within—

1. Nothing, or anything.

The Bravest—grope a little—
And sometimes hit a Tree
Directly in the Forehead— 15
But as they learn to see—

Either the Darkness alters—
Or something in the sight
Adjusts itself to Midnight—
And Life steps almost straight. 20
1862 *1935*

465

I heard a Fly buzz—when I died—
The Stillness in the Room
Was like the Stillness in the Air—
Between the Heaves of Storm—

The Eyes around—had wrung them dry— 5
And Breaths were gathering firm
For that last Onset—when the King
Be witnessed—in the Room—

I willed my Keepsakes—Signed away
What portion of me be 10
Assignable—and then it was
There interposed a Fly—

With Blue—uncertain stumbling Buzz—
Between the light—and me—
And then the Windows failed—and then 15
I could not see to see—
ca. 1862

712

Because I could not stop for Death—
He kindly stopped for me—

The Carriage held but just Ourselves—
And Immortality.

We slowly drove—He knew no haste   5
And I had put away
My labor and my leisure too,
For His Civility—

We passed the School, where Children strove
At Recess—in the Ring—   10
We passed the Fields of Gazing Grain—
We passed the Setting Sun—

Or rather—He passed Us—
The Dews drew quivering and chill—
For only Gossamer, my Gown—   15
My Tippet—only Tulle[1]—

We paused before a House that seemed
A Swelling of the Ground—
The Roof was scarcely visible—
The Cornice—in the Ground—   20

Since then—'tis Centuries—and yet
Feels shorter than the Day
I first surmised the Horses' Heads
Were toward Eternity—

                              ca. 1863

John Donne
1572–1631

> *Donne wrote poems for a coterie of friends, an elite society, and
> circulated them only in manuscript. Those included here were
> not published until two years after his death. Donne's poems "The
> Canonization" and "The Flea" both depict a love affair remarkable*

---

1. Thin silk. *Tippet:* a shawl.

for the age, perhaps for any age, and their bawdy conceits are striking even today. "A Valediction: Forbidding Mourning" is less cheerful but equally suggestive and intricate. To understand these "metaphysical" poems, as Donne's style of startling, extended metaphors (or conceits) came to be called, you must patiently unravel the intricate comparisons. His Holy Sonnets, exemplified here by "Death, be not proud" and "Batter my heart," express a piety belied by the love poems, though they were possibly written around the same time.

Song

Go, and catch a falling star,
   Get with child a mandrake root,[1]
Tell me, where all past years are,
   Or who cleft the Devil's foot,
Teach me to hear Mermaids singing,   5
   Or to keep off envies stinging,
      And find
      What wind
Serves to advance an honest mind.

If thou beest borne to strange sights,   10
   Things invisible to see,
Ride ten thousand days and nights,
   Till age snow white hairs on thee,
Thou, when thou retorn'st, wilt tell me
All strange wonders that befell thee,   15
      And swear
      No where
Lives a woman true, and fair.

If though findst one, let me know,
   Such a pilgrimage were sweet;   20

---

1. The roots of this plant sometimes resemble the legs of a human, sometimes the male genitalia. These resemblances probably account for its popularity in magical potions related to human fertility.

Yet do not, I would not go,
  Though at next door we might meet,
Though she were true, when you met her,
And last, till you write your letter,
    Yet she   25
    Will be
False, ere I come, to two, or three.

                                        1633

The Canonization[1]

  For God's sake hold your tongue, and let me love,
    Or chide my palsy, or my gout,
My five gray hairs, or ruined fortune, flout,
    With wealth your state, your mind with arts improve,
      Take you a course, get you a place,[2]   5
      Observe his honor, or his grace,
Or the King's real, or his stampèd face
    Contemplate; what you will, approve,
    So you will let me love.

Alas, alas, who's injured by my love?   10
    What merchant's ships have my sighs drowned?
Who says my tears have overflowed his ground?
    When did my colds a forward spring remove?[3]
      When did the heats which my veins fill
      Add one more to the plaguy bill?[4]   15
Soldiers find wars, and lawyers find out still
    Litigious men, which quarrels move,
    Though she and I do love.

---

1. Candidates for sainthood are canonized only after they have undergone a rigorous scrutiny in which a "devil's advocate" exposes all the defects that might undermine such a pronouncement.

2. An appointment. *Take you a course*: pursue a career.

3. Possible reference to the chill a rejected lover feels when given a "cold shoulder." The speaker's "colds" have not robbed the early spring of its warmth.

4. A public list of plague victims during an epidemic.

Call us what you will, we are made such by love;
   Call her one, me another fly,   20
We're tapers too, and at our own cost die,[5]
   And we in us find the eagle and the dove.
     The phoenix riddle hath more wit
     By us: we two being one, are it.
So, to one neutral thing both sexes fit.   25
   We die and rise the same, and prove
   Mysterious by this love.

We can die by it, if not live by love,
   And if unfit for tombs and hearse
Our legend be, it will be fit for verse;   30
   And if no piece of chronicle we prove,
     We'll build in sonnets pretty rooms;
     As well a well-wrought urn becomes
The greatest ashes, as half-acre tombs;[6]
   And by these hymns, all shall approve   35
   Us canonized for love.

And thus invoke us: You whom reverend love
   Made one another's hermitage;
You, to whom love was peace, that now is rage;[7]
   Who did the whole world's soul contract, and drove   40
     Into the glasses of your eyes
     (So made such mirrors, and such spies,
That they did all to you epitomize)[8]
   Countries, towns, courts: Beg from above
   A pattern of your love!   45

1633

5. A conventional metaphor for orgasm and a reference to the contemporary superstition that each ejaculation cost a man one day of life.

6. I.e., the pretty sonnets will contain their story, just as urns store ashes as well as giant mausoleums do.

7. I.e., lust.

8. Putting *epitomize* between *did* and *all* will help make sense of this line. A too-simple paraphrase of this and the preceding three lines might read, "whose eyes have seen it all."

The Flea[1]

Mark but this flea, and mark in this,
How little that which thou deniest me is;
It sucked me first, and now sucks thee,
And in this flea, our two bloods mingled be;
Thou know'st that this cannot be said   5
A sin, nor shame nor loss of maidenhead,
   Yet this enjoys before it woo,[2]
     And pampered swells with one blood made of two,[3]
     And this, alas, is more than we would do.

Oh stay, three lives in one flea spare,   10
Where we almost, yea more than married are.
This flea is you and I, and this
Our marriage bed, and marriage temple is;
Though parents grudge, and you, we are met,
And cloisered in these living walls of jet.[4]   15
   Though use make you apt to kill me,
     Let not to that, self murder added be,
     And sacrilege, three sins in killing three.

Cruel and sudden, hast thou since
Purpled thy nail, in blood of innocence?   20
Wherein could this flea guilty be,
Except in that drop which it sucked from thee?
Yet thou triumph'st, and say'st that thou
Find'st not thy self, nor me the weaker now;
   'Tis true, then learn how false, fears be;   25
     Just so much honor, when thou yield'st to me,
      Will waste, as this flea's death took life from thee.[5]

1633

1. A conventional item in Renaissance love poetry. Typically, the speaker envies the flea for its ability to roam the beloved's body at will, a liberty denied the speaker.

2. I.e., the flea does not have to court the woman before he "enjoys" her.

3. In the Renaissance, doctors believed that pregnancy resulted from the man's blood mixing with the woman's during intercourse.

4. I.e., the black body of the flea.

5. I.e., having sex with the speaker will hurt the woman's honor about as much as the flea's death lessened her life.

A Valediction: Forbidding Mourning[1]

As virtuous men pass mildly away,
    And whisper to their souls to go,
Whilst some of their sad friends do say
    The breath goes now, and some say, no;

So let us melt, and make no noise,   5
    No tear-floods, nor sigh-tempests move,
'Twere profanation of our joys
    To tell the laity our love.

Moving of th' earth brings harms and fears,
    Men reckon what it did and meant;   10
But trepidation of the spheres,[2]
    Though greater far, is innocent.

Dull sublunary[3] lovers' love
    (Whose soul is sense) cannot admit
Absence, because it doth remove   15
    Those things which elemented[4] it.

But we by a love so much refined
    That our selves know not what it is,
Inter-assurèd of the mind,
    Care less, eyes, lips, and hands to miss.   20

Our two souls therefore, which are one,
    Though I must go, endure not yet
A breach, but an expansion,
    Like gold to airy thinness beat.

1. Some evidence suggests that Donne wrote this poem in 1611 when he had to leave his wife to take a trip to the Continent.
2. Geocentric astronomers trying to explain why the planets did not orbit the earth in perfect circles like the stars suggested that they periodically and suddenly stopped themselves and reversed their direction.
3. Beneath the moon's orbit, and thus earthly as opposed to heavenly; in other words, subject to decay and corruption.
4. I.e., composed.

If they be two, they are two so   25
  As stiff twin compasses[5] are two;
Thy soul, the fixed foot, makes no show
  To move, but doth, if th' other do.

And though it in the center sit,
  Yet when the other far doth roam,   30
It leans and hearkens after it,
  And grows erect, as that comes home.

Such wilt thou be to me, who must
  Like th' other foot, obliquely run.
Thy firmness makes my circle just,   35
  And makes me end where I begun.

                                        1633

Holy Sonnets

10

Death, be not proud, though some have callèd thee
Mighty and dreadful, for thou are not so;
For those whom thou think'st thou dost overthrow
Die not, poor Death, nor yet canst thou kill me.
From rest and sleep, which but thy pictures be,   5
Much pleasure; then from thee much more must flow,
And soonest our best men with thee do go,
Rest of their bones, and soul's delivery.
Thou art slave to fate, chance, kings, and desperate men,
And dost with poison, war, and sickness dwell,   10
And poppy or charms can make us sleep as well
And better than thy stroke; why swell'st thou then?
One short sleep past, we wake eternally,
And death shall be no more; Death, thou shalt die.

                                        1633

5. I.e., compasses used to draw circles, not to find magnetic north.

14

Batter my heart, three-personed God;[1] for you
As yet but knock, breathe, shine, and seek to mend;
That I may rise and stand, o'erthrow me, and bend
Your force to break, blow, burn, and make me new.
I, like an usurped town, to another due,   5
Labor to admit you, but O, to no end;
Reason, your viceroy in me, me should defend,
But is captived, and proves weak or untrue.
Yet dearly I love you, and would be loved fain,[2]
But am betrothed unto your enemy.   10
Divorce me, untie or break that knot again;
Take me to you, imprison me, for I,
Except you enthrall me, never shall be free,
Nor ever chaste, except you ravish me.

1633

Mark Doty
b. 1953

*The modern gay rights movement in the United States began with
the Stonewall riot in New York City in 1969, and throughout the
1970s gays and lesbians made rapid progress casting off the main-
stream culture's prejudice and discrimination. Doty spent those
years in Manhattan, the epicenter of the movement. By the early
1980s, though, heady excitement and confidence gave way to a
strange immunodeficiency disease. By 1986, scientists identified
what we know now as human immunodeficiency virus (HIV) as
the cause of acquired immunodeficiency syndrome (AIDS). Nearly
every gay man in New York knew someone who had HIV or had
died of AIDS. Because HIV/AIDS was often transmitted by spe-
cific behaviors—specifically unprotected sex and the sharing of drug
needles—it carried the stigma of social opprobrium in the 1980s
and early 1990s. This poem enters into the public, moral debate
about the disease. Doty's partner, Willy Roberts, tested positive for*

1. The Father, Son, and Holy Spirit.   2. I.e., with pleasure.

HIV in 1989, and this poem was published shortly after, in 1991,
before Roberts suffered the symptoms of AIDS. He died in 1994,
crushing Doty with grief.

Tiara

Peter died in a paper tiara
cut from a book of princess paper dolls;
he loved royalty, sashes

and jewels. *I don't know,*
he said, when he woke in the hospice,   5
I was watching the Bette Davis[1] film festival

on Channel 57 and then—
At the wake, the tension broke
when someone guessed

the casket closed because   10
he was *in there in a big wig*
and heels, someone said,

You know he's always late,
he probably isn't here yet—
he's still fixing his makeup.   15

And someone said he asked for it.
Asked for it—
when all he did was go down

into the salt tide
of wanting as much as he wanted,   20
giving himself over so drunk

---

1. A glamorous movie star (1908–1989) known more for her compelling, melodramatic acting style than for her beauty. By the 1980s, she was an icon in gay culture and a favorite among female impersonators.

or stoned it almost didn't matter who,
though they were beautiful,
stampeding into him in the simple,

ravishing music of their hurry.   25
I think heaven is perfect stasis
poised over the realms of desire,

where dreaming and waking men lie
on the grass while wet horses
roam among them, huge fragments   30

of the music we die into
in the body's paradise.
Sometimes we wake not knowing

how we came to lie here,
or who has crowned us with these temporary, —   35
precious stones. And given

the world's perfectly turned shoulders,
the deep hollows blued by longing,
given the irreplaceable silk

of horses rippling in orchards,   40
fruit thundering and chiming down,
given the ordinary marvels of form

and gravity, what could he do,
what could any of us ever do
but ask for it?   45

1991

Rita Dove

b. 1952

"The House Slave" explores the ambiguous position of planta-
tion slaves who worked in the master's "big house" rather than
the fields in the pre–Civil War South. The life of a house slave
was often less difficult and dangerous than the field hand's and
sometimes allowed for a measure of education. House workers
enjoyed a high status among slaves, but because their ascendency
depended on their closeness to their aristocratic owners, it was
often accompanied by feelings of guilt. Perhaps this poem sug-
gests an analogue in the status of the economically successful,
modern-day African American. Dove based her poetry sequence
Thomas and Beulah *(1987), which won the Pulitzer Prize and*
the wide general audience that follows such recognition, on the
lives of her grandparents. "Daystar" is one of the Beulah *poems*
in the collection. "Demeter's Prayer to Hades" alludes to the
Greek myth in which Hades, the god of the underworld and
the dead, kidnaps Demeter's daughter, Persephone, for his wife.
Demeter, the goddess of the harvest, is devastated, and so the
vegetative world wastes away while she searches for her child.
Ultimately, a compromise is reached: Persephone remains in the
underworld only for the winter, which renews Demeter's grief
each year. The poem comes from Dove's 1992 collection Mother
Love, *which mixes the ancient with the modern, as if the mythi-*
cal characters were expressed in the elements and language of
contemporary life.

The House Slave

The first horn lifts its arm over the dew-lit grass
and in the slave quarters there is a rustling—
children are bundled into aprons, cornbread

and water gourds grabbed, a salt pork breakfast taken.
I watch them driven into the vague before-dawn   5
while their mistress sleeps like an ivory toothpick

and Massa dreams of asses, rum and slave-funk.
I cannot fall asleep again. At the second horn,
the whip curls across the backs of the laggards—

sometimes my sister's voice, unmistaken, among them.   10
"Oh! pray," she cries. "Oh! pray!" Those days
I lie on my cot, shivering in the early heat,

and as the fields unfold to whiteness,
and they spill like bees among the fat flowers,
I weep. It is not yet daylight.   15

1987

Daystar

She wanted a little room for thinking:
but she saw diapers steaming on the line,
a doll slumped behind the door.

So she lugged a chair behind the garage
to sit out the children's naps.   5

Sometimes there were things to watch—
the pinched armor of a vanished cricket,
a floating maple leaf. Other days
she stared until she was assured
when she closed her eyes   10
she'd see only her own vivid blood.

She had an hour, at best, before Liza appeared
pouting from the top of the stairs.
And just *what* was mother doing
out back with the field mice? Why,   15

building a palace. Later
that night when Thomas rolled over and
lurched into her, she would open her eyes
and think of the place that was hers

for an hour—where 20
she was nothing,
pure nothing, in the middle of the day.
1987

Demeter's Prayer to Hades

This alone is what I wish for you: knowledge.
To understand each desire has an edge,
to know we are responsible for the lives
we change. No faith comes without cost,
no one believes without dying. 5
Now for the first time
I see clearly the trail you planted,
what ground opened to waste,
though you dreamed a wealth
of flowers. 10
        There are no curses—only mirrors
held up to the souls of gods and mortals.
And so I give up this fate, too.
Believe in yourself,
go ahead—see where it gets you. 15
1992

Denise Duhamel
b. 1961
Known for what she calls the "personal or confessional" quality of her poems, Duhamel cites Sharon Olds, Sylvia Plath, and Anne Sexton as influences. From reading Olds's poetry, she learned that she didn't need to use "big symbols to mask my real feelings." Instead, she "can just say it." Much of Duhamel's work revises old fairy tales, myths, and contemporary cultural icons (like Barbie dolls). Her work is, in some ways, outside the mainstream of today's poetic trends. This poem is from Smile!, *her first book, which she completed six years before it found a publisher in 1993. Another book,* Kinky, *which has now gone through multiple printings, was rejected fifty-four times.*

Song for All the Would-Have-Been Princesses

Consider the gall of the bullfrog,
throatily calling at night for a mate,
longing for a kiss from a Beauty
that could change his fate. Some say a frog
is the male sex. And girls   5
who kindly put their lips to its
are promised to get over their fears.
But what about the cowfrog?
No mammary glands, no sweet milk, all her eggs
outside herself—not a frog in history   10
ever turned into a princess by a peck
on the cheek from an innocent boy,
as though female royalty and luck
sprout from other stuff. Once, before the Ranidae
were green and slimy, a young she-frog,   15
acting on impulse, shyly flirted with a prince.
she batted her eyes, big and bright as flash bulbs,
but, busily adjusting his white mink capelet,
the prince said to someone in his court,
"Get this commoner out of here! Does she not realize   20
such a scandal could cost me my throne?!"
And like St. Brigid, the defeated she-frog
might have mumbled, "Please God,
make me ugly, so I will no longer tempt men.
So I will no longer be tempted."   25
As though for a cowfrog, a would-be princess,
desire itself is shameful.

1993

Bob Dylan
b. 1941

> *Bob Dylan wrote "The Times They Are A-Changin'" in 1962, when*
> *he was twenty-one years old. The United States was taking over*
> *France's role in the Vietnam War, the civil rights movement was*

well under way, and what came to be called a "generation gap"
seemed to have opened between America's young people and their
parents. In a quick series of albums beginning in 1962, Dylan trans-
formed the possibilities for popular music, giving it a legitimacy
that put it alongside other recognized works of literature. "Tangled
Up in Blue," which Dylan presents as autobiographical—not in
literal detail but in mood and effect—was written in 1974 and first
appeared on Dylan's album Blood on the Tracks.

The Times They Are A-Changin'

Come gather 'round people
Wherever you roam
And admit that the waters
Around you have grown
And accept it that soon   5
You'll be drenched to the bone.
If your time to you
Is worth savin'
Then you better start swimmin'
Or you'll sink like a stone   10
For the times they are a-changin'.

Come writers and critics
Who prophesize with your pen
And keep your eyes wide
The chance won't come again   15
And don't speak too soon
For the wheel's still in spin
And there's no tellin' who
That it's namin'.
For the loser now   20
Will be later to win
For the times they are a-changin'.

Come senators, congressmen
Please heed the call

Don't stand in the doorway   25
Don't block up the hall
For he that gets hurt
Will be he who has stalled
There's a battle outside
And it is ragin'.   30
It'll soon shake your windows
And rattle your walls
For the times they are a-changin'.

Come mothers and fathers
Throughout the land   35
And don't criticize
What you can't understand
Your sons and your daughters
Are beyond your command
Your old road is   40
Rapidly agin'.
Please get out of the new one
If you can't lend your hand
For the times they are a-changin'.

The line it is drawn   45
The curse it is cast
The slow one now
Will later be fast
As the present now
Will later be past   50
The order is
Rapidly fadin'.
And the first one now
Will later be last
For the times they are a-changin'.   55

1962

Tangled Up in Blue

Early one mornin' the sun was shinin',
I was layin' in bed
Wond'rin' if she'd changed at all
If her hair was still red.
Her folks they said our lives together   5
Sure was gonna be rough
They never did like Mama's homemade dress
Papa's bankbook wasn't big enough.
And I was standin' on the side of the road
Rain fallin' on my shoes   10
Heading out for the East Coast
Lord knows I've paid some dues gettin' through,
Tangled up in blue.

She was married when we first met
Soon to be divorced   15
I helped her out of a jam, I guess,
But I used a little too much force.
We drove that car as far as we could
Abandoned it out West
Split up on a dark sad night   20
Both agreeing it was best.
She turned around to look at me
As I was walkin' away
I heard her say over my shoulder
"We'll meet again someday on the avenue,"   25
Tangled up in blue.

I had a job in the great north woods
Working as a cook for a spell
But I never did like it all that much
And one day the ax just fell.   30
So I drifted down to New Orleans
Where I happened to be employed
Workin' for a while on a fishin' boat
Right outside of Delacroix.

But all the while I was alone   35
The past was close behind,
I seen a lot of women
But she never escaped my mind, and I just grew
Tangled up in blue.

She was workin' in a topless place   40
And I stopped in for a beer,
I just kept lookin' at the side of her face
In the spotlight so clear.
And later on as the crowd thinned out
I's just about to do the same,   45
She was standing there in back of my chair
Said to me, "Don't I know your name?"
I muttered somethin' underneath my breath,
She studied the lines on my face.
I must admit I felt a little uneasy   50
When she bent down to tie the laces of my shoe,
Tangled up in blue.

She lit a burner on the stove and offered me a pipe
"I thought you'd never say hello," she said
"You look like the silent type."   55
Then she opened up a book of poems
And handed it to me
Written by an Italian poet
From the thirteenth century.
And every one of them words rang true   60
And glowed like burnin' coal
Pourin' off of every page
Like it was written in my soul from me to you,
Tangled up in blue.

I lived with them on Montague Street   65
In a basement down the stairs,
There was music in the cafes at night
And revolution in the air.
Then he started into dealing with slaves

And something inside of him died.   70
She had to sell everything she owned
And froze up inside.
And when finally the bottom fell out
I became withdrawn,
The only thing I knew how to do   75
Was to keep on keepin' on like a bird that flew,
Tangled up in blue.

So now I'm goin' back again,
I got to get to her somehow.
All the people we used to know   80
They're an illusion to me now.
Some are mathematicians
Some are carpenter's wives.
Don't know how it all got started,
I don't know what they're doin' with their lives.   85
But me, I'm still on the road
Headin' for another joint
We always did feel the same,
We just saw it from a different point of view,
Tangled up in blue.   90

                                 1974

T. S. (*Thomas Stearns*) Eliot
1888–1965

*Eliot was working on his Ph.D. in philosophy at Harvard when he
began writing "The Love Song of J. Alfred Prufrock." When he trav-
eled to London, he met Ezra Pound, who persuaded the Chicago-
based* Poetry *magazine to publish "Prufrock" in 1915. The poem
established Eliot as one of the new poets using a "modern" style that
refused to make any concessions to what we might call the "com-
mon reader." "Prufrock," like most of Eliot's poetry, is characterized
by striking conceits (like the simile in lines 2–3) and allusions to
literary tradition (such as* Hamlet *and the* Bible*). Eliot's poetry
may be disconcerting on a first read: because he leaves out logical*

links and signposts between images, it can be hard to figure out the literal level of "Prufrock." Even so, the poem is easier to understand than it first appears. Gauging Prufrock's character will give you a fair estimate of the "modern" or "anti-hero" Eliot helped define: the sensitive figure crippled by his insight into human character.

The Love Song of J. Alfred Prufrock

*S'io credesse che mia risposta fosse
A persona che mai tornasse al mondo,
Questa fiamma staria senza piu scosse.
Ma perciocche giammai di questo fondo
Non torno vivo alcun, s'i'odo il vero,
Senza tema d'infamia ti rispondo.*[1]

Let us go then, you and I,
When the evening is spread out against the sky
Like a patient etherised upon a table;
Let us go, through certain half-deserted streets,
The muttering retreats   5
Of restless nights in one-night cheap hotels
And sawdust restaurants with oyster-shells:
Streets that follow like a tedious argument
Of insidious intent
To lead you to an overwhelming question . . .   10
Oh, do not ask, "What is it?"
Let us go and make our visit.

In the room the women come and go
Talking of Michelangelo.

The yellow fog that rubs its back upon the window-panes,   15
The yellow smoke that rubs its muzzle on the window-panes

---

1. Dante, *Inferno* 27.61–66; spoken by Guido da Montefeltro, whom Dante and Virgil find among the false counselors (each spirit is concealed within a flame): "If I thought my answer were given / to anyone who would ever return to the world, / this flame would stand still without moving any further. / But since never from this abyss / has anyone ever returned alive, if what I hear is true, / without fear of infamy I answer you."

Licked its tongue into the corners of the evening,
Lingered upon the pools that stand in drains,
Let fall upon its back the soot that falls from chimneys,
Slipped by the terrace, made a sudden leap,   20
And seeing that it was a soft October night,
Curled once about the house, and fell asleep.

And indeed there will be time
For the yellow smoke that slides along the street,
Rubbing its back upon the window-panes;   25
There will be time, there will be time
To prepare a face to meet the faces that you meet;
There will be time to murder and create,
And time for all the works and days of hands
That lift and drop a question on your plate;   30
Time for you and time for me,
And time yet for a hundred indecisions,
And for a hundred visions and revisions,
Before the taking of a toast and tea.

In the room the women come and go   35
Talking of Michelangelo.

And indeed there will be time
To wonder, "Do I dare?" and, "Do I dare?"
Time to turn back and descend the stair,
With a bald spot in the middle of my hair—   40
(They will say: "How his hair is growing thin!")
My morning coat, my collar mounting firmly to the chin,
My necktie rich and modest, but asserted by a simple pin—
(They will say: "But how his arms and legs are thin!")
Do I dare   45
Disturb the universe?
In a minute there is time
For decisions and revisions which a minute will reverse.

For I have known them all already, known them all—
Have known the evenings, mornings, afternoons,   50

I have measured out my life with coffee spoons;
I know the voices dying with a dying fall[2]
Beneath the music from a farther room.
    So how should I presume?

And I have known the eyes already, known them all—   55
The eyes that fix you in a formulated phrase,
And when I am formulated, sprawling on a pin,
When I am pinned and wriggling on the wall,
Then how should I begin
To spit out all the butt-ends of my days and ways?   60
    And how should I presume?

And I have known the arms already, known them all—
Arms that are braceleted and white and bare
(But in the lamplight, downed with light brown hair!)
Is it perfume from a dress   65
That makes me so digress?
Arms that lie along a table, or wrap about a shawl.
    And should I then presume?
    And how should I begin?

    .   .   .   .   .   .

Shall I say, I have gone at dusk through narrow streets   70
And watched the smoke that rises from the pipes
Of lonely men in shirt-sleeves, leaning out of windows? . . .

I should have been a pair of ragged claws
Scuttling across the floors of silent seas.

    .   .   .   .   .

And the afternoon, the evening, sleeps so peacefully!   75
Smoothed by long fingers,
Asleep . . . tired . . . or it malingers,
Stretched on the floor, here beside you and me.
Should I, after tea and cakes and ices,
Have the strength to force the moment to its crisis?   80

2. An echo of Shakespeare's *Twelfth Night* (1.1.1–4): "If music be the food of love, play
on. . . . That strain again, it had a dying fall."

But though I have wept and fasted, wept and prayed,
Though I have seen my head (grown slightly bald) brought in
    upon a platter,[3]
I am no prophet—and here's no great matter;
I have seen the moment of my greatness flicker,
And I have seen the eternal Footman hold my coat, and snicker,   85
And in short, I was afraid.

And would it have been worth it, after all,
After the cups, the marmalade, the tea,
Among the porcelain, among some talk of you and me,
Would it have been worth while,   90
To have bitten off the matter with a smile,
To have squeezed the universe into a ball
To roll it toward some overwhelming question,
To say: "I am Lazarus, come from the dead,
Come back to tell you all, I shall tell you all"—   95
If one, settling a pillow by her head,
    Should say: "That is not what I meant at all.
    That is not it, at all."

And would it have been worth it, after all,
Would it have been worth while,   100
After the sunsets and the dooryards and the sprinkled streets,
After the novels, after the teacups, after the skirts that trail
    along the floor—
And this, and so much more?—
It is impossible to say just what I mean!
But as if a magic lantern threw the nerves in patterns on a
    screen: 105
Would it have been worth while
If one, settling a pillow or throwing off a shawl,
And turning toward the window, should say:
    "That is not it at all,
    That is not what I meant, at all."   110

     .   .   .   .   .   .

3. At her request, King Herod gave his daughter, Salome, the head of John the Baptist on a serving plate (Matthew 14.1–12).

No! I am not Prince Hamlet, nor was meant to be;
Am an attendant lord, one that will do
To swell a progress,[4] start a scene or two,
Advise the prince; no doubt, an easy tool,
Deferential, glad to be of use,   115
Politic, cautious, and meticulous;
Full of high sentence, but a bit obtuse;
At times, indeed, almost ridiculous—
Almost, at times, the Fool.

I grow old . . . I grow old . . .   120
I shall wear the bottoms of my trousers rolled.

Shall I part my hair behind? Do I dare to eat a peach?
I shall wear white flannel trousers, and walk upon the beach.
I have heard the mermaids singing, each to each.

I do not think that they will sing to me.   125

I have seen them riding seaward on the waves
Combing the white hair of the waves blown back
When the wind blows the water white and black.

We have lingered in the chambers of the sea
By sea-girls wreathed with seaweed red and brown   130
Till human voices wake us, and we drown.

                        1917

Thomas Sayers Ellis
b. 1963

*Ellis grew up in Washington, D.C., and was educated at Harvard
and Brown Universities, where he counted among his teachers
the great poets Seamus Heaney and Derek Walcott. But his poems
cut against the grain of tradition—"all their stanzas look alike,"*

---

4. I.e., to enlarge the group accompanying a lord with one more body, as might be done
with bit actors on the Elizabethan stage.

the refrain of one of his more famous poems, refers to the canon of great poets, and he's probably closer to rap than he is to Wordsworth. At one reading he called this poem an "ode to my favorite conjunction," but that joke belies the more serious theme: the poem appears in his 2010 collection Skin, Inc. *which is subtitled,* Identity Repair Poems. *"Or," begins almost as if designating categories of race one might check off on some government form. "Oreo," for instance, means someone with black skin (on the outside) who thinks and reacts like a white person (on the inside).*

Or,

Or Oreo, or
worse. Or ordinary.
Or your choice
of category

    or   5
    Color

or any color
other than Colored
or Colored Only.
Or "Of Color"   10

    or
    Other

or theory or discourse
or oral territory.
Oregon or Georgia   15
or Florida Zora[1]

---

1. Probably Zora Neale Hurston (1891–1960), a Floridian, who as a folklorist and fiction writer contributed to the Harlem Renaissance of African American artists in the 1920s. *Their Eyes Were Watching God* (1937) is her most famous novel.

or
Opportunity

or born poor
or Corporate. Or Moor.   20
Or a Noir Orpheus[2]
or Senghor[3]

or
Diaspora

or a horrendous   25
and tore-up journey.
Or performance. Or allegory's armor
of ignorant comfort

or
Worship   30

or reform or a sore chorus.
Or Electoral Corruption
or important ports
of Yoruba[4] or worry

or   35
Neighbor

or fear of . . .
of terror or border.
Or all organized
minorities.   40

2010

2. Greek god often associated with music and song. The 1959 film, *Orfeu Negro* (*Black Orpheus*), won an Academy Award for best foreign film and the Palme d'Or at the Cannes Film Festival.

3. Léopold Sédar Senghor (1906–2001), poet and first president of Senegal (1960–1980).

4. Ethnicity, culture, and language of as many as fifty million people in southwestern Nigeria and Benin. In the eighteenth and nineteenth centuries, Yorubaland constituted part of the "slave coast" of West African, where Europeans established several slave depots.

Louise Erdrich
b. 1954

In an interview, Erdrich explained that the children speaking in "Indian Boarding School: The Runaways" have "been taken from their homes [and] their cultures by the Bureau of Indian Affairs." Earlier in this century, such schools attempted to acclimate Native American children to mainstream American life by obliterating their culture. The speaker in "Captivity" is a European woman captured by Native Americans. While you might think that her natural reaction to being rescued would be relief, the speaker's response is more complex. She is suspended between cultures, and her dream suggests some ambivalence. Erdrich herself has one foot in each culture: she has both German and Chippewa ancestors.

Indian Boarding School: The Runaways

Home's the place we head for in our sleep.
Boxcars stumbling north in dreams
don't wait for us. We catch them on the run.
The rails, old lacerations that we love,
shoot parallel across the face and break   5
just under Turtle Mountains.[1] Riding scars
you can't get lost. Home is the place they cross.

The lame guard strikes a match and makes the dark
less tolerant. We watch through cracks in boards
as the land starts rolling, rolling till it hurts   10
to be here, cold in regulation clothes.
We know the sheriff's waiting at midrun
to take us back. His car is dumb and warm.
The highway doesn't rock, it only hums
like a wing of long insults. The worn-down welts   15
of ancient punishments lead back and forth.

All runaways wear dresses, long green ones,
the color you would think shame was. We scrub

1. In North Dakota, the home of one band of Chippewa Indians.

the sidewalks down because it's shameful work.
Our brushes cut the stone in watered arcs   20
and in the soak frail outlines shiver clear
a moment, things us kids pressed on the dark
face before it hardened, pale, remembering
delicate old injuries, the spines of names and leaves.

1987

Captivity

> *He (my captor) gave me a bisquit, which I put in my pocket, and not daring to eat it, buried it under a log, fearing he had put something in it to make me love him.*
> —from the narrative of the captivity of Mrs. Mary Rowlandson, who was taken prisoner by the Wampanoag when Lancaster, Massachusetts, was destroyed, in the year 1676

The stream was swift, and so cold
I thought I would be sliced in two.
But he dragged me from the flood
by the ends of my hair.
I had grown to recognize his face.   5
I could distinguish it from the others.
There were times I feared I understood
his language, which was not human,
and I knelt to pray for strength.

We were pursued! By God's agents   10
or pitch devils I did not know.
Only that we must march.
Their guns were loaded with swan shot.
I could not suckle and my child's wail
put them in danger.   15
He had a woman
with teeth black and glittering.
She fed the child milk of acorns.
The forest closed, the light deepened.

I told myself that I would starve   20
before I took food from his hands
but I did not starve.
One night
he killed a deer with a young one in her
and gave me to eat of the fawn.   25
It was so tender,
the bones like the stems of flowers,
that I followed where he took me.
The night was thick. He cut the cord
that bound me to the tree.   30

After that the birds mocked.
Shadows gaped and roared
and the trees flung down
their sharpened lashes.
He did not notice God's wrath.   35
God blasted fire from half-buried stumps.
I hid my face in my dress, fearing He would burn us all
but this, too, passed.

Rescued, I see no truth in things.
My husband drives a thick wedge   40
through the earth, still it shuts
to him year after year.
My child is fed of the first wheat.
I lay myself to sleep
on a Holland-laced pillowbeer.   45
I lay to sleep.
And in the dark I see myself
as I was outside their circle.

They knelt on deerskins, some with sticks,
and he led his company in the noise   50
until I could no longer bear
the thought of how I was.
I stripped a branch
and struck the earth,

in time, begging it to open   55
to admit me
as he was
and feed me honey from the rock.

1989

Martín Espada
b. 1957

> *Espada's father was a Puerto Rican political activist in Brooklyn,*
> *New York, and when Espada earned his law degree, he took on the*
> *cases of poor tenants in their disputes with landlords. He brings*
> *that kind of political action to poetry, insisting that poems can*
> *make visible the Hispanics who tend to disappear in mainstream*
> *American culture. "How is it possible," he asks, "that 40 million*
> *people can also be invisible?" This poem examines the condition of*
> *Hispanic art and artists in America and the economic reality that*
> *underpins their condition. Consider the title of the pawnshop,*
> *"Liberty Loan" and the role of credit in the lives of the poor.*

Latin Night at the Pawnshop

Chelsea, Massachusetts,
Christmas, 1987

The apparition of a salsa band
gleaming in the Liberty Loan
pawnshop window:

Golden trumpet,
silver trombone,   5
congas, maracas, tambourine,
all with price tags dangling
like the city morgue ticket
on a dead man's toe.

1987

Nikky Finney
b. 1957

Born in Conway, South Carolina, Finney grew up in the Jim Crow era, when many southern whites stubbornly refused political, economic, educational, and social opportunity to their fellow black citizens. Her parents were middle-class professionals working actively for civil rights. The 1968 Orangeburg Massacre, in which state troopers killed three young black men who were protesting a segregated bowling alley, helped form her understanding of American politics. If you've heard of Kent State (where four white anti–Vietnam War protesters were killed by National Guardsmen) but have not heard of Orangeburg, Finney wants to speak to you. She writes many of her poems, including "Left," to make sure stories and names and truths that usually do not "make it to air" are heard. "Don't leave the arena to the fools," she says, quoting Toni Cade Bambara. The context for this poem is the Hurricane Katrina disaster, which flooded New Orleans in 2005, killing nearly two thousand people and displacing hundreds of thousands. The poor bore the worst of the consequences, and government agencies all the way up to President George W. Bush were criticized for the inadequacy of their response.

Left

Eenee Menee Mainee Mo!

    —RUDYARD KIPLING, "A COUNTING-OUT-SONG,"

    IN *LAND AND SEA TALES FOR SCOUTS AND GUIDES*, 1923

    The woman with cheerleading legs
has been left for dead. She hot paces a roof,
four days, three nights, her leaping fingers,
helium arms rise & fall, pulling at the week-
old baby in the bassinet, pointing to the eighty-   5
two-year-old grandmother, fanning & raspy
in the New Orleans Saints folding chair,

        Eenee Menee Mainee Mo!

Three times a day the helicopter flies
by in a low crawl. The grandmother insists on   10
not being helpless, so she waves a white hand-
kerchief that she puts on and takes off her head
toward the cameraman and the pilot who
remembers well the art of his mirrored-eyed
posture in his low-flying helicopter: Bong Son,   15
Dong Ha, Pleiku, Chu Lai. He makes a slow
Vietcong dip & dive, a move known in Rescue
as the Observation Pass.

The roof is surrounded by broken-levee
water. The people are dark but not broken. Starv-   20
ing, abandoned, dehydrated, brown & cumulous,
but not broken. The four-hundred-year-old
anniversary of observation begins, again—

    Eenee Menee Mainee Mo!
    Catch a—   25

The woman with pom-pom legs waves
her uneven homemade sign:

    Pleas Help Pleas

and even if the *e* has been left off the *Pleas e*

do you know simply   30
by looking at her
that it has been left off
because she can't spell
(and therefore is not worth saving)
or was it because the water was rising so fast;   35
there wasn't time?

    Eenee Menee Mainee Mo!
    Catch a—a—

The low-flying helicopter does not know
the answer. It catches all of this on patriotic tape,   40
but does not land, and does not drop dictionary,
or ladder.

Regulations require an *e* be at the end
of any *Pleas e* before any national response
can be taken.   45

Therefore, it takes four days before
the national council of observers will consider
dropping one bottle of water, or one case
of dehydrated baby formula, on the roof
where the *e* has rolled off into the flood,   50

(but obviously not splashed loud enough)

where four days later not the mother,
not the baby girl,
but the determined hanky waver,   55
whom they were both named for,
(and after) has now been covered up
with a green plastic window awning,
pushed over to the side
right where the missing *e* was last seen.   60

My mother said to pick
The very best one!

What else would you call it,
Mr. Every-Child-Left-Behind.

Anyone you know   65
ever left off or put on
an *e* by mistake

Potato Po tato e

     In the future observation helicopters
will leave the well-observed South and fly   70
In Kanye-West-Was-Finally-Right formation.
They will arrive over burning San Diego.

     The fires there will be put out *so well,*
The people there will wait *in a civilized manner.*
And they will receive *foie gras* and *free massage*   75
for all their trouble, while their houses don't
flood, but instead burn *calmly* to the ground.

The grandmothers were right
about everything.

People who outlived bullwhips & Bull   80
Connor, historically afraid of water and routinely
fed to crocodiles, left in the sun on the sticky tar-
heat of roofs to roast like pigs, surrounded by
forty feet of churning water, in the summer
of 2005, while the richest country in the world   85
played the old observation game, studied
the situation: wondered by committee what to do;
counted, in private, by long historical division;
speculated whether or not some people are surely
born ready, accustomed to flood, famine, fear.   90

       My mother said to pick
       The very best one
       And you are not it!

     After all, it was only po' New Orleans,
old bastard city of funny spellers. Nonswimmers   95
with squeeze-box accordion accents. Who would
be left alive to care ?

                      2011

Carolyn Forché
b. 1950

In 1978, supported by a Guggenheim Fellowship, Forché traveled to El Salvador and produced her award-winning The Country Between Us *(1981), which included "The Colonel." Beginning in 1960, El Salvador was ruled by a series of repressive military governments, and the country was in civil war by the late 1970s. Colonel Arturo Armando Molina ruled until 1977, when he was replaced by the extremely repressive General Carlos Humberto Romero, who, in turn, was ousted by a coup in 1979. This is the only example of a prose poem in this book, and it can be taken as a good representative of the genre. Usually, prose poems are about this length, and they often relate an anecdotal incident.*

The Colonel

What you have heard is true. I was in his house. His wife carried a tray of coffee and sugar. His daughter filed her nails, his son went out for the night. There were daily papers, pet dogs, a pistol on the cushion beside him. The moon swung bare on its black cord over the house. On the television was a cop show. It was in English. Broken[5] bottles were embedded in the walls around the house to scoop the kneecaps from a man's legs or cut his hands to lace. On the windows there were gratings like those in liquor stores. We had dinner, rack of lamb, good wine, a gold bell was on the table for calling the maid. The maid brought green mangoes, salt, a type of bread. I[10] was asked how I enjoyed the country. There was a brief commercial in Spanish. His wife took everything away. There was some talk of how difficult it had become to govern. The parrot said hello on the terrace. The colonel told it to shut up, and pushed himself from the table. My friend said to me with his eyes: say nothing. The colonel[15] returned with a sack used to bring groceries home. He spilled many human ears on the table. They were like dried peach halves. There is no other way to say this. He took one of them in his hands, shook it in our faces, dropped it into a water glass. It came alive there. I am tired of fooling around he said. As for the rights of anyone, tell your[20] people they can go fuck themselves.[1] He swept the ears to the floor with his arm and held the last of his wine in the air.

Something for your poetry, no? he said. Some of the ears on the floor caught this scrap of his voice. Some of the ears on the floor were pressed to the ground.   25

1981

Robert Frost

1874–1963

Frost's formal style and rural subjects helped make his poetry particularly accessible to a popular reading audience. Even so, you must be careful to gauge the tone of the selections printed here: Frost's poems are darker than his reputation might suggest. Many deal with the isolation and loneliness of the human condition. For instance, do not forget that the memorable line in "Mending Wall," "Good fences make good neighbors," is uttered by "an old-stone savage armed . . . [and moving] in darkness." Likewise, you may have seen the last three lines of "The Road Not Taken" quoted on a poster in high school, where it exhorted you to be an individual. But be careful to consider the context of those lines and ask yourself, Will the speaker, in "ages hence," be lying to himself? Though his rural subjects, as in "After Apple-Picking," "Out, Out—," and "Birches," often spark comparisons to those of the Romantic poets a hundred years earlier, Frost was no worshiper of nature. "Design," for example, which Frost wrote when he was sixty-two, is a Petrarchan sonnet that could be written only in the post-Darwinian age because it takes seriously the possibility that the complexity of the natural world is random.

---

1. Between 1976 and 1980, President Jimmy Carter's emphasis on human rights in American foreign policy complicated U.S. relations with dictatorial regimes in Central and South American countries such as El Salvador.

After Apple-Picking

My long two-pointed ladder's sticking through a tree
Toward heaven still,
And there's a barrel that I didn't fill
Beside it, and there may be two or three
Apples I didn't pick upon some bough.   5
But I am done with apple-picking now.
Essence of winter sleep is on the night,
The scent of apples: I am drowsing off.
I cannot rub the strangeness from my sight
I got from looking through a pane of glass   10
I skimmed this morning from the drinking trough
And held against the world of hoary grass.
It melted, and I let it fall and break.
But I was well
Upon my way to sleep before it fell,   15
And I could tell
What form my dreaming was about to take.
Magnified apples appear and disappear,
Stem end and blossom end,
And every fleck of russet showing clear.   20
My instep arch not only keeps the ache,
It keeps the pressure of a ladder-round.
I feel the ladder sway as the boughs bend.
And I keep hearing from the cellar bin
The rumbling sound   25
Of load on load of apples coming in.
For I have had too much
Of apple-picking: I am overtired
Of the great harvest I myself desired.
There were ten thousand thousand fruit to touch,   30
Cherish in hand, lift down, and not let fall.
For all
That struck the earth,
No matter if not bruised or spiked with stubble,
Went surely to the cider-apple heap   35
As of no worth.

One can see what will trouble
This sleep of mine, whatever sleep it is.
Were he not gone,
The woodchuck could say whether it's like his   40
Long sleep, as I describe its coming on,
Or just some human sleep.

                                        1914

Mending Wall

Something there is that doesn't love a wall,
That sends the frozen-ground-swell under it,
And spills the upper boulders in the sun;
And makes gaps even two can pass abreast.
The work of hunters is another thing: 5
I have come after them and made repair
Where they have left not one stone on a stone,
But they would have the rabbit out of hiding,
To please the yelping dogs. The gaps I mean,
No one has seen them made or heard them made,   10
But at spring mending-time we find them there.
I let my neighbor know beyond the hill;
And on a day we meet to walk the line
And set the wall between us once again.
We keep the wall between us as we go.   15
To each the boulders that have fallen to each.
And some are loaves and some so nearly balls
We have to use a spell to make them balance:
'Stay where you are until our backs are turned!'
We wear our fingers rough with handling them.   20
Oh, just another kind of outdoor game,
One on a side. It comes to little more:
There where it is we do not need the wall:
He is all pine and I am apple orchard.
My apple trees will never get across   25
And eat the cones under his pines, I tell him.
He only says, 'Good fences make good neighbors.'
Spring is the mischief in me, and I wonder

If I could put a notion in his head:
'*Why* do they make good neighbors? Isn't it   30
Where there are cows? But here there are no cows.
Before I built a wall I'd ask to know
What I was walling in or walling out,
And to whom I was like to give offense.
Something there is that doesn't love a wall,   35
That wants it down.' I could say 'Elves' to him,
But it's not elves exactly, and I'd rather
He said it for himself. I see him there
Bringing a stone grasped firmly by the top
In each hand, like an old-stone savage armed.   40
He moves in darkness as it seems to me,
Not of woods only and the shade of trees.
He will not go behind his father's saying,
And he likes having thought of it so well
He says again, 'Good fences make good neighbors.'   45

1914

"Out, Out—"

The buzz saw snarled and rattled in the yard
And made dust and dropped stove-length sticks of wood,
Sweet-scented stuff when the breeze drew across it.
And from there those that lifted eyes could count
Five mountain ranges one behind the other   5
Under the sunset far into Vermont.
And the saw snarled and rattled, snarled and rattled,
As it ran light, or had to bear a load.
And nothing happened: day was all but done.
Call it a day, I wish they might have said   10
To please the boy by giving him the half hour
That a boy counts so much when saved from work.
His sister stood beside them in her apron
To tell them "Supper." At the word, the saw,
As if to prove saws knew what supper meant,   15
Leaped out at the boy's hand, or seemed to leap—
He must have given the hand. However it was,

Neither refused the meeting. But the hand!
The boy's first outcry was a rueful laugh,
As he swung toward them holding up the hand,   20
Half in appeal, but half as if to keep
The life from spilling. Then the boy saw all—
Since he was old enough to know, big boy
Doing a man's work, though a child at heart—
He saw all spoiled. "Don't let him cut my hand off—   25
The doctor, when he comes. Don't let him, sister!"
So. But the hand was gone already.
The doctor put him in the dark of ether.
He lay and puffed his lips out with his breath.
And then—the watcher at his pulse took fright.   30
No one believed. They listened at his heart.
Little—less—nothing!—and that ended it.
No more to build on there. And they, since they
Were not the one dead, turned to their affairs.

1916

The Road Not Taken

Two roads diverged in a yellow wood,
And sorry I could not travel both
And be one traveler, long I stood
And looked down one as far as I could
To where it bent in the undergrowth;   5

Then took the other, as just as fair,
And having perhaps the better claim,
Because it was grassy and wanted wear;
Though as for that the passing there
Had worn them really about the same,   10

And both that morning equally lay
In leaves no step had trodden black.
Oh, I kept the first for another day!
Yet knowing how way leads on to way,
I doubted if I should ever come back.   15

I shall be telling this with a sigh
Somewhere ages and ages hence:
Two roads diverged in a wood, and I—
I took the one less traveled by,
And that has made all the difference.   20

                    1916

Birches

When I see birches bend to left and right
Across the lines of straighter darker trees,
I like to think some boy's been swinging them.
But swinging doesn't bend them down to stay
As ice-storms do. Often you must have seen them   5
Loaded with ice a sunny winter morning
After a rain. They click upon themselves
As the breeze rises, and turn many-colored
As the stir cracks and crazes their enamel.
Soon the sun's warmth makes them shed crystal shells   10
Shattering and avalanching on the snow-crust—
Such heaps of broken glass to sweep away
You'd think the inner dome of heaven had fallen.
They are dragged to the withered bracken by the load,
And they seem not to break; though once they are bowed 15
So low for long, they never right themselves:
You may see their trunks arching in the woods
Years afterwards, trailing their leaves on the ground
Like girls on hands and knees that throw their hair
Before them over their heads to dry in the sun.   20
But I was going to say when Truth broke in
With all her matter-of-fact about the ice-storm
I should prefer to have some boy bend them
As he went out and in to fetch the cows—
Some boy too far from town to learn baseball,   25
Whose only play was what he found himself,
Summer or winter, and could play alone.
One by one he subdued his father's trees
By riding them down over and over again

Until he took the stiffness out of them,   30
And not one but hung limp, not one was left
For him to conquer. He learned all there was
To learn about not launching out too soon
And so not carrying the tree away
Clear to the ground. He always kept his poise   35
To the top branches, climbing carefully
With the same pains you use to fill a cup
Up to the brim, and even above the brim.
Then he flung outward, feet first, with a swish,
Kicking his way down through the air to the ground.   40
So was I once myself a swinger of birches.
And so I dream of going back to be.
It's when I'm weary of considerations,
And life is too much like a pathless wood
Where your face burns and tickles with the cobwebs   45
Broken across it, and one eye is weeping
From a twig's having lashed across it open.
I'd like to get away from earth awhile
And then come back to it and begin over.
May no fate willfully misunderstand me   50
And half grant what I wish and snatch me away
Not to return. Earth's the right place for love:
I don't know where it's likely to go better.
I'd like to go by climbing a birch tree,
And climb black branches up a snow-white trunk   55
Toward heaven, till the tree could bear no more,
But dipped its top and set me down again.
That would be good both going and coming back.
One could do worse than be a swinger of birches.

1916

Stopping by Woods on a Snowy Evening

Whose woods these are I think I know.
His house is in the village though;
He will not see me stopping here
To watch his woods fill up with snow.

My little horse must think it queer   5
To stop without a farmhouse near
Between the woods and frozen lake
The darkest evening of the year.

He gives his harness bells a shake
To ask if there is some mistake.   10
The only other sound's the sweep
Of easy wind and downy flake.

The woods are lovely, dark and deep,
But I have promises to keep,
And miles to go before I sleep,   15
And miles to go before I sleep.

1923

Design

I found a dimpled spider, fat and white,
On a white heal-all,[1] holding up a moth
Like a white piece of rigid satin cloth—
Assorted characters of death and blight
Mixed ready to begin the morning right,   5
Like the ingredients of a witches' broth—
A snow-drop spider, a flower like a froth,
And dead wings carried like a paper kite.

What had that flower to do with being white,
The wayside blue and innocent heal-all?   10
What brought the kindred spider to that height,
Then steered the white moth thither in the night?
What but design of darkness to appall?—
If design govern in a thing so small.

1936

---

1. One of a variety of plants in the mint family; the flowers are usually violet-blue.

The Silken Tent

She is as in a field a silken tent
At midday when a sunny summer breeze
Has dried the dew and all its ropes relent,
So that in guys it gently sways at ease,
And its supporting central cedar pole,   5
That is its pinnacle to heavenward
And signifies the sureness of the soul,
Seems to owe naught to any single cord,
But strictly held by none, is loosely bound
By countless silken ties of love and thought   10
To everything on earth the compass round,
And only by one's going slightly taut
In the capriciousness of summer air
Is of the slightest bondage made aware.

1942

Zulfikar Ghose
b. 1935

> *Ghose, an American immigrant born and raised in what is now Pakistan, has claimed that he writes best "when I have nothing to say but have a desire to write a poem, a pressure of form within my mind, so that I look for images through which that form might emerge." He published "Autobiography in Late Middle Age" in* Illuminations, *an international poetry magazine, in 1992, when he was fifty-seven years old.*

Autobiography in Late Middle Age

Little hair and that steel-grey like a horseshoe
around the head just above the ears but most
incongruously small tufts of black hair plug
the earholes and sprout from the flared nostrils;
and of course wrinkles, bifocals, and not   5
inconspicuous dental work go with one's age.

But that's what you see of me when you stop
at the traffic lights and become indulgent
when I take my time to cross the road, you smile
to show your patience towards the elderly;　　　　　　　　10
or when I sit next to you in the airplane,
preferring the aisle seat for quick access
to the toilet, and you decide to be tolerant
of fussy quirks and clumsiness with the lunch tray
that might send bits of ice from my scotch into your lap,　　15
you make a secret resolve to be on your guard
against the unpredictable accidents of old age.
Stranger, you know nothing! Have you seen me
striding across the lawn behind the power mower
declaiming from the fourth book of Virgil's　　　　　　　20
Aeneid[1] with such metrical beauty that my breath
seems to come from the heavy-scented blooms
of the honeysuckle? You cannot guess the sweetness
there is in my tongue that awakens in young flesh
the quickened pulse of desire. Know, stranger, of my　　25
secret power. There are days when I drive out West
in my sports car and there hitting the straight
road in the middle of the desert free of traffic cops
I turn high the volume on a Maria Callas[2] tape
and there in the desert singing *O Patria mia*　　　　　30
with her I aim for the horizon at one hundred
and twenty miles an hour. Time stops then
on that flat disc of sand bisected by the still
arrow of the road as if the planet had halted
and I'd become the ageless exile singing　　　　　　　35
of a land of green hills and perfumed rivers.

1992

1. In this part of his epic poem, the Roman poet Virgil (70–19 B.C.E.) recounts the love affair between the Trojan hero Aeneas and Dido, the queen of Carthage. After the fall of Troy, Aeneas set out to found the city of Rome, stopping in Carthage along the way, where he meets Dido, who tempts him to remain in Africa. But Aeneas, refusing to delay his heaven-appointed fate, leaves the queen, who kills herself in despair.

2. One of the most celebrated divas of the twentieth century. She famously sang "O Patria Mia," an aria from the third act of Giuseppe Verdi's *Aida*. The title character, the princess of Ethiopia, is a captive slave in Egypt. In the song she laments her conquered homeland.

Allen Ginsberg
1926–1998

"A Supermarket in California" appeared in Ginsberg's provocative
Howl and Other Poems *(1956), a volume that made Ginsberg*
famous at least partly because its publisher was tried for obscenity
and acquitted. That book put him in the company of Jack Kerouac
and the other Beat writers centered in San Francisco. In the 1960s
he became a well-known figure among hippies and one of the voices
of the counterculture generation: Ginsberg coined the term flower
power. *As this poem makes clear, Ginsberg consciously echoes Walt*
Whitman and assumed for himself the long beard and sandals of
the prophet. Here he questions whether the consumer society of
modern America is the same country Whitman celebrated a hun-
dred years earlier.

A Supermarket in California

What thoughts I have of you tonight, Walt Whitman, for I
walked down the sidestreets under the trees with a headache
self-conscious looking at the full moon.

In my hungry fatigue, and shopping for images, I went
into the neon fruit supermarket, dreaming of your
enumerations!

What peaches and what penumbras! Whole families
shopping at night! Aisles full of husbands! Wives in the
avocados, babies in the tomatoes!—and you, García Lorca,[1]
what were you doing down by the watermelons?

I saw you, Walt Whitman, childless, lonely old grubber,
poking among the meats in the refrigerator and eyeing the
grocery boys.

I heard you asking questions of each: Who killed the pork
chops? What price bananas? Are you my Angel?   5

---

1. Federico García Lorca (1898–1936), avant-garde Spanish poet and playwright who was
killed by a fascist militia in the early days of the Spanish Civil War. His works were banned
in Spain until 1953.

I wandered in and out of the brilliant stacks of cans
following you, and followed in my imagination by the store
detective.
We strode down the open corridors together in our solitary
fancy tasting artichokes, possessing every frozen delicacy, and
never passing the cashier.

Where are we going, Walt Whitman? The doors close in an
hour. Which way does your beard point tonight?
(I touch your book and dream of our odyssey in the
supermarket and feel absurd.)
Will we walk all night through solitary streets? The trees add
shade to shade, lights out in the houses, we'll both be lonely.   10
Will we stroll dreaming of the lost America of love past blue
automobiles in driveways, home to our silent cottage?
Ah, dear father, graybeard, lonely old courage-teacher, what
America did you have when Charon² quit poling his ferry and
you got out on a smoking bank and stood watching the boat
disappear on the black waters of Lethe?

1956

Thomas Gray
1716–1771

*"Elegy Written in a Country Churchyard," Gray's best-known
poem, was written to mourn the death of his close friend Richard
West, who died of tuberculosis in 1742. Though "Elegy" represents
one of Gray's earliest efforts at writing poetry, it was revised for five
years before publication. When the public finally read the poem,
Gray became an immediate celebrity. This elegy is unusual in that
it considers not the death of an individual or human mortality in
general but the deaths of a particular group of people: commoners.*

---

2. One of the rivers of Hades, whose waters made drinkers forget their lives. In Greek
mythology, Charon ferried dead souls across the river Acheron (or Styx) to their final destina-
tion, Hades.

Elegy Written in a Country Churchyard

The curfew tolls the knell of parting day,
    The lowing herd wind slowly o'er the lea,
The plowman homeward plods his weary way,
    And leaves the world to darkness and to me.

Now fades the glimmering landscape on the sight,   5
    And all the air a solemn stillness holds,
Save where the beetle wheels his droning flight,
    And drowsy tinklings lull the distant folds;

Save that from yonder ivy-mantled tower
    The moping owl does to the moon complain   10
Of such, as wandering near her secret bower,
    Molest her ancient solitary reign.

Beneath those rugged elms, that yew tree's shade,
    Where heaves the turf in many a moldering heap,
Each in his narrow cell forever laid,   15
    The rude forefathers of the hamlet sleep.

The breezy call of incense-breathing morn,
    The swallow twittering from the straw-built shed,
The cock's shrill clarion, or the echoing horn,
    No more shall rouse them from their lowly bed.   20

For them no more the blazing hearth shall burn,
    Or busy housewife ply her evening care;
No children run to lisp their sire's return,
    Or climb his knees the envied kiss to share.

Oft did the harvest to their sickle yield,   25
    Their furrow oft the stubborn glebe has broke;
How jocund did they drive their team afield!
    How bowed the woods beneath their sturdy stroke!

Let not Ambition mock their useful toil,
    Their homely joys, and destiny obscure;   30
Nor Grandeur hear with a disdainful smile
    The short and simple annals of the poor.

The boast of heraldry, the pomp of power,
    And all that beauty, all that wealth e'er gave,
Awaits alike the inevitable hour.   35
    The paths of glory lead but to the grave.

Nor you, ye proud, impute to these the fault,
    If Memory o'er their tomb no trophies raise,
Where through the long-drawn aisle and fretted vault
    The pealing anthem swells the note of praise.   40

Can storied urn or animated bust
    Back to its mansion call the fleeting breath?
Can Honor's voice provoke the silent dust,
    Or Flattery soothe the dull cold ear of Death?

Perhaps in this neglected spot is laid   45
    Some heart once pregnant with celestial fire;
Hands that the rod of empire might have swayed,
    Or waked to ecstasy the living lyre.

But Knowledge to their eyes her ample page
    Rich with the spoils of time did ne'er unroll;   50
Chill Penury repressed their noble rage,
    And froze the genial current of the soul.

Full many a gem of purest ray serene,
    The dark unfathomed caves of ocean bear:
Full many a flower is born to blush unseen,   55
    And waste its sweetness on the desert air.

Some village Hampden¹ that with dauntless breast
    The little tyrant of his fields withstood;

---

1. Leader of the opposition to Charles I in the controversy over ship money; he was killed in battle in the civil wars.

Some mute inglorious Milton[2] here may rest,
Some Cromwell[3] guiltless of his country's blood.   60

The applause of listening senates to command,
    The threats of pain and ruin to despise,
To scatter plenty o'er a smiling land,
    And read their history in a nation's eyes,

Their lot forbade; nor circumscribed alone   65
    Their growing virtues, but their crimes confined;
Forbade to wade through slaughter to a throne,
    And shut the gates of mercy on mankind,

The struggling pangs of conscious truth to hide,
    To quench the blushes of ingenuous shame,   70
Or heap the shrine of Luxury and Pride
    With incense kindled at the Muse's flame.

Far from the madding crowd's ignoble strife,
    Their sober wishes never learned to stray;
Along the cool sequestered vale of life   75
    They kept the noiseless tenor of their way.

Yet even these bones from insult to protect
    Some frail memorial still erected nigh,
With uncouth rhymes and shapeless sculpture decked,
    Implores the passing tribute of a sigh.   80

Their name, their years, spelt by the unlettered Muse,
    The place of fame and elegy supply:
And many a holy text around she strews,
    That teach the rustic moralist to die.

2. John Milton (1608–1674), English poet, author of *Paradise Lost*, and secretary of foreign tongues during the regime of Oliver Cromwell.

3. Oliver Cromwell (1599–1658), leader of Parliament's army in the brutal English Civil War; later he was lord protector, or dictator, of England.

For who to dumb Forgetfulness a prey,   85
    This pleasing anxious being e'er resigned,
Left the warm precincts of the cheerful day,
    Nor cast one longing lingering look behind?

On some fond breast the parting soul relies,
    Some pious drops the closing eye requires;   90
Even from the tomb the voice of Nature cries,
    Even in our ashes live their wonted fires.

For thee, who mindful of the unhonored dead
    Dost in these lines their artless tale relate;
If chance, by lonely contemplation led,   95
    Some kindred spirit shall inquire thy fate,

Haply some hoary-headed swain may say,
    "Oft have we seen him at the peep of dawn
Brushing with hasty steps the dews away
    To meet the sun upon the upland lawn.   100

"There at the foot of yonder nodding beech
    That wreathes its old fantastic roots so high,
His listless length at noontide would he stretch,
    And pore upon the brook that babbles by.

"Hard by yon wood, now smiling as in scorn,   105
    Muttering his wayward fancies he would rove,
Now drooping, woeful wan, like one forlorn,
    Or crazed with care, or crossed in hopeless love.

"One morn I missed him on the customed hill,
    Along the heath and near his favorite tree;   110
Another came; nor yet beside the rill,
    Nor up the lawn, nor at the wood was he;

"The next with dirges due in sad array
    Slow through the churchway path we saw him borne.
Approach and read (for thou canst read) the lay,   115
    Graved on the stone beneath yon aged thorn."

The Epitaph

Here rests his head upon the lap of Earth
A youth to Fortune and to Fame unknown.
Fair Science frowned not on his humble birth,
And Melancholy marked him for her own.　　　　　120

Large was his bounty, and his soul sincere,
Heaven did a recompense as largely send:
He gave to Misery all he had, a tear,
He gained from Heaven ('twas all he wished) a friend.

No farther seek his merits to disclose,　　　　　125
Or draw his frailties from their dread abode
(There they alike in trembling hope repose),
The bosom of his Father and his God.

1751

Thomas Hardy
1840–1928

 Hardy wrote "Hap" in 1866, just seven years after Darwin's On the Origin of Species, *though the poem was not published until 1898. Clearly, this Petrarchan sonnet is inspired by Darwin's theory that human beings are the result of random, natural forces rather than a divine plan. "Hap" is short for happenstance, or chance. "The Convergence of the Twain" and "Channel Firing" are both occasional poems, or poems triggered by historical events. The sinking of the* Titanic *in 1912 gave Western society reason to reflect on its place in the universe and relation to God. "Channel Firing" comments on the English navy's gunnery practice in April 1914, just four months before the war everyone expected, World War I, finally erupted.*

Hap

If but some vengeful god would call to me
From up the sky, and laugh: "Thou suffering thing,
Know that thy sorrow is my ecstasy,
That thy love's loss is my hate's profiting!"

Then would I bear it, clench myself, and die,   5
Steeled by the sense of ire unmerited;
Half-eased in that a Powerfuller than I
Had willed and meted me the tears I shed.

But not so. How arrives it joy lies slain,
And why unblooms the best hope ever sown?   10
—Crass Casualty obstructs the sun and rain,
And dicing Time for gladness casts a moan. . . .
These purblind Doomsters had as readily strown
Blisses about my pilgrimage as pain.

1898

The Convergence of the Twain

Lines on the Loss of the Titanic[1]

I

In a solitude of the sea
Deep from human vanity,
And the Pride of Life that planned her, stilly couches she.

II

Steel chambers, late the pyres
Of her salamandrine fires,[2]   5
Cold currents thrid,[3] and turn to rhythmic tidal lyres.

---

1. On April 15, 1912, the R.M.S. *Titanic* sank on its maiden voyage from Southampton to New York. The ship was thought to be unsinkable because it was constructed with many water-tight sections. It struck an iceberg, which tore a long gash in its side, and quickly sank.

2. According to legend, salamanders can live in fire. The boilers of the *Titanic* were similarly remarkable for burning though they were under water, so to speak.

3. I.e., thread.

III

Over the mirrors meant
To glass the opulent
The sea-worm crawls—grotesque, slimed, dumb, indifferent.

IV

Jewels in joy designed   10
To ravish the sensuous mind
Lie lightless, all their sparkles bleared and black and blind.

V

Dim moon-eyed fishes near
Gaze at the gilded gear
And query: "What does this vaingloriousness down here?"   15

VI

Well: while was fashioning
This creature of cleaving wing,
The Immanent Will that stirs and urges everything

VII

Prepared a sinister mate
For her—so gaily great—   20
A Shape of Ice, for the time far and dissociate.

VIII

And as the smart ship grew
In stature, grace, and hue,
In shadowy silent distance grew the Iceberg too.

IX

Alien they seemed to be: 25
No mortal eye could see
The intimate welding of their later history.

X

Or sign that they were bent
By paths coincident
On being anon twin halves of one august event,   30

XI

'Till the Spinner of the Years
Said "Now!" And each one hears,
And consummation comes, and jars two hemispheres.
                                                           1912

Channel Firing

That night your great guns, unawares,
Shook all our coffins as we lay,
And broke the chancel window-squares,
We thought it was the Judgment-day.

And sat upright. While drearisome   5
Arose the howl of wakened hounds:
The mouse let fall the altar-crumb,
The worms drew back into the mounds,

The glebe cow drooled. Till God called, "No;
It's gunnery practice out at sea   10
Just as before you went below;
The world is as it used to be:

"All nations striving strong to make
Red war yet redder. Mad as hatters

They do no more for Christés sake   15
Than you who are helpless in such matters.

"That this is not the judgment-hour
For some of them's a blessed thing,
For if it were they'd have to scour
Hell's floor for so much threatening. . . .   20

"Ha, ha. It will be warmer when
I blow the trumpet (if indeed
I ever do; for you are men,
And rest eternal sorely need)."

So down we lay again. "I wonder,   25
Will the world ever saner be,"
Said one, "than when He sent us under
In our indifferent century!"

And many a skeleton shook his head.
"Instead of preaching forty year,"   30
My neighbour Parson Thirdly said,
"I wish I had stuck to pipes and beer."

Again the guns disturbed the hour,
Roaring their readiness to avenge,
As far inland as Stourton Tower,[1]   35
And Camelot, and starlit Stonehenge.[2]
                    1914

---

1. Sometimes called King Alfred's Tower, built in 1772, it stands 170 feet above the Wiltshire farmlands, more than twenty miles from the sea. It commemorates the Saxon victory over invading Danes in 878.

2. The stone-age ruin located near Stourton Tower. Camelot was the mythical capital of King Arthur, located somewhere in southern England.

Joy Harjo
b. 1951

"The Woman Hanging from the Thirteenth Floor Window" was published in Harjo's 1983 book She Had Some Horses. *Most buildings in the United States do not have a thirteenth floor. Considered unlucky, that number is skipped. Discussing this poem, Harjo has said that "Repetition has always been used, ceremonially." She intends that the litany of phrases will "make the poem lift off the page and enter into the listener much like a song or chant."*

The Woman Hanging from the Thirteenth Floor Window

She is the woman hanging from the 13th floor
window. Her hands are pressed white against the
concrete moulding of the tenement building. She
hangs from the 13th floor window in east Chicago,
with a swirl of birds over her head. They could   5
be a halo, or a storm of glass waiting to crush her.

She thinks she will be set free.

The woman hanging from the 13th floor window
on the east side of Chicago is not alone.
She is a woman of children, of the baby, Carlos,   10
and of Margaret, and of Jimmy who is the oldest,
She is her mother's daughter and her father's son.
She is several pieces between the two husbands
she has had. She is all the women of the apartment
building who stand watching her, watching themselves.   15

When she was young she ate wild rice on scraped down
plates in warm wood rooms. It was in the farther
north and she was the baby then. They rocked her.

She sees Lake Michigan lapping at the shores of
herself. It is a dizzy hole of water and the rich   20

live in tall glass houses at the edge of it. In some
places Lake Michigan speaks softly, here, it just sputters
and butts itself against the asphalt. She sees
other buildings just like hers. She sees other
women hanging from many-floored windows   25
counting their lives in the palms of their hands
and in the palms of their children's hands.

She is the woman hanging from the 13th floor window
on the Indian side of town. Her belly is soft from
her children's births, her worn levis swing down below   30
her waist, and then her feet, and then her heart.
She is dangling.

The woman hanging from the 13th floor hears voices.
They come to her in the night when the lights have gone
dim. Sometimes they are little cats mewing and scratching   35
at the door, sometimes they are her grandmother's voice,
and sometimes they are gigantic men of light whispering
to her to get up, to get up, to get up. That's when she wants
to have another child to hold onto in the night, to be able
to fall back into dreams.   40

And the woman hanging from the 13th floor window
hears other voices. Some of them scream out from below
for her to jump, they would push her over. Others cry softly
from the sidewalks, pull their children up like flowers and gather
them into their arms. They would help her, like themselves.   45

But she is the woman hanging from the 13th floor window,
and she knows she is hanging by her own fingers, her
own skin, her own thread of indecision.

She thinks of Carlos, of Margaret, of Jimmy.
She thinks of her father, and of her mother.   50
She thinks of all the women she has been, of all
the men. She thinks of the color of her skin, and
of Chicago streets, and of waterfalls and pines.

She thinks of moonlight nights, and of cool spring storms.
Her mind chatters like neon and northside bars.　　　　55
She thinks of the 4 a.m. lonelinesses that have folded
her up like death, discordant, without logical and
beautiful conclusion. Her teeth break off at the edges.
She would speak.

The woman hangs from the 13th floor window crying for　60
the lost beauty of her own life. She sees the
sun falling west over the grey plane of Chicago.
She thinks she remembers listening to her own life
break loose, as she falls from the 13th floor
window on the east side of Chicago, or as she　　　　65
climbs back up to claim herself again.

1983

Robert Hayden

1913–1980

> *Hayden's birth parents gave him up for adoption when he was two
> years old, and "Those Winter Sundays" recounts his youth growing
> up in the working-class Detroit home of his adoptive family. Much
> of Hayden's work deals with racial injustice in America, but, as he
> declared, he wanted to be a black poet "the way [W. B.] Yeats was
> an Irish poet." That is, he wanted his sensibility to be suffused with
> a racial awareness and his work to be political in a broad sense of
> that word, but he allows neither to narrow the scope of his work.
> No reader of the 1962 book in which Hayden published "Those
> Winter Sundays" could ignore the racial injustices that kept this
> family poor. But at the same time Hayden does not reserve "love's
> austere and lonely offices" for working-class black Americans.*

Those Winter Sundays

Sundays too my father got up early
and put his clothes on in the blueblack cold,
then with cracked hands that ached

from labor in the weekday weather made
banked fires blaze. No one ever thanked him.   5
I'd wake and hear the cold splintering, breaking.
When the rooms were warm, he'd call,
and slowly I would rise and dress,
fearing the chronic angers of that house,

Speaking indifferently to him,   10
who had driven out the cold
and polished my good shoes as well.
What did I know, what did I know
of love's austere and lonely offices?

                                              1962

Terrance Hayes
b. 1971

> *"The poet," Hayes explains, "should never be the person with the saber*
> *saying, 'Everybody let's go this way.'" Despite his claim, Hayes's work*
> *is both political and forward looking. An African American who*
> *grew up in postsegregation South Carolina, he attended mixed-race*
> *schools and, like the speaker in this poem, was a basketball player,*
> *making the All-American academic team when he was at Coker*
> *College. His first book of poems was published in 1999, so he is,*
> *basically, a twenty-first-century poet, working in what is sometimes*
> *called a "postracial" America. That term is unfortunate because race*
> *clearly still influences most Americans' identities, but often in differ-*
> *ent ways from how it did before the civil rights movement. Poems*
> *like "Talk" help contemporary audiences negotiate those differences.*
> *That's how poet Mary Carr, for instance, introduced Hayes's poem*
> *to a* Washington Post *audience in 2008, just after Barack Obama*
> *won the Democratic nomination for the presidency.*

Talk

like a nigger now, my white friend, M, said
after my M.L.K. and Ronald Reagan impersonations,
the two of us alone and shirtless in the locker room,

and if you're thinking my knuckles knocked
a few times against his jaw or my fingers knotted   5
at his throat, you're wrong because I pretended

I didn't hear him, and when he didn't ask it again,
we slipped into our middle school uniforms
since it was November, the beginning

of basketball season, and jogged out   10
onto the court to play together
in that vision all Americans wish for

their children, and the point is we slipped
into our uniform harmony, and spit out *Go Team!,*
our hands stacked on and beneath the hands   15

of our teammates and that was as close
as I have come to passing for one
of the members of The Dream, my white friend

thinking I was so far from that word
that he could say it to me, which I guess   20
he could since I didn't let him taste the salt

and iron in the blood, I didn't teach him
what it's like to squint through a black eye,
and if I had I wonder if he would have grown

up to be the kind of white man who believes   25
all blacks are thugs or if he would have learned
to bite his tongue or let his belly be filled

by shame, but more importantly, would I be
the kind of black man who believes silence
is worth more than talk or that it can be   30

a kind of grace, though I'm not sure
that's the kind of black man I've become,
and in any case, M, wherever you are,

I'd just like to say I heard it, but let it go
because I was afraid to lose our friendship   35
or afraid we'd lose the game—which we did anyway.

2006

Seamus Heaney

b. 1939–2013

*Heaney put "Digging" on the first page of his first book in 1966,
suggesting he meant it to inaugurate and justify his vocation. For
Ireland's Catholics, potatoes are rich symbols: they represent both
the sustenance of the earth and the terrible famines in the 1840s
under England's colonial rule. The Irish cut "turf" from peat bogs
to burn in their stoves and fireplaces like coal. Heaney discov-
ered in these peat bogs a rich symbol of the unwritten, almost
racial history of the Irish. In large part due to his so-called bog
poems, the public recognized Heaney as Ireland's most impor-
tant poet. Nevertheless, he was criticized for not commenting
on the "troubles" between Catholics and Protestants that flared
in 1969. Heaney responded with* North *in 1975, but it hardly
endorsed militant nationalism. In* North, *the bogs figure as the
racial memory bank of Celts: the bog woman in "Punishment"
is an ancient Celt unearthed in modern times. The archaeologi-
cal evidence suggests that she was ritually executed for adultery.
The women chained to the rails are contemporary Catholics who
were tarred, shaved, and stripped naked by soldiers in the Irish
Republican Army for the crime of dating British soldiers. In "The
Skunk" Heaney pays comical tribute to his wife, exploding the
conventions of love poetry. "A Call," written after Heaney won
the Nobel Prize in Literature, is a fine companion poem to his
inaugural "Digging."*

Digging

Between my finger and my thumb
The squat pen rests; snug as a gun.

Under my window, a clean rasping sound
When the spade sinks into gravelly ground:
My father, digging. I look down   5

Till his straining rump among the flowerbeds
Bends low, comes up twenty years away
Stooping in rhythm through potato drills[1]
Where he was digging.

The coarse boot nestled on the lug, the shaft   10
Against the inside knee was levered firmly.
He rooted out tall tops, buried the bright edge deep
To scatter new potatoes that we picked
Loving their cool hardness in our hands.

By god, the old man could handle a spade.   15
Just like his old man.

My grandfather cut more turf in a day
Than any other man on Toner's bog.
Once I carried him milk in a bottle
Corked sloppily with paper. He straightened up   20
To drink it, then fell to right away
Nicking and slicing neatly, heaving sods
Over his shoulder, going down and down
For the good turf. Digging.

The cold smell of potato mould, the squelch and slap   25
Of soggy peat, the curt cuts of an edge
Through living roots awaken in my head.
But I've no spade to follow men like them.

Between my finger and my thumb
The squat pen rests.   30
I'll dig with it.

                                        1966

1. Small furrows in which seeds are sown.

The Tollund Man[1]

I

Some day I will go to Aarhus[2]
To see his peat-brown head,
The mild pods of his eye-lids,
His pointed skin cap.

In the flat country nearby   5
Where they dug him out,
His last gruel of winter seeds
Caked in his stomach,

Naked except for
The cap, noose and girdle,   10
I will stand a long time.
Bridegroom to the goddess,

She tightened her torc[3] on him
And opened her fen,
Those dark juices working   15
Him to a saint's kept body,

Trove of the turfcutters'
Honeycombed workings.
Now his stained face
Reposes at Aarhus.   20

---

1. The mummified corpse of a Celt from the fourth century B.C.E. discovered in a Danish bog in 1950 by farmers digging peat for their stoves.

2. Or Arhus, a city in Denmark. Heaney visited a museum there, which had the Tollund man on display.

3. Collar or necklace. The Tollund man was found with a leather noose around his neck, indicating that he was probably executed.

II

I could risk blasphemy,
Consecrate the cauldron bog
Our holy ground and pray
Him to make germinate

The scattered, ambushed   25
Flesh of labourers,
Stockinged corpses
Laid out in the farmyards,

Tell-tale skin and teeth
Flecking the sleepers   30
Of four young brothers, trailed
For miles along the lines.

III

Something of his sad freedom
As he rode the tumbril
Should come to me, driving,   35
Saying the names

Tollund, Grauballe, Nebelgard,[4]
Watching the pointing hands
Of country people,
Not knowing their tongue.   40

Out there in Jutland[5]
In the old man-killing parishes
I will feel lost,
Unhappy and at home.
                     1972

---

4. Places where the mummified remains of ancient Celts have been found.

5. Region in Denmark where many Celtic artifacts have been unearthed from peat bogs.

Punishment

I can feel the tug
of the halter at the nape
of her neck, the wind
on her naked front.

It blows her nipples   5
to amber beads,
it shakes the frail rigging
of her ribs.

I can see her drowned
body in the bog,   10
the weighing stone,
the floating rods and boughs.

Under which at first
she was a barked sapling
that is dug up   15
oak-bone, brain-firkin:[1]

her shaved head
like a stubble of black corn,
her blindfold a soiled bandage,
her noose a ring   20

to store
the memories of love.
Little adulteress,
before they punished you

you were flaxen-haired,   25
undernourished, and your
tar-black face was beautiful.
My poor scapegoat,

1. A small wooden cask or vessel.

I almost love you
but would have cast, I know,   30
the stones of silence.
I am the artful voyeur

of your brain's exposed
and darkened combs,
your muscles' webbing   35
and all your numbered bones:

I who have stood dumb
when your betraying sisters,
cauled in tar,
wept by the railings,   40

who would connive
in civilized outrage
yet understand the exact
and tribal, intimate revenge.
      1975

The Skunk

Up, black, striped and damasked like the chasuble
At a funeral Mass, the skunk's tail
Paraded the skunk. Night after night
I expected her like a visitor.

The refrigerator whinnied into silence.   5
My desk light softened beyond the verandah.
Small oranges loomed in the orange tree.
I began to be tense as a voyeur.

After eleven years I was composing
Love-letters again, broaching the word 'wife'   10
Like a stored cask, as if its slender vowel
Had mutated into the night earth and air

Of California.[1] The beautiful, useless
Tang of eucalyptus spelt your absence.
The aftermath of a mouthful of wine   15
Was like inhaling you off a cold pillow.

And there she was, the intent and glamorous,
Ordinary, mysterious skunk,
Mythologized, demythologized,
Snuffing the boards five feet beyond me.   20

It all came back to me last night, stirred
By the sootfall of your things at bedtime,
Your head-down, tail-up hunt in a bottom drawer
For the black plunge-line nightdress.
                              1979

A Call

'Hold on,' she said, 'I'll just run out and get him.
The weather here's so good, he took the chance
To do a bit of weeding.'
                    So I saw him
Down on his hands and knees beside the leek rig,   5
Touching, inspecting, separating one
Stalk from the other, gently pulling up
Everything not tapered, frail and leafless,
Pleased to feel each little weed-root break,
But rueful also . . .   10

               Then found myself listening to
The amplified grave ticking of hall clocks
Where the phone lay unattended in a calm
Of mirror glass and sunstruck pendulums . . .

---

1. Heaney often traveled to California to teach at the University of California, Berkeley.

And found myself then thinking: if it were nowadays,   15
This is how Death would summon Everyman.

Next thing he spoke and I nearly said I loved him.

1996

Felicia Dorothea Hemans
1793–1835

> *"Casabianca," first published in 1826, commemorates an event during a sea battle between England and France in 1798. Giocante, the young son of the French admiral Louis de Casabianca, died during the Battle of the Nile, when the powder magazine of the ship* L'Orient *exploded. The poem quickly became one of the most popular in England and America, and for over a hundred years young students were required to study its edifying lesson. For a hundred years young students rebelled by composing their own ridiculous parodies.*

Casabianca

The boy stood on the burning deck
  Whence all but he had fled;
The flame that lit the battle's wreck,
  Shone round him o'er the dead.

Yet beautiful and bright he stood,   5
  As born to rule the storm;
A creature of heroic blood,
  A proud, though child-like form.

The flames rolled on—he would not go,
  Without his Father's word;   10
That Father, faint in death below,
  His voice no longer heard.

He called aloud:—"Say, Father, say
  If yet my task is done?"
He knew not that the chieftain lay   15
  Unconscious of his son.

"Speak, Father!" once again he cried,
  "If I may yet be gone!
And"—but the booming shots replied,
  And fast the flames rolled on.   20

Upon his brow he felt their breath,
  And in his waving hair,
And looked from that lone post of death,
  In still, yet brave despair;

And shouted but once more aloud,   25
  "My Father! must I stay?"
While o'er him fast, through sail and shroud,
  The wreathing fires made way.

They wrapt the ship in splendour wild,
  They caught the flag on high,   30
And streamed above the gallant child,
  Like banners in the sky.

There came a burst of thunder-sound—
  The boy—oh! where was he?
Ask of the winds that far around   35
  With fragments strewed the sea!—

With mast, and helm, and pennon fair,
  That well had borne their part—
But the noblest thing which perished there
  Was that young faithful heart!   40

1826

George Herbert
1593–1633

Herbert was one of the "metaphysical" poets led by John Donne. Herbert's poems exhibit highly polished conceits and the careful attention to the poetic form typical of that school. On his deathbed, Herbert expressed the hope that his poetry might improve the life of "any dejected poor soul." "The Collar" displays a psychological depth and subtlety we expect from the metaphysicals.

The Collar

I struck the board[1] and cried, "No more;
    I will abroad!
  What? shall I ever sigh and pine?
My lines and life are free, free as the road,
  Loose as the wind, as large as store.[2]   5
      Shall I be still in suit?[3]
Have I no harvest but a thorn
To let me blood, and not restore
What I have lost with cordial[4] fruit?
      Sure there was wine   10
  Before my sighs did dry it; there was corn
    Before my tears did drown it.
  Is the year only lost to me?
    Have I no bays[5] to crown it,
No flowers, no garlands gay? All blasted?   15
    All wasted?
  Not so, my heart; but there is fruit,
    And thou hast hands.
  Recover all thy sigh-blown age
On double pleasures: leave thy cold dispute   20
Of what is fit, and not. Forsake thy cage,
      Thy rope of sands,

---

1. Table.
2. A storehouse.
3. In service to another.

4. Reviving, restorative.
5. Laurel wreaths of triumph.

Which petty thoughts have made, and made to thee
   Good cable, to enforce and draw,
      And be thy law,   25
While thou didst wink and wouldst not see.
      Away! take heed;
      I will abroad.
Call in thy death's-head[6] there; tie up thy fears.
      He that forbears   30
   To suit and serve his need,
      Deserves his load."
But as I raved and grew more fierce and wild
      At every word,
Methought I heard one calling, *Child!*   35
      And I replied, *My Lord.*

                          1633

Robert Herrick
1591–1674

   Herrick carried on a slow life as a country minister until the Puritans took over England in the 1640s. Then he was deprived of his parish and forced to return to London, where he prepared his verse for publication. More than fourteen hundred poems—including the three here—came out at once in 1648. Public opinion during the Puritan regime was not likely to praise his poems "of youth, of love, and . . . of cleanly wantonness," as Herrick described his own work. Actually, no one noticed his poems, not even to condemn their salaciousness. He was ignored until the nineteenth century. "To the Virgins to Make Much of Time" is a seduction poem using the conventional carpe diem *strategy, just as "Upon Julia's Clothes" is a typical poem in praise of the speaker's beloved. But "Delight in Disorder" suggests that underlying these conventions is a distinct philosophy of life. In the mind of a seventeenth-century reader, the word* precise *in the last line would have called up images of Puritans and their ethic.*

---

6. *Memento mori,* a skull intended to remind people of their mortality.

Delight in Disorder

A sweet disorder in the dress
Kindles in clothes a wantonness.
A lawn[1] about the shoulders thrown
Into a fine distractiòn;
An erring lace, which here and there   5
Enthralls the crimson stomacher;[2]
A cuff neglectful, and thereby
Ribbons to flow confusedly;
A winning wave, deserving note,
In the tempestuous petticoat;   10
A careless shoestring, in whose tie
I see a wild civility;
Do more bewitch me than when art
Is too precise in every part.

                              1648

To the Virgins, to Make Much of Time

Gather ye rosebuds while ye may,
    Old time is still a-flying;
And this same flower that smiles today
    Tomorrow will be dying.

The glorious lamp of heaven, the sun,   5
    The higher he's a-getting,
The sooner will his race be run,
    And nearer he's to setting.

That age is best which is the first,
    When youth and blood are warmer;   10

---

1. A piece of fine linen.
2. A fancy garment, often studded with jewels, worn over a woman's chest and usually under a lace bodice.

But being spent, the worse, and worst
  Times still succeed the former.

Then be not coy, but use your time,
  And, while ye may, go marry;
For, having lost but once your prime,   15
  You may forever tarry.
        1648

Upon Julia's Clothes

Whenas in silks my Julia goes,
Then, then, methinks, how sweetly flows
That liquefaction of her clothes.

Next, when I cast mine eyes, and see
That brave vibration, each way free,   5
O, how that glittering taketh me!
        1648

Tony Hoagland
b. 1953

> *Hoagland is conscious of his place—of the place of many poets of his generation—in the development of American literature. They are halfway between the confessional, personal poetry of the previous generation, which, when it devolves into convention, is "inadvertently sentimental and narcissistic," and the "poetry of lyric-associative fragment, "favored by poets who came of age in the 1990s and 2000s, for whom "organized narration [is] considered inadequate to our contemporary experience." Influenced by writers like John Ashbury, today's young poets, according to Hoagland, string together "motley data—i. e. experience—[that] doesn't add up to a story." Perhaps the closest (though not perfect) example in this volume of this kind of "elliptical" poet is Emily Rosko. In contrast, Hoagland sets out to write a more coherent, verse featuring*

narrative—with traditional, accessible, often strongly emotional stories—such as in "History of Desire."

History of Desire

When you're seventeen, and drunk
on the husky, late-night flavor
of your first girlfriend's voice
along the wires of the telephone

what else to do but steal   5
your father's El Dorado from the drive,
and cruise out to the park on Driscoll Hill?
Then climb the county water tower

and aerosol her name in spraycan orange
a hundred feet above the town?   10
Because only the letters of that word,
DORIS, next door to yours,

in yard-high, iridescent script,
are amplified enough to tell the world
who's playing lead guitar   15
in the rock band of your blood.

You don't consider for a moment
the shock in store for you in 10 A.D.,
a decade after Doris, when,
out for a drive on your visit home,   20

you take the Smallville Road, look up
and see *RON LOVES DORIS*
still scorched upon the reservoir.
This is how history catches up—

by holding still until you   25
bump into yourself.

What makes you blush, and shove
the pedal of the Mustang

almost through the floor
as if you wanted to spray gravel   30
across the features of the past,
or accelerate into oblivion?

Are you so out of love that you
can't move fast enough away?
But if desire is acceleration,   35
experience is circular as any

Indianapolis. We keep coming back
to what we are—each time older,
more freaked out, or less afraid.
And you are older now.   40

You should stop today.
In the name of Doris, stop.

                              1992

Gerard Manley Hopkins
1844–1889

*At twenty-two years old, against his parents' will, Hopkins con-
verted to Catholicism, and a few years later he joined the Jesuit
order and burned all his poems. With his rector's blessing he com-
posed ten sonnets on nature in 1877, including "God's Grandeur"
and "The Windhover," each remarkable for its striking rhythms.
Hopkins called it "sprung rhythm," which he developed from
ancient Welsh verse that combines in each line any number of
lightly stressed syllables with a set number of stressed syllables. Yet
more striking are Hopkins's conceits, which were like nothing any-
one else was writing in Victorian England. In fact, the poems
were not published until 1918, when they found proper compan-
ions with modern poems, like Eliot's and Pound's. Margaret in*

"Spring and Fall" is not based on a real girl; Hopkins invented her when he wrote the poem on September 7, 1880. "God's Grandeur," "The Windhover," and "Spring and Fall" all come to us from letters Hopkins sent to Robert Bridges, a fellow poet, who saved them for posterity. Hopkins called "Pied Beauty" a "curtal sonnet," which he defined as having proportions "resembling those of the sonnet proper, namely 6 + 4 instead of 8 + 6, with however a halfline tailpiece."

God's Grandeur

The world is charged with the grandeur of God.
   It will flame out, like shining from shook foil;[1]
   It gathers to a greatness, like the ooze of oil
Crushed. Why do men then now not reck[2] his rod?
Generations have trod, have trod, have trod;   5
   And all is seared with trade; bleared, smeared with toil;
   And wears man's smudge and shares man's smell: the soil
Is bare now, nor can foot feel, being shod.

And for all this, nature is never spent;
   There lives the dearest freshness deep down things;   10
And though the last lights off the black West went
   Oh, morning, at the brown brink eastward, springs—
Because the Holy Ghost over the bent
   World broods with warm breast and with ah! bright wings.
1877   *1918*

---

1. In a letter to Robert Bridges (January 4, 1883), Hopkins says: "I mean foil in its sense of leaf or tinsel, and no other word whatever will give the effect I want. Shaken goldfoil gives off broad glares like sheet lightning and also, and this is true of nothing else, owing to its zigzag dints and crossings and network of small many cornered facets, a sort of fork lightning too."

2. Reckon; the sense here is, "Why do men not heed the threat of his punishment?"

The Windhover[1]

To Christ Our Lord

I caught this morning morning's minion, kingdom
  of daylight's dauphin, dapple-dawn-drawn Falcon, in his
    riding
Of the rolling level underneath him steady air, and striding
High there, how he rung upon the rein of a wimpling wing
In his ecstasy! then off, off forth on swing,   5
  As a skate's heel sweeps smooth on a bow-bend: the hurl
    and gliding
Rebuffed the big wind. My heart in hiding
Stirred for a bird,—the achieve of, the mastery of the thing!

Brute beauty and valour and act, oh, air, pride, plume, here
  Buckle![2] AND the fire that breaks from thee then, a billion   10
Times told lovelier, more dangerous, O my chevalier!

No wonder of it; shéer plód makes plough down sillion[3]
Shine, and blue-bleak embers, ah my dear,
  Fall, gall themselves, and gash gold-vermilion.
1877   *1918*

Pied Beauty

Glory be to God for dappled things—
  For skies of couple-colour as a brinded cow;
    For rose-moles all in stipple upon trout that swim;

---

1. "A name for the kestrel [a species of small hawk], from its habit of hovering or hanging with its head to the wind" (*O.E.D.*).

2. Can be understood two ways: either the elements in line 9 are fastened together as if by a buckle, or they crumble as a support might buckle. The verb also can be read as an indicative or an imperative, as if the speaker were either describing an action or commanding it.

3. The plowed furrow in a field; with certain soils, a freshly plowed field will gleam with reflected sunlight.

Fresh-firecoal chestnut-falls; finches' wings;
    Landscape plotted and pieced—fold, fallow, and plough;   5
    And áll trádes, their gear and tackle and trim.

All things counter, original, spare, strange;
    Whatever is fickle, freckled (who knows how?)
        With swift, slow; sweet, sour; adazzle, dim;
He fathers-forth whose beauty is past change: 10
                  Praise him.
1877   *1918*

Spring and Fall

    To a Young Child

Márgarét, áre you gríeving
Over Goldengrove unleaving?
Leáves, líke the things of man, you
With your fresh thoughts care for, can you?
Áh! ás the heart grows older   5
It will come to such sights colder
By and by, nor spare a sigh
Though worlds of wanwood leafmeal[1] lie;
And yet you *will* weep and know why.
Now no matter, child, the name: 10
Sórrow's spríngs áre the same.
Nor mouth had, no nor mind, expressed
What heart heard of, ghost guessed:
It ís the blight man was born for,
It is Margaret you mourn for.   15
1880   *1918*

---

1. Partially decayed fallen leaves.

A. E. (Alfred Edward) Housman
1859–1936

> Housman was tormented for years by his love for his college room-
> mate and close friend, Moses Jackson. When Jackson went to India
> to make his fortune and marry, Housman transferred his affections
> to Jackson's brother, who died unexpectedly. This event might have
> triggered Housman's burst of creative energy in the mid-1890s,
> which produced all of these poems. The speaker in these poems is
> Terence Hearsay, a youth from Shropshire, a county that figures in
> the English imagination the way the states Iowa or Nebraska might
> in the American. "1887" commemorates the fiftieth anniversary
> of Queen Victoria's reign, and its apparent endorsement of empire
> made Housman's book popular when England went to war against
> the Boers in South Africa. English soldiers dead in the foreign fields
> had these poems buttoned in their pockets. Housman was an atheist,
> which calls into question the advice Terence gives in "To an Athlete
> Dying Young" and "Shot? So quick, so clean an ending?" (Housman
> wrote these about the same time that Oscar Wilde was convicted
> of homosexuality in a sensational trial and sentenced to two years
> of hard labor, which makes Terence's approval of the suicide more
> understandable.) These celebrations of the dead should be read in
> the context of "Terence, this is stupid stuff . . . ," which suggests that
> the speaker might not be entirely sincere. The speaker in "A Shropshire
> Lad II: Loveliest of trees" might be closer to the poet's own voice.

1887

From Clee[1] to heaven the beacon burns,
  The shires have seen it plain,
From north and south the sign returns
  And beacons burn again.

Look left, look right, the hills are bright,   5
  The dales are light between,

---

1. The Clee Hills are a long ridge in Shropshire, England, that give a commanding view
of the surrounding country.

Because 'tis fifty years to-night
   That God has saved the Queen.

Now, when the flame they watch not towers
   About the soil they trod,   10
Lads, we'll remember friends of ours
   Who shared the work with God.

To skies that knit their heartstrings right,
   To fields that bred them brave,
The saviours come not home to-night: 15
   Themselves they could not save.

It dawns in Asia, tombstones show
   And Shropshire names are read;
And the Nile spills his overflow
   Beside the Severn's[2] dead.   20

We pledge in peace by farm and town
   The Queen they served in war,
And fire the beacons up and down
   The land they perished for.

"God save the Queen" we living sing,   25
   From height to height 'tis heard;
And with the rest your voices ring,
   Lads of the Fifty-third.[3]

Oh, God will save her, fear you not:
   Be you the men you've been,   30
Get you the sons your fathers got,
   And God will save the Queen.

                     1896

---

2. The river that divides England from Wales.

3. A British army unit of soldiers from Shropshire.

To an Athlete Dying Young

The time you won your town the race
We chaired you through the market-place;
Man and boy stood cheering by,
And home we brought you shoulder-high.

Today, the road all runners come,   5
Shoulder-high we bring you home,
And set you at your threshold down,
Townsman of a stiller town.

Smart lad, to slip betimes away
From fields where glory does not stay   10
And early though the laurel grows
It withers quicker than the rose.

Eyes the shady night has shut
Cannot see the record cut,
And silence sounds no worse than cheers   15
After earth has stopped the ears:

Now you will not swell the rout
Of lads that wore their honours out,
Runners whom renown outran
And the name died before the man.   20

So set, before its echoes fade,
The fleet foot on the sill of shade,
And hold to the low lintel up
The still-defended challenge-cup.

And round that early-laurelled head   25
Will flock to gaze the strengthless dead,
And find unwithered on its curls
The garland briefer than a girl's.

1896

Shot? So quick, so clean an ending?

Shot? so quick, so clean an ending?
  Oh that was right, lad, that was brave:
Yours was not an ill for mending,
  'Twas best to take it to the grave.

Oh you had forethought, you could reason,   5
  And saw your road and where it led,
And early wise and brave in season
  Put the pistol to your head.

Oh soon, and better so than later
  After long disgrace and scorn,   10
You shot dead the household traitor,
  The soul that should not have been born.

Right you guessed the rising morrow
  And scorned to tread the mire you must:
Dust's your wages, son of sorrow,   15
  But men may come to worse than dust.

Souls undone, undoing others,—
  Long time since the tale began.
You would not live to wrong your brothers:
  Oh lad, you died as fits a man.   20

Now to your grave shall friend and stranger
  With ruth and some with envy come:
Undishonoured, clear of danger,
  Clean of guilt, pass hence and home.

Turn safe to rest, no dreams, no waking;   25
  And here, man, here's the wreath I've made.
'Tis not a gift that's worth the taking,
  But wear it and it will not fade.

                              1896

"Terence, this is Stupid Stuff . . ."

"Terence, this is stupid stuff:
You eat your victuals fast enough;
There can't be much amiss, 'tis clear,
To see the rate you drink your beer.
But oh, good Lord, the verse you make,   5
It gives a chap the belly-ache.
The cow, the old cow, she is dead;
It sleeps well, the hornéd head:
We poor lads, 'tis our turn now
To hear such tunes as killed the cow.   10
Pretty friendship 'tis to rhyme
Your friends to death before their time
Moping melancholy mad:
Come, pipe a tune to dance to, lad."

Why, if 'tis dancing you would be,   15
There's brisker pipes than poetry.
Say, for what were hop-yards[1] meant,
Or why was Burton built on Trent?[2]
Oh many a peer of England[3] brews
Livelier liquor than the Muse,   20
And malt does more than Milton can
To justify God's ways to man.
Ale, man, ale's the stuff to drink
For fellows whom it hurts to think:
Look into the pewter pot   25
To see the world as the world's not.
And faith, 'tis pleasant till 'tis past:
The mischief is that 'twill not last.
Oh I have been to Ludlow fair[4]

---

1. Fields growing hops, an ingredient in beer.

2. An English town associated with breweries, similar to Milwaukee in American culture.

3. A member of the House of Lords; the sense here is that many of England's noblemen made their money by manufacturing liquor.

4. A popular festival in the town of Ludlow, Shropshire.

And left my necktie God knows where,   30
And carried halfway home, or near,
Pints and quarts of Ludlow beer:
Then the world seemed none so bad,
And I myself a sterling lad;
And down in lovely muck I've lain,   35
Happy till I woke again.
Then I saw the morning sky:
Heigho, the tale was all a lie;
The world, it was the old world yet,
I was I, my things were wet,   40
And nothing now remained to do
But begin the game anew.

   Therefore, since the world has still
Much good, but much less good than ill,
And while the sun and moon endure   45
Luck's a chance, but trouble's sure,
I'd face it as a wise man would,
And train for ill and not for good.
'Tis true, the stuff I bring for sale
Is not so brisk a brew as ale: 50
Out of a stem that scored the hand
I wrung it in a weary land.
But take it: if the smack is sour,
The better for the embittered hour;
It should do good to heart and head   55
When your soul is in my soul's stead;
And I will friend you, if I may,
In the dark and cloudy day.

   There was a king reigned in the East:
There, when kings will sit to feast,   60
They get their fill before they think
With poisoned meat and poisoned drink.
He gathered all that springs to birth
From the many-venomed earth;
First a little, thence to more,   65

He sampled all her killing store;
And easy, smiling, seasoned sound,
Sate the king when healths went round.
They put arsenic in his meat
And stared aghast to watch him eat;   70
They poured strychnine in his cup
And shook to see him drink it up:
They shook, they stared as white's their shirt:
Them it was their poison hurt.
—I tell the tale that I heard told.   75
Mithridates, he died old.[5]

                                        1896

A Shropshire Lad II: Loveliest of trees, the cherry now

Loveliest of trees, the cherry now
Is hung with bloom along the bough,
And stands about the woodland ride
Wearing white for Eastertide.[1]

Now, of my threescore years and ten,   5
Twenty will not come again,
And take from seventy springs a score,
It only leaves me fifty more.

And since to look at things in bloom
Fifty springs are little room,   10
About the woodlands I will go
To see the cherry hung with snow.

                                        1896

---

5. In the first century B.C.E., King Mithridates VI took small doses of poison until he developed an immunity to it.

1. The fifty-day peroid after Easter in the Christian calender.

Langston Hughes
1902–1967

> *Not long after he graduated from high school, Hughes published "The Negro Speaks of Rivers" in the political magazine* The Crisis. *The poem counters white views of blacks as a primitive race without history by linking African Americans to ancient black civilizations. Hughes went to Columbia University, where he began meeting the leaders of the Harlem Renaissance, a movement among African American artists in literature, music, painting, dance, and the like. In 1926, at just twenty-four years old, Hughes published an essay in the widely circulated, leftist paper* The Nation, *which argued that African Americans should create a "racial art." That concept was controversial in the 1920s because many intellectuals, black and white, thought that subcultures should dissolve themselves in the American mainstream. "Dream Boogie," "Harlem," and "Theme for English B" came much later in Hughes's career, after he had established himself as one of America's most successful poets, but both illustrate what he called for in 1926. Hughes wanted these and the other poems in* Montage of a Dream Deferred *(1951) to express contemporary Harlem by borrowing from the "current of Afro-American popular music . . . jazz, ragtime, swing, blues, boogie-woogie, and be-bop."*

The Negro Speaks of Rivers

(*To W. E. B. Du Bois*)[1]

I've known rivers:
I've known rivers ancient as the world and older than the
    flow of human blood in human veins.
My soul has grown deep like the rivers.

I bathed in the Euphrates when dawns were young.
I built my hut near the Congo and it lulled me to sleep.   5

---

1. American historian, educator, and activist (1868–1963); and one of the founders of the NAACP.

I looked upon the Nile and raised the pyramids above it.
I heard the singing of the Mississippi when Abe Lincoln
    went down to New Orleans, and I've seen its muddy
    bosom turn all golden in the sunset.

I've known rivers:
Ancient, dusky rivers.

My soul has grown deep like the rivers.   10

1926

Dream Boogie

Good morning, daddy!
Ain't you heard
The boogie-woogie rumble
Of a dream deferred?

Listen closely: 5
You'll hear their feet
Beating out and beating out a—

    You think
    It's a happy beat?

Listen to it closely:
Ain't you heard   10
something underneath
like a—

    What did I say?

Sure,
I'm happy!   15
Take it away!

Hey, pop!
Re-bop!
Mop!   20

Y-e-a-h!
                              1951

Harlem

What happens to a dream deferred?

Does it dry up
like a raisin in the sun?
Or fester like a sore—
And then run?
Does it stink like rotten meat?   5
Or crust and sugar over—
like a syrupy sweet?

Maybe it just sags
like a heavy load.   10

Or does it explode?
                              1951

Theme for English B

The instructor said,

　　　Go home and write
　　　a page tonight.
　　　And let that page come out of you—
　　　Then, it will be true.   5

I wonder if it's that simple?
I am twenty-two, colored, born in Winston-Salem.
I went to school there, then Durham, then here

to this college on the hill above Harlem
I am the only colored student in my class.   10
The steps from the hill lead down into Harlem,
through a park, then I cross St. Nicholas,
Eighth Avenue, Seventh, and I come to the Y,[1]
the Harlem Branch Y, where I take the elevator
up to my room, sit down, and write this page: 15

It's not easy to know what is true for you or me
at twenty-two, my age. But I guess I'm what
I feel and see and hear, Harlem, I hear you:
hear you, hear me—we two—you, me, talk on this page.
(I hear New York, too.) Me—who?   20
Well, I like to eat, sleep, drink, and be in love.
I like to work, read, learn, and understand life.
I like a pipe for a Christmas present,
or records—Bessie,[2] bop, or Bach.
I guess being colored doesn't make me *not* like   25
the same things other folks like who are other races.
So will my page be colored that I write?
Being me, it will not be white.
But it will be
a part of you, instructor.   30
You are white—
yet a part of me, as I am a part of you.
That's American.
Sometimes perhaps you don't want to be a part of me.
Nor do I often want to be a part of you.   35
But we are, that's true!
I guess you learn from me—
although you're older—and white—
and somewhat more free.

This is my page for English B.   40

1951

1. The YMCA (Young Men's Christian
Association), which, in addition to gym facili-
ties, would provide inexpensive rooms to rent.

2. Bessie Smith (1894?–1937), American
blues singer.

Gary Jackson

b. 1981

Poet Yusef Komunyakaa says that Jackson's voice is "uniquely shaped and tuned for the twenty-first century," a "world of sped-up motion" and "virtual reality." The speaker in "Luke Cage Tells It Like It Is" is Marvel Comic's first major black character. Wrongly imprisoned by a failed judicial system, Cage purchased his liberty by subjecting himself to experimentation that turned him from an ordinary man, Carl Lucas, into a shadowy parallel to the super-soldier superhero, Captain America. Invented in 1972 in the first years of a desegregated United States, Cage illustrated for white readers the parallel, unequal universe inhabited by black Americans, while also providing African American children with one of the first black protagonists in the comic genre—a hero to help shape their own identities. This poem strips away yet another layer of constructed reality: though eventually some blacks writers told Cage's stories, his identity and stories were first scripted by white men.

Luke Cage Tells It Like It Is

Don't believe everything you read
The exploits you find in my comic
are no more probable
than snow in Sunnyvale.
I'm not as black as you dream.   5

But a body has to make a living.
And I play the part
better than any. I know
the dangers of believing
every shade of black you see.   10

In this issue
there's a Mandingo of a man,
dark like olives,
voice as deep as a desert valley

in the dead of night. He smiles   15
as if he wants to bite your throat,
holds back his teeth
with those bubblegum lips
he can't help but lick, leaving
the thinnest film of saliva   20
on the surface.
He's slick
and he's bold
and he's everything you imagine he should be.

Sometimes, you want to be him,   25
want to see yourself in the silver gleam of his image
and other times you want to be wanted by him.

Crave his brand of desire,
his form of righteousness,
bringing a little black to the world   30
one *motherfucker* at a time.

No matter how three-dimensional he seems,
know that behind every *jive turkey* uttered
there is not a black mouth, but a white one,
one that dictates who he calls *Nigger,*   35
to temper the perfect tone of black.

This is the cruelest trick.
Even now, I'm defined by the borders
of my panels, the hue of sienna ink,
an assembly of lines, a rendering of man   40
splayed across your page.

2010

James Weldon Johnson

1871–1938

> Johnson wrote "Lift Every Voice and Sing" as a tribute to Abraham Lincoln, and the African American children of the Jacksonville, Florida, school where he was principal recited it on Lincoln's birthday in 1900. It grew in popularity, leading to its adoption by the NAACP as its official song in 1920. (Johnson administered the NAACP from 1920 to 1930.) Over the generations it was sung as a hymn in churches, at public events and meetings, and so on, until it came to be known as "the black National Anthem." It was a standard among civil rights activists in the 1960s. Written in an era in which many of the rights blacks won after the Civil War had been eroded by white supremacists in southern states and even in the federal government, the poem was more of a protest than a victory song. The NAACP was founded in the midst of that political climate, when black Americans found themselves once again having to insist to a hostile society that the United States was their native land. The poem is still potent today: its last stanza was recited at President Barak Obama's inauguration in 2008.

Lift Every Voice and Sing

Lift every voice and sing
Till earth and heaven ring,
Ring with the harmonies of Liberty;
Let our rejoicing rise
High as the listening skies,   5
Let it resound loud as the rolling sea.
Sing a song full of the faith that the dark past has taught us,
Sing a song full of the hope that the present has brought us.
Facing the rising sun of our new day begun,
Let us march on till victory is won.   10

Stony the road we trod,
Bitter the chastening rod,
Felt in the days when hope unborn had died;
Yet with a steady beat,

Have not our weary feet   15
Come to the place for which our fathers sighed?
We have come over a way that with tears has been watered,
We have come, treading our path through the blood of the
    slaughtered,
Out from the gloomy past,
Till now we stand at last   20
Where the white gleam of our bright star is cast.

God of our weary years,
God of our silent tears,
Thou who hast brought us thus far on the way;
Thou who hast by Thy might   25
Led us into the light,
Keep us forever in the path, we pray.
Lest our feet stray from the places, our God, where we met
    Thee,
Lest, our hearts drunk with the wine of the world, we forget
    Thee;
Shadowed beneath Thy hand,   30
May we forever stand.
True to our God,
True to our native land.

1900

Ben Jonson
1572–1637

> *Jonson, a contemporary of Shakespeare, gathered around himself England's first "school" of literature, the Cavaliers, characterized by their classical learning and frank, playful treatment of sexual themes, a direct challenge to the Puritan ethic of seventeenth-century England. "Song: To Celia" is a translation stitched together from various parts of the* Epistles *of Philostratus, an ancient Greek philosopher. The key to the poem is how the speaker (and you) interpret the symbolic action in lines 9–16. "On My First Daughter" is an epitaph: a poem that might have been carved on a tombstone. We do not know if Jonson really had a daughter, but his son, Benjamin, died in 1603 on his seventh birthday.*

Song: To Celia

Drink to me only with thine eyes,
And I will pledge with mine;
Or leave a kiss but in the cup,
And I'll not look for wine.
The thirst that from the soul doth rise,   5
Doth ask a drink divine:
But might I of Jove's nectar sup,
I would not change for thine.
I sent thee late a rosy wreath,
Not so much honoring thee,   10
As giving it a hope, that there
It could not withered be.
But thou thereon did'st only breathe,
And sent'st it back to me;
Since when it grows and smells, I swear,   15
Not of itself, but thee.

                              1616

On My First Daughter

Here lies, to each her parents' ruth,
Mary, the daughter of their youth;
Yet all heaven's gifts being heaven's due,
It makes the father less to rue.
At six months' end she parted hence   5
With safety of her innocence;
Whose soul heaven's queen, whose name she bears,
In comfort of her mother's tears,
Hath placed amongst her virgin-train:
Where, while that severed doth remain,[1]   10
This grave partakes the fleshly birth;
Which cover lightly, gentle earth!

                              1616

---

1. The severing of the soul from the body is only temporary, according to orthodoxy. They will reunite at the end of time.

Julie Kane

b. 1952

Kane grew up in an Irish American family in Boston, New Jersey, and New York. "Happy times in my family," she says, "often meant standing around a piano and singing old Irish songs." "The Good Women" recounts a sad time, but Irish Catholic culture still fills the room. This poem comes from Kane's first book, Body and Soul *(1987), and it uses the confessional tone perfected by Kane's teacher at Boston University, Anne Sexton, who advised her to be "emotionally honest in your poems. . . . [Y]ou can't ever worry that you're acting undignified or that someone might not like the you that is in your poems." One way to interpret this poem is to determine why the "you" who is speaking does not count herself among the "good women" and instead accuses herself of being the "betrayer of my race." Another Irish Catholic poet, Seamus Heaney, explores how poets can be betrayers in his 1975 poem "Punishment." Similarly, he contemplates breaking long cultural and family traditions in "Digging." It might be helpful to compare the Irish American woman speaker in Kane's poem to the Irish male persona speaking in Heaney's confessional poems.*

The Good Women

Three out of four
are named Mary,
these good Irish women
who surface at wakes
like earthworms after rain.
Death makes them bake
turkeys, casseroles,
applesauce cakes.
They breathe the thick
incense of flowers
for strength, dispense
prayers like milk
from each massive breast.
Black becomes them.
Red-haired, broad-hipped

for easy babies,
I stand among them,
betrayer of my race:
I whose God bless you's
have no authority behind them
am awkward as the corpse
in this army of grace.

1987

John Keats
1795–1821

>One evening in October 1816, the twenty-one-year-old Keats
>stayed up late with his former teacher reading George Chapman's
>translation of Homer. The vigor of the Elizabethan poetry aston-
>ished Keats. After walking home at dawn, Keats wrote "On First
>Looking into Chapman's Homer" in about an hour and sent it to
>his teacher, who found the Petrarchan sonnet waiting for him at
>breakfast. The foreboding of his own death expressed in "When I
>Have Fears," written in January 1818, intensified later that year,
>when Keats nursed his younger brother through the final stages of
>tuberculosis. Then came the great burst of writing that produced
>the other poems here. In them you can trace Keats's evolving atti-
>tude toward death: first "To Sleep," "Ode to a Nightingale," and
>"Ode on a Grecian Urn," written about the same time; then "To
>Autumn," written less than a year before his own death.

On First Looking into Chapman's Homer

Much have I traveled in the realms of gold,
   And many goodly states and kingdoms seen;
   Round many western islands have I been
Which bards in fealty to Apollo[1] hold.
Oft of one wide expanse had I been told
   That deep-browed Homer ruled as his demesne;[2]   5
   Yet did I never breathe its pure serene

---

1. God of poetic inspiration.   2. I.e., domain.

Till I heard Chapman speak out loud and bold:
Then felt I like some watcher of the skies
   When a new planet swims into his ken;   10
Or like stout Cortez[3] when with eagle eyes
   He stared at the Pacific—and all his men
Looked at each other with a wild surmise—
   Silent, upon a peak in Darien.[4]

                       1816

When I Have Fears

When I have fears that I may cease to be
   Before my pen has gleaned my teeming brain,
Before high-piléd books, in charact'ry,
   Hold like rich garners the full-ripened grain;
When I behold, upon the night's starred face,   5
   Huge cloudy symbols of a high romance,
And think that I may never live to trace
   Their shadows, with the magic hand of chance;
And when I feel, fair creature of an hour,
   That I shall never look upon thee more,   10
Never have relish in the faery power
   Of unreflecting love!—then on the shore
Of the wide world I stand alone, and think
Till Love and Fame to nothingness do sink.
1818   *1848*

To Sleep

O soft embalmer of the still midnight,
   Shutting with careful fingers and benign
Our gloom-pleas'd eyes, embower'd from the light,
   Enshaded in forgetfulness divine:

---

3. Keats is confusing Cortez with Balboa, who was the first European to see the Pacific Ocean.

4. A region in Panama.

O soothest[1] Sleep! if so it please thee, close,   5
    In midst of this thine hymn, my willing eyes,
Or wait the Amen ere thy poppy[2] throws
    Around my bed its lulling charities.
Then save me or the passed day will shine
    Upon my pillow, breeding many woes: 10
Save me from curious conscience, that still hoards
    Its strength for darkness, burrowing like the mole;
Turn the key deftly in the oiled wards,
    And seal the hushed casket of my soul.
1819   *1838*

Ode to a Nightingale

1

My heart aches, and a drowsy numbness pains
    My sense, as though of hemlock I had drunk,
Or emptied some dull opiate to the drains
    One minute past, and Lethe-wards[1] had sunk:
'Tis not through envy of thy happy lot,   5
    But being too happy in thine happiness—
        That thou, light-wingéd Dryad[2] of the trees,
            In some melodious plot
Of beechen green, and shadows numberless,
    Singest of summer in full-throated ease.   10

2

O, for a draught of vintage! that hath been
    Cooled a long age in the deep-delvéd earth,
Tasting of Flora and the country green,
    Dance, and Provençal song, and sunburnt mirth!
O for a beaker full of the warm South,   15

---

1. Softest.
2. Opium is made from the dried juice
of the opium poppy.

1. Toward the river Lethe, whose waters
in Hades bring the dead forgetfulness.
2. A tree spirit in Greek mythology.

Full of the true, the blushful Hippocrene,[3]
  With beaded bubbles winking at the brim,
    And purple-stainéd mouth;
That I might drink, and leave the world unseen,
  And with thee fade away into the forest dim: 20

3

Fade far away, dissolve, and quite forget
  What thou among the leaves hast never known,
The weariness, the fever, and the fret
  Here, where men sit and hear each other groan;
Where palsy shakes a few, sad, last gray hairs,   25
  Where youth grows pale, and specter-thin, and dies,
    Where but to think is to be full of sorrow
      And leaden-eyed despairs,
Where Beauty cannot keep her lustrous eyes,
  Or new Love pine at them beyond tomorrow.   30

4

Away! away! for I will fly to thee,
  Not charioted by Bacchus[4] and his pards,
But on the viewless wings of Poesy,
  Though the dull brain perplexes and retards:
Already with thee! tender is the night,   35
  And haply the Queen-Moon is on her throne,
    Clustered around by all her starry Fays;
      But here there is no light,
Save what from heaven is with the breezes blown
  Through verdurous glooms and winding mossy ways.   40

3. The fountain of the Muses (goddesses of poetry and the arts) on Mount Helicon in Greece; its waters inspire poets.

4. The god of wine was often depicted in a chariot drawn by leopards ("pards").

5

I cannot see what flowers are at my feet,
  Nor what soft incense hangs upon the boughs,
But, in embalméd darkness, guess each sweet
  Wherewith the seasonable month endows
The grass, the thicket, and the fruit tree wild;   45
  White hawthorn, and the pastoral eglantine;
Fast fading violets covered up in leaves;
  And mid-May's eldest child,
The coming musk-rose, full of dewy wine,
  The murmurous haunt of flies on summer eves.   50

6

Darkling I listen; and for many a time
  I have been half in love with easeful Death,
Called him soft names in many a muséd rhyme,
  To take into the air my quiet breath;
Now more than ever seems it rich to die,   55
  To cease upon the midnight with no pain,
    While thou art pouring forth thy soul abroad
      In such an ecstasy!
Still wouldst thou sing, and I have ears in vain—
  To thy high requiem become a sod.   60

7

Thou wast not born for death, immortal Bird!
  No hungry generations tread thee down;
The voice I hear this passing night was heard
  In ancient days by emperor and clown:
Perhaps the selfsame song that found a path   65
  Through the sad heart of Ruth,[5] when, sick for home,
    She stood in tears amid the alien corn;
      The same that ofttimes hath

---

5. In the Old Testament, a woman of great loyalty and modesty who, as a stranger in Judah, won a husband while gleaning in the barley fields ("the alien corn," line 67).

Charmed magic casements, opening on the foam
   Of perilous seas, in faery lands forlorn.   70

8

Forlorn! the very word is like a bell
   To toll me back from thee to my sole self!
Adieu! the fancy cannot cheat so well
   As she is famed to do, deceiving elf.
Adieu! adieu! thy plaintive anthem fades   75
   Past the near meadows, over the still stream,
      Up the hill side; and now 'tis buried deep
         In the next valley-glades:
Was it a vision, or a waking dream?
   Fled is that music:—Do I wake or sleep?   80
1820

Ode on a Grecian Urn

1

Thou still unravished bride of quietness,
   Thou foster child of silence and slow time,
Sylvan historian, who canst thus express
   A flowery tale more sweetly than our rhyme:
What leaf-fringed legend haunts about thy shape   5
   Of deities or mortals, or of both,
      In Tempe or the dales of Arcady?[1]
   What men or gods are these? What maidens loath?
What mad pursuit? What struggle to escape?
   What pipes and timbrels? What wild ecstasy?   10

2

Heard melodies are sweet, but those unheard
   Are sweeter; therefore, ye soft pipes, play on;
Not to the sensual ear, but, more endeared,
   Pipe to the spirit ditties of no tone:

---

1. The Greeks considered Tempe and Arcadia to be perfect examples of rural landscapes.

Fair youth, beneath the trees, thou canst not leave   15
　Thy song, nor ever can those trees be bare;
　　Bold Lover, never, never canst thou kiss,
Though winning near the goal—yet, do not grieve;
　She cannot fade, though thou hast not thy bliss,
　Forever wilt thou love, and she be fair!   20

　　　　　　　　3

Ah, happy, happy boughs! that cannot shed
　Your leaves, nor ever bid the Spring adieu;
And, happy melodist, unweariéd,
　Forever piping songs forever new;
More happy love! more happy, happy love!   25
　Forever warm and still to be enjoyed,
　　Forever panting, and forever young;
All breathing human passion far above,
　That leaves a heart high-sorrowful and cloyed,
　　A burning forehead, and a parching tongue.   30

　　　　　　　　4

Who are these coming to the sacrifice?
　To what green altar, O mysterious priest,
Lead'st thou that heifer lowing at the skies,
　And all her silken flanks with garlands dressed?
What little town by river or sea shore,   35
　Or mountain-built with peaceful citadel,
　　Is emptied of this folk, this pious morn?
And, little town, thy streets forevermore
　Will silent be; and not a soul to tell
　　Why thou art desolate, can e'er return.   40

　　　　　　　　5

O Attic shape! Fair attitude! with brede[2]
　Of marble men and maidens overwrought,

---

2. I.e., woven pattern. "Attic": Greek, especially Athenian.

With forest branches and the trodden weed;
  Thou, silent form, dost tease us out of thought
As doth eternity: Cold Pastoral!   45
  When old age shall this generation waste,
    Thou shalt remain, in midst of other woe
  Than ours, a friend to man, to whom thou say'st,
"Beauty is truth, truth beauty,"—that is all
  Ye know on earth, and all ye need to know.   50

1820

To Autumn

1

Season of mists and mellow fruitfulness,
  Close bosom-friend of the maturing sun;
Conspiring with him how to load and bless
  With fruit the vines that round the thatch-eaves run;
To bend with apples the mossed cottage-trees,   5
  And fill all fruit with ripeness to the core;
    To swell the gourd, and plump the hazel shells
  With a sweet kernel; to set budding more,
And still more, later flowers for the bees,
Until they think warm days will never cease,   10
    For Summer has o'er-brimmed their clammy cells.

2

Who hath not seen thee oft amid thy store?
  Sometimes whoever seeks abroad may find
Thee sitting careless on a granary floor,
  Thy hair soft-lifted by the winnowing wind;   15
Or on a half-reaped furrow sound asleep,
  Drowsed with the fume of poppies, while thy hook
    Spares the next swath and all its twinéd flowers:
And sometimes like a gleaner thou dost keep
  Steady thy laden head across a brook;   20

Or by a cider-press, with patient look,
Thou watchest the last oozings hours by hours.

3

Where are the songs of Spring? Aye, where are they?
Think not of them, thou hast thy music too—
While barréd clouds bloom the soft-dying day,   25
    And touch the stubble-plains with rosy hue;
Then in a wailful choir the small gnats mourn
    Among the river sallows, borne aloft
        Or sinking as the light wind lives or dies;
And full-grown lambs loud bleat from hilly bourn;   30
    Hedge crickets sing; and now with treble soft
    The redbreast whistles from a garden-croft;
        And gathering swallows twitter in the skies.

                                            1820

Jane Kenyon
1947–1995

*Kenyon, who lived her last twenty-three years on her husband's fam-
ily farm in New Hampshire, is noted for her attention to the routine
details of everyday life and the rhythms of nature observed on a farm,
which link her to other rural poets like Robert Frost and Seamus
Heaney. Because she suffered depression, many readers see a parallel
with the poems of Sylvia Plath, while others see her poems as work-
ing out a reconciliation with mortality in a way that John Keats did.
Kenyon acknowledged her debt to Keats and wrote several variations
on his ode "To Autumn." All of these elements are evident in the brief
lyric "The Suitor." Writing a short memoir of their marriage, Kenyon's
husband, the poet Donald Hall, explains, "We did not spend our days
gazing into each other's eyes . . . [M]ost of the time our gazes met
and entwined as they looked at a third thing. Third things are essen-
tial to marriages . . . John Keats can be a third thing, or the Boston
Symphony Orchestra, or Dutch interiors, or Monopoly." After naps,
Hall writes, "we loaded up books and blankets and walked across*

*Route 4 and the old railroad to the steep slippery bank that led down
to our private beach on Eagle Pond." That bucolic setting was one of
their third things. Kenyon died of leukemia at the age of forty-seven.*

The Suitor

We lie back to back. Curtains
lift and fall,
like the chest of someone sleeping.
Wind moves the leaves of the box elder;
they show their light undersides,   5
turning all at once
like a school of fish.
Suddenly I understand that I am happy.
For months this feeling
has been coming closer, stopping   10
for short visits, like a timid suitor.

1978

Galway Kinnell

1927–2014

*Kinnell was often compared to the Romantic poets, like William
Wordsworth, and neoromantics, like Yeats and Frost. Kinnell was
famous for his attention to natural detail and delight in simple,
ordinary acts, such as displayed in "Blackberry Eating." "Earthly
creatures" and his "own children" were inspirations to his poetry.
Kinnell said that it is "through something radiant in our lives
that we have been able to dream of paradise, that we have been
able to invent the realm of eternity," and his poetry often captures
these radiances. This pursuit of what Kinnell himself called sacred
accounts for the interest that religious intellectuals have shown in
his poetry.*

Blackberry Eating

I love to go out in late September
among the fat, overripe, icy, black blackberries

to eat blackberries for breakfast,
the stalks very prickly, a penalty
they earn for knowing the black art   5
of blackberry making; and as I stand among them
lifting the stalks to my mouth, the ripest berries
fall almost unbidden to my tongue,
as words sometimes do, certain peculiar words
like *strengths* or *squinched* or *broughamed*,   10
many-lettered, one-syllabled lumps,
which I squeeze, squinch open, and splurge well
in the silent, startled, icy, black language
of blackberry eating in late September.

1980

After Making Love We Hear Footsteps

For I can snore like a bullhorn
or play loud music
or sit up talking with any reasonably sober Irishman
and Fergus will only sink deeper
into his dreamless sleep, which goes by all in one flash,   5
but let there be that heavy breathing
or a stifled come-cry anywhere in the house
and he will wrench himself awake
and make for it on the run—as now, we lie together,
after making love, quiet, touching along the length of our
    bodies,   10
familiar touch of the long-married,
and he appears—in his baseball pajamas, it happens,
the neck opening so small
he has to screw them on, which one day may make him wonder
about the mental capacity of baseball players—   15
and flops down between us and hugs and snuggles himself
    to sleep,
his face gleaming with satisfaction at being this very child.

In the half darkness we look at each other
and smile

and touch arms across his little, startlingly muscled body—   20
this one whom habit of memory propels to the ground of his
   making,
sleeper only the mortal sounds can sing awake,
this blessing love gives again into our arms.

1980

Etheridge Knight
1931–1991

*All poets use sound and intend for their works to be read aloud, but
Etheridge did so even more than most. Poetry that stays on the page,
"mainly analyzing and blah blah blah on college campuses," he
said dismissively, is elitist, in "some ivory tower." Writing in what
might be called a vernacular, never forgetting that black men were
his primary audience, Knight tried to write poetry that would get
up off the page. His technique derives from the blues songs he heard
growing up, and to understand "The Idea of Ancestry" you must
read it aloud, using the slashes to help you find the bluesy rhythms.
"The repetition that goes down in [poems] when they're said aloud,"
Knight explained, "causes a certain activity. When you say some-
thing aloud, the physical activity of repeating it is the basic blues
form."*

The Idea of Ancestry

I

Taped to the wall of my cell are 47 pictures: 47 black
faces: my father, mother, grandmothers (1 dead), grand-
fathers (both dead), brothers, sisters, uncles, aunts,
cousins (1st & 2nd), nieces, and nephews. They stare
across the space at me sprawling on my bunk. I know   5
their dark eyes, they know mine. I know their style,
they know mine. I am all of them, they are all of me;
they are farmers, I am a thief, I am me, they are thee.

I have at one time or another been in love with my mother,
1 grandmother, 2 sisters, 2 aunts (I went to the asylum),   10
and 5 cousins. I am now in love with a 7-yr-old niece
(she sends me letters written in large block print, and
her picture is the only one that smiles at me).

I have the same name as 1 grandfather, 3 cousins, 3 nephews,
and 1 uncle. The uncle disappeared when he was 15, just took   15
off and caught a freight (they say). He's discussed each year
when the family has a reunion, he causes uneasiness in
the clan, he is an empty space. My father's mother, who is 93
and who keeps the Family Bible with everybody's birth dates
(and death dates) in it, always mentions him. There is no   20
place in her Bible for "whereabouts unknown."

2

Each fall the graves of my grandfathers call me, the brown
hills and red gullies of mississippi send out their electric
messages, galvanizing my genes. Last yr/like a salmon quitting
the cold ocean-leaping and bucking up his birthstream/I   25
hitchhiked my way from LA with 16 caps in my pocket and a
monkey on my back. And I almost kicked it with the kinfolks.
I walked barefooted in my grandmother's backyard/I smelled
    the old
land and the woods/I sipped cornwhiskey from fruit jars with
    the men/
I flirted with the women/I had a ball till the caps ran out   30
and my habit came down. That night I looked at my
    grandmother
and split/my guts were screaming for junk/but I was almost
contented/I had almost caught up with me.
(The next day in Memphis I cracked a croaker's crib[1] for a fix.)
This yr there is a gray stone wall damming my stream, and
    when the falling leaves stir my genes,   35

---

1. I.e., "I broke into a doctor's house."

I pace my cell or flop on my bunk
and stare at 47 black faces across the space. I am all of them,
they are all of me, I am me, they are thee, and I have no
children to float in the space between.

1968

Yusef Komunyakaa

b. 1947

Komunyakaa was an army correspondent during the Vietnam War. The speaker in "Facing It" is visiting the Vietnam Veterans Memorial in Washington, D.C., two long, low arms of polished black granite on which are engraved the names of the American dead. Compare the African American speaker's reflection in the granite to the white veteran's image, which floats toward the speaker. "We Never Know" describes in disturbingly sexual terms the experience of killing someone. The speaker is an American soldier; the dead man is either North Vietnamese or a Viet Cong soldier. To make sense of this poem, you might determine how this experience has affected the American. Just as Langston Hughes's "Dream Boogie" translates into words the syncopated rhythm and the spirit of jazz, the first three stanzas of "Blue Dementia" reflect the mood and style of blues lyrics, which rely on repetitions. The genre is borne out of and voices the suffering of blacks in the American South and in the ghettos of northern cities.

Facing It

My black face fades,
hiding inside the black granite.
I said I wouldn't,
dammit: No tears.
I'm stone. I'm flesh.   5
My clouded reflection eyes me
like a bird of prey, the profile of night
slanted against morning. I turn
this way—the stone lets me go.
I turn that way—I'm inside   10
the Vietnam Veterans Memorial

again, depending on the light
to make a difference.
I go down the 58,022 names,
half-expecting to find   15
my own in letters like smoke.
I touch the name Andrew Johnson;
I see the booby trap's white flash.
Names shimmer on a woman's blouse
but when she walks away   20
the names stay on the wall.
Brushstrokes flash, a red bird's
wings cutting across my stare.
The sky. A plane in the sky.
A white vet's image floats   25
closer to me, then his pale eyes
look through mine. I'm a window.
He's lost his right arm
inside the stone. In the black mirror
a woman's trying to erase names: 30
No, she's brushing a boy's hair.

                                    1988

We Never Know

He danced with tall grass
for a moment, like he was swaying
with a woman. Our gun barrels
glowed white-hot.
When I got to him,   5
a blue halo
of flies had already claimed him.
I pulled the crumbled photograph
from his fingers.
There's no other way   10
to say this: I fell in love.
The morning cleared again,
except for a distant mortar
& somewhere choppers taking off.

I slid the wallet into his pocket   15
& turned him over, so he wouldn't be
kissing the ground.

1988

Blue Dementia

In the days when a man
would hold a swarm of words
inside his belly, nestled
against his spleen, singing.

In the days of night riders   5
when life tongued a reed
till blues & sorrow song
called out of the deep night:
Another man done gone.
Another man done gone.   10

In the days when one could lose oneself
all up inside love that way,
& then moan on the bone
till the gods cried out in someone's sleep.

Today,   15
already I've seen three dark-skinned men
discussing the weather with demons
& angels, gazing up at the clouds
& squinting down into iron grates
along the fast streets of luminous encounters.   20

I double-check my reflection in plate glass
& wonder, Am I passing another
Lucky Thompson or Marion Brown[1]

---

1. Eli Thompson (1924–2005) and Marion Brown (1931–2010) were jazz saxophonists.
Though both were successful recording artists, neither made very much money, and their
illness-plagued waning years were difficult. Thompson, who suffered from Alzheimer's dis-
ease, was homeless for a time near the end of his life.

cornered by a blue dementia,
another dark-skinned man   25
who woke up dreaming one morning
& then walked out of himself
dreaming? Did this one dare
to step on a crack in the sidewalk,
to turn a midnight corner & never come back   30
whole, or did he try to stare down a look
that shoved a blade into his heart?
I mean, I also know something
about night riders & catgut. Yeah,
honey, I know something about talking with ghosts.   35

2011

Maxine Kumin

b. 1925–2014

Kumin won the Pulitzer Prize in 1973 for Up Country: Poems
of New England, *her fourth book of poems, which included
"Woodchucks." The first group of poems in the book was inspired
by her property in rural New Hampshire. She created the persona
of the hermit, the person fleeing human society and, like Henry
David Thoreau, taking up residence among the plants and ani-
mals of a country place. The speaker in "Woodchucks" is all the
more surprising given the cluster of nature-loving poems within
which it dwells.*

Woodchucks

Gassing the woodchucks didn't turn out right.
The knockout bomb from the Feed and Grain Exchange
was featured as merciful, quick at the bone
and the case we had against them was airtight,
both exits shoehorned shut with puddingstone,   5
but they had a sub-sub-basement out of range.

Next morning they turned up again, no worse
for the cyanide than we for our cigarettes
and state-store Scotch, all of us up to scratch.
They brought down the marigolds as a matter of course   10
and then took over the vegetable patch
nipping the broccoli shoots, beheading the carrots.

The food from our mouths, I said, righteously thrilling
to the feel of the .22, the bullets' neat noses.
I, a lapsed pacifist fallen from grace   15
puffed with Darwinian pieties for killing,
now drew a bead on the littlest woodchuck's face.
He died down in the everbearing roses.

Ten minutes later I dropped the mother. She
flipflopped in the air and fell, her needle teeth   20
still hooked in a leaf of early Swiss chard.
Another baby next. O one-two-three
the murderer inside me rose up hard,
the hawkeye killer came on stage forthwith.

There's one chuck left. Old wily fellow, he keeps   25
me cocked and ready day after day after day.
All night I hunt his humped-up form. I dream
I sight along the barrel in my sleep.
If only they'd all consented to die unseen
gassed underground the quiet Nazi way.   30

1973

Letitia Elizabeth Landon
1802–1836

*Landon was one of the most popular poets of her generation, who
succeeded the Romantics, like Lord Byron and Percy Shelley. The
poets of the 1820s and 1830s have been negatively compared to
their predecessors for having an "inclination toward [orthodox]
morality, . . . peaceful domestic virtues, idyllic intimacy, lack of
passion, coziness, contendedness, innocent drollery, conservatism,*

[and] resignation." Perhaps this attitude resulted from Landon's relationship to her readers. Publishing many of her poems in a cheap magazine, the Literary Gazette, *she was among the first of Britain's poets to actually make a living as a writer by appealing to a larger, less-educated audience. Only recently have scholars begun to reexamine the work of writers like Landon.*

Revenge

Ay, gaze upon her rose-wreathed hair,
    And gaze upon her smile;
Seem as you drank the very air
    Her breath perfumed the while:

And wake for her the gifted line,   5
    That wild and witching lay,
And swear your heart is as a shrine,
    That only owns her sway.

'Tis well: I am revenged at last,—
    Mark you that scornful cheek,—   10
The eye averted as you pass'd,
    Spoke more than words could speak.

Ay, now by all the bitter tears
    That I have shed for thee,—
The racking doubts, the burning fears,—   15
    Avenged they well may be—

By the nights pass'd in sleepless care,
    The days of endless woe;
All that you taught my heart to bear,
    All that yourself will know.   20

I would not wish to see you laid
    Within an early tomb;
I should forget how you betray'd,
    And only weep your doom:

But this is fitting punishment,   25
    To live and love in vain,—
Oh my wrung heart, be thou content,
    And feed upon his pain.

Go thou and watch her lightest sigh,—
    Thine own it will not be;   30
And bask beneath her sunny eye,—
    It will not turn on thee.

'Tis well: the rack, the chain, the wheel,
    Far better had'st thou proved;
Ev'n I could almost pity feel,   35
    For thou art not beloved.
                          1829

The Little Shroud

She put him on a snow-white shroud,
    A chaplet on his head;
And gather'd early primroses
    To scatter o'er the dead.

She laid him in his little grave—   5
    'Twas hard to lay him there,
When spring was putting forth its flowers,
    And every thing was fair.

She had lost many children—now
    The last of them was gone;   10
And day and night she sat and wept
    Beside the funeral stone.

One midnight, while her constant tears
    Were falling with the dew,
She heard a voice, and lo! her child   15
    Stood by her weeping too!

His shroud was damp, his face was white:
  He said,—"I cannot sleep,
Your tears have made my shroud so wet;
  Oh, mother, do not weep!"   20

Oh, love is strong!—the mother's heart
  Was filled with tender fears;
Oh, love is strong!—and for her child
  Her grief restrained its tears.

One eve a light shone round her bed,   25
  And there she saw him stand—
Her infant, in his little shroud,
  A taper in his hand.

"Lo! mother, see my shroud is dry,
  And I can sleep once more!"   30
And beautiful the parting smile ·
  The little infant wore.

And down within the silent grave
  He laid his weary head;
And soon the early violets   35
  Grew o'er his grassy bed.

                    1832

Philip Larkin
1922–1985

> *Larkin was part of a wave of English writers who, in the 1950s
> and after, reacted against modernists like T. S. Eliot and Ezra
> Pound and strove to write in an easier, less academic style. An
> aubade celebrates the coming of dawn, but clearly Larkin uses
> the term ironically because the coming of another sunrise terrifies
> the speaker. These poems—and much of Larkin's work—explore the
> concerns particular to the existentialist philosophers who were bur-
> dened by the terrible experience of World War II. But ever since*

Darwin suggested we shared an ancestor with apes, many men and women have had to confront and somehow resolve the dilemmas articulated by Larkin.

Church Going

Once I am sure there's nothing going on
I step inside, letting the door thud shut.
Another church: matting, seats, and stone,
And little books; sprawling of flowers, cut
For Sunday, brownish now; some brass and stuff   5
Up at the holy end; the small neat organ;
And a tense, musty, unignorable silence,
Brewed God knows how long. Hatless, I take off
My cycle clips[1] in awkward reverence.

Move forward, run my hand around the font.   10
From where I stand, the roof looks almost new—
Cleaned, or restored? Someone would know: I don't.
Mounting the lectern, I peruse a few
Hectoring large-scale verses, and pronounce
"Here endeth" much more loudly than I'd meant.   15
The echoes snigger briefly. Back at the door
I sign the book, donate an Irish sixpence.
Reflect the place was not worth stopping for.

Yet stop I did: in fact I often do,
And always end much at a loss like this,   20
Wondering what to look for; wondering, too,
When churches fall completely out of use
What we shall turn them into, if we shall keep
A few cathedrals chronically on show,
Their parchment, plate and pyx in locked cases,   25
And let the rest rent-free to rain and sheep.
Shall we avoid them as unlucky places?

---

1. The removable clasps holding the cuffs of pants tight so they don't tangle in the bike's chain.

Or , after dark, will dubious women come
To make their children touch a particular stone;
Pick simples[2] for a cancer; or on some   30
Advised night see walking a dead one?
Power of some sort or other will go on
In games, in riddles, seemingly at random;
But superstition, like belief, must die,
And what remains when disbelief has gone?   35
Grass, weedy pavement, brambles, buttress, sky,

A shape less recognisable each week,
A purpose more obscure. I wonder who
Will be the last, the very last, to seek
This place for what it was, one of the crew   40
That tap and jot and know what rood-lofts[3] were?
Some ruin-bibber, randy for antique,
Or Christmas-addict, counting on a whiff
Of gown-and-bands and organ-pipes and myrrh?
Or will he be my representative,   45

Bored, uninformed, knowing the ghostly silt
Dispersed, yet tending to this cross of ground
Through suburb scrub because it held unspilt
So long and equably what since is found
Only in separation—marriage, and birth,   50
And death, and thoughts of these—for whom was built
This special shell? For, though I've no idea
What this accoutred frowsty barn is worth,
It pleases me to stand in silence here;

A serious house on serious earth it is,   55
In whose blent air all our compulsions meet,
Are recognised, and robed as destinies.
And that much never can be obsolete,

2. Medicinal herbs.   3. Upper galleries at the end of the naves
                                       in churches.

Since someone will forever be surprising
A hunger in himself to be more serious,   60
And gravitating with it to this ground,
Which, he once heard, was proper to grow wise in,
If only that so many dead lie round.

1955

High Windows

When I see a couple of kids
And guess he's fucking her and she's
Taking pills or wearing a diaphragm,
I know this is paradise

Everyone old has dreamed of all their lives—   5
Bonds and gestures pushed to one side
Like an outdated combine harvester,
And everyone young going down the long slide

To happiness, endlessly. I wonder if
Anyone looked at me, forty years back,   10
And thought, *That'll be the life;*
No God any more, or sweating in the dark

About hell and that, or having to hide
What you think of the priest. He
And his lot will all go down the long slide   15
Like free bloody birds. And immediately

Rather than words comes the thought of high windows:
The sun-comprehending glass,
And beyond it, the deep blue air, that shows
Nothing, and is nowhere, and is endless.   20

1974

Aubade

I work all day, and get half-drunk at night.
Waking at four to soundless dark, I stare.
In time the curtain-edges will grow light.
Till then I see what's really always there:
Unresting death, a whole day nearer now,   5
Making all thought impossible but how
And where and when I shall myself die.
Arid interrogation: yet the dread
Of dying, and being dead,
Flashes afresh to hold and horrify.   10

The mind blanks at the glare. Not in remorse
—The good not done, the love not given, time
Torn off unused—nor wretchedly because
An only life can take so long to climb
Clear of its wrong beginnings, and may never;   15
But at the total emptiness for ever,
The sure extinction that we travel to
And shall be lost in always. Not to be here,
Not to be anywhere,
And soon; nothing more terrible, nothing more true.   20

This is a special way of being afraid
No trick dispels. Religion used to try,
That vast moth-eaten musical brocade
Created to pretend we never die,
And specious stuff that says *No rational being*   25
Can fear a thing it will not feel, not seeing
That this is what we fear—no sight, no sound,
No touch or taste or smell, nothing to think with,
Nothing to love or link with,
The anaesthetic from which none come round.   30

And so it stays just on the edge of vision,
A small unfocused blur, a standing chill

That slows each impulse down to indecision.
Most things may never happen: this one will,
And realisation of it rages out   35
In furnace-fear when we are caught without
People or drink. Courage is no good:
It means not scaring others. Being brave
Lets no one off the grave.
Death is no different whined at than withstood.   40

Slowly light strengthens, and the room takes shape.
It stands plain as a wardrobe, what we know,
Have always known, know that we can't escape,
Yet can't accept. One side will have to go.
Meanwhile telephones crouch, getting ready to ring   45
In locked-up offices, and all the uncaring
Intricate rented world begins to rouse.
The sky is white as clay, with no sun.
Work has to be done.
Postmen like doctors go from house to house.   50

1977

Li-Young Lee

b. 1957

Lee combines a variety of traditions, from Chinese poetry to Walt Whitman, to whom he is often compared. For the Chinese influence, you might compare the concluding stanzas of "Visions and Interpretations" to Pound's translation of the Chinese poem "The River-Merchant's Wife." Despite this affinity with old forms, "Visions and Interpretations" is one of the few examples of postmodern poetry in this volume. One of the poem's main concerns is the nature of poetry and its relation to real experience. This poem is, among other things, about writing poems. "The Gift" is an excellent example of the emotive power of simple diction and mundane incident. Among the poem's striking features is the juxtaposition of a son's love for his father with a husband's love for his wife.

"Eating Alone" and "Eating Together" both appeared in Lee's book
The Rose, and while each can stand alone, they can also be consid-
ered companion pieces.

Eating Alone

I've pulled the last of the year's young onions.
The garden is bare now. The ground is cold,
brown and old. What is left of the day flames
in the maples at the corner of my
eye. I turn, a cardinal vanishes.   5
By the cellar door, I wash the onions,
then drink from the icy metal spigot.

Once, years back, I walked beside my father
among the windfall pears. I can't recall
our words. We may have strolled in silence. But   10
I still see him bend that way—left hand braced
on knee, creaky—to lift and hold to my
eye a rotten pear. In it, a hornet
spun crazily, glazed in slow, glistening juice.

It was my father I saw this morning   15
waving to me from the trees. I almost
called to him, until I came close enough
to see the shovel, leaning where I had
left it, in the flickering, deep green shade.

White rice steaming, almost done. Sweet green peas   20
fried in onions. Shrimp braised in sesame
oil and garlic. And my own loneliness.
What more could I, a young man, want.

                                        1986

Eating Together

In the steamer is the trout
seasoned with slivers of ginger,

two sprigs of green onion, and sesame oil.
We shall eat it with rice for lunch,
brothers, sister, my mother who will   5
taste the sweetest meat of the head,
holding it between her fingers
deftly, the way my father did
weeks ago. Then he lay down
to sleep like a snow-covered road   10
winding through pines older than him,
without any travelers, and lonely for no one.

                                        1986

Visions and Interpretations

Because this graveyard is a hill,
I must climb up to see my dead,
stopping once midway to rest
beside this tree.

It was here, between the anticipation   5
of exhaustion, and exhaustion,
between vale and peak,
my father came down to me

and we climbed arm in arm to the top.
He cradled the bouquet I'd brought,   10
and I, a good son, never mentioned his grave,
erect like a door behind him.

And it was here, one summer day, I sat down
to read an old book. When I looked up
from the noon-lit page, I saw a vision   15
of a world about to come, and a world about to go.

Truth is, I've not seen my father
since he died, and, no, the dead
do not walk arm in arm with me.

If I carry flowers to them, I do so without their help,   20
the blossoms not always bright, torch-like,
but often heavy as sodden newspaper.

Truth is, I came here with my son one day,
and we rested against this tree,
and I fell asleep, and dreamed   25

a dream which, upon my boy waking me, I told.
Neither of us understood.
Then we went up.

Even this is not accurate.
Let me begin again: 30

Between two griefs, a tree.
Between my hands, white chrysanthemums, yellow
     chrysanthemums.

The old book I finished reading
I've since read again and again.

And what was far grows near,   35
and what is near grows more dear,

and all of my visions and interpretations
depend on what I see,

and between my eyes is always
the rain, the migrant rain.   40
                                                    1986

The Gift

To pull the metal splinter from my palm
my father recited a story in a low voice.
I watched his lovely face and not the blade.

Before the story ended, he'd removed
the iron sliver I thought I'd die from.   5

I can't remember the tale,
but hear his voice still, a well
of dark water, a prayer.
And I recall his hands,
two measures of tenderness   10
he laid against my face,
the flames of discipline
he raised above my head.

Had you entered that afternoon
you would have thought you saw a man   15
planting something in a boy's palm,
a silver tear, a tiny flame.
Had you followed that boy
you would have arrived here,
where I bend over my wife's right hand.   20

Look how I shave her thumbnail down
so carefully she feels no pain.
Watch as I lift the splinter out.
I was seven when my father
took my hand like this,   25
and I did not hold that shard
between my fingers and think,
Metal that will bury me,
christen it Little Assassin,
Ore Going Deep for My Heart.   30
And I did not lift up my wound and cry,
Death visited here!
I did what a child does
when he's given something to keep.
I kissed my father.   35

1986

Robert Lowell

1917–1977

"Skunk Hour" contrasts the human and natural worlds in Castine, Maine, where Lowell had a summer residence. He composed it in the summer of 1957, after Elizabeth Bishop encouraged him to write in a looser, less formal style. The poem breaks with the impersonal style instituted by T. S. Eliot, a style that was still popular among many prominent American poets in the 1950s. In fact, Lowell's poem could in some sense be considered confessional: Lowell had bipolar disorder, also known as manic depression, and in the fall of 1957, extremely manic, he checked himself into a psychiatric hospital in Boston. "For the Union Dead" commemorates Robert Gould Shaw and his Civil War regiment of African Americans. Shaw and many of the men in his command died assaulting a beachfort protecting Charleston, South Carolina, from Union siege. Their bravery and devotion provided a model of heroism and virtue that the city of Boston celebrated in 1897 when it erected the statue described in the poem.

Skunk Hour

(For Elizabeth Bishop)

Nautilus Island's hermit
heiress still lives through winter in her Spartan cottage;
her sheep still graze above the sea.
Her son's a bishop. Her farmer
is first selectman in our village;   5
she's in her dotage.

Thirsting for
the hierarchic privacy
of Queen Victoria's century,
she buys up all   10
the eyesores facing her shore,
and lets them fall.

The season's ill—
we've lost our summer millionaire,
who seemed to leap from an L. L. Bean   15
catalogue. His nine-knot yawl
was auctioned off to lobstermen.
A red fox stain covers Blue Hill.

And now our fairy
decorator brightens his shop for fall;   20
his fishnet's filled with orange cork,
orange, his cobbler's bench and awl;
there is no money in his work,
he'd rather marry.

One dark night,   25
my Tudor Ford climbed the hill's skull;
I watched for love-cars. Lights turned down,
they lay together, hull to hull,
where the graveyard shelves on the town. . . .
My mind's not right.   30

A car radio bleats,
"Love, O careless Love. . . ." I hear
my ill-spirit sob in each blood cell,
as if my hand were at its throat. . . .
I myself am hell;   35
nobody's here—

only skunks, that search
in the moonlight for a bite to eat.
They march on their soles up Main Street:
white stripes, moonstruck eyes' red fire   40
under the chalk-dry and spar spire
of the Trinitarian Church.

I stand on top
of our back steps and breathe the rich air—

a mother skunk with her column of kittens swills the garbage
    pail.   45
She jabs her wedge-head in a cup
of sour cream, drops her ostrich tail,
and will not scare.

1959

For the Union Dead

"Relinquunt Omnia Servare Rem Publicam." [1]

The old South Boston Aquarium stands
in a Sahara of snow now. Its broken windows are boarded.
The bronze weathervane cod has lost half its scales.
The airy tanks are dry.

Once my nose crawled like a snail on the glass;   5
my hand tingled
to burst the bubbles
drifting from the noses of the cowed, compliant fish.

My hand draws back. I often sigh still
for the dark downward and vegetating kingdom   10
of the fish and reptile. One morning last March,
I pressed against the new barbed and galvanized

fence on the Boston Common. Behind their cage,
yellow dinosaur steamshovels were grunting
as they cropped up tons of mush and grass   15
to gouge their underworld garage.

Parking spaces luxuriate like civic
sandpiles in the heart of Boston.
A girdle of orange, Puritan-pumpkin colored girders
braces the tingling Statehouse,   20

1. They sacrificed all to serve the republic (Latin).

shaking over the excavations, as it faces Colonel Shaw
and his bell-cheeked Negro infantry
on St. Gaudens'[2] shaking Civil War relief,
propped by a plank splint against the garage's earthquake.

Two months after marching through Boston,   25
half the regiment was dead;
at the dedication,
William James[3] could almost hear the bronze Negroes breathe.

Their monument sticks like a fishbone
in the city's throat.   30
Its Colonel is as lean
as a compass-needle.

He has an angry wrenlike vigilance,
a greyhound's gentle tautness;
he seems to wince at pleasure,   35
and suffocate for privacy.

He is out of bounds now. He rejoices in man's lovely,
peculiar power to choose life and die—
when he leads his black soldiers to death,
he cannot bend his back.   40

On a thousand small town New England greens,
the old white churches hold their air
of sparse, sincere rebellion; frayed flags
quilt the graveyards of the Grand Army of the Republic.

The stone statues of the abstract Union Soldier   45
grow slimmer and younger each year—
wasp-waisted, they doze over muskets
and muse through their sideburns . . .

2. Augustus Saint-Gaudens (1848–
1907), French artist who sculpted a num-
ber of Civil War monuments, including the
Shaw memorial described here.

3. Boston psychologist and philosopher
(1842–1910).

Shaw's father wanted no monument
except the ditch,   50
where his son's body was thrown
and lost with his "niggers."

The ditch is nearer.
There are no statues for the last war here;
on Boylston Street, a commercial photograph   55
shows Hiroshima boiling

over a Mosler Safe,[4] the "Rock of Ages"
that survived the blast. Space is nearer.
When I crouch to my television set,
the drained faces of Negro school-children rise like balloons.   60

Colonel Shaw
is riding on his bubble,
he waits
for the blessèd break.

The Aquarium is gone. Everywhere,   65
giant finned cars nose forward like fish;
a savage servility
slides by on grease.

1959

Susan Ludvigson
b. 1942

> *Ludvigson says that the images in her poetry come from her child-*
> *hood and her dreams and credits "learning to listen to one's inner*
> *ear and trusting to the unconscious." "After Love" was published in*
> Everything Winged Must Be Dreaming *(1993). Winged crea-*
> *tures appear in many of the poems, either on the literal level or, as*
> *here, in a metaphor. That context emphasizes Ludvigson's decision*

4. Probably an advertising photograph depicting an undamaged safe, manufactured by the
Mosler Safe Company of Ohio, amid the ruins of Hiroshima, the first of two Japanese cities
destroyed by atomic bombs at the end of World War II.

to compare reason to a moth rather than some other animal. You
might ask yourself: Why not a pheasant or a peacock or a swallow
or an angel, which appear in her other poems?

After Love

She remembers how reason
escaped from the body,
flew out with a sigh,
went winging up
to a corner of the ceiling   5
and fluttered there,
a moth, a translucence,
waiting.
She did not hear it
return, did not see   10
but felt its brush
against her breasts
quieter, quieter,
until it slipped
back in, powdered   15
wings intact.
                    1993

Archibald MacLeish
1892–1982

When MacLeish published "Ars Poetica" (The art of poetry), it
became a sort of manifesto for the American, mid-century poets asso-
ciated with New Criticism (represented in this volume by Williams,
Moore, Lowell, Bishop, Ransom, and Stevens). "Ars Poetica" erects the
pillars of New Critical aesthetics: that poetry, because it is experienced
rather than interpreted, is something completely different from ordi-
nary language (and therefore does not convey a meaning in the way
we think of, for example, a political speech meaning *something); that*
the proper subject matter of poetry is the universal, timeless truths of
the human heart, like grief and love; and that these truths are con-
veyed through images (an "empty doorway" for "grief "). Reforming

society, then, according to MacLeish and the New Critics, is not the business of poetry. For this reason, some of the more political poets in this volume would dispute the philosophy presented in "Ars Poetica."

Ars Poetica

A poem should be palpable and mute
As a globed fruit,

⁕

Dumb
As old medallions to the thumb,

Silent as the sleeve-worn stone   5
Of casement ledges where the moss has grown—

A poem should be wordless
As the flight of birds.

⁕

A poem should be motionless in time
As the moon climbs,   10

Leaving, as the moon releases
Twig by twig the night-entangled trees,

Leaving, as the moon behind the winter leaves,
Memory by memory the mind—

A poem should be motionless in time   15
As the moon climbs.

⁕

A poem should be equal to:
Not true.

For all the history of grief
An empty doorway and a maple leaf.   20

For love
The leaning grasses and two lights above the sea—

A poem should not mean
But be.

1926

Ed Madden

b. 1963

*"Sunday Morning, Wadmalaw" is the one example in this volume of
an epithalamium, which is a poem celebrating the occasion of a mar-
riage. It is also an aubade, a morning poem, and you might inter-
pret it alongside Philip Larkin's poem in the same genre. Wadmalaw
Island sits along the South Carolina coast, surrounded by marshes,
between the barrier island Kiawah and the mainland. The tides
mentioned in the poem, being inland, would be gentle and quiet.*

Sunday Morning, Wadmalaw

for Teresa and Fred, June 1998

I

The way the day began: a white sun, white sky,
the chatter and prattle of martins a kind of artless consecration

for the dawn. The guests woke slowly, each in turn; some
huddled over rituals of coffee, one wandered down the dirt path

to mass, others out to the dock, where I waited, expectant,   5
for the slow apparition of a white heron, flying

out of the sun. On such days, we reach for metaphor, something
to represent the way two people may decide to be

together. And so I waited on the deck for the white bird, before
it became a bird or white or near. Floral pediments from the   10
  wedding

remained on the porch, small towers of sunflower, palmetto,
    fern—
and vervain from the island's fields, a bloom like purple ash.

II

The bride waited at the end of a corridor of moss-draped oak,
her neck thin and graceful as the heron's, and nothing fragile

about her smile. She tossed her bouquet of magnolia into the
    river,   15
where it floated, only to be rescued later by a nephew

when it reached the muddy shore, the return of something
too beautiful to happen only once, as if every trajectory

had its return, every prodigal his home. Told he was next
to marry, the nephew threw it back to the tides, the deepening
    dark.   20

III

Photos capture an evening disappearing: her parents leaning
into a whisper; his parents leading a line dance; the beauty

of a man, barefoot and tan, whose slate-blue shirt echoed the hue
of his eyes; the quiet groom, the shining bride—memory an album
of nameless faces, an index of images and scents—mango
    cocktails   25
late in the evening, the dock moving beneath me like a lover.

IV

I broke a bloom of vervain to take home—its purple tipped
with a speck of blue, the color of the sky, the morning after

the wedding, a cloudless blue lightening to white at the horizon.
The tide dawdled along the dock, the purple martins dithering,   30

a screen door slammed, the air was bright and hot, and not
prepared for anything—other than the bride and groom's
  expected visit

to say goodbyes—and then the surprise of the white heron
flying slowly from the sun, white on white, followed

moments later by another, a reply, the repetition   35
required by fate, and perhaps I thought—or hoped—its mate.

2006

Christopher Marlowe
1564–1593

  Marlowe was Shakespeare's contemporary and his chief rival as playwright. "The Passionate Shepherd to His Love" circulated in manuscript throughout London's literary circles, as was the case with many poems in the Elizabethan era (it was not published until eight years after Marlowe's untimely death in a bar fight). Its original audience, then, was aristocrats (both men and women) and well-educated men of letters, and it was widely read by these groups. "The Passionate Shepherd" is the best example in this volume of the pastoral lyric—a popular form in the Elizabethan age. No one would mistake the shepherds for real people.

The Passionate Shepherd to His Love

Come live with me and be my love,
And we will all the pleasures prove
That valleys, groves, hills, and fields,
Woods, or steepy mountain yields.

And we will sit upon the rocks,   5
Seeing the shepherds feed their flocks,

By shallow rivers to whose falls
Melodious birds sing madrigals.

And I will make thee beds of roses
And a thousand fragrant posies,   10
A cap of flowers, and a kirtle
Embroidered all with leaves of myrtle;

A gown made of the finest wool
Which from our pretty lambs we pull;
Fair lined slippers for the cold,   15
With buckles of the purest gold;

A belt of straw and ivy buds,
With coral clasps and amber studs:
And if these pleasures may thee move,
Come live with me, and be my love.   20

The shepherds' swains shall dance and sing
For thy delight each May morning:
If these delights thy mind may move,
Then live with me and be my love.

                          1599, 1600

Andrew Marvell
1621–1678

> *Marvell, a friend of John Milton, published little during his life-time: his housekeeper, who represented herself as his widow, brought out a collection of his poems after his death. The speaker in "To His Coy Mistress" is the persona speaking in a conventional* carpe diem *poem: the artful seducer. In fact, this poem is probably the most famous example of its kind in the English language. Note how the poem breaks down into a logical, three-point argument: "If," "but," "therefore."*

To His Coy Mistress

   Had we but world enough, and time,
This coyness, lady, were no crime.
We would sit down, and think which way
To walk, and pass our long love's day.
Thou by the Indian Ganges'[1] side   5
Shouldst rubies[2] find; I by the tide
Of Humber would complain. I would
Love you ten years before the flood,
And you should, if you please, refuse
Till the conversion of the Jews.   10
My vegetable[3] love should grow
Vaster than empires and more slow;
An hundred years should go to praise
Thine eyes, and on thy forehead gaze;
Two hundred to adore each breast,   15
But thirty thousand to the rest;
An age at least to every part,
And the last age should show your heart.
For, lady, you deserve this state,
Nor would I love at lower rate.   20
   But at my back I always hear
Time's wingèd chariot hurrying near;
And yonder all before us lie
Deserts of vast eternity.
Thy beauty shall no more be found;   25
Nor, in thy marble vault, shall sound
My echoing song; then worms shall try
That long-preserved virginity,
And your quaint[4] honor turn to dust,
And into ashes all my lust: 30

---

1. A river in northern India.
2. Thought to help preserve virginity.
3. I.e., characterized by plantlike growth.
4. Has several meanings, including fine, elegant, fastidious, and oversubtle; also with a pun on the Middle English noun *queynte*, meaning "a woman's genitals."

The grave's a fine and private place,
But none, I think, do there embrace.
   Now therefore, while the youthful hue
Sits on thy skin like morning dew,
And while thy willing soul transpires   35
At every pore with instant fires,
Now let us sport us while we may,
And now, like amorous birds of prey,
Rather at once our time devour
Than languish in his slow-chapped power.   40
Let us roll all our strength and all
Our sweetness up into one ball,
And tear our pleasures with rough strife
Through the iron gates of life:
Thus, though we cannot make our sun   45
Stand still, yet we will make him run.
        1681

Claude McKay
1889–1948
   This poem was published in McKay's 1922 Harlem Shadows. *If we take the speaker to be McKay himself, he is a black immigrant from Jamaica. But the ambivalence expressed here is not necessarily that of an alien; McKay was part of the Harlem Renaissance, a 1920s black arts movement as rich as any cultural flourishing in America's history. Aspects of the renaissance were political, and McKay's criticism comes from a socialist perspective. He probably had Percy Shelley's "Ozymandias" in mind when he wrote this poem, thus it might help to read this poem alongside Shelley's.*

America

Although she feeds me bread of bitterness,
And sinks into my throat her tiger's tooth,
Stealing my breath of life, I will confess
I love this cultured hell that tests my youth!

Her vigor flows like tides into my blood,   5
Giving me strength erect against her hate.
Her bigness sweeps my being like a flood.
Yet as a rebel fronts a king in state,
I stand within her walls with not a shred
Of terror, malice, not a word of jeer.   10
Darkly I gaze into the days ahead,
And see her might and granite wonders there,
Beneath the touch of Time's unerring hand,
Like priceless treasures sinking in the sand.

1922

Edna St. Vincent Millay

1892–1950

> *Millay exemplified the rakish free spirit of Greenwich Village in
> the years during and after World War I. She took many lovers and
> wrote frankly about them in her verse. "I, being born a woman"
> expresses the relative sexual freedom and self-possession of the "new
> woman." "What Lips My Lips Have Kissed" was the fifth of a
> sequence of eight sonnets that helped win her the Pulitzer Prize
> in 1922. The season motif appears throughout the sequence: the
> third sonnet begins with these lines: "I know I am but summer to
> your heart, / And not the full four seasons of the year[.]" "Love Is
> Not All" was part of a 1931 sequence,* Fatal Interview. *Though
> its rhyme scheme indicates it is a Shakespearean sonnet, the poem
> seems to divide like a Petrarchan sonnet.*

What Lips My Lips Have Kissed

What lips my lips have kissed, and where, and why,
I have forgotten, and what arms have lain
Under my head till morning; but the rain
Is full of ghosts tonight, that tap and sigh
Upon the glass and listen for reply,   5
And in my heart there stirs a quiet pain
For unremembered lads that not again

Will turn to me at midnight with a cry.
Thus in the winter stands the lonely tree,
Nor knows what birds have vanished one by one,   10
Yet knows its boughs more silent than before:
I cannot say what loves have come and gone,
I only know that summer sang in me
A little while, that in me sings no more.

1922

I, Being Born a Woman and Distressed

I, being born a woman and distressed
By all the needs and notions of my kind,
Am urged by your propinquity to find
Your person fair, and feel a certain zest
To bear your body's weight upon my breast: 5
So subtly is the fume of life designed,
To clarify the pulse and cloud the mind,
And leave me once again undone, possessed.
Think not for this, however, the poor treason
Of my stout blood against my staggering brain,   10
I shall remember you with love, or season
My scorn with pity,—let me make it plain:
I find this frenzy insufficient reason
For conversation when we meet again.

1923

Love Is Not All: It Is Not Meat nor Drink

Love is not all: it is not meat nor drink
Nor slumber nor a roof against the rain;
Nor yet a floating spar to men that sink
And rise and sink and rise and sink again;
Love can not fill the thickened lung with breath,   5
Nor clean the blood, nor set the fractured bone;
Yet many a man is making friends with death
Even as I speak, for lack of love alone.

It well may be that in a difficult hour,
Pinned down by pain and moaning for release,   10
Or nagged by want past resolution's power,
I might be driven to sell your love for peace,
Or trade the memory of this night for food.
It well may be. I do not think I would.

1931

John Milton
1608–1674

Milton wrote "When I Consider How My Light Is Spent" after going blind around 1651. His eyesight deteriorated while he was writing political pamphlets defending Parliament's 1649 execution of King Charles I, though it would be fair to say he considered the king's downfall to be God's work because Charles was overthrown by a Puritan revolution that was as much religious and cultural as it was political. Milton's fortunes fell when the monarchy was restored in 1660. Blind and poor, he wrote his greatest work, the epic Paradise Lost, *which was instantly recognized by English audiences as a work worthy of Homer or Virgil when it was published in 1667. When his short lyrics, including this one, were first published in 1673, readers would have known Milton as England's famous blind epic poet.*

When I Consider How My Light Is Spent

When I consider how my light is spent
    Ere half my days, in this dark world and wide,
    And that one talent which is death to hide
    Lodged with me useless, though my soul more bent
To serve therewith my Maker, and present   5
    My true account, lest he returning chide;
    "Doth God exact day-labor, light denied?"
    I fondly ask; but Patience to prevent

That murmur, soon replies, "God doth not need
 Either man's work or his own gifts; who best   10
Bear his mild yoke, they serve him best. His state
Is kingly. Thousands at his bidding speed
And post o'er land and ocean without rest:
They also serve who only stand and wait."

           1673

Marianne Moore
1887–1972

In "The Steeple-Jack" Moore uses an unusual "syllabic" method. The opening stanza unfolds as one complete sentence. The subsequent stanzas mirror that form in the number of syllables per line, but the syntax of the subsequent sentences move against this pattern in a counterrhythm. Moore's career paralleled Pound's and Eliot's, and as editor of the influential Dial *magazine, she mentored many of America's mid-century poets—people like Elizabeth Bishop. The way she framed her question about poetry's importance is, then, somewhat surprising, especially when you consider "Poetry" along-side a work like MacLeish's "Ars Poetica." It is difficult to gauge her attitude toward those things "that we do not admire" because we can't understand them: the "immovable critic" of course is a figure of some contempt, but Moore's famous love of the Dodgers suggests that the frivolity and inutility of the baseball fan is something the speaker admires.*

Poetry

I, too, dislike it: there are things that are important beyond all
  this fiddle.
Reading it, however, with a perfect contempt for it, one
  discovers in
it after all, a place for the genuine.
 Hands that can grasp, eyes
  that can dilate, hair that can rise   5
   if it must, these things are important not because a

high-sounding interpretation can be put upon them but
    because they are
  useful. When they become so derivative as to become
    unintelligible,
the same thing may be said for all of us, that we
    do not admire what   10
    we cannot understand: the bat
      holding on upside down or in quest of something to

eat, elephants pushing, a wild horse taking a roll, a tireless wolf
  under a tree, the immovable critic twitching his skin like a
    horse that feels a flea, the base-
  ball fan, the statistician—   15
    nor is it valid
      to discriminate against "business documents and

school-books"; all these phenomena are important. One must
    make a distinction
  however: when dragged into prominence by half poets, the
    result is not poetry,
nor till the poets among us can be   20
    "literalists of
  the imagination"—above
    insolence and triviality and can present

for inspection, "imaginary gardens with real toads in them,"
    shall we have
  it. In the meantime, if you demand on the one hand,   25
  the raw material of poetry in
    all its rawness and
    that which is on the other hand
      genuine, then you are interested in poetry.

1921, 1935

The Steeple-Jack

Revised, 1961

Dürer[1] would have seen a reason for living
    in a town like this, with eight stranded whales
to look at; with the sweet sea air coming into your house
on a fine day, from water etched
    with waves as formal as the scales   5
on a fish.

One by one in two's and three's, the seagulls keep
    flying back and forth over the town clock,
or sailing around the lighthouse without moving their wings—
rising steadily with a slight   10
    quiver of the body—or flock
mewing where

a sea the purple of the peacock's neck is
    paled to greenish azure as Dürer changed
the pine green of the Tyrol to peacock blue and guinea   15
gray. You can see a twenty-five-
    pound lobster; and fish nets arranged
to dry. The

whirlwind fife-and-drum of the storm bends the salt
    marsh grass, disturbs stars in the sky and the   20
star on the steeple; it is a privilege to see so
much confusion. Disguised by what
    might seem the opposite, the sea-
side flowers and

trees are favored by the fog so that you have   25
    the tropics at first hand: the trumpet vine,
foxglove, giant snapdragon, a salpiglossis that has

---

1. Albrecht Dürer (1471–1528), German artist best known for his woodcut prints and engravings. Presumably, the "etched" water (line 4) resembles one of his works.

spots and stripes; morning-glories, gourds,
    or moon-vines trained on fishing twine
at the back door: 30

cattails, flags, blueberries and spiderwort,
    striped grass, lichens, sunflowers, asters, daisies—
yellow and crab-claw ragged sailors with green bracts—toad-plant,
petunias, ferns; pink lilies, blue
    ones, tigers; poppies; black sweet-peas.   35
The climate

is not right for the banyan, frangipani, or
    jack-fruit trees; or for exotic serpent
life. Ring lizard and snakeskin for the foot, if you see fit;
but here they've cats, not cobras, to   40
    keep down the rats. The diffident
little newt

with white pin-dots on black horizontal spaced-
    out bands lives here; yet there is nothing that
ambition can buy or take away. The college student   45
named Ambrose sits on the hillside
    with his not-native books and hat
and sees boats

at sea progress white and rigid as if in
    a groove. Liking an elegance of which   50
the source is not bravado, he knows by heart the antique
sugar-bowl shaped summerhouse of
    interlacing slats, and the pitch
of the church

spire, not true, from which a man in scarlet lets   55
    down a rope as a spider spins a thread;
he might be part of a novel, but on the sidewalk a
sign says C.J. Poole, Steeple Jack,
    in black and white; and one in red
and white says   60

Danger. The church portico has four fluted
     columns, each a single piece of stone, made
modester by whitewash. This would be a fit haven for
waifs, children, animals, prisoners,
     and presidents who have repaid   65
sin-driven

senators by not thinking about them. The
     place has a schoolhouse, a post-office in a
store, fish-houses, hen-houses, a three-masted
     schooner on   70
the stocks. The hero, the student,
     the steeple jack, each in his way,
is at home.

It could not be dangerous to be living
     in a town like this, of simple people,   75
who have a steeple-jack placing danger signs by the church
while he is gilding the solid-
     pointed star, which on a steeple
stands for hope.

                                             1935, 1961

Pablo Neruda
1904–1973

*Poet and politician, Neruda was beloved by his readers and alter-
natively hated or embraced by the rulers of his home country, Chile.
Neruda skirted danger for all his adult life. He consistently supported
communist causes: the Spanish Civil War, Joseph Stalin's Russia,
Fidel Castro's revolution in Cuba, and Che Guevera's guerilla activi-
ties in Bolivia. All the while he was writing poetry, from Whitman-
esque epics to love poems. Amid some controversy, he was awarded
the Nobel Prize for Literature in 1971. In the 1950s, he wrote
three books of odes, from which "Ode to My Suit" is taken. Many
of them looked at simple, everyday objects with splendor rendered in
simple, everyday language. The image of the bullet in this poem is not*

outlandish: the poet's death was investigated to determine if he was
poisoned by someone in the right-wing Pinochet regime that staged a
coup against the elected socialist government Neruda supported.

Ode to My Suit[1]

Every morning, suit,
you are waiting on a chair
to be filled
by my vanity, my love,
my hope, my body.   5
Still
only half awake
I leave the shower
to shrug into your sleeves,
my legs seek   10
the hollow of your legs,
and thus embraced
by your unfailing loyalty
I take my morning walk,
work my way into my poetry;   15
from my windows I see
the things,
men, women,
events and struggles
constantly shaping me,   20
constantly confronting me,
setting my hands to the task,
opening my eyes,
creasing my lips,
and in the same way,   25
suit,
I am shaping you,
poking out your elbows,
wearing you threadbare,
and so your life grows   30

1. Translated by Margret Sayers Pelen.

in the image of my own.
In the wind
you flap and hum
as if you were my soul,
in bad moments   35
you cling
to my bones,
abandoned, at nighttime
darkness and dream
people with their phantoms   40
your wings and mine.
I wonder
whether some day
an enemy
bullet   45
will stain you with my blood,
for then
you would die with me,
but perhaps
it will be   50
less dramatic,
simple,
and you will grow ill,
suit,
with me,   55
grow older
with me, with my body,
and together
we will be lowered
into the earth.   60
That's why
every day
I greet you
with respect and then
you embrace me and I forget you,   65
because we are one being
and shall be always
in the wind, through the night,

the streets and the struggle,
one body,   70
maybe, maybe, one day, still.
                    1954

Sharon Olds
b. 1942

*"Sex without Love" and "The One Girl at the Boys' Party" appeared
in Olds's second volume,* The Dead and the Living. *The book is a
sort of biography of its speaker, who seems to be Olds herself. We learn
of the speaker's alcoholic, abusive father; her suffering mother and
sister; her miscarriage and abortion. The two poems are among the
"Poems for the Living." "Sex without Love," in a sequence called "The
Men," is sandwiched between two poems describing sexual ecstasy
between the speaker and her husband—that is, sex with love—which
should help you determine the speaker's tone. "The One Girl at the
Boys' Party" is one of twenty poems about "The Children." "I Go
Back to May 1937" appeared in Olds's 1987* The Gold Cell, *and of
the poems here it best exemplifies her confessional style. Perhaps more
than any other living poet, Olds frankly reveals the intimate thoughts
and feelings most of us refuse to acknowledge.*

Sex without Love

How do they do it, the ones who make love
without love? Beautiful as dancers,
gliding over each other like ice-skaters
over the ice, fingers hooked
inside each other's bodies, faces   5
red as steak, wine, wet as the
children at birth whose mothers are going to
give them away. How do they come to the
come to the come to the God come to the
still waters, and not love   10
the one who came there with them, light
rising slowly as steam off their joined
skin? These are the true religious,

the purists, the pros, the ones who will not
accept a false Messiah, love the   15
priest instead of the God. They do not
mistake the lover for their own pleasure,
they are like great runners: they know they are alone
with the road surface, the cold, the wind,
the fit of their shoes, their over-all cardio-   20
vascular health—just factors, like the partner
in the bed, and not the truth, which is the
single body alone in the universe
against its own best time.

1984

The One Girl at the Boys' Party

When I take our girl to the swimming party
I set her down among the boys. They tower and
bristle, she stands there smooth and sleek,
her math scores unfolding in the air around her.
They will strip to their suits, her body hard and   5
indivisible as a prime number,
they'll plunge in the deep end, she'll subtract
her height from ten feet, divide it into
hundreds of gallons of water, the numbers
bouncing in her mind like molecules of chlorine   10
in the bright blue pool. When they climb out,
her ponytail will hand its pencil lead
down her back, her narrow silk suit
with hamburgers and french fries printed on it
will glisten in the brilliant air, and they will   15
see her sweet face, solemn and
sealed, a factor of one, and she will
see their eyes, two each,
their legs, two each, and the curves of their sexes,
one each, and in her head she'll be doing her   20
wild multiplying, as the drops
sparkle and fall to the power of a thousand from her body.

1984

I Go Back to May 1937

I see them standing at the formal gates of their colleges,
I see my father strolling out
under the ochre sandstone arch, the
red tiles glinting like bent
plates of blood behind his head, I   5
see my mother with a few light books at her hip
standing at the pillar made of tiny bricks with the
wrought-iron gate still open behind her, its
sword-tips black in the May air,
they are about to graduate, they are about to get married,   10
they are kids, they are dumb, all they know is they are
innocent, they would never hurt anybody.
I want to go up to them and say Stop,
don't do it—she's the wrong woman,
he's the wrong man, you are going to do things   15
you cannot imagine you would ever do,
you are going to do bad things to children,
you are going to suffer in ways you never heard of,
you are going to want to die. I want to go
up to them there in the late May sunlight and say it,   20
her hungry pretty blank face turning to me,
her pitiful beautiful untouched body,
his arrogant handsome blind face turning to me,
his pitiful beautiful untouched body,
but I don't do it. I want to live. I   25
take them up like the male and female
paper dolls and bang them together
at the hips like chips of flint as if to
strike sparks from them, I say
Do what you are going to do, and I will tell about it.   30

1987

Judith Ortiz Cofer

b. 1952

> *"The Latin Deli: An Ars Poetica" provides a title for Ortiz Cofer's 1993 book—the subtitle is* Telling the Lives of Barrio Women—*and it begins that collection of poems, memoirs, and stories, occupying the space of a preface or perhaps an invocation of the muse. The poem and the analogy of the deli itself illustrate what's sometimes invisible from a mainstream perspective: the multiplicity of cultures and experiences that make up Hispanic America. Pay careful attention to how language functions for these economic and political exiles. You might compare the significance of language in this poem to that in Diaz's "Abecedarian Requiring Further Examination."*

The Latin Deli: An Ars Poetica

Presiding over a formica counter,
plastic Mother and Child[1] magnetized
to the top of an ancient register,
the heady mix of smells from the open bins
of dried codfish, the green plantains   5
hanging in stalks like votive offerings,
she is the Patroness of Exiles,
a woman of no-age who was never pretty,
who spends her days selling canned memories
while listening to the Puerto Ricans complain   10
that it would be cheaper to fly to San Juan
than to buy a pound of Bustelo coffee here,
and to Cubans perfecting their speech
of a "glorious return" to Havana—where no one
has been allowed to die and nothing to change until then;   15
to Mexicans who pass through, talking lyrically
of *dólares* to be made in El Norte—
                                        all wanting the comfort
of spoken Spanish, to gaze upon the family portrait
of her plain wide face, her ample bosom   20
resting on her plump arms, her look of maternal interest
as they speak to her and each other

---

1. Statuette of Saint Mary and the baby Jesus.

of their dreams and their disillusions—
how she smiles understanding,
when they walk down the narrow aisles of her store   25
reading the labels of packages aloud, as if
they were the names of lost lovers: *Suspiros*,
Merengues,[2] the stale candy of everyone's childhood.
                                     She spends her days
slicing *jamón y queso* and wrapping it in wax paper   30
tied with string: plain ham and cheese
that would cost less at the A&P,[3] but it would not satisfy
the hunger of the fragile old man lost in the folds
of his winter coat, who brings her lists of items
that he reads to her like poetry, or the others,   35
whose needs she must divine, conjuring up products
from places that now exist only in their hearts—
closed ports she must trade with.

                                            1993

Wilfred Owen

1893–1918

    Owen enlisted in the British Army to fight the Germans in World War I, was dispatched to the front, sickened, and was sent to Scotland to recuperate, where he wrote "Dulce Et Decorum Est" in October 1917. Originally he dedicated it to Jessie Pope, an author of children's books and editor of patriotic war poems; Pope is probably the "friend" in line 25. Owen was returned to the front and killed a week before the cease-fire. This poem was not published until 1920, when it came to be heard as, essentially, the plea of a dead soldier.

Dulce Et Decorum Est

Bent double, like old beggars under sacks,
Knock-kneed, coughing like hags, we cursed through sludge,
Till on the haunting flares we turned our backs
And towards our distant rest began to trudge.

   2. Also called suspiros (line 27); meringue sweets.   3. Chain of supermarkets in the Mid-Atlantic region of the United States.

Men marched asleep. Many had lost their boots   5
But limped on, blood-shod. All went lame; all blind;
Drunk with fatigue; deaf even to the hoots
Of tired, outstripped Five-Nines[1] that dropped behind.

Gas! Gas! Quick, boys!—An ecstasy of fumbling,
Fitting the clumsy helmets just in time;   10
But someone still was yelling out and stumbling,
And flound'ring like a man in fire or lime . . .
Dim, through the misty panes[2] and thick green light,
As under a green sea, I saw him drowning.

In all my dreams, before my helpless sight,   15
He plunges at me, guttering, choking, drowning.
If in smothering dreams you too could pace
Behind the wagon that we flung him in,
And watch the white eyes writhing in his face,
His hanging face, like a devil's sick of sin;   20
If you could hear, at every jolt, the blood
Come gargling from the froth-corrupted lungs,
Obscene as cancer, bitter as the cud
Of vile, incurable sores on innocent tongues,—
My friend, you would not tell with such high zest   25
To children ardent for some desperate glory,
The old Lie: Dulce et decorum est
Pro patria mori.[3]

1920

Marge Piercy
b. 1936

*In her poetry and prose, Piercy engages with social myths that she
believes inform the behavior of women and men. She has rewrit-
ten traditional stories and, in "Barbie doll," offers a critical look
at a female icon. "Barbie doll" eschews subtlety in favor of shock,*

1. I.e., 5.9-inch caliber shells.
2. Of the gas mask's celluloid window.

3. Owen translated this popular Latin
motto as "It is sweet and meet to die for
one's country. Sweet and decorous!"

but this poem is more complex than you might at first think. For example, it seems obvious that we are meant to read the last two lines ironically. But why does Piercy use the word consummation *rather than* ending? *The third stanza compares the woman's good nature to a fan belt—a striking metaphor. How are the two similar? What does a fan belt do? How does it wear out?*

Barbie doll

This girlchild was born as usual
and presented dolls that did pee-pee
and miniature GE stoves and irons
and wee lipsticks the color of cherry candy.
Then in the magic of puberty, a classmate said: 5
You have a great big nose and fat legs.

She was healthy, tested intelligent,
possessed strong arms and back,
abundant sexual drive and manual dexterity.
She went to and fro apologizing.   10
Everyone saw a fat nose on thick legs.

She was advised to play coy,
exhorted to come on hearty,
exercise, diet, smile and wheedle.
Her good nature wore out   15
like a fan belt.
So she cut off her nose and her legs
and offered them up.

In the casket displayed on satin she lay
with the undertaker's cosmetics painted on,   20
a turned-up putty nose,
dressed in a pink and white nightie.
Doesn't she look pretty? everyone said.
Consummation at last.
To every woman a happy ending.   25

1973

Sylvia Plath

1932–1963

> *In England on a Fulbright scholarship, at twenty-four years old, Plath married the British poet Ted Hughes. She finished writing "Metaphors" on March 20, 1959, just after she discovered to her disappointment that she wasn't pregnant. "Daddy" was written on October 12, 1962, shortly after she decided to divorce Hughes. "Lady Lazarus" was written in the same month, and it references Plath's suicide attempt when she was in college. Most critics, however, do not consider either of these poems to be truly confessional—that is, they are not strictly autobiographical; references, for example, to Nazi concentration camps and their crematoria suggests that "Daddy" is a fictional apostrophe, and "Lady Lazarus" is a dramatic monologue. Nevertheless, when she finished "Daddy," Plath declared, "It is over. . . . My life can begin." But before "Daddy" appeared in print, Plath, who was living in London with her two young children, committed suicide. She was thirty.*

Metaphors

I'm a riddle in nine syllables,
An elephant, a ponderous house,
A melon strolling on two tendrils.
O red fruit, ivory, fine timbers!
This loaf's big with its yeasty rising.   5
Money's new-minted in this fat purse.
I'm a means, a stage, a cow in calf.
I've eaten a bag of green apples,
Boarded the train there's no getting off.

1961

Lady Lazarus

I have done it again.
One year in every ten
I manage it—

A sort of walking miracle, my skin
Bright as a Nazi lampshade,[1]   5
My right foot

A paperweight,
My face a featureless, fine
Jew linen.

Peel off the napkin   10
O my enemy.
Do I terrify?—

The nose, the eye pits, the full set of teeth?
The sour breath
Will vanish in a day.   15

Soon, soon the flesh
The grave cave ate will be
At home on me

And I a smiling woman.
I am only thirty.   20
And like the cat I have nine times to die.

This is Number Three.
What a trash
To annihilate each decade.

What a million filaments.   25
The peanut-crunching crowd
Shoves in to see

Them unwrap me hand and foot—
The big strip tease.
Gentleman, ladies,   30

1. It was commonly believed after World War II that the Nazis had used the skin of Jews killed at the concentration camp in Buchenwald to make lampshades.

These are my hands,
My knees.
I may be skin and bone,

Nevertheless, I am the same, identical woman.
The first time it happened I was ten.   35
It was an accident.

The second time I meant
To last it out and not come back at all.
I rocked shut

As a seashell.   40
They had to call and call
And pick the worms off me like sticky pearls.

Dying
Is an art, like everything else.
I do it exceptionally well.   45

I do it so it feels like hell.
I do it so it feels real.
I guess you could say I've a call.

It's easy enough to do it in a cell.
It's easy enough to do it and stay put.   50
It's the theatrical

Comeback in broad day
To the same place, the same face, the same brute
Amused shout:

"A miracle!"   55
That knocks me out.
There is a charge

For the eyeing of my scars, there is a charge
For the hearing of my heart—
It really goes.   60

And there is a charge, a very large charge,
For a word or a touch
Or a bit of blood

Or a piece of my hair or my clothes.
So, so, Herr Doktor.   65
So, Herr Enemy.

I am your opus,
I am your valuable,
The pure gold baby

That melts to a shriek.   70
I turn and burn.
Do not think I underestimate your great concern.

Ash, ash—
You poke and stir.
Flesh, bone, there is nothing there—   75

A cake of soap,
A wedding ring,
A gold filling.

Herr God, Herr Lucifer,
Beware   80
Beware.

Out of the ash
I rise with my red hair
And I eat men like air.

                              1965

Daddy

You do not do, you do not do
Any more, black shoe
In which I have lived like a foot

For thirty years, poor and white,
Barely daring to breathe or Achoo.   5

Daddy, I have had to kill you.
You died before I had time——
Marble-heavy, a bag full of God,
Ghastly statue with one gray toe[1]
Big as a Frisco seal   10

And a head in the freakish Atlantic
Where it pours bean green over blue
In the waters off beautiful Nauset.
I used to pray to recover you.
Ach, du.[2]   15

In the German tongue, in the Polish town
Scraped flat by the roller
Of wars, wars, wars.
But the name of the town is common.
My Polack friend   20

Says there are a dozen or two.
So I never could tell where you
Put your foot, your root,
I never could talk to you.
The tongue stuck in my jaw.   25

It stuck in a barb wire snare.
Ich, ich, ich, ich,[3]
I could hardly speak.
I thought every German was you.
And the language obscene   30

An engine, an engine
Chuffing me off like a Jew.

1. Plath's father's toe turned black from gangrene.   2. Ah, you (German).

3. I, I, I, I (German).

A Jew to Dachau, Auschwitz, Belsen.[4]
I began to talk like a Jew.
I think I may well be a Jew.   35

The snows of the Tyrol, the clear beer of Vienna
Are not very pure or true.
With my gypsy ancestress and my weird luck
And my Taroc pack[5] and my Taroc pack
I may be a bit of a Jew.   40

I have always been scared of *you*,
With your Luftwaffe,[6] your gobbledygoo.
And your neat moustache
And your Aryan eye, bright blue.
Panzer[7]-man, panzer-man, O You—   45

Not God but a swastika
So black no sky could squeak through.
Every woman adores a Fascist,
The boot in the face, the brute
Brute heart of a brute like you.   50

You stand at the blackboard, daddy,
In the picture I have of you,
A cleft in your chin instead of your foot
But no less a devil for that, no not
Any less the black man who   55

Bit my pretty red heart in two.
I was ten when they buried you.
At twenty I tried to die
And get back, back, back to you.
I thought even the bones would do.   60

---

4. German concentration camps where millions of Jews were murdered during World War II.

5. Tarot cards, used for fortune telling.

6. The German air force.

7. "Armor" (German); during World War II usually referring to the German armored tank corps.

But they pulled me out of the sack,
And they stuck me together with glue,
And then I knew what to do.
I made a model of you,
A man in black with a Meinkampf[8] look   65

And a love of the rack and the screw.
And I said I do, I do.
So daddy, I'm finally through.
The black telephone's off at the root,
The voices just can't worm through.   70

If I've killed one man, I've killed two—
The vampire who said he was you
And drank my blood for a year,
Seven years, if you want to know.
Daddy, you can lie back now.   75

There's a stake in your fat black heart
And the villagers never liked you.
They are dancing and stamping on you.
They always *knew* it was you.
Daddy, daddy, you bastard, I'm through.   80
                    1965

Li Po
701-762

> *Li Po grew up in the Sichuan Province of China and spent much of his life wandering the cities of the Yangzi River Valley. He participated in political intrigues in the court of the emperor and was at one point sentenced to death for treason before the sentence was commuted to exile; eventually, he was pardoned. Li lived a dissolute life, often drunk, and wrote poems celebrating the senses' delights.*

8. *Mein Kampf* (My struggle) is the title of Hitler's political autobiography and Nazi polemic, written before his rise to power.

American poet and critic Ezra Pound translated "Ch'ang-Kan Village Song" from a Japanese translation from the Chinese and published it under the title, "The River-Merchant's Wife: A Letter" (you can compare Hinton's translation here to Pound's on p. 255. Pound prized the crisp, precise images of this classic Chinese poet over the grander, often rhetorical and abstract flourishes of some Romantic and Victorian poets. Pound's boosterism helped popularize Li Po's style among twentieth-century Western poets.

Ch'ang-Kan Village Song[1]

These bangs not yet reaching my eyes,
I played at our gate, picking flowers,

and you came on your horse of bamboo,
circling the well, tossing green plums.

We lived together here in Ch'ang-kan,   5
two little people without suspicions.

At fourteen, when I became your wife,
so timid and betrayed I never smiled,

I faced wall and shadow, eyes downcast.
A thousand pleas: I ignored them all.   10

At fifteen, my scowl began to soften.
I wanted us mingled as dust and ash,

and you always stood fast here for me,
no tower vigils awaiting your return.

At sixteen, you sailed far off to distant   15
Yen-yü Rock in Ch'ü-t'ang Gorge,[2] fierce

---

1. Translated by David Hinton. Ch'ang-Kan is a town on the Yangtze River near today's Nanjing, not far from the coast.

2. A steep canyon on the Yangtze River, deep in China's interior in the Sichuan Province.

June waters impossible, and howling
gibbons called out into the heavens.

At our gate, where you lingered long,
moss buried your tracks one by one,   20

deep green moss I can't sweep away.
And autumn's come early. Leaves fall.

It's September now. Butterflies appear
in the west garden. They fly in pairs,

and it hurts. I sit heart-stricken   25
at the bloom of youth in my old face.

Before you start back from out beyond
all those gorges, send a letter home.

I'm not saying I'd go far to meet you,
no further than Ch'ang-feng Sands.   30
                                    750

Edgar Allan Poe
1809–1849

*Poe wrote "The Raven" in a deliberate attempt to become famous.
He didn't want the poem to be too high for popular or too low
for critical taste, so it is not surprising that between January and
March 1845, it was published both in a New York newspaper and
in two literary journals. "The Raven" earned him little money, but
it did establish Poe as a celebrity. Though ravens are conventionally
associated with evil, Poe's symbolism, like Coleridge's, is psychologi-
cal. Poe attempts to convey in the sound of the words the mel-
ancholy and foreboding felt by the speaker. Likewise, in "Annabel
Lee," Poe wants the sound of the poem to help convey its mean-
ing. Meaning, then, is as much a mood as it is an idea. Poe wrote
"Annabel Lee" in May 1849, not long before he died.*

The Raven

Once upon a midnight dreary, while I pondered, weak and weary,
Over many a quaint and curious volume of forgotten lore—
While I nodded, nearly napping, suddenly there came a tapping,
As of some one gently rapping, rapping at my chamber door.
" 'Tis some visiter," I muttered, "tapping at my chamber door—   5
                Only this and nothing more."

Ah, distinctly I remember it was in the bleak December;
And each separate dying ember wrought its ghost upon the floor.
Eagerly I wished the morrow;—vainly I had sought to borrow
From my books surcease of sorrow—sorrow for the lost
    Lenore—   10
For the rare and radiant maiden whom the angels name
    Lenore—
                Nameless *here* for evermore.

And the silken, sad, uncertain rustling of each purple curtain
Thrilled me—filled me with fantastic terrors never felt before;
So that now, to still the beating of my heart, I stood repeating   15
" 'Tis some visiter entreating entrance at my chamber door—
Some late visiter entreating entrance at my chamber door;—
                This it is and nothing more."

Presently my soul grew stronger; hesitating then no longer,
"Sir," said I, "or Madam, truly your forgiveness I implore;   20
But the fact is I was napping, and so gently you came rapping,
And so faintly you came tapping, tapping at my chamber door,
That I scarce was sure I heard you"—here I opened wide the
    door;—
                Darkness there and nothing more.

Deep into that darkness peering, long I stood there wondering,
    fearing,   25
Doubting, dreaming dreams no mortal ever dared to dream
    before;

But the silence was unbroken, and the stillness gave no token,
And the only word there spoken was the whispered word,
    "Lenore?"
This I whispered, and an echo murmured back the word,
    "Lenore!"
                Merely this and nothing more.   30

Back into the chamber turning, all my soul within me burning,
Soon again I heard a tapping somewhat louder than before.
"Surely," said I, "surely that is something at my window lattice;
Let me see, then, what thereat is, and this mystery explore—
Let my heart be still a moment and this mystery explore;—   35
              'Tis the wind and nothing more!"

Open here I flung the shutter, when, with many a flirt and
    flutter,
In there stepped a stately Raven of the saintly days of yore;
Not the least obeisance made he; not a minute stopped or
    stayed he;
But, with mien of lord or lady, perched above my chamber
    door—
                           40
Perched upon a bust of Pallas[1] just above my chamber door—
           Perched, and sat, and nothing more.

Then this ebony bird beguiling my sad fancy into smiling,
By the grave and stern decorum of the countenance it wore,
"Though thy crest be shorn and shaven, thou," I said, "art sure
    no craven,   45
Ghastly grim and ancient Raven wandering from the Nightly
    shore—
Tell me what thy lordly name is on the Night's Plutonian[2]
    shore!"
           Quoth the Raven "Nevermore."

Much I marvelled this ungainly fowl to hear discourse so plainly,
Though its answer little meaning—little relevancy bore;   50

---

1. Athena, Greek goddess of wisdom and the arts.   2. Black. Pluto was the Greek god of the underworld.

For we cannot help agreeing that no living human being
Ever yet was blessed with seeing bird above his chamber door—
Bird or beast upon the sculptured bust above his chamber door,
                    With such name as "Nevermore."

But the Raven, sitting lonely on the placid bust, spoke only   55
That one word, as if his soul in that one word he did outpour.
Nothing farther then he uttered—not a feather then he
    fluttered—
Till I scarcely more than muttered "Other friends have flown
    before—
On the morrow *he* will leave me, as my Hopes have flown
    before."
                    Then the bird said "Nevermore."   60

Startled at the stillness broken by reply so aptly spoken,
"Doubtless," said I, "what it utters is its only stock and store
Caught from some unhappy master whom unmerciful Disaster
Followed fast and followed faster till his songs one burden bore—
Till the dirges of his Hope that melancholy burden bore   65
                    Of 'Never—nevermore.' "

But the Raven still beguiling my sad fancy into smiling,
Straight I wheeled a cushioned seat in front of bird, and bust
    and door;
Then, upon the velvet sinking, I betook myself to linking
Fancy unto fancy, thinking what this ominous bird of yore—   70
What this grim, ungainly, ghastly, gaunt, and ominous bird of
    yore
                    Meant in croaking "Nevermore."

This I sat engaged in guessing, but no syllable expressing
To the fowl whose fiery eyes now burned into my bosom's core;
This and more I sat divining, with my head at ease reclining   75
On the cushion's velvet lining that the lamp-light gloated o'er,
But whose velvet-violet lining with the lamp-light gloating o'er,
                    She shall press, ah, nevermore!

Then, methought, the air grew denser, perfumed from an
    unseen censer
Swung by seraphim whose foot-falls tinkled on the tufted
    floor.   80
"Wretch," I cried, "thy God hath lent thee—by these angels he
    hath sent thee
Respite—respite and nepenthe[3] from thy memories of Lenore;
Quaff, oh quaff this kind nepenthe and forget this lost Lenore!"
              Quoth the Raven "Nevermore."

"Prophet!" said I, "thing of evil!—prophet still, if bird or
    devil!—   85
Whether Tempter sent, or whether tempest tossed thee here
    ashore,
Desolate yet all undaunted, on this desert land enchanted—
On this home by Horror haunted—tell me truly, I implore—
Is there—*is* there balm in Gilead?—tell me—tell me, I
    implore!"
              Quoth the Raven "Nevermore."   90

"Prophet!" said I, "thing of evil!—prophet still, if bird or devil!
By that Heaven that bends above us—by that God we both
    adore—
Tell this soul with sorrow laden if, within the distant Aidenn,
It shall clasp a sainted maiden whom the angels name
    Lenore—
Clasp a rare and radiant maiden whom the angels name
    Lenore."   95
              Quoth the Raven "Nevermore."

"Be that word our sign of parting, bird or fiend!" I shrieked,
    upstarting—
"Get thee back into the tempest and the Night's Plutonian
    shore!
Leave no black plume as a token of that lie thy soul hath
    spoken!

---

3. Oblivion-inducing drug.

Leave my loneliness unbroken!—quit the bust above my door!   100
Take thy beak from out my heart, and take thy form from off
   my door!"
                 Quoth the Raven "Nevermore."

And the Raven, never flitting, still is sitting, *still* is sitting
On the pallid bust of Pallas just above my chamber door;
And his eyes have all the seeming of a demon's that is
   dreaming,   105
And the lamp-light o'er him streaming throws his shadow on
   the floor;
And my soul from out that shadow that lies floating on the
   floor
              Shall be lifted—nevermore!
                   1845

Annabel Lee

It was many and many a year ago,
   In a kingdom by the sea,
That a maiden there lived whom you may know
   By the name of Annabel Lee;
And this maiden she lived with no other thought   5
   Than to love and be loved by me.

She was a child and *I* was a child,
   In this kingdom by the sea,
But we loved with a love that was more than love—
   I and my Annabel Lee—   10
With a love that the wingéd seraphs of Heaven
   Coveted her and me.

And this was the reason that, long ago,
   In this kingdom by the sea,
A wind blew out of a cloud by night   15
   Chilling my Annabel Lee;
So that her highborn kinsmen came
   And bore her away from me,

To shut her up in a sepulchre
    In this kingdom by the sea.   20

The angels, not half so happy in Heaven,
    Went envying her and me:
Yes! that was the reason (as all men know,
    In this kingdom by the sea)
That the wind came out of the cloud, chilling   25
    And killing my Annabel Lee.

But our love it was stronger by far than the love
    Of those who were older than we—
    Of many far wiser than we—
And neither the angels in Heaven above   30
    Nor the demons down under the sea,
Can ever dissever my soul from the soul
    Of the beautiful Annabel Lee:

For the moon never beams without bringing me dreams
    Of the beautiful Annabel Lee;   35
And the stars never rise but I see the bright eyes
    Of the beautiful Annabel Lee;
And so, all the night-tide, I lie down by the side
Of my darling, my darling, my life and my bride,
    In her sepulchere there by the sea—   40
    In her tomb by the side of the sea.

                           1849, 1850

Ezra Pound

1885–1972

> *In 1915, Pound translated a number of poems from Chinese ideo-graphs, and with these poems—which deposit all meaning in con-crete images—he meant to release himself from what he considered the tyranny of iambic pentameter. The rhythm of "The River-Merchant's Wife: A Letter," which is a translation of an eighth-century poem by Li Po, is based on syntax, not meter. The rhythmic*

unit is the sentence, not the foot, and it typically makes up a single line. For "In a Station of the Metro," Pound borrowed the technique of juxtaposed images from Japanese haiku (a three-line poem of five, seven, and five syllables). He attempted to express through the image of the petals what he felt watching beautiful faces, one after another, emerge from the Concorde station of the Paris subway. The image of the petals is meant to be equivalent to the emotion he wanted to express.

The River-Merchant's Wife: A Letter

While my hair was still cut straight across my forehead
I played about the front gate, pulling flowers.
You came by on bamboo stilts, playing horse,
You walked about my seat, playing with blue plums.

And we went on living in the village of Chokan: 5
Two small people, without dislike or suspicion.
At fourteen I married My Lord you.
I never laughed, being bashful.
Lowering my head, I looked at the wall.
Called to, a thousand times, I never looked back.   10

At fifteen I stopped scowling,
I desired my dust to be mingled with yours
Forever and forever and forever.
Why should I climb the look out?

At sixteen you departed,   15
You went into far Ku-to-yen, by the river of swirling eddies,
And you have been gone five months.
The monkeys make sorrowful noise overhead.

You dragged your feet when you went out.
By the gate now, the moss is grown, the different mosses,   20
Too deep to clear them away!
The leaves fall early this autumn, in wind.
The paired butterflies are already yellow with August

Over the grass in the West garden;
They hurt me. I grow older.   25
If you are coming down through the narrows of the river
    Kiang,
Please let me know beforehand,
And I will come out to meet you
                As far as Cho-fu-Sa.

                                By *Rihaku*
                                 1915

In a Station of the Metro

The apparition of these faces in the crowd;
Petals on a wet, black bough.
                           1916

D. A. Powell
b. 1963

    "Mass for Pentecost: Canticle for Birds & Water" *is the last in Powell's*
Useless Landscape or a Guide for Boys *(2012), a collection of poems
that oscillate between the rural Central Valley of California and the
gay community of San Francisco. Jumbled together are the hedonism
of the 1980s laced with the intimations of mortality brought on by
the AIDS epidemic as well as the natural imagery of the countryside
and the rich symbolism and rituals of Catholicism. A canticle is a
song, such as a hymn, fashioned from verses in the Bible. In the Chris-
tian calendar, Pentecost Sunday ends the Easter season. According to
the New Testament, the resurrected Jesus remained on Earth until
Ascension Thursday, forty days after Easter, when he ascended into
Heaven. Ten days later, somewhat fearful and lost, the disciples holed
up in an upper room, when the Holy Spirit descended upon them in
fire and wind, inspiring them to spread the word of Christ.*

Mass for Pentecost: Canticle for Birds & Waters

There is no cause to grieve among the living or the dead,
    so long as there is music in the air.

And where the water and the air divide, I'll take you there.
    The levee aureate with yellow thistles.
White moth, wasp and dragonfly.   5
        We could not wish unless it were on wings.
Give us our means and point us toward the sun.

Will the spirit come to us now in the pewter paten[1] of the air,
        the fluted call of dabbler drakes, the deadpan honk
            of the white-fronted goose, the tule goose.   10
Tongues confused in the matchstick rushes.
        High, high the baldpate cries, and in the air,
and in the air, the red-winged blackbirds chase the damselflies.

Triumph over death with me. And we'll divide the air.

                                                    2011

John Crowe Ransom
1888–1974

> As a college professor, Ransom trained a generation of southern
> writers who formed the core of the New Critical movement in liter-
> ature. Aristocratic and traditional in politics and culture, the New
> Critics instituted the methods of close reading still taught in most
> English departments, though their insistence on a poem's autonomy
> from its poet and from its cultural context is largely rejected today.
> Ransom wrote "Bells for John Whiteside's Daughter" in the spring
> of 1924 after he watched a neighbor's daughter playing outside and
> imagined the aftermath of her death.

Bells for John Whiteside's Daughter

There was such speed in her little body,
And such lightness in her footfall,

---

1. In a Catholic Mass, a metal plate on which the bread (the host) rests while it is conse-
crated. In the language of Catholic theology, after transubstantiation the paten and chalice
become the sepulcher for the body and blood of Christ.

It is no wonder her brown study[1]
Astonishes us all.

Her wars were bruited[2] in our high window.   5
We looked among orchard trees and beyond
Where she took arms against her shadow,
Or harried unto the pond

The lazy geese, like a snow cloud
Dripping their snow on the green grass,   10
Tricking and stopping, sleepy and proud,
Who cried in goose, Alas,

For the tireless heart within the little
Lady with rod that made them rise
From their noon apple-dreams and scuttle   15
Goose-fashion under the skies!

But now go the bells, and we are ready,
In one house we are sternly stopped
To say we are vexed at her brown study,
Lying so primly propped.   20

                        1924

Adrienne Rich
1929–2012

   "Aunt Jennifer's Tigers" was published in the 1951 volume A
Change of World. *In his foreword to that book, W. H. Auden
wrote that Rich's poems "are neatly and modestly dressed, speak qui-
etly but do not mumble, respect their elders but are not cowed by
them." Though such a poem as this displays Rich's dominant theme,
her early poetry was mostly noted for being precise, tightly wrought,
and, in comparison to her later work, politically unthreatening.*

---

   1. Moody or even melancholic state of   2. I.e., loudly voiced.
deep thought.

"Diving into the Wreck" is the title poem of Rich's collection of poems from 1971 to 1972, which won the National Book Award. It firmly established her as a great American poet, with some critics calling the poem "a modern classic," others considering it one of the great poems of the age. But that volume also made Rich a lightning rod for political debate. "The School Among the Ruins," the title poem of Rich's collection of poems from 2000 to 2004, and "Transparencies," also from that collection, exhibit the same passion and political engagement that "Diving into the Wreck" announced thirty years earlier.

Aunt Jennifer's Tigers

Aunt Jennifer's tigers prance across a screen,
Bright topaz denizens of a world of green.
They do not fear the men beneath the tree;
They pace in sleek chivalric certainty.

Aunt Jennifer's fingers fluttering through her wool   5
Find even the ivory needle hard to pull.
The massive weight of Uncle's wedding band
Sits heavily upon Aunt Jennifer's hand.

When Aunt is dead, her terrified hands will lie
Still ringed with ordeals she was mastered by.   10
The tigers in the panel that she made
Will go on prancing, proud and unafraid.

1951

Diving into the Wreck

First having read the book of myths,
and loaded the camera,
and checked the edge of the knife-blade,
I put on
the body-armor of black rubber   5
the absurd flippers

the grave and awkward mask.
I am having to do this
not like Cousteau with his
assiduous team   10
aboard the sun-flooded schooner
but here alone.

There is a ladder.
The ladder is always there
hanging innocently   15
close to the side of the schooner.
We know what it is for,
we who have used it.
Otherwise
it's a piece of maritime floss   20
some sundry equipment.

I go down.
Rung after rung and still
the oxygen immerses me
the blue light   25
the clear atoms
of our human air.
I go down.
My flippers cripple me,
I crawl like an insect down the ladder   30
and there is no one
to tell me when the ocean
will begin.

First the air is blue and then
it is bluer and then green and then   35
black I am blacking out and yet
my mask is powerful
it pumps my blood with power
the sea is another story
the sea is not a question of power   40
I have to learn alone

to turn my body without force
in the deep element.

And now: it is easy to forget
what I came for   45
among so many who have always
lived here
swaying their crenellated fans
between the reefs
and besides   50
you breathe differently down here.

I came to explore the wreck.
The words are purposes.
The words are maps.
I came to see the damage that was done   55
and the treasures that prevail.
I stroke the beam of my lamp
slowly along the flank
of something more permanent
than fish or weed   60

the thing I came for:
the wreck and not the story of the wreck
the thing itself and not the myth
the drowned face always staring
toward the sun   65
the evidence of damage
worn by salt and sway into this threadbare beauty
the ribs of the disaster
curving their assertion
among the tentative haunters.   70

This is the place.
And I am here, the mermaid whose dark hair
streams black, the merman in his armored body
We circle silently
about the wreck   75

we dive into the hold
I am she: I am he

whose drowned face sleeps with open eyes
whose breasts still bear the stress
whose silver, copper, vermeil cargo lies   80
obscurely inside barrels
half-wedged and left to rot
we are the half-destroyed instruments
that once held to a course
the water-eaten log   85
the fouled compass

We are, I am, you are
by cowardice or courage
the one who find our way
back to this scene   90
carrying a knife, a camera
a book of myths
in which
our names do not appear.

                                        1972
                                          .

The School Among the Ruins

     Beirut.Baghdad.Sarajevo.Bethlehem.Kabul. Not of course here.

                    I

Teaching the first lesson and the last
—great falling light of summer will you last
longer than schooltime?
When children flow
in columns at the doors   5
BOYS GIRLS and the busy teachers

open or close high windows
with hooked poles   drawing darkgreen shades

closets unlocked, locked
questions unasked, asked, when   10

love of the fresh impeccable
sharp-pencilled   yes
order without cruelty

a street on earth   neither heaven nor hell
busy with commerce and worship   15
young teachers walking to school

fresh bread and early-open foodstalls

                              2

When the offensive rocks the sky when nightglare
misconstrues day and night when lived-in
rooms from the upper city   20
tumble cratering lower streets

cornices of olden ornament   human debris
when fear vacuums out the streets

When the whole town flinches
blood on the undersole thickening to glass   25

Whoever crosses   hunched   knees bent   a contested zone
knows why she does this suicidal thing

School's now in session day and night
children sleep
in the classrooms   teachers rolled close   30

                              3

How the good teacher loved
his school   the students
the lunchroom with fresh sandwiches

lemonade and milk
the classroom   glass cages   35
of moss and turtles
teaching responsibility

A morning breaks without bread or fresh-poured milk
parents or lesson plans

diarrhea first question of the day   40
children shivering   it's September
Second question: where is my mother?

                                4

One: I don't know where your mother
is   Two: I don't know
why they are trying to hurt us   45
Three: or the latitude and longitude
of their hatred   Four: I don't know if we
hate them as much   I think there's more toilet paper
in the supply closet   I'm going to break it open
Today this is your lesson: 50
write as clearly as you can
your name   home street   and number
down on this page
No you can't go home yet
but you aren't lost   55
this is our school

I'm not sure what we'll eat
we'll look for healthy roots and greens
searching for water though the pipes are broken   60

                                5

There's a young cat sticking
her head through window bars

she's hungry like us
but can feed on mice
her bronze erupting fur
speaks of a life already wild   65

her golden eyes
don't give quarter   She'll teach us   Let's call her
Sister
when we get milk we'll give her some

6

I've told you, let's try to sleep in this funny camp   70
All night pitiless pilotless things go shrieking
above us to somewhere

Don't let your faces turn to stone
Don't stop asking me why
Let's pay attention to our cat   she needs us   75

Maybe tomorrow the bakers can fix their ovens

7

"We sang them to naps   told stories   made
shadow-animals with our hands

wiped human debris off boots and coats
sat learning by heart the names   80
some were too young to write
some had forgotten how"
2001

Transparencies

That the meek word like the righteous word can bully
that an Israeli soldier interviewed years

after the first Intifada[1] could mourn on camera
what under orders he did, saw done, did not refuse
that another leaving Beit Jala[2] could scrawl   5
on a wall: *We are truely sorry for the mess we made*
is merely routine   word that would cancel deed
That human equals innocent and guilty
That we grasp for innocence whether or no
is elementary   That words can translate into broken bones   10
That the power to hurl words is a weapon
That the body can be a weapon
any child on playground knows   That asked your favorite
                                       word in a game

you always named a thing, a quality, *freedom* or *river*   15
(never a pronoun never *God* or *War*)
is taken for granted   That word and body
are all we have to lay on the line
That words are windowpanes in a ransacked hut, smeared
by time's dirty rains, we might argue   20
likewise that words are clear as glass till the sun strikes it
                                       blinding

But that in a dark windowpane you have seen your face
That when you wipe your glasses the text grows clearer
That the sound of crunching glass comes at the height of the
                                       wedding   25

That I can look through glass
into my neighbor's house
but not my neighbor's life
That glass is sometimes broken to save lives
That a word can be crushed like a goblet underfoot   30
is only what it seems, part question, part answer: how
                                       you live it

                                                   2002

1. A large-scale uprising from 1987 to 1993 of Palestinians in Gaza, the West Bank, and Jerusalem against Israeli rule. Over a thousand Palestinians were killed in the fighting with Israeli troops.
2. A small city on the West Bank.

Edwin Arlington Robinson
1869–1935

> *In 1897 Robinson published at his own expense* The Children of
> the Night, *which included "Richard Cory." The book was largely
> ignored until President Theodore Roosevelt happened across a copy
> and, attracted by what he considered a masculine style and pro-
> gressive sentiments, started promoting Robinson—to the chagrin of
> some members of the literary community, who thought Robinson
> was second rate. Many poets in the twentieth century, following
> the lead of Eliot and Pound, thought that if a poem was straight-
> forward and appealed to the mass market, it must be bad. Thus
> "Richard Cory" provides a good opportunity to reflect on poetry's
> purpose and definition.*

Richard Cory

Whenever Richard Cory went down town,
We people on the pavement looked at him:
He was a gentleman from sole to crown,
Clean favored, and imperially slim.

And he was always quietly arrayed,   5
And he was always human when he talked;
But still he fluttered pulses when he said,
"Good-morning," and he glittered when he walked.

And he was rich—yes, richer than a king—
And admirably schooled in every grace: 10
In fine, we thought that he was everything
To make us wish that we were in his place.

So on we worked, and waited for the light,
And went without the meat, and cursed the bread;
And Richard Cory, one calm summer night,   15
Went home and put a bullet through his head.

1869

Mary Robinson
1758–1800

"January, 1795" should be placed in the company of other Roman-
tic poems, such as Wordsworth's "The World Is Too Much with Us,"
Shelley's "Song (to the men of England)," and Blake's Songs of
Experience, *that describe the contemporary world, diagnosing the*
ills of the poet's society. Robinson's poem was composed at a time
when England's aristocracy was especially worried about popular
uprisings. Following the French Revolution in 1789, new modes
in politics and culture challenged what was often characterized by
Robinson's generation as the "old regime" throughout Europe.

January, 1795

Pavement slipp'ry, people sneezing,
Lords in ermine, beggars freezing;
Titled gluttons dainties carving,
Genius in a garret starving.

Lofty mansions, warm and spacious;   5
Courtiers cringing and voracious;
Misers scarce the wretched heeding;
Gallant soldiers fighting, bleeding.

Wives who laugh at passive spouses;
Theatres, and meeting-houses;
Balls, where simp'ring misses languish;   10
Hospitals, and groans of anguish.

Arts and sciences bewailing;
Commerce drooping, credit failing;
Placemen[1] mocking subjects loyal;   15
Separations, weddings royal.

Authors who can't earn a dinner;
Many a subtle rogue a winner;

1. Men who had government jobs given to them by virtue of their political party
affiliations.

Fugitives for shelter seeking;
Misers hoarding, tradesmen breaking. 20

Taste and talents quite deserted;
All the laws of truth perverted;
Arrogance o'er merit soaring;
Merit silently deploring.

Ladies gambling night and morning; 25
Fools the works of genius scorning;
Ancient dames for girls mistaken,
Youthful damsels quite forsaken.

Some in luxury delighting;
More in talking than in fighting; 30
Lovers old, and beaux decrepid;
Lordlings empty and insipid.

Poets, painters, and musicians;
Lawyers, doctors, politicians:
Pamphlets, newspapers, and odes, 35
Seeking fame by diff'rent roads.

Gallant souls with empty purses;
Gen'rals only fit for nurses;
School-boys, smit with martial spirit,
Taking place of vet'ran merit. 40

Honest men who can't get places,
Knaves who shew unblushing faces;
Ruin hasten'd, peace retarded;
Candor spurn'd, and art rewarded.
                    1806

Theodore Roethke
1908–1963

> Roethke's "Greenhouse Poems," which include "Root Cellar," reflect his childhood observations in Saginaw, Michigan, where his father owned a greenhouse. The bulbs and shoots are some of those "minimal creatures" in which Roethke delighted and which characterize most of his poetry. What raises this poem above mere (though vivid) description is that it joins "evil" to these things that would not "give up life." "My Papa's Waltz" initiated a group of seven autobiographical poems that express the poet's dissatisfaction with human society. Even so, it is very difficult to determine the speaker's attitude toward his father. "The Waking" is one of the few examples in this volume of a villanelle, an unusual form of three-line stanzas, with the last line of each a repetition.

Root Cellar

Nothing would sleep in that cellar, dank as a ditch,
Bulbs broke out of boxes hunting for chinks in the dark,
Shoots dangled and drooped,
Lolling obscenely from mildewed crates,
Hung down long yellow evil necks, like tropical snakes.   5
And what a congress of stinks!
Roots ripe as old bait,
Pulpy stems, rank, silo-rich,
Leaf-mold, manure, lime, piled against slippery planks.
Nothing would give up life: 10
Even the dirt kept breathing a small breath.

1948

My Papa's Waltz

The whiskey on your breath
Could make a small boy dizzy;
But I hung on like death:
Such waltzing was not easy.

We romped until the pans   5
Slid from the kitchen shelf;
My mother's countenance
Could not unfrown itself.

The hand that held my wrist
Was battered on one knuckle;   10
At every step you missed
My right ear scraped a buckle.

You beat time on my head
With a palm caked hard by dirt,
Then waltzed me off to bed   15
Still clinging to your shirt.
                    1948

The Waking

I wake to sleep, and take my waking slow.
I feel my fate in what I cannot fear.
I learn by going where I have to go.

We think by feeling. What is there to know?
I hear my being dance from ear to ear.   5
I wake to sleep, and take my waking slow.

Of those so close beside me, which are you?
God bless the Ground! I shall walk softly there,
And learn by going where I have to go.

Light takes the Tree; but who can tell us how? 10
The lowly worm climbs up a winding stair;
I wake to sleep, and take my waking slow.

Great Nature has another thing to do
To you and me; so take the lively air,
And, lovely, learn by going where to go.   15

This shaking keeps me steady. I should know.
What falls away is always. And is near.
I wake to sleep, and take my waking slow.
I learn by going where I have to go.

                                        1953

Emily Rosko
b. 1979

The first word in the first poem of Rosko's first collection, Raw
Goods Inventory *(2006) is* detritus, *which Rosko considers a
statement of her method. She presents little bits, fragments, images
that have washed up like things from the sea, not quite randomly
but not linked by a clear narrative either. Her method is related to
that used by Eliot in "J. Alfred Prufrock," and* The Waste Land,
*(and quite different from something like Hoagland's "History of
Desire," which relies on narrative as a cohesive principle); she
requires us to do half the work, to figure out how to make our own
sense of the fragments, thereby assigning the reader an important
role in producing the meaning of the poem. Still, the poet does pro-
vide directions; in an interview Rosko suggested that the titles of her
poems can guide the reader, as it does for "Even before your Elbow
knocked Over the Glass."*

Even before Your Elbow Knocked Over The Glass

First, there were the broken pieces.
You said, don't you think I know

what I'm doing? To which I replied,
don't you feel most alone when we're in

this together? Under the eave, wasps   5
are constructing a nest, gray paper

out of spit, so much of the body
is in their work. See how

the legs move, bending and praying.
You said, don't you think I know   10

when you're trying to change the subject?
I could make a building out of my despair.

We could acquire a nice piece of land
and sit on it. There are a thousand blades

of grass, each one waiting   15
to be claimed. As I always say,

you said, if you commit one sin, then
you commit them all. To which I said,

how many absolutes do we have proof
of? The sky has never looked bluer.   20

What is the significance of that?
It means I might walk out on you

yet. What, you asked. Nothing,
I said, I said nothing. What is there

to say anyway, except in the sunlight,   25
I could see the glass fall even before

your elbow knocked it over.
This is always how it happens, certain

ideas are never fully formed.
This is some mess, you said.   30

To which I said, there are lives
that go on this way. Then we went

down on our knees, and
in that manner, we began.

2003

Christina Rossetti
1830–1894

"After Death" was written in 1849 and is typical of Rossetti's early works' obsession with an early death. Though critics have tried, none have successfully linked her love poems to a real-life love affair. Her break with her fiancé, James Collinson, did not take place until the year after she wrote this poem, and the break came at her urging, not his. "A Birthday" was one of a few poems that Rossetti published in Macmillan's Magazine, *helping to launch her career, in 1861.*

After Death

The curtains were half drawn, the floor was swept
   And strewn with rushes, rosemary and may
   Lay thick upon the bed on which I lay,
Where thro' the lattice ivy-shadows crept.
He leaned above me, thinking that I slept   5
   And could not hear him; but I heard him say:
   "Poor child, poor child:" and as he turned away
Came a deep silence, and I knew he wept.

He did not touch the shroud, or raise the fold
   That hid my face, or take my hand in his,   10
     Or ruffle the smooth pillows for my head:
     He did not love me living; but once dead
   He pitied me; and very sweet it is
To know he still is warm tho' I am cold.
1849   *1862*

A Birthday

My heart is like a singing bird
   Whose nest is in a watered shoot;
My heart is like an apple tree
   Whose boughs are bent with thickset fruit;
My heart is like a rainbow shell   5

That paddles in a halcyon sea;
My heart is gladder than all these
Because my love is come to me.

Raise me a dais of silk and down;
   Hang it with vair and purple dyes;   10
Carve it in doves and pomegranates,
   And peacocks with a hundred eyes;
Work it in gold and silver grapes,
   In leaves and silver fleurs-de-lys;
Because the birthday of my life   15
   Is come, my love is come to me.
                 1861, 1862

Anne Sexton
1928–1974

> *Sexton is best known for her confessional poetry, which frankly exposes the intimate details of a woman's life. But "Her Kind" departs from Sexton's typically autobiographical technique by making an analogy with the historical persecution of witches. Coming from Boston, Sexton would have been well aware of the trials— and the consequent executions—of witches in seventeenth-century Massachusetts. Historians today believe that many "witches" were no more dangerous than women who somehow threatened a patriarchal order in society—midwives, for example, who offered people an alternative to credentialed doctors, especially by supplying women with folk methods of birth control.*

Her Kind

I have gone out, a possessed witch,
haunting the black air, braver at night;
dreaming evil, I have done my hitch
over the plain houses, light by light:
lonely thing, twelve-fingered, out of mind.   5
A woman like that is not a woman, quite.
I have been her kind.

I have found the warm caves in the woods,
filled them with skillets, carvings, shelves,
closets, silks, innumerable goods;   10
fixed the suppers for the worms and the elves:
whining, rearranging the disaligned.
A woman like that is misunderstood.
I have been her kind.

I have ridden in your cart, driver,   15
waved my nude arms at villages going by,
learning the last bright routes, survivor
where your flames still bite my thigh
and my ribs crack where your wheels wind.
A woman like that is not ashamed to die.   20
I have been her kind.

                                    1958

William Shakespeare

1564–1616

Readers have long argued the identities of the speaker and listener in his sonnets, but with so little evidence of Shakespeare's life no one can prove or disprove that the poems are autobiographical. The 1609 edition is dedicated "TO THE ONLIE BEGETTER OF THESE INSUING SONNETS MR W. H.," whose identity has eluded the most careful scholars. Many candidates have been suggested, but none has been proven. It is clear that in the first 126 sonnets an older man addresses a younger man and urges him to marry. The relationship between these two men is intimate—some readers think they are sexually intimate, others do not. Sonnet 18 gives us Shakespeare's version of a conventional poetic boast: that the poet bestows immortality on his subject. In Sonnet 29 Shakespeare continues lauding the young man. Here, his friendship refreshes the poet. Sonnet 73 is a fine example of how a Shakespearean sonnet can develop an idea in successive, related images, each expressed in a quatrain. Sonnet 116 speaks to the enduring quality of love. You may be able to detect in Sonnet 129 a tone different from

that in the preceding sonnets. This is because, in Sonnets 127–152,
the speaker addresses a female persona who has come to be called
"the dark lady" on account of her complexion and bawdy habits.
Sonnet 130 satirizes the conventions of love poetry that exaggerate
the beloved's beauty. The mistress is not necessarily ugly; these terms
seem so negative merely because they are realistic.

18

Shall I compare thee to a summer's day?
Thou art more lovely and more temperate:
Rough winds do shake the darling buds of May,
And summer's lease hath all too short a date;
Sometimes too hot the eye of heaven shines,   5
And often is his gold complexion dimmed;
And every fair from fair sometimes declines,
By chance or nature's changing course untrimmed;[1]
But thy eternal summer shall not fade,
Nor lose possession of that fair thou ow'st;   10
Nor shall death brag thou wand'rest in his shade,
When in eternal lines to Time thou grow'st:[2]
   So long as men can breathe, or eyes can see,
   So long lives this, and this gives life to thee.
1609

29

When, in disgrace with fortune and men's eyes,
I all alone beweep my outcast state,
And trouble deaf heaven with my bootless[1] cries,
And look upon myself, and curse my fate,
Wishing me like to one more rich in hope,   5
Featured like him, like him with friends possessed,
Desiring this man's art and that man's scope,

1. Divested of its beauty.   1. I.e., futile.
2. I.e., when you are grafted to Time in
this immortal poetry.

With what I most enjoy contented least;
Yet in these thoughts myself almost despising,
Haply I think on thee—and then my state,   10
Like to the lark at break of day arising
From sullen earth, sings hymns at heaven's gate;
    For thy sweet love rememb'red such wealth brings
    That then I scorn to change my state with kings.

1609

55

Not marble, nor the gilded monuments
Of princes, shall outlive this powerful rhyme;
But you shall shine more bright in these contents
Than unswept stone, besmeared with sluttish time.
When wasteful war shall statues overturn,   5
And broils root out the work of masonry,
Nor Mars his sword nor war's quick fire shall burn
The living record of your memory.
'Gainst death and all-oblivious enmity
Shall you pace forth; your praise shall still find room   10
Even in the eyes of all posterity
That wear this world out to the ending doom.
    So, till the judgment that yourself arise,
    You live in this, and dwell in lovers' eyes.

1609

73

That time of year thou mayst in me behold
When yellow leaves, or none, or few, do hang
Upon those boughs which shake against the cold,
Bare ruined choirs, where late the sweet birds sang.
In me thou see'st the twilight of such day   5
As after sunset fadeth in the west;
Which by and by black night doth take away,
Death's second self, that seals up all in rest.

In me thou see'st the glowing of such fire,
That on the ashes of his youth doth lie,   10
As the deathbed whereon it must expire,
Consumed with that which it was nourished by.
   This thou perceiv'st, which makes thy love more strong,
   To love that well which thou must leave ere long.
                                             1609

116

Let me not to the marriage of true minds
Admit impediments. Love is not love
Which alters when it alteration finds,
Or bends with the remover to remove:
Oh, no! it is an ever-fixèd mark,   5
That looks on tempests and is never shaken;
It is the star to every wandering bark,
Whose worth's unknown, although his height be taken.
Love's not Time's fool, though rosy lips and cheeks
Within his bending sickle's compass come;   10
Love alters not with his brief hours and weeks,
But bears it out even to the edge of doom.
   If this be error and upon me proved,
   I never writ, nor no man ever loved.
                                             1609

129

Th' expense of spirit in a waste of shame
Is lust in action; and till action, lust
Is perjured, murd'rous, bloody, full of blame,
Savage, extreme, rude, cruel, not to trust;
Enjoyed no sooner but despisèd straight: 5
Past reason hunted; and no sooner had,
Past reason hated, as a swallowed bait,
On purpose laid to make the taker mad:
Mad in pursuit, and in possession so;

Had, having, and in quest to have, extreme;   10
A bliss in proof and proved, a very woe;
Before, a joy proposed; behind, a dream.
    All this the world well knows; yet none knows well
    To shun the heaven that leads men to this hell.

1609

130

My mistress' eyes are nothing like the sun;
Coral is far more red than her lips' red;
If snow be white, why then her breasts are dun;[1]
If hairs be wires, black wires grow on her head.
I have seen roses damasked, red and white,   5
But no such roses see I in her cheeks;
And in some perfumes is there more delight
Than in the breath that from my mistress reeks.
I love to hear her speak, yet well I know
That music hath a far more pleasing sound;   10
I grant I never saw a goddess go;
My mistress, when she walks, treads on the ground.
    And yet, by heaven, I think my love as rare
    As any she belied with false compare.

1609

Percy Bysshe Shelley
1792–1822

> *In late 1817, Shelley and another poet, Horace Smith, challenged each other to write a poem about a statue of Ramses II, the Egyptian pharoah whom Moses and the Jews escaped in Exodus (Ozymandias is his Greek name). Shelley's poem, with obvious implications for contemporary politics (England had recently defeated Napoleon and so dominated Europe), was published in Leigh Hunt's radical newspaper* The Examiner *in February 1818. "Ode to the West Wind" was*

---

1. I.e., dull grayish brown.

inspired by an autumn storm Shelley witnessed on the edge of a wood near Florence. The last lines might refer to Shelley's labors on behalf of the working classes; though an aristocrat himself, he hoped for the overthrow of the privileged classes. Shelley wrote "Song (to the men of England)" in 1819, not long after the Peterloo Massacre, a notorious moment in English history when the army fired on a crowd of protesting workers. He could not publish it in his lifetime or he would have been prosecuted for sedition. Shelley concluded his "Defense of Poetry" with these lines: "Poets are . . . the trumpets which sing to battle, and feel not what they inspire: the influence which is moved not, but moves. Poets are the unacknowledged legislators of the World."

Ozymandias

I met a traveler from an antique land
Who said: Two vast and trunkless legs of stone
Stand in the desert . . . Near them, on the sand,
Half sunk, a shattered visage lies, whose frown,
And wrinkled lip, and sneer of cold command,   5
Tell that its sculptor well those passions read
Which yet survive, stamped on these lifeless things,
The hand that mocked them, and the heart that fed:
And on the pedestal these words appear:
"My name is Ozymandias, king of kings: 10
Look on my works, ye Mighty, and despair!"
Nothing beside remains. Round the decay
Of that colossal wreck, boundless and bare
The lone and level sands stretch far away.

1818

Ode to the West Wind

I

O wild West Wind, thou breath of Autumn's being,
Thou, from whose unseen presence the leaves dead
Are driven, like ghosts from an enchanter fleeing,

Yellow, and black, and pale, and hectic red,
Pestilence-stricken multitudes: O thou, 5
Who chariotest to their dark wintry bed

The wingéd seeds, where they lie cold and low,
Each like a corpse within its grave, until
Thine azure sister of the Spring shall blow

Her clarion¹ o'er the dreaming earth, and fill 10
(Driving sweet buds like flocks to feed in air)
With living hues and odors plain and hill:

Wild Spirit, which art moving everywhere;
Destroyer and preserver; hear, oh, hear!

2

Thou on whose stream, mid the steep sky's commotion, 15
Loose clouds like earth's decaying leaves are shed,
Shook from the tangled boughs of Heaven and Ocean,

Angels of rain and lightning: there are spread
On the blue surface of thine aëry surge,
Like the bright hair uplifted from the head 20

Of some fierce Maenad,² even from the dim verge
Of the horizon to the zenith's height,
The locks of the approaching storm. Thou dirge

Of the dying year, to which this closing night
Will be the dome of a vast sepulcher, 25
Vaulted with all thy congregated might

Of vapors, from whose solid atmosphere
Black rain, and fire, and hail will burst: oh, hear!

1. Melodious trumpet call.
2. Frenzied dancer, worshiper of Dionysus (Greek god of wine and fertility).

3

Thou who didst waken from his summer dreams
The blue Mediterranean, where he lay,   30
Lulled by the coil of his crystálline streams,

Beside a pumice isle in Baiae's bay,
And saw in sleep old palaces and towers
Quivering within the wave's intenser day,

All overgrown with azure moss and flowers   35
So sweet, the sense faints picturing them! Thou
For whose path the Atlantic's level powers

Cleave themselves into chasms, while far below
The sea-blooms and the oozy woods which wear
The sapless foliage of the ocean, know   40

Thy voice, and suddenly grow gray with fear,
And tremble and despoil themselves: oh, hear!

4

If I were a dead leaf thou mightest bear;
If I were a swift cloud to fly with thee;
A wave to pant beneath thy power, and share   45

The impulse of thy strength, only less free
Than thou, O uncontrollable! If even
I were as in my boyhood, and could be

The comrade of thy wanderings over Heaven,
As then, when to outstrip thy skyey speed   50
Scarce seemed a vision; I would ne'er have striven

As thus with thee in prayer in my sore need.
Oh, lift me as a wave, a leaf, a cloud!
I fall upon the thorns of life! I bleed!

A heavy weight of hours has chained and bowed   55
One too like thee: tameless, and swift, and proud.

                              5

Make me thy lyre,[3] even as the forest is:
What if my leaves are falling like its own!
The tumult of thy mighty harmonies

Will take from both a deep, autumnal tone,   60
Sweet though in sadness. Be thou, Spirit fierce,
My spirit! Be thou me, impetuous one!

Drive my dead thoughts over the universe
Like withered leaves to quicken a new birth!
And, by the incantation of this verse,   65

Scatter, as from an unextinguished hearth
Ashes and sparks, my words among mankind!
Be through my lips to unawakened earth

The trumpet of a prophecy! O Wind,
If Winter comes, can Spring be far behind?   70
                              1820

Song

       to the men of England

                              I

Men of England, wherefore plough
For the lords who lay ye low?
Wherefore weave with toil and care,
The rich robes your tyrants wear?

---

3. Small harp traditionally used to accompany songs and recited poems.

II

Wherefore feed, and clothe, and save,   5
From the cradle to the grave,
Those ungrateful drones who would
Drain your sweat—nay, drink your blood!

III

Wherefore, Bees of England, forge
Many a weapon, chain, and scourge,   10
That these stingless drones may spoil
The forced produce of your toil?

IV

Have ye leisure, comfort, calm,
Shelter, food, love's gentle balm?
Or what is it ye buy so dear   15
With your pain and with your fear?

V

The seed ye sow, another reaps;
The wealth ye find, another keeps;
The robes ye weave, another wears;
The arms ye forge, another bears.   20

VI

Sow seed,—but let no tyrant reap;
Find wealth,—let no impostor heap;
Weave robes,—let not the idle wear;
Forge arms,—in your defence to bear.

VII

Shrink to your cellars, holes, and cells;   25
In halls ye deck, another dwells.
Why shake the chains ye wrought? Ye see
The steel ye tempered glance on ye.

VIII

With plough and spade, and hoe and loom,
Trace your grave, and build your tomb,   30
And weave your winding-sheet, till fair
England be your sepulchre.

1839

Sir Philip Sidney
1554–1586

> *The sonnet sequence* Astrophil and Stella *was inspired by Sidney's love for the young Penelope Devereaux, who eventually was married, against her will, to one of Sidney's political and romantic rivals. Sidney probably wrote the sequence in the early 1580s, and it circulated in manuscript during his lifetime. Its posthumous publication in 1598 popularized sonnet sequences in England. A sonnet sequence or cycle typically includes a series of poems that chronicle the varying emotions of a lover in his pursuit of a reluctant or unavailable beloved, tracing a vague narrative of the affair's progress (or lack of progress).*

Astrophil and Stella[1]

I

Loving in truth, and fain in verse my love to show,
That she dear she might take some pleasure of my pain,

---

1. I.e.,: Star Lover and Star.

Pleasure might cause her read, reading might make her know,
Knowledge might pity win, and pity grace obtain,
I sought fit words to paint the blackest face of woe: 5
Studying inventions fine, her wits to entertain,
Oft turning others' leaves, to see if thence would flow
Some fresh and fruitful showers upon my sunburned brain.
But words came halting forth, wanting Invention's stay;
Invention, Nature's child, fled stepdame Study's blows;   10
And others' feet still seemed but strangers in my way.
Thus, great with child to speak, and helpless in my throes,
Biting my truant pen, beating myself for spite:
"Fool," said my Muse to me, "look in thy heart, and write."

                                                                                    1598

Stevie Smith
1902–1971

> *Much of Smith's poetry, like much of all poetry, is preoccupied with
> death. She attributed this feature to her illness as a young girl,
> tubercular peritonitis, which required her to be sequestered for a
> long while in an asylum. "Not Waving but Drowing" is based on a
> newspaper account of an actual drowning, during which a swim-
> mer's gestures for help were misinterpreted.*

Not Waving but Drowning

Nobody heard him, the dead man,
But still he lay moaning:
I was much further out than you thought
And not waving but drowning.

Poor chap, he always loved larking   5
And now he's dead
It must have been too cold for him his heart gave way,
They said.

Oh, no no no, it was too cold always
(Still the dead one lay moaning)   10
I was much too far out all my life
And not waving but drowning.

1957

Tracy K. Smith
b. 1972

> *When Smith's father brought home a book of images from deep*
> *space taken by the Hubble Telescope, she realized that the stuff of*
> *science fiction had become the stuff of science. This poem was pub-*
> *lished in her 2011, Pulitzer Prize–winning collection called* Life
> on Mars. *(The Hubble photograph of the Cone Nebula supplies her*
> *cover art.) The title, "My God, It's Full of Stars," alludes to Arthur*
> *C. Clarke's* 2001: A Space Odyssey; *near the end of that novel, an*
> *astronaut stares into a gigantic monolith on the far side of Jupiter*
> *and discovers that it's a gate into interstellar space. But the "it" of*
> *the first line in this poem is even more enigmatic. Several poems in*
> Life on Mars *use the pronoun this way, with no antecedent. But*
> *one poem, "It & Co.," gives us a hint of its cosmological and theo-*
> *logical scope: "We / Have gone looking for It everywhere," Smith*
> *writes, "In Bibles and bandwidth."*

My God, It's Full of Stars

I

We like to think of it as parallel to what we know,
Only bigger. One man against the authorities.
Or one man against a city of zombies. One man

Who is not, in fact, a man, sent to understand
The caravan of men now chasing him like red ants   5
Let loose down the pants of America. Man on the run.

Man with a ship to catch, a payload to drop,
This message going out to all of space. . . . Though
Maybe it's more like life below the sea: silent,

Buoyant, bizarrely benign. Relics   10
Of an outmoded design. Some like to imagine
A cosmic mother watching through a spray of stars,

Mouthing *yes, yes* as we toddle toward the light,
Biting her lip if we teeter at some ledge. Longing
To sweep us to her breast, she hopes for the best   15

While the father storms through adjacent rooms
Ranting with the force of Kingdom Come,
Not caring anymore what might snap us in its jaw.

Sometimes, what I see is a library in a rural community.
All the tall shelves in the big open room. And the pencils   20
In a cup at Circulation, gnawed on by the entire population.

The books have lived here all along, belonging
For weeks at a time to one or another in the brief sequence
Of family names, speaking (at night mostly) to a face,

A pair of eyes. The most remarkable lies.   25

2

Charlton Heston[1] is waiting to be let in. He asked once politely.
A second time with force from the diaphragm. The third time,
He did it like Moses: arms raised high, face an apocryphal white.

---

1. Actor (1923–2008) who starred in many epic movies, including *The Ten Command-
ments* (1956), in which he played Moses. Here the poem also alludes to his science fiction
films: *Planet of the Apes* (1968) and its sequels and especially *The Omega Man* (1971).

Shirt crisp, suit trim, he stoops a little coming in,
Then grows tall. He scans the room. He stands until I gesture, 30
Then he sits. Birds commence their evening chatter. Someone
    fires

Charcoals out below. He'll take a whiskey if I have it. Water
    if I don't.
I ask him to start from the beginning, but he goes only
    halfway back.
That was the future once, he says. *Before the world went upside
    down.*

Hero, survivor, God's right hand man, I know he sees the blank 35
Surface of the moon where I see a language built from brick
    and bone.
He sits straight in his seat, takes a long, slow high-thespian
    breath,

Then lets it go. *For all I know, I was the last true man on this
    earth.* And:
May I smoke? The voices outside soften. Planes jet past
    heading off or back.
Someone cries that she does not want to go to bed.
    Footsteps overhead. 40

A fountain in the neighbor's yard babbles to itself, and the
    night air
Lifts the sound indoors. *It was another time*, he says, picking
    up again.
We were pioneers. Will you fight to stay alive here, riding the earth

Toward God knows where? I think of Atlantis buried under
    ice, gone
One day from sight, the shore from which it rose now glacial
    and stark. 45
Our eyes adjust to the dark.

3

Perhaps the great error is believing we're alone,
That the others have come and gone —a momentary blip—
When all along, space might be choc full of traffic,
Bursting at the seams with energy we neither feel   50
Nor see, flush against us, living, dying, deciding,
Setting solid feet down on planets everywhere,
Bowing to the great stars that command, pitching stones
At whatever are their moons. They live wondering
If they are the only ones, knowing only the wish to know,   55
And the great black distance they—we—flicker in.

Maybe the dead know, their eyes widening at last,
Seeing the high beams of a million galaxies flick on
At twilight. Hearing the engines flare, the horns
Not letting up, the frenzy of being. I want it to be   60
One notch below bedlam, like a radio without a dial.
Wide open, so everything floods in at once.
And sealed tight, so nothing escapes. Not even time,
Which should curl in on itself and loop around like smoke.
So that I might be sitting now beside my father   65
As he raises a lit match to the bowl of his pipe
For the first time in the winter of 1959.

4

In those last scenes of Kubrick's *2001*
When Dave is whisked into the center of space,
Which unfurls in an aurora of orgasmic light   70
Before opening wide, like a jungle orchid
For a love-struck bee, then goes liquid,
Paint in-water, and then gauze wafting out and off,
Before, finally, the night tide, luminescent
And vague, swirls in, and on and on. . . .   75

In those last scenes, as he floats
Above Jupiter's vast canyons and seas,

Over the lava strewn plains and mountains
Packed in ice, that whole time, he doesn't blink.
In his little ship, blind to what he rides, whisked   80
Across the wide-screen of unparcelled time,
Who knows what blazes through his mind?
Is it still his life he moves through, or does
That end at the end of what he can name?

On set, it's shot after shot till Kubrick is happy,   85
Then the costumes go back on their racks
And the great gleaming set goes black.

5

When my father worked on the Hubble Telescope, he said
They operated like surgeons: scrubbed and sheathed
In papery green, the room a clean cold, and bright white.   90

He'd read Larry Niven[2] at home, and drink scotch on the rocks,
His eyes exhausted and pink. These were the Reagan years,
When we lived with our finger on The Button[3] and struggled

To view our enemies as children. My father spent whole seasons
Bowing before the oracle-eye, hungry for what it would find.   95
His face lit-up whenever anyone asked, and his arms would rise

As if he were weightless, perfectly at ease in the never-ending
Night of space. On the ground, we tied postcards to balloons
For peace. Prince Charles married Lady Di. Rock Hudson died.

We learned new words for things. The decade changed.   100

2. Laurence van Cott Niven (b. 1938), science fiction writer.
3. President Reagan reversed a decade of nuclear weapons treaties and detente by reinstituting the arms race and calling the U.S.S.R. the "evil empire."

The first few pictures came back blurred, and I felt ashamed
For all the cheerful engineers, my father and his tribe.
  The second time,
The optics jibed[4]. We saw to the edge of all there is—

So brutal and alive it seemed to comprehend us back.

2011

Susan B. A. Somers-Willett
b. 1973

> *Somers-Willett's poems often adopt the point of view of famous characters and historical figures. For instance; one speaker is a fusion of Ophelia [from Shakespeare's* Hamlet*) and a New Orleans drag queen. A series of poems come in Joan of Arc's voice, while yet another poem explores Albert Einstein's point of view. "Radium: Aubade," like the Einstein poem, was published in Somers-Willett's 2009 book,* Quiver, *which exemplifies poetry's new fascination with scientific knowledge and language (see, for example, Tracy K. Smith's "My God, It's Full of Stars"). An aubade is an esoteric poetic form—a poem written at daybreak, often from the point of view of lovers parting. Here an age dawns, not a day, and the rays of sun are replaced by the radioactive emissions of radium, discovered by Marie Curie in 1902 and a likely factor in her death in 1934.*

Radium: Aubade

Now all of Paris begs
to tremble in my
artificial light,
the bellies of pianos
churning their   5
fin de siècle blues—

---

4. Not until after the Hubble Telescope was launched into space in 1990 was a flaw discovered in its gigantic primary mirror; the problem was corrected by astronauts in January 1994.

I am pressed
to a woman's ailing
temple and like
the city, I incandesce.   10

What could I give
these two who burned
a ton of earth to an atom
and who so perilously shook
the glass in which my   15
blue light shon?[1]

With such ostentation, I pass
into them and through
the body of the world
playing my eighty-eight
keys to prove it.   20

I open my mouth
to crow
the dawn atomic.

                    2009

Edmund Spenser
1552–1599

> *Sonnet 75 ("One day I wrote her name upon the strand") is one in
> Spenser's sonnet sequence* Amoretti, *which celebrates his love affair
> with Elizabeth Boyle. It is unique in the Renaissance sonnet tradi-
> tion for detailing a successful romance: Spenser and Boyle's love led
> to their marriage. The speaker in this poem, then, is not the typical
> sonneteer, the lover trying to woo or adore from afar an unwilling
> or unavailable beloved. Of the nearly ninety poems in the sequence,
> this one is the best known. Like Sidney's* Astrophil *and* Stella *and
> some of Shakespeare's sonnets included in this volume, the poem
> discusses not only love but also the role of poetry in the world.*

---

1. In 1902, Curie needed a ton of pitchblende to distill one-tenth of a gram of radium
chloride, and in 1910 she was able to isolate radium itself.

Amoretti

75

One day I wrote her name upon the strand
But came the waves and washed it away:
Again I wrote it with a second hand,
But came the tide, and made my pains his prey.
Vain man, said she, that doest in vain assay   5
A mortal thing so to immortalize!
For I my self shall like to this decay,
And eek[1] my name be wiped out likewise.
Not so (quod I) let baser things devise
To die in dust, but you shall live by fame: 10
My verse your virtues rare shall eternize,
And in the heavens write your glorious name;
Where, whenas death shall all the world subdue,
Our love shall live, and later life renew.

1595

Bruce Springsteen
b. 1949

Springsteen's songs celebrate the outcast, the working-class dreamer. "The River," the title song to Springsteen's acclaimed 1980 album, is an excellent example of a contemporary ballad, and like "Sir Patrick Spens," it tells a story with terse details. "Born in the U.S.A." is the title track of an album that topped Billboard's *chart in the summer of 1984, ten years after the American withdrawal from the Vietnam War. In a famous case of misinterpretation, first the conservative columnist George Will and then Ronald Reagan, who was running for president on the slogan "It's morning in America," invoked Springsteen's "message of hope." Springsteen repudiated Reagan's interpretation three days later at a concert in Pittsburgh.*

1. Also.

The River

I come from down in the valley[1]
Where mister, when you're young
They bring you up to do
Like your daddy done

Me and Mary we met in high school   5
When she was just seventeen
We'd drive out of this valley
Down to where the fields were green

We'd go down to the river
And into the river we'd dive   10
Oh down to the river we'd ride

Then I got Mary pregnant
And, man, that was all she wrote
And for my 19th birthday
I got a union card and a wedding coat   15

We went down to the courthouse
And the judge put it all to rest
No wedding day smiles, no walk down the aisle
No flowers, no wedding dress

That night we went down to the river   20
And into the river we'd dive
Oh down to the river we did ride

I got a job working construction
For the Johnstown Company
But lately there ain't been much work   25
On account of the economy

1. As becomes clear in line 24, this song is set in Johnstown, Pennsylvania, the site of a
devastating flood in 1889 that decimated the working-class community located in the valley
bellow the manmade lake (Lake Conemaugh) that was the site of a fishing and hunting lodge
for the town's wealthy.

Now all them things that seemed so important
Well, mister they vanished right into the air
Now I just act like I don't remember
Mary acts like she don't care   30

But I remember us riding in my brother's car
Her body tan and wet down at the reservoir
At night on them banks I'd lie awake
And pull her close just to feel each breath she'd take

Now those memories come back to haunt me   35
They haunt me like a curse
Is a dream a lie if it don't come true
Or is it something worse

That sends me down to the river
Though I know the river is dry   40
That sends me down to the river tonight
Down to the river
My baby and I
Oh down to the river we ride

1980

Born in the U.S.A.

Born down in a dead man's town
The first kick I took was when I hit the ground
You end up like a dog that's been beat too much
Till you spend half your life just covering up

Born in the U.S.A.   5
I was born in the U.S.A.
I was born in the U.S.A.
Born in the U.S.A.

Got in a little hometown jam
So they put a rifle in my hand   10

Sent me off to a foreign land
To go and kill the yellow man

Born in the U.S.A.
I was born in the U.S.A.
I was born in the U.S.A.   15
I was born in the U.S.A.
Born in the U.S.A.

Come back home to the refinery
Hiring man says "Son if it was up to me"
Went down to see my V.A. man[1]   20
He said "Son, don't you understand"

I had a brother at Khe Sahn fighting off the Viet Cong[2]
They're still there, he's all gone

He had a woman he loved in Saigon
I got a picture of him in her arms now   25

Down in the shadow of the penitentiary
Out by the gas fires of the refinery
I'm ten years burning down the road
Nowhere to run ain't got nowhere to go

Born in the U.S.A.   30
I was born in the U.S.A.
Born in the U.S.A.
I'm a long gone Daddy in the U.S.A.
Born in the U.S.A.

---

1. A representative of the Veterans Administration; one of the V.A.'s duties is to counsel soldiers readjusting to civilian life after discharge.

2. South Vietnamese communist guerrillas fighting with different tactics from, but in the same cause as, the North Vietnamese soldiers. Khe Sahn was a remote outpost held by U.S. Marines from 1962 on, the site of a four-month battle between the United States and North Vietnam in early 1968. The Marine base at Khe Sahn was completely surrounded for a time, and was supported largely by the Air Force, until a land-based operation broke through to relieve the garrison in March. Over seven hundred Americans died, and more than ten thousand North Vietnamese.

Born in the U.S.A.   35
Born in the U.S.A.
I'm a cool rocking Daddy in the U.S.A.
1984

William Stafford
1914–1993
> *After Stafford published his first book at age forty-six, readers quickly recognized and noted his extraordinary moral authority. "Traveling through the Dark" tells the story of something that actually happened to Stafford while he was driving the seventy-mile mountain road home from a Wednesday night class in Oregon. Stafford said he wanted to "deliver for the reader something of the loneliness and the minimum scope for action we all have in extreme situations."*

Traveling through the Dark

Traveling through the dark I found a deer
dead on the edge of the Wilson River road.
It is usually best to roll them into the canyon:
that road is narrow; to swerve might make more dead.

By glow of the tail-light I stumbled back of the car   5
and stood by the heap, a doe, a recent killing;
she had stiffened already, almost cold.
I dragged her off; she was large in the belly.

My fingers touching her side brought me the reason—
her side was warm; her fawn lay there waiting,   10
alive, still, never to be born.
Beside that mountain road I hesitated.

The car aimed ahead its lowered parking lights;
under the hood purred the steady engine.

I stood in the glare of the warm exhaust turning red;   15
around our group I could hear the wilderness listen.

I thought hard for us all—my only swerving—,
then pushed her over the edge into the river.

1962

Wallace Stevens
1879–1955

*Stevens is famous for the beautiful sounds his lines produce: read
these poems aloud without worrying about meaning, and you'll hear
the fine rhythms. "Thirteen Ways of Looking at a Blackbird" was
first published in 1917, the same year T. S. Eliot published "The
Love Song of J. Alfred Prufrock," and together they inaugurated
a modern aspect in poetry, the strange discontinuity of juxtaposed
images. Stevens's technique here has been likened to Japanese haiku,
and it was surely influenced by modern ideas about knowledge,
which suggested that truth can be represented only through multiple
perspectives. (The poem was later included in Stevens's 1923 col-
lection* Harmonium, *which included the other poems here.) "The
Snow Man" was first published in 1921. "Anecdote of the Jar" dis-
plays the kind of contrast between the human and natural worlds
that is typical of Romantic poetry, like Wordsworth's "Nutting." In
a letter, Stevens explained that "Sunday Morning" is "simply an
expression of paganism, although, of course, I did not think that I
was expressing paganism when I wrote it." Likewise, "The Emperor
of Ice-Cream" seems to deny the orthodox, Christian view of life
and death.*

Thirteen Ways of Looking at a Blackbird

I

Among twenty snowy mountains,
The only moving thing
Was the eye of the blackbird.

II

I was of three minds,
Like a tree   5
In which there are three blackbirds.

III

The blackbird whirled in the autumn winds.
It was a small part of the pantomime.

IV

A man and a woman
Are one.   10
A man and a woman and a blackbird
Are one.

V

I do not know which to prefer,
The beauty of inflections
Or the beauty of innuendoes,   15
The blackbird whistling
Or just after.

VI

Icicles filled the long window
With barbaric glass.
The shadow of the blackbird   20
Crossed it, to and fro.
The mood
Traced in the shadow
An indecipherable cause.

VII

O thin men of Haddam,[1]   25
Why do you imagine golden birds?
Do you not see how the blackbird
Walks around the feet
Of the women about you?

VIII

I know noble accents   30
And lucid, inescapable rhythms;
But I know, too,
That the blackbird is involved
In what I know.

IX

When the blackbird flew out of sight,   35
It marked the edge
Of one of many circles.

X

At the sight of blackbirds
Flying in a green light,
Even the bawds of euphony   40
Would cry out sharply.

XI

He rode over Connecticut
In a glass coach.
Once, a fear pierced him,

1. A small town just outside Hartford, Connecticut.

In that he mistook   45
The shadow of his equipage
For blackbirds.

XII

The river is moving.
The blackbird must be flying.

XIII

It was evening all afternoon.   50
It was snowing
And it was going to snow.
The blackbird sat
In the cedar-limbs.

1917

The Snow Man

One must have a mind of winter
To regard the frost and the boughs
Of the pine-trees crusted with snow;

And have been cold a long time
To behold the junipers shagged with ice,   5
The spruces rough in the distant glitter

Of the January sun; and not to think
Of any misery in the sound of the wind,
In the sound of a few leaves,

Which is the sound of the land   10
Full of the same wind
That is blowing in the same bare place

For the listener, who listens in the snow,
And, nothing himself, beholds
Nothing that is not there and the nothing that is.   15
1921

Anecdote of the Jar

I placed a jar in Tennessee,
And round it was, upon a hill.
It made the slovenly wilderness
Surround that hill.

The wilderness rose up to it,   5
And sprawled around, no longer wild.
The jar was round upon the ground
And tall and of a port in air.

It took dominion everywhere.
The jar was gray and bare.   10
It did not give of bird or bush,
Like nothing else in Tennessee.
1923

Sunday Morning

I

Complacencies of the peignoir, and late
Coffee and oranges in a sunny chair,
And the green freedom of a cockatoo
Upon a rug mingle to dissipate
The holy hush of ancient sacrifice.   5
She dreams a little, and she feels the dark
Encroachment of that old catastrophe,
As a calm darkens among water-lights.
The pungent oranges and bright, green wings
Seem things in some procession of the dead,   10

Winding across wide water, without sound.
The day is like wide water, without sound,
Stilled for the passing of her dreaming feet
Over the seas, to silent Palestine,
Dominion of the blood and sepulchre.[1]   15

2

Why should she give her bounty to the dead?
What is divinity if it can come
Only in silent shadows and in dreams?
Shall she not find in comforts of the sun,
In pungent fruit and bright, green wings, or else   20
In any balm or beauty of the earth,
Things to be cherished like the thought of heaven?
Divinity must live within herself:
Passions of rain, or moods in falling snow;
Grievings in loneliness, or unsubdued   25
Elations when the forest blooms; gusty
Emotions on wet roads on autumn nights;
All pleasures and all pains, remembering
The bough of summer and the winter branch.
These are the measures destined for her soul.   30

3

Jove in the clouds had his inhuman birth.
No mother suckled him, no sweet land gave
Large-mannered motions to his mythy mind
He moved among us, as a muttering king,
Magnificent, would move among his hinds,   35
Until our blood, commingling, virginal,
With heaven, brought such requital to desire
The very hinds discerned it, in a star.

1. I.e., the holy sepulcher, the cave in Jerusalem where Jesus was entombed; much blood was shed during the Crusades (eleventh to thirteenth centuries) as Christians attempted to gain control of Palestine.

Shall our blood fail? Or shall it come to be
The blood of paradise? And shall the earth   40
Seem all of paradise that we shall know?
The sky will be much friendlier then than now,
A part of labor and a part of pain,
And next in glory to enduring love,
Not this dividing and indifferent blue.   45

4

She says, "I am content when wakened birds,
Before they fly, test the reality
Of misty fields, by their sweet questionings;
But when the birds are gone, and their warm fields
Return no more, where, then, is paradise?"   50
There is not any haunt of prophecy,
Nor any old chimera² of the grave,
Neither the golden underground, nor isle
Melodious, where spirits gat them home,
Nor visionary south, nor cloudy palm   55
Remote on heaven's hill, that has endured
As April's green endures; or will endure
Like her remembrance of awakened birds,
Or her desire for June and evening, tipped
By the consummation of the swallow's wings.   60

5

She says, "But in contentment I still feel
The need of some imperishable bliss."
Death is the mother of beauty; hence from her,
Alone, shall come fulfilment to our dreams
And our desires. Although she strews the leaves   65
Of sure obliteration on our paths,
The path sick sorrow took, the many paths

---

2. In Greek mythology, a monster with a lion's head, goat's body, and serpent's tail. Also, an illusion or fabrication of the mind.

Where triumph rang its brassy phrase, or love
Whispered a little out of tenderness,
She makes the willow shiver in the sun   70
For maidens who were wont to sit and gaze
Upon the grass, relinquished to their feet.
She causes boys to pile new plums and pears
On disregarded plate. The maidens taste
And stray impassioned in the littering leaves.   75

6

Is there no change of death in paradise?
Does ripe fruit never fall? Or do the boughs
Hang always heavy in that perfect sky,
Unchanging, yet so like our perishing earth,
With rivers like our own that seek for seas   80
They never find, the same receding shores
That never touch with inarticulate pang?
Why set the pear upon those river-banks
Or spice the shores with odors of the plum?
Alas, that they should wear our colors there,   85
The silken weavings of our afternoons,
And pick the strings of our insipid lutes!
Death is the mother of beauty, mystical,
Within whose burning bosom we devise
Our earthly mothers waiting, sleeplessly.   90

7

Supple and turbulent, a ring of men
Shall chant in orgy on a summer morn
Their boisterous devotion to the sun,
Not as a god, but as a god might be,
Naked among them, like a savage source.   95
Their chant shall be a chant of paradise,
Out of their blood, returning to the sky;
And in their chant shall enter, voice by voice,

The windy lake wherein their lord delights,
The trees, like serafin, and echoing hills,   100
That choir among themselves long afterward.
They shall know well the heavenly fellowship
Of men that perish and of summer morn.
And whence they came and whither they shall go
The dew upon their feet shall manifest.   105

                              8

She hears, upon that water without sound,
A voice that cries, "The tomb in Palestine
Is not the porch of spirits lingering.
It is the grave of Jesus, where he lay."
We live in an old chaos of the sun,   110
Or old dependency of day and night,
Or island solitude, unsponsored, free,
Of that wide water, inescapable.
Deer walk upon our mountains, and the quail
Whistle about us their spontaneous cries;   115
Sweet berries ripen in the wilderness;
And, in the isolation of the sky,
At evening, casual flocks of pigeons make
Ambiguous undulations as they sink,
Downward to darkness, on extended wings.   120
                              1923

The Emperor of Ice-Cream

Call the roller of big cigars,
The muscular one, and bid him whip
In kitchen cups concupiscent curds.
Let the wenches dawdle in such dress
As they are used to wear, and let the boys   5
Bring flowers in last month's newspapers.
Let be be finale of seem
The only emperor is the emperor of ice-cream.

Take from the dresser of deal[1]
Lacking the three glass knobs, that sheet   10
On which she embroidered fantails once
And spread it so as to cover her face.
If her horny feet protrude, they come
To show how cold she is, and dumb.
Let the lamp affix its beam.   15
The only emperor is the emperor of ice-cream.
                                                    1923

Anne Stevenson
b. 1933

> *"The Victory" is an autobiographical poem in the style of confes-
> sional poetry, like that of Sylvia Plath. What Stevenson said of
> Plath might be said of her own poetry: she "unwittingly helped
> inaugurate the fashion for therapeutic confession, which soon took
> the field in women's poetry and owed more to Sigmund Freud and
> the spread of feminism than to any major poet." Stevenson trained
> as a musician, but early in her adult life she began to lose her hear-
> ing, and though she eventually lost most of her ability to hear, she
> reports that "poems still come to me as tunes in the head. Words fall
> into rhythms before they make sense. It often happens that I dis-
> cover what a poem is about through a process of listening to what
> its rhythms are telling me."*

The Victory

I thought you were my victory
though you cut me like a knife
when I brought you out of my body
into your life.

Tiny antagonist, gory,   5
blue as a bruise. The stains

---

1. I.e., pine or firwood.

of your cloud of glory
bled from my veins.

How can you dare, blind thing,
blank insect eyes?   10
You barb the air. You sting
with bladed cries.

Snail. Scary knot of desires.
Hungry snarl. Small son.
Why do I have to love you?   15
How have you won?

                              1974

Rabindranath Tagore
1861–1941

*Born into a wealthy Calcutta family when the English ruled India,
Tagore became, by 1900, the most beloved and celebrated poet writ-
ing in the Bengali language. Though he did not scorn traditional,
classical forms of Sanskrit poetry, Tagore favored a more democratic
type of verse accessible to all over the more learned poetry that can
appeal only to elites in India's caste system, like himself. The poems
also are anticolonial because, though Tagore was partially educated
in England, his poems refuse to submit local culture to a suppos-
edly superior one imposed by the West. To understand how Tagore
might have been read in India, you might consider reading him
alongside American poets like Baca, Diaz, and Finney. This poem
comes from a book of Tagore's short lyrics,* Gitanjali, *published in
English in England in 1912, and W. B. Yeats wrote the introduc-
tion to that volume. One year later, Tagore was the first Asian to
win the Nobel Prize for Literature. Though Yeats conceded that his
poems were "[t]he work of a supreme culture," he further insisted
that "they yet appear as much the growth of the common soil as
the grass and the rushes," seeing a primitivism Yeats thought had
disappeared from the hypermodern West. In* Gitanjali *it is clear
the speaker in the poem is speaking to God in the same manner we*

find in many of the Jewish psalms. The first lyric in Gitanjali *also compares the poet to a flute: "This little flute of a reed . . . thou hast breathed through it melodies eternally new."*

Song VII ("My song has put off her adornments")

My song has put off her adornments.
She has no pride of dress and decoration.
Ornaments would mar our union;
they would come between thee and me;
their jingling would drown thy whispers.   5

My poet's vanity dies in shame before thy sight.
O master poet, I have sat down at thy feet.
Only let me make my life simple and straight,
like a flute of reed for thee to fill with music.

1912

Alfred, Lord Tennyson
1809–1892

"Ulysses" broke with the Romantic practice of autobiographical poetry—the speaker is a character and the poem is a dramatic monologue. What Ulysses thinks is not necessarily what Tennyson thinks. Nevertheless, many critics think Tennyson's friend Arthur Hallam, who died in 1833, inspired the lines about Achilles, and the rousing conclusion to the poem was taken at face value by Tennyson's Victorian readers. The poem alludes to Dante's version of Ulysses's final journey: he sailed across the Atlantic toward Purgatory, and God sank his ship to punish him for the impudence of the act. "The Charge of the Light Brigade" celebrates an actual battle during the Crimean War. On October 25, 1854, during the Battle of Balaclava, confusing orders were relayed to the British cavalry, which led the Light Brigade to make a futile assault on an impregnable Russian position. Of about 670 men, 245 were casualties, and fewer than 200 of their horses survived. The disaster was followed by a huge public outcry against the incompetence that led

to such a waste of lives. Tennyson, in publishing this poem in the newspapers, offered his interpretation of the events. "Crossing the Bar" was written in 1889, near the end of Tennyson's life, and he left instructions that it should conclude all posthumous collections of his poetry. The "bar" is the sandbar that forms naturally at the mouth of a harbor; it can be crossed safely only at high tide.

Ulysses

It little profits that an idle king,
By this still hearth, among these barren crags,
Matched with an aged wife, I mete and dole
Unequal laws unto a savage race,
That hoard, and sleep, and feed, and know not me.   5

    I cannot rest from travel: I will drink
Life to the lees: all times I have enjoyed
Greatly, have suffered greatly, both with those
That loved me, and alone; on shore, and when
Through scudding drifts the rainy Hyades[1]   10
Vext the dim sea: I am become a name;
For always roaming with a hungry heart
Much have I seen and known; cities of men
And manners, climates, councils, governments,
Myself not least, but honored of them all;   15
And drunk delight of battle with my peers,
Far on the ringing plains of windy Troy.
I am a part of all that I have met;
Yet all experience is an arch wherethrough
Gleams that untravelled world whose margin fades   20
For ever and for ever when I move.
How dull it is to pause, to make an end,
To rust unburnished, not to shine in use!
As though to breathe were life! Life piled on life
Were all too little, and of one to me   25

---

1. A group of stars in the constellation Taurus, believed to foretell the coming of rain when they rose with the sun.

Little remains: but every hour is saved
From that eternal silence, something more,
A bringer of new things; and vile it were
For some three suns to store and hoard myself,
And this gray spirit yearning in desire   30
To follow knowledge like a sinking star,
Beyond the utmost bound of human thought.

   This is my son, mine own Telemachus,
To whom I leave the scepter and the isle—
Well-loved of me, discerning to fulfill   35
This labor, by slow prudence to make mild
A rugged people, and through soft degrees
Subdue them to the useful and the good.
Most blameless is he, centered in the sphere
Of common duties, decent not to fail   40
In offices of tenderness, and pay
Meet adoration to my household gods,
When I am gone. He works his work, I mine.

   There lies the port; the vessel puffs her sail:
There gloom the dark, broad seas. My mariners,   45
Souls that have toiled, and wrought, and thought with me—
That ever with a frolic welcome took
The thunder and the sunshine, and opposed
Free hearts, free foreheads—you and I are old;
Old age hath yet his honor and his toil;   50
Death closes all: but something ere the end,
Some work of noble note, may yet be done,
Not unbecoming men that strove with Gods.
The lights begin to twinkle from the rocks:
The long day wanes: the slow moon climbs: the deep   55
Moans round with many voices. Come, my friends,
'Tis not too late to seek a newer world.
Push off, and sitting well in order smite
The sounding furrows; for my purpose holds
To sail beyond the sunset, and the baths   60
Of all the western stars, until I die.

It may be that the gulfs will wash us down:
It may be we shall touch the Happy Isles,[2]
And see the great Achilles, whom we knew.
Though much is taken, much abides; and though 65
We are not now that strength which in old days
Moved earth and heaven; that which we are, we are,
One equal temper of heroic hearts,
Made weak by time and fate, but strong in will
To strive, to seek, to find, and not to yield. 70

1842

The Charge of the Light Brigade

I

Half a league, half a league,
    Half a league onward,
All in the valley of Death
    Rode the six hundred.
'Forward, the Light Brigade! 5
Charge for the guns!' he said;
Into the valley of Death
    Rode the six hundred.

II

'Forward, the Light Brigade!'
Was there a man dismay'd? 10
Not tho' the soldier knew
    Some one had blunder'd:
Their's not to make reply,
Their's not to reason why,
Their's but to do and die; 15
Into the valley of Death
    Rode the six hundred.

2. The Islands of the Blessed, the abode after death of those favored by the gods, especially heroes and patriots.

III

Cannon to right of them,
Cannon to left of them,
Cannon in front of them   20
   Volley'd and thunder'd;
Storm'd at with shot and shell,
Boldly they rode and well,
Into the jaws of Death,
Into the mouth of Hell   25
   Rode the six hundred.

IV

Flash'd all their sabres bare,
Flash'd as they turn'd in air,
Sabring the gunners there,
Charging an army, while   30
   All the world wonder'd:
Plunged in the battery-smoke
Right thro' the line they broke;
Cossack and Russian
Reel'd from the sabre-stroke   35
   Shatter'd and sunder'd.
Then they rode back, but not,
   Not the six hundred.

V

Cannon to right of them,
Cannon to left of them,   40
Cannon behind them
   Volley'd and thunder'd;
Storm'd at with shot and shell,
While horse and hero fell,
They that had fought so well   45
Came thro' the jaws of Death
Back from the mouth of Hell,

All that was left of them,
   Left of six hundred.

      VI

When can their glory fade?   50
O the wild charge they made!
   All the world wonder'd.
Honour the charge they made!
Honour the Light Brigade,
   Noble six hundred!   55
          1854

Crossing the Bar

Sunset and evening star,
   And one clear call for me!
And may there be no moaning of the bar,
   When I put out to sea,

But such a tide as moving seems asleep,   5
   Too full for sound and foam,
When that which drew from out the boundless deep
   Turns again home.

Twilight and evening bell,
   And after that the dark!   10
And may there be no sadness of farewell,
   When I embark;

For though from out our bourne of Time and Place
   The flood may bear me far,
I hope to see my Pilot face to face   15
   When I have crossed the bar.
          1889

Dylan Thomas
1914–1953

> *Thomas was as sensitive as any poet to aging. He wrote "The Force That through the Green Fuse Drives the Flower" when he was just twenty. At the ripe old age of thirty-nine he said that he was "old, small, dark, intelligent, and darting-doting-dotting-eyed, balding and tooth-lessing." Much of his poetry came from his memories of childhood. Fern Hill was a country farm, a largish, peasant plot with a damp, dark, creaky house on the side of a hill, rented by an aunt and uncle. Thomas spent summers there in childhood, and remembered it as an Edenic farm in "Fern Hill." Thomas wrote "Do Not Go Gentle into That Good Night" while watching his father, the once proud and fiery schoolteacher "who had a violent and quite personal dislike for God," wither, grow powerless, then die.*

The Force That Through the Green Fuse Drives the Flower

The force that through the green fuse drives the flower
Drives my green age; that blasts the roots of trees
Is my destroyer.
And I am dumb to tell the crooked rose
My youth is bent by the same wintry fever.   5

The force that drives the water through the rocks
Drives my red blood; that dries the mouthing streams
Turns mine to wax.
And I am dumb to mouth unto my veins
How at the mountain spring the same mouth sucks.   10

The hand that whirls the water in the pool
Stirs the quicksand; that ropes the blowing wind
Hauls my shroud sail.
And I am dumb to tell the hanging man
How of my clay is made the hangman's lime.   15

The lips of time leech to the fountain head;
Love drips and gathers, but the fallen blood
Shall calm her sores.
And I am dumb to tell a weather's wind
How time has ticked a heaven round the stars.   20

And I am dumb to tell the lover's tomb
How at my sheet goes the same crooked worm.
                                        1934

Fern Hill

Now as I was young and easy under the apple boughs
About the lilting house and happy as the grass was green,
        The night above the dingle[1] starry,
                Time let me hail and climb
                Golden in the heydays of his eyes,   5
And honoured among wagons I was prince of the apple towns
And once below a time I lordly had the trees and leaves
                Trail with daisies and barley
                Down the rivers of the windfall light.

And as I was green and carefree, famous among the barns   10
About the happy yard and singing as the farm was home,
        In the sun that is young once only,
                Time let me play and be
                Golden in the mercy of his means,
And green and golden I was huntsman and herdsman, the
        calves   15
Sang to my horn, the foxes on the hills barked clear and cold,
                And the sabbath rang slowly
                In the pebbles of the holy streams.

All the sun long it was running, it was lovely, the hay
Fields high as the house, the tunes from the chimneys, it was
        air   20

1. Small wooded valley.

And playing, lovely and watery
  And fire green as grass.
  And nightly under the simple stars
As I rode to sleep the owls were bearing the farm away,
All the moon long I heard, blessed among stables, the
   night jars[2]   25
  Flying with the ricks,[3] and the horses
   Flashing into the dark.

And then to awake, and the farm, like a wanderer white
With the dew, come back, the cock on his shoulder: it was all
  Shining, it was Adam and maiden,   30
   The sky gathered again
  And the sun grew round that very day.
So it must have been after the birth of the simple light
In the first, spinning place, the spellbound horses walking warm
  Out of the whinnying green stable   35
   On to the fields of praise.

And honoured among foxes and pheasants by the gay house
Under the new made clouds and happy as the heart was long,
  In the sun born over and over,
   I ran my heedless ways,   40
  My wishes raced through the house high hay
And nothing I cared, at my sky blue trades, that time allows
In all his tuneful turning so few and such morning songs
  Before the children green and golden
   Follow him out of grace,   45

Nothing I cared, in the lamb white days, that time would take me
Up to the swallow thronged loft by the shadow of my hand,
  In the moon that is always rising,
   Nor that riding to sleep
  I should hear him fly with the high fields 50
And wake to the farm forever fled from the childless land.

2. Nocturnal birds.   3. Haystacks.

Oh as I was young and easy in the mercy of his means,
  Time held me green and dying
  Though I sang in my chains like the sea.
1946

Do Not Go Gentle into That Good Night

Do not go gentle into that good night,
Old age should burn and rave at close of day;
Rage, rage against the dying of the light.

Though wise men at their end know dark is right,
Because their words had forked no lightning they   5
Do not go gentle into that good night.

Good men, the last wave by, crying how bright
Their frail deeds might have danced in a green bay,
Rage, rage against the dying of the light.

Wild men who caught and sang the sun in flight,   10
And learn, too late, they grieved it on its way,
Do not go gentle into that good night.

Grave men, near death, who see with blinding sight
Blind eyes could blaze like meteors and be gay,
Rage, rage against the dying of the light.   15

And you, my father, there on the sad height,
Curse, bless, me now with your fierce tears, I pray.
Do not go gentle into that good night.
Rage, rage against the dying of the light.
1952

Natasha Trethewey
b. 1966

> *Very much a Southern writer, Trethewey often explores the experience of mixed-race Americans (like herself) or gives voice to the lives of the poor, such as in her award-winning first book,* Domestic Work. *But this poem, from the 2006 collection,* Native Guard, *is more personal than political: when Trethewey was nineteen and attending the University of Georgia, her mother was killed by her stepfather, a violent and abusive man who ruled over Trethewey's adolescence. Trethewey was asleep when the murder took place. She wrote the poem when she returned to her hometown Decatur about nineteen years after the crime. Elegies are typically formal, even somewhat stately, but this poem's form is more than usually precise. You might consider how it affects your experience of reading and making sense of the poem.*

Myth

I was asleep while you were dying.
It's as if you slipped through some rift, a hollow
I make between my slumber and my waking,

the Erebus I keep you in, still trying
not to let go. You'll be dead again tomorrow,
but in dreams you live. So I try taking

you back into morning. Sleep-heavy, turning,
my eyes open, I find you do not follow.
Again and again, this constant forsaking.

*

Again and again, this constant forsaking:
my eyes open, I find you do not follow.
You back into morning, sleep-heavy, turning.

But in dreams you live. So I try taking,
not to let go. You'll be dead again tomorrow.
The Erebus I keep you in—still, trying—

I make between my slumber and my waking.
It's as if you slipped through some rift, a hollow.
I was asleep while you were dying.

2006

Catherine Tufariello
b. 1963

> *Tufariello's poem commemorates the White Rose movement—a*
> *group of five students, including Hans and Sophie Scholl, at the*
> *University of Munich who, inspired by their detestation of Hitler's*
> *tyranny, the cruelty of Germany's war machine, a deep religious sen-*
> *sibility, and their hopes for a confederated Europe, secretly distrib-*
> *uted up to nine thousand anti-Nazi leaflets throughout Germany.*
> *The Gestapo was intent on discovering the authors and distributors*
> *of these leaflets when, on February 18, 1943, the Scholls recklessly*
> *littered school hallways with copies of their sixth leaflet. They nearly*
> *escaped detection, but discovering a few sheets in their case, climbed*
> *to the top of a staircase and dumped the last few through the air.*
> *Unfortunately, the janitor saw this gesture and they were caught,*
> *interrogated, and beheaded.*

February 18, 1943

In memory of Hans and Sophie Scholl, leaders of the White Rose
student resistance movement, executed February 22, 1943.

I imagine how easily you could have gotten away,
Standing in the Ludwigstraße in the sun
That improbably springlike February day,
The not-quite-empty suitcase slung
Between you—like two students on holiday,   5
Let out of class, on your way to catch a train.
Relieved and out of breath,
You stood for a moment blinking in the sun,
Tasting the early spring that caught all Munich unawares
After bleak weeks of cold.   10

How hopeful the light must have looked, how far from death.
Was it that you suddenly felt young?
—Another nose-thumbing at the omnipotent State!
Or was it the recklessness of the desperate?
Not furtively, but in the pale spun-gold   15
Of full daylight, like farmers casting grain,
You'd left your leaflets scattered on the floors
In the hallways, on windowsills, at the doors
Of the lecture rooms, and, ignoring their stony stares,
In the marble laps of Ludwig and Leopold.   20
Was it the change in weather
That made your glances catch, a glance that said
Almost gaily, *Why waste any?* so that instead
Of slipping away as planned, you raced together
Back to the empty hall,   25
And up the stairs, to let the last ones fall?

I imagine, then, how you leaned from the great height
Of the gallery railing into a well of light;
How, giddy with boldness and vertigo,
You popped the latch, and—hurriedly this time—scooped   30
The leftover handfuls out.
For a few seconds, the pages must have swooped
Like wind-torn blossoms, sideways in the air,
Filling the gallery with a storm of white,
While under the skylight with its square of blue   35
Your arms were still flung wide;
And while, rounding a corner down below,
For just a moment, the porter, Jakob Schmid,
Must have stopped to stare,
Not indignant yet, but merely shocked,   40
Blinded for an instant by the glare,
Before he recovered himself and did
His job as he'd been taught;
Before milling students spilled into the hall
From morning lectures, but not quite fast enough;   45
Before Schmid gave a shout,
And surging forward in the tumult, caught

The dark-haired young man's shoulder in a rough
Policeman's grip that would not be shaken off,
Though he didn't try, and the girl stayed by his side;   50
Before, in a sudden hush, the crowd withdrew,
And the doors all locked.

2003

Derek Walcott

b. 1930

> *A Latin primer is a textbook meant for young scholars of that dead European language. Images and words from the primer recur throughout the poem of the same name, including in the concluding image of Roman ruins. This poem is similar to Wordsworth's "The Tables Turned," exploring the conflict between natural living and scholarly study, but in this case the conflict is complicated by the issue of race—the culture the speaker learns and teaches is, in a sense, not his own. A variation on this theme animates "White Magic," which compares the folk beliefs in the Caribbean to those in Western cultures, and "The Light of the World," which details one of Walcott's return visits to his native St. Lucia.*

A Latin Primer

(In Memoriam: H. D. Boxill)

I had nothing against which
to notch the growth of my work
but the horizon, no language
but the shallows in my long walk

home, so I shook all the help   5
my young right hand could use
from the sand-crusted kelp
of distant literatures.

The frigate bird[1] my phoenix,
I was high on iodine,
one drop from the sun's murex
stained the foam's fabric wine;

ploughing white fields of surf
with a boy's shins, I kept
staggering as the shelf
of sand under me slipped,

then found my deepest wish
in the swaying words of the sea,
and the skeletal fish
of that boy is ribbed in me;

but I saw how the bronze
dusk of imperial palms
curled their fronds into questions
over Latin exams.

I hated signs of scansion.
Those strokes across the line
drizzled on the horizon
and darkened discipline.

They were like Mathematics
that made delight Design,
arranging the thrown sticks
of stars to sine and cosine.

Raging, I'd skip a pebble
across the sea's page; it still
scanned its own syllable:
trochee, anapest, dactyl.

1. A Caribbean species that cannot swim and is clumsy on land. It can spend up to a week in the air without landing, and it often rides the currents of a weather front, presaging changes in the weather.

Miles, foot soldier. *Fossa,*
a trench or a grave. My hand
hefts a last sand bomb to toss
at slowly fading sand.   40

I failed Matriculation
in Maths; passed it; after that,
I taught Love's basic Latin:
Amo, amas, amat.

In tweed jacket and tie   45
a master at my college
I watched the old words dry
like seaweed on the page.

I'd muse from the roofed harbour
back to my desk, the boys'   50
heads plunged in paper
softly as porpoises.

The discipline I preached
made me a hypocrite;
their lithe black bodies, beached,   55
would die in dialect;

I spun the globe's meridian,
showed its sealed hemispheres,
but where were those brows heading
when neither world was theirs?   60

Silence clogged my ears
with cotton, a cloud's noise;
I climbed white tiered arenas
trying to find my voice,

and I remember: it was on a   65
Saturday near noon, at Vigie,

that my heart, rounding the corner
of Half-Moon Battery,[2]

stopped to watch the foundry
of midday cast in bronze   70
the trunk of a gommier tree
on a sea without seasons,

while ochre Rat Island[3]
was nibbling the sea's lace,
that a frigate bird came sailing   75
through a tree's net, to raise

its emblem in the cirrus,
named with the common sense
of fishermen: sea scissors,
Fregata magnificens,   80

ciseau-la-mer, the patois
for its cloud-cutting course;
and that native metaphor
made by the strokes of oars,

with one wing beat for scansion,   85
that slowly levelling V
made one with my horizon
as it sailed steadily

beyond the sheep-nibbled columns
of fallen marble trees,   90
or the roofless pillars once
sacred to Hercules.

1987

2. Vigie and Half-Moon Battery are in   3. In St. Lucia.
St. Lucia, Wallcott's birthplace.

White Magic

(For Leo St. Helene)

The *gens-gagée* kicks off her wrinkled skin.
Clap her soul in a jar! The half-man wolf
can trot with bending elbows, rise, and grin
in lockjawed lycanthropia.[1] Censers dissolve
the ground fog with its whistling, wandering souls,   5
the unbaptized, unfinished, and uncursed
by holy fiat. The island's griots[2] love
our mushroom elves, the devil's parasols
who creep like grubs from a trunk's rotten holes,
their mouths a sewn seam, their clubfeet reversed.   10
Exorcism cannot anachronize
those signs we hear past midnight in a wood
where a pale woman like a blind owl flies
to her forked branch, with scarlet moons for eyes
bubbling with doubt. You heard a silver splash?   15
It's nothing. If it slid from mossed rocks
dismiss it as a tired crab, a fish,
unless our water-mother with dank locks
is sliding under this page below your pen,
only a simple people think they happen.   20
Dryads and hamadryads[3] were engrained
in the wood's bark, in papyrus, and this paper;
but when our dry leaves crackle to the deer-
footed, hobbling hunter, Papa Bois,[4]
he's just Pan's[5] clone, one more translated satyr.   25
The crone who steps from her jute sugar sack
(though you line moonlit lintels with white flour),
the *beau l'homme* creeping towards you, front to back,

---

1. The malady that results in one's becoming a werewolf.
2. Caribbean bards who carry on the oral traditions of folk culture.
3. Two types of tree spirits in Greek mythology.

4. A character in Trinidadian folklore, the hairy man of the forest.
5. A bacchanalian god in Roman mythology, half goat, half man.

the ferny footed, faceless, mouse-eared elves,
these fables of the backward and the poor   30
marbled by moonlight, will grow white and richer.
Our myths are ignorance, theirs are literature.

                                        1987

The Light of the World

> *Kaya[1] now, got to have kaya now,*
> *Got to have kaya now,*
> *For the rain is falling.*
> —Bob Marley

Marley was rocking on the transport's stereo
and the beauty was humming the choruses quietly.
I could see where the lights on the planes of her cheek
streaked and defined them; if this were a portrait
you'd leave the highlights for last, these lights   5
silkened her black skin; I'd have put in an earring,
something simple, in good gold, for contrast, but she
wore no jewelry. I imagined a powerful and sweet
odour coming from her, as from a still panther,
and the head was nothing else but heraldic.   10
When she looked at me, then away from me politely
because any staring at strangers is impolite,
it was like a statue, like a black Delacroix's[2]
Liberty Leading the People, the gently bulging
whites of her eyes, the carved ebony mouth,   15
the heft of the torso solid, and a woman's,
but gradually even that was going in the dusk,
except the line of her profile, and the highlit cheek,
and I thought, O Beauty, you are the light of the world!

It was not the only time I would think of that phrase   20
in the sixteen-seater transport that hummed between

1. A spicy cuisine native to the Carib-
bean islands.
2. Eugene Delacroix (1798–1863), French
Romantic painter. His *Liberty Leading the*

People commemorates the failed 1832 French
Revolution; the central figure in the painting
is a bare-chested woman leading the revolu-
tionaries in a street battle.

Gros-Islet[3] and the Market, with its grit of charcoal
and the litter of vegetables after Saturday's sales,
and the roaring rum shops, outside whose bright doors
you saw drunk women on pavements, the saddest of all things,   25
winding up their week, winding down their week.
The Market, as it closed on this Saturday night,
remembered a childhood of wandering gas lanterns
hung on poles at street corners, and the old roar
of vendors and traffic, when the lamplighter climbed,   30
hooked the lantern on its pole and moved on to another,
and the children turned their faces to its moth, their
eyes white as their nighties; the Market
itself was closed in its involved darkness
and the shadows quarrelled for bread in the shops,   35
or quarrelled for the formal custom of quarrelling
in the electric rum shops. I remember the shadows.

The van was slowly filling in the darkening depot.
I sat in the front seat, I had no need for time.
I looked at two girls, one in a yellow bodice   40
and yellow shorts, with a flower in her hair,
and lusted in peace, the other less interesting.
That evening I had walked the streets of the town
where I was born and grew up, thinking of my mother
with her white hair tinted by the dyeing dusk,   45
and the tilting box houses that seemed perverse
in their cramp; I had peered into parlours
with half-closed jalousies, at the dim furniture,
Morris chairs, a centre table with wax flowers,
and the lithograph of *Christ of the Sacred Heart*,   50
vendors still selling to the empty streets—
sweets, nuts, sodden chocolates, nut cakes, mints.

An old woman with a straw hat over her headkerchief
hobbled towards us with a basket; somewhere,
some distance off, was a heavier basket   55

---

3. A town on the northern tip of St. Lucia.

that she couldn't carry. She was in a panic.
She said to the driver: *"Pas quittez moi à terre,"*
which is, in her patois: "Don't leave me stranded,"
which is, in her history and that of her people:
"Don't leave me on earth," or, by a shift of stress: 60
"Don't leave me the earth" [for an inheritance];
"Pas quittez moi à terre, Heavenly transport,
Don't leave me on earth, I've had enough of it."
The bus filled in the dark with heavy shadows
that would not be left on earth; no, that would be left   65
on the earth, and would have to make out.
Abandonment was something they had grown used to.

And I had abandoned them, I knew that there
sitting in the transport, in the sea-quiet dusk,
with men hunched in canoes, and the orange lights   70
from the Vigie headland, black boats on the water;
I, who could never solidify my shadow
to be one of their shadows, had left them their earth,
their white rum quarrels, and their coal bags,
their hatred of corporals, of all authority.   75
I was deeply in love with the woman by the window.
I wanted to be going home with her this evening.
I wanted her to have the key to our small house
by the beach at Gros-Islet; I wanted her to change
into a smooth white nightie that would pour like water   80
over the black rocks of her breasts, to lie
simply beside her by the ring of a brass lamp
with a kerosene wick, and tell her in silence
that her hair was like a hill forest at night,
that a trickle of rivers was in her armpits,   85
that I would buy her Benin if she wanted it,
and never leave her on earth. But the others, too.

Because I felt a great love that could bring me to tears,
and a pity that prickled my eyes like a nettle,
I was afraid I might suddenly start sobbing   90
on the public transport with the Marley going,

and a small boy peering over the shoulders
of the driver and me at the lights coming,
at the rush of the road in the country darkness,
with lamps in the houses on the small hills,   95
and thickets of stars; I had abandoned them,
I had left them on earth, I left them to sing
Marley's songs of a sadness as real as the smell
of rain on dry earth, or the smell of damp sand,
and the bus felt warm with their neighbourliness,   100
their consideration, and the polite partings.

in the light of its headlamps. In the blare,
in the thud-sobbing music, the claiming scent
that came from their bodies. I wanted the transport
to continue forever, for no one to descend   105
and say a good night in the beams of the lamps
and take the crooked path up to the lit door,
guided by fireflies; I wanted her beauty
to come into the warmth of considerate wood,
to the relieved rattling of enamel plates   110
in the kitchen, and the tree in the yard,
but I came to my stop. Outside the Halcyon Hotel.
The lounge would be full of transients like myself.
Then I would walk with the surf up the beach.
I got off the van without saying good night.   115
Good night would be full of inexpressible love.
They went on in their transport, they left me on earth.

Then, a few yards ahead, the van stopped. A man
shouted my name from the transport window.
I walked up towards him. He held out something.   120
A pack of cigarettes had dropped from my pocket.
He gave it to me. I turned, hiding my tears.
There was nothing they wanted, nothing I could give them
but this thing I have called "The Light of the World."

1987

Alice Walker
b. 1944

The speaker in "Women" stands in much the same position that Walker herself did in 1961: a black woman who was a first-generation college student looking back at the previous generation of black women, whose world was far more limited by white supremacy. Primarily known as a fiction writer, Walker published her most famous and hugely successful novel, The Color Purple, in 1982. Walker considers herself a "womanist," a term she coined in 1983 to distinguish herself from mainstream feminists she felt focused too much on the rights and experiences of middle-class white women. Walker's brand of feminism seeks to expose and change the racist and class-based prejudices that have impeded the lives of women of color in America.

Women

They were women then
My mama's generation
Husky of voice—Stout of
Step
With fists as well as   5
Hands
How they battered down
Doors
And ironed
Starched white   10
Shirts
How they led
Armies
Headragged Generals
Across mined   15
Fields
Booby-trapped
Kitchens
To discover books
Desks   20
A place for us

How they knew what we
Must know
Without knowing a page
Of it   25
Themselves.

1973

Phillis Wheatley

1753–1784

> *Published when she was just nineteen, Wheatley's first book of poems,*
> *which included* On Being Brought from Africa to America,
> *amazed contemporaries: no one had seen anyone like her before. After*
> *Phillis was kidnapped from West Africa and enslaved when she was*
> *six years old, the Wheatley family in Boston bought her and forced*
> *her into a new identity, yet also recognized her genius, educated*
> *her, and encouraged her writing. With their patronage, she startled*
> *white readers by defying the prevailing racial stereotypes in Europe*
> *and white America. Incredulous publishers demanded proof of her*
> *authorship, while writers such as Voltaire recognized her as an intel-*
> *lectual equal to whites. Many critics today note the ways she infused*
> *her own African roots, early memories, and experience as a slave*
> *into the language, religious iconography, and poetic forms foisted on*
> *her by an oppressive and alien culture, subtly displaying the tension*
> *between an imposed and a personally constructed identity.*

On Being Brought from Africa to America

'Twas mercy brought me from my *Pagan* land,
Taught my benighted soul to understand
That there's a God, that there's a *Saviour* too:
Once I redemption neither sought nor knew.
Some view our sable race with scornful eye,
"Their colour is a diabolic die."
Remember, *Christians*, *Negros*, black as *Cain*,
May be refin'd, and join th' angelic train.

1768

Walt Whitman
1819–1892

> *The first edition of Whitman's only book of poetry,* Leaves of Grass, *published privately and with the type set by himself, came out in 1855. (As he wrote more poems and revised the old, Whitman republished* Leaves of Grass *many times.) The longest poem in the volume was the yet-untitled "Song of Myself," and it revolutionized American poetry, inaugurating "free verse." But even more radical was the encyclopedic content of this national poem. Only the beginning is reprinted here, but it should give you a good sense of what Whitman was up to in the poem. "A Noiseless Patient Spider" demonstrates that* free *does not mean "random." For example, note the similar syntax in lines 4 and 8, which connects the action of the spider to that of the speaker's soul. This poem is an apostrophe: the speaker is talking to his soul. Its meaning depends on the comparison of the soul to the spider. You should ask yourself why Whitman chose a spider and not, say, a bird building a nest or a lion stalking its prey. During the Civil War, Whitman visited his brother, a wounded Union soldier, in Virginia, and subsequently spent most of his time tending to the wounded in Washington hospitals. "Cavalry Crossing a Ford" is one of the poems that came from this experience. "When I Heard the Learn'd Astronomer" is a latter-day Romantic poem, very similar in theme to Wordsworth's "The Tables Turned" and its pronouncement on science: "We murder to dissect."*

From Song of Myself

1

I celebrate myself, and sing myself,
And what I assume you shall assume,
For every atom belonging to me as good belongs to you.

I loafe and invite my soul,
I lean and loafe at my ease observing a spear of summer grass.   5
My tongue, every atom of my blood, form'd from this soil, this
    air,

Born here of parents born here from parents the same, and their
    parents the same,
I, now thirty-seven years old in perfect health begin,
Hoping to cease not till death.
Creeds and schools in abeyance,   10
Retiring back a while sufficed at what they are, but never
    forgotten,
I harbor for good or bad, I permit to speak at every hazard,
Nature without check with original energy.

2

Houses and rooms are full of perfumes, the shelves are
    crowded with perfumes,
I breathe the fragrance myself and know it and like it,   15
The distillation would intoxicate me also, but I shall not let it.

The atmosphere is not a perfume, it has no taste of the
    distillation, it is odorless,
It is for my mouth forever, I am in love with it,
I will go to the bank by the wood and become undisguised and
    naked,
I am mad for it to be in contact with me.   20

The smoke of my own breath,
Echoes, ripples, buzz'd whispers, love-root, silk-thread, crotch
    and vine,
My respiration and inspiration, the beating of my heart, the
    passing of blood and air through my lungs,
The sniff of green leaves and dry leaves, and of the shore and
    dark-color'd sea-rocks, and of hay in the barn,
The sound of the belch'd words of my voice loos'd to the eddies
    of the wind,   25
A few light kisses, a few embraces, a reaching around of arms,
The play of shine and shade on the trees as the supple boughs
    wag,

The delight alone or in the rush of the streets, or along the
    fields and hill-sides,
The feeling of health, the full-noon trill, the song of me rising
    from bed and meeting the sun.

Have you reckon'd a thousand acres much? have you reckon'd
    the earth much?   30
Have you practis'd so long to learn to read?
Have you felt so proud to get at the meaning of poems?

Stop this day and night with me and you shall possess the
    origin of all poems,
You shall possess the good of the earth and sun, (there are
    millions of suns left,)
You shall no longer take things at second or third hand, nor
    look through the eyes of the dead, nor feed on the
    spectres in books,   35
You shall not look through my eyes either, nor take things
    from me,
You shall listen to all sides and filter them from your self.

3

I have heard what the talkers were talking, the talk of the
    beginning and the end,
But I do not talk of the beginning or the end.

There was never any more inception than there is now,   40
Nor any more youth or age than there is now,
And will never be any more perfection than there is now,
Nor any more heaven or hell than there is now.

Urge and urge and urge,
Always the procreant urge of the world.   45

Out of the dimness opposite equals advance, always substance
    and increase, always sex,

Always a knit of identity, always distinction, always a breed of
life.

To elaborate is no avail, learn'd and unlearn'd feel that it is so.

Sure as the most certain sure, plumb in the uprights, well
entretied, braced in the beams,
Stout as a horse, affectionate, haughty, electrical,   50
I and this mystery here we stand.

Clear and sweet is my soul, and clear and sweet is all that is not
my soul.

Lack one lacks both, and the unseen is proved by the seen,
Till that becomes unseen and receives proof in its turn.

Showing the best and dividing it from the worst age vexes age,   55
Knowing the perfect fitness and equanimity of things, while
they discuss I am silent, and go bathe and admire myself.
Welcome is every organ and attribute of me, and of any man
hearty and clean,
Not an inch nor a particle of an inch is vile, and none shall be
less familiar than the rest.

I am satisfied—I see, dance, laugh, sing;
As the hugging and loving bed-fellow sleeps at my side through
the night, and withdraws at the peep of the day with
stealthy tread,   60
Leaving me baskets cover'd with white towels swelling the house
with their plenty,
Shall I postpone my acceptation and realization and scream at
my eyes,
That they turn from gazing after and down the road,
And forthwith cipher and show me to a cent,
Exactly the value of one and exactly the value of two, and
which is ahead?   65

4

Trippers and askers surround me,
People I meet, the effect upon me of my early life or the ward
    and city I live in, or the nation,
The latest dates, discoveries, inventions, societies, authors old
    and new,
My dinner, dress, associates, looks, compliments, dues,
The real or fancied indifference of some man or woman I love,   70
The sickness of one of my folks or of myself, or ill-doing or
    loss or lack of money, or depressions or exaltations,
Battles, the horrors of fratricidal war, the fever of doubtful
    news, the fitful events;
These come to me days and nights and go from me again,
But they are not the Me myself.

Apart from the pulling and hauling stands what I am,   75
Stands amused, complacent, compassionating, idle, unitary,
Looks down, is erect, or bends an arm on an impalpable
    certain rest,
Looking with side-curved head curious what will come next,
Both in and out of the game and watching and wondering at
    it.

Backward I see in my own days where I sweated through fog
    with linguists and contenders,   80

I have no mockings or arguments, I witness and wait.

5

I believe in you my soul, the other I am must not abase itself
    to you,
And you must not be abased to the other.

Loafe with me on the grass, loose the stop from your throat,
Not words, not music or rhyme I want, not custom or
    lecture, not even the best,   85

Only the lull I like, the hum of your valved voice.
I mind how once we lay such a transparent summer morning,
How you settled your head athwart my hips and gently turn'd
    over upon me,
And parted the shirt from my bosom-bone, and plunged your
    tongue to my bare-stript heart,
And reach'd till you felt my beard, and reach'd till you held my
    feet.   90
Swiftly arose and spread around me the peace and knowledge
    that pass all the argument of the earth,
And I know that the hand of God is the promise of my own,
And I know that the spirit of God is the brother of my own,
And that all the men ever born are also my brothers, and the
    women my sisters and lovers,
And that a kelson of the creation is love,   95
And limitless are leaves stiff or drooping in the fields,
And brown ants in the little wells beneath them,
And mossy scabs of the worm fence, heap'd stones, elder,
    mullein and poke-weed.

6

A child said *What is the grass?* fetching it to me with full hands,
How could I answer the child? I do not know what it is any
    more than he.   100

I guess it must be the flag of my disposition, out of hopeful
    green stuff woven.

Or I guess it is the handkerchief of the Lord,
A scented gift and remembrancer designedly dropt,
Bearing the owner's name someway in the corners, that we
    may see and remark, and say *Whose?*

Or I guess the grass is itself a child, the produced babe of the
    vegetation.   105

Or I guess it is a uniform hieroglyphic,
And it means, Sprouting alike in broad zones and narrow
zones,
Growing among black folks as among white,
Kanuck, Tuckahoe, Congressman, Cuff, I give them the same,
I receive them the same.

And now it seems to me the beautiful uncut hair of graves. 110

Tenderly will I use you curling grass,
It may be you transpire from the breasts of young men,
It may be if I had known them I would have loved them,
It may be you are from old people, or from offspring taken
soon out of their mothers' laps.
And here you are the mothers' laps. 115
This grass is very dark to be from the white heads of old
mothers,
Darker than the colorless beards of old men,
Dark to come from under the faint red roofs of mouths.

O I perceive after all so many uttering tongues,
And I perceive they do not come from the roofs of mouths for
nothing. 120

I wish I could translate the hints about the dead young men
and women,
And the hints about old men and mothers, and the offspring
taken soon out of their laps.

What do you think has become of the young and old men?
And what do you think has become of the women and
children?

They are alive and well somewhere, 125
The smallest sprout shows there is really no death,
And if ever there was it led forward life, and does not wait at
the end to arrest it,
And ceas'd the moment life appear'd.

All goes onward and outward, nothing collapses,
And to die is different from what any one supposed, and
      luckier.   130

7

Has any one supposed it lucky to be born?
I hasten to inform him or her it is just as lucky to die, and I
      know it.

I pass death with the dying and birth with the new-wash'd
      babe, and am not contain'd between my hat and boots,
And peruse manifold objects, no two alike and every one
      good,
The earth good and the stars good, and their adjuncts all
      good.   135

I am not an earth nor an adjunct of an earth,
I am the mate and companion of people, all just as immortal
      and fathomless as myself,
(They do not know how immortal, but I know.)

Every kind for itself and its own, for me mine male and
      female,
For me those that have been boys and that love women,   140
For me the man that is proud and feels how it stings to be
      slighted,
For me the sweet-heart and the old maid, for me mothers and
      the mothers of mothers,
For me lips that have smiled, eyes that have shed tears,
For me children and the begetters of children.

Undrape! you are not guilty to me, nor stale nor discarded,   145
I see through the broadcloth and gingham whether or no,
And am around, tenacious, acquisitive, tireless, and cannot be
      shaken away.

1855

A Noiseless Patient Spider

A noiseless patient spider,
I mark'd where on a little promontory it stood isolated,
Mark'd how to explore the vacant vast surrounding,
It launch'd forth filament, filament, filament, out of itself,
Ever unreeling them, ever tirelessly speeding them. 5

And you O my soul where you stand,
Surrounded, detached, in measureless oceans of space,
Ceaselessly musing, venturing, throwing, seeking the spheres
        to connect them,
Till the bridge you will need be form'd, till the ductile anchor
        hold,
Till the gossamer thread you fling catch somewhere, O my
        soul. 10

1881

When I Heard the Learn'd Astronomer

When I heard the learn'd astronomer,
When the proofs, the figures, were ranged in columns before
        me,
When I was shown the charts and diagrams, to add, divide,
        and measure them,
When I sitting heard the astronomer where he lectured with
        much applause in the lecture-room,
How soon unaccountable I became tired and sick, 5
Till rising and gliding out I wander'd off by myself,
In the mystical moist night-air, and from time to time,
Look'd up in perfect silence at the stars.

1865

Cavalry Crossing a Ford

A line in long array where they wind betwixt green islands,
They take a serpentine course, their arms flash in the sun—
        hark to the musical clank,

Behold the silvery river, in it the splashing horses loitering stop
      to drink,
Behold the brown-faced men, each group, each person a
      picture, the negligent rest on the saddles,
Some emerge on the opposite bank, others are just entering
      the ford—while,   5
Scarlet and blue and snowy white,
The guidon flags flutter gayly in the wind.

1865

Richard Wilbur
b. 1921

*Influenced by the seventeenth-century metaphysical poets and the
ironic stances of his contemporaries, Wilbur composes poetry with
precision, wit, and a keen attention to meter. Of "Love Calls Us
to the Things of This World" Wilbur wrote, "You must imagine
the poem as occurring at perhaps seven-thirty in the morning; the
scene is a bedroom high up in a city apartment building; outside
the bedroom window, the first laundry of the day is being yanked
across the sky and one has been awakened by the squeaking pulleys
of the laundry-line."*

Love Calls Us to the Things of This World

    The eyes open to a cry of pulleys,
And spirited from sleep, the astounded soul
Hangs for a moment bodiless and simple
As false dawn.
              Outside the open window
The morning air is all awash with angels.   5

    Some are in bed-sheets, some are in blouses,
Some are in smocks: but truly there they are.
Now they are rising together in calm swells
Of halcyon feeling, filling whatever they wear
With the deep joy of their impersonal breathing;   10

Now they are flying in place, conveying
The terrible speed of their omnipresence, moving
And staying like white water; and now of a sudden
They swoon down into so rapt a quiet
That nobody seems to be there.
                    The soul shrinks   15

From all that it is about to remember,
From the punctual rape of every blessèd day
And cries,
        "Oh, let there be nothing on earth but laundry,
Nothing but rosy hands in the rising steam
And clear dances done in the sight of heaven."   20

Yet, as the sun acknowledges
With a warm look the world's hunks and colors,
The soul descends once more in bitter love
To accept the waking body, saying now
In a changed voice as the man yawns and rises,   25

"Bring them down from their ruddy gallows;
Let there be clean linen for the backs of thieves;
Let lovers go fresh and sweet to be undone,
And the heaviest nuns walk in a pure floating
Of dark habits,
        keeping their difficult balance."   30
                  1956

William Carlos Williams
1883–1963
In 1923 Williams broke with his fellow modern poets by publishing Spring and All, *perhaps in response to what he considered T. S. Eliot's great catastrophe,* The Waste Land. *"Spring and All," the first poem in the volume, seems to comment on the opening of Eliot's poem, "April is the cruelest month." But Williams explained that he did not want his poems to communicate ideas. They were*

"[t]o refine, to clarify, to intensify that eternal moment in which we alone live" through contact with things. "The Red Wheelbarrow," the twenty-second poem (none had a title in the original book), is, perhaps, his best attempt to achieve that intensity.

Spring and All

By the road to the contagious hospital
under the surge of the blue
mottled clouds driven from the
northeast—a cold wind. Beyond, the
waste of broad, muddy fields   5
brown with dried weeds, standing and fallen

patches of standing water
the scattering of tall trees

All along the road the reddish
purplish, forked, upstanding, twiggy   10
stuff of bushes and small trees
with dead, brown leaves under them
leafless vines—

Lifeless in appearance, sluggish
dazed spring approaches—   15

They enter the new world naked,
cold, uncertain of all
save that they enter. All about them
the cold, familiar wind—

Now the grass, tomorrow   20
the stiff curl of wildcarrot leaf
One by one objects are defined—
It quickens: clarity, outline of leaf

But now the stark dignity of
entrance—Still, the profound change   25

has come upon them: rooted, they
grip down and begin to awaken
                    1923

The Red Wheelbarrow

so much depends
upon

a red wheel
barrow

glazed with rain   5
water

beside the white
chickens.
              1923

This Is Just to Say

I have eaten
the plums
that were in
the icebox

and which   5
you were probably
saving
for breakfast

Forgive me
they were delicious   10
so sweet
and so cold
          1934

William Wordsworth

1770–1850

It would be difficult to overstate Wordsworth's revolutionary impor-
tance to poetry written in English. He was the central figure in the
Romantic movement, which reversed many long-accepted beliefs.
For example, compare Wordsworth's use of the sonnet form (in
"The World Is Too Much with Us") to Shakespeare's or Sidney's.
Wordsworth's (and Samuel Coleridge's) Lyrical Ballads lowered
poetic diction to simple, ordinary language and widened the scope
of poetry to include simple, rural subjects like farmers, flowers, and
children. "The Tables Turned" exemplifies this new, unlearned style,
just as "I Wandered Lonely as a Cloud" illustrates the new range of
subject matter for Romantic poets. "She Dwelt among the Untrod-
den Ways" and "Lucy Gray" may be taken as typical Romantic
poems in sentiment and style. "Lines, composed a few miles above
Tintern Abbey" (commonly referred to as "Tintern Abbey"), was
unusual among the "lyrical ballads" for being philosophical and
sophisticated in vocabulary in syntax; it experimented with a new
technique: the poem seems to record the poet's spontaneous thoughts
as they interact with the world. That technique is the foundation of
the Romantic, or irregular, ode, which molds each stanza's structure
to the speaker's fluctuating thoughts and moods. "Nutting" expresses
what was, in Wordsworth's day, a new attitude toward nature.
Before the Romantic movement, most thought the natural world
was a hostile, dangerous power that threatend human beings.

The Tables Turned

Up! up! my Friend, and quit your books;
Or surely you'll grow double:
Up! up! my Friend, and clear your looks;
Why all this toil and trouble?

The sun, above the mountain's head,   5
A freshening lustre mellow
Through all the long green fields has spread,
His first sweet evening yellow.

Books! 'tis a dull and endless strife:
Come, hear the woodland linnet,   10
How sweet his music! on my life,
There's more of wisdom in it.

And hark! how blithe the throstle sings!
He, too, is no mean preacher:
Come forth into the light of things,   15
Let Nature be your Teacher.

She has a world of ready wealth,
Our minds and hearts to bless—
Spontaneous wisdom breathed by health,
Truth breathed by cheerfulness.   20

One impulse from a vernal wood
May teach you more of man,
Of moral evil and of good,
Than all the sages can.

Sweet is the lore which Nature brings;   25
Our meddling intellect
Mis-shapes the beauteous forms of things:—
We murder to dissect.

Enough of Science and of Art;
Close up those barren leaves;   30
Come forth, and bring with you a heart
That watches and receives.

1798

Lines

*composed a few miles above Tintern Abbey,
on revisiting the Banks of the Wye
during a tour. July 13, 1798*

Five years have past; five summers, with the length
Of five long winters! and again I hear

These waters, rolling from their mountain-springs
With a soft inland murmur.—Once again
Do I behold these steep and lofty cliffs,   5
That on a wild secluded scene impress
Thoughts of more deep seclusion; and connect
The landscape with the quiet of the sky.
The day is come when I again repose
Here, under this dark sycamore, and view   10
These plots of cottage-ground, these orchard-tufts,
Which at this season, with their unripe fruits,
Are clad in one green hue, and lose themselves
'Mid groves and copses. Once again I see
These hedge-rows, hardly hedge-rows, little lines   15
Of sportive wood run wild: these pastoral farms,
Green to the very door; and wreaths of smoke
Sent up, in silence, from among the trees!
With some uncertain notice, as might seem
Of vagrant dwellers in the houseless woods,   20
Or of some Hermit's cave, where by his fire
The Hermit sits alone.
                                        These beauteous forms,
Through a long absence, have not been to me
As is a landscape to a blind man's eye: 25
But oft, in lonely rooms, and 'mid the din
Of towns and cities, I have owed to them
In hours of weariness, sensations sweet,
Felt in the blood, and felt along the heart;
And passing even into my purer mind,   30
With tranquil restoration:—feelings too
Of unremembered pleasure: such, perhaps,
As have no slight or trivial influence
On that best portion of a good man's life,
His little, nameless, unremembered, acts   35
Of kindness and of love. Nor less, I trust,
To them I may have owed another gift,
Of aspect more sublime; that blessed mood,
In which the burthen of the mystery,
In which the heavy and the weary weight   40
Of all this unintelligible world,

Is lightened:—that serene and blessed mood,
In which the affections gently lead us on,—
Until, the breath of this corporeal frame
And even the motion of our human blood   45
Almost suspended, we are laid asleep
In body, and become a living soul:
While with an eye made quiet by the power
Of harmony, and the deep power of joy,
We see into the life of things.   50
                     If this
Be but a vain belief, yet, oh! how oft—
In darkness and amid the many shapes
Of joyless daylight; when the fretful stir
Unprofitable, and the fever of the world,   55
Have hung upon the beatings of my heart—
How oft, in spirit, have I turned to thee,
O sylvan Wye! thou wanderer thro' the woods,
How often has my spirit turned to thee!
  And now, with gleams of half-extinguished thought,   60
With many recognitions dim and faint,
And somewhat of a sad perplexity,
The picture of the mind revives again:
While here I stand, not only with the sense
Of present pleasure, but with pleasing thoughts   65
That in this moment there is life and food
For future years. And so I dare to hope,
Though changed, no doubt, from what I was when first
I came among these hills; when like a roe
I bounded o'er the mountains, by the sides   70
Of the deep rivers, and the lonely streams,
Wherever nature led: more like a man
Flying from something that he dreads, than one
Who sought the thing he loved. For nature then
(The coarser pleasures of my boyish days,   75
And their glad animal movements all gone by)
To me was all in all.—I cannot paint
What then I was. The sounding cataract
Haunted me like a passion: the tall rock,
The mountain, and the deep and gloomy wood,   80

Their colours and their forms, were then to me
An appetite; a feeling and a love,
That had no need of a remoter charm,
By thought supplied, nor any interest
Unborrowed from the eye.—That time is past, 85
And all its aching joys are now no more,
And all its dizzy raptures. Not for this
Faint I, nor mourn nor murmur; other gifts
Have followed; for such loss, I would believe,
Abundant recompense. For I have learned 90
To look on nature, not as in the hour
Of thoughtless youth; but hearing often-times
The still, sad music of humanity,
Nor harsh nor grating, though of ample power
To chasten and subdue. And I have felt 95
A presence that disturbs me with the joy
Of elevated thoughts; a sense sublime
Of something far more deeply interfused,
Whose dwelling is the light of setting suns,
And the round ocean and the living air, 100
And the blue sky, and in the mind of man;
A motion and a spirit, that impels
All thinking things, all objects of all thought,
And rolls through all things. Therefore am I still
A lover of the meadows and the woods, 105
And mountains; and of all that we behold
From this green earth; of all the mighty world
Of eye, and ear,—both what they half create,
And what perceive; well pleased to recognise
In nature and the language of the sense, 110
The anchor of my purest thoughts, the nurse,
The guide, the guardian of my heart, and soul
Of all my moral being.   Nor perchance,
If I were not thus taught, should I the more 115
Suffer my genial spirits[1] to decay:

1. Natural disposition.

For thou art with me here upon the banks
Of this fair river; thou my dearest Friend,
My dear, dear Friend; and in thy voice I catch
The language of my former heart, and read   120
My former pleasures in the shooting lights
Of thy wild eyes. Oh! yet a little while
May I behold in thee what I was once,
My dear, dear Sister! and this prayer I make,
Knowing that Nature never did betray   125
The heart that loved her; 't is her privilege,
Through all the years of this our life, to lead
From joy to joy: for she can so inform
The mind that is within us, so impress
With quietness and beauty, and so feed   130
With lofty thoughts, that neither evil tongues,
Rash judgments, nor the sneers of selfish men,
Nor greetings where no kindness is, nor all
The dreary intercourse of daily life,
Shall e'er prevail against us, or disturb   135
Our cheerful faith, that all which we behold
Is full of blessings. Therefore let the moon
Shine on thee in thy solitary walk;
And let the misty mountain-winds be free
To blow against thee: and, in after years,   140
When these wild ecstasies shall be matured
Into a sober pleasure; when thy mind
Shall be a mansion for all lovely forms,
Thy memory be as a dwelling-place
For all sweet sounds and harmonies; oh! then,   145
If solitude, or fear, or pain, or grief,
Should be thy portion, with what healing thoughts
Of tender joy wilt thou remember me,
And these my exhortations! Nor, perchance—
If I should be where I no more can hear   150
Thy voice, nor catch from thy wild eyes these gleams
Of past existence—wilt thou then forget
That on the banks of this delightful stream
We stood together; and that I, so long

A worshipper of Nature, hither came   155
Unwearied in that service: rather say
With warmer love—oh! with far deeper zeal
Of holier love. Nor wilt thou then forget,
That after many wanderings, many years
Of absence, these steep woods and lofty cliffs,   160
And this green pastoral landscape, were to me
More dear, both for themselves and for thy sake!
                                         1798

She Dwelt among the Untrodden Ways

She dwelt among the untrodden ways
   Beside the springs of Dove,
A Maid whom there were none to praise
   And very few to love:

A violet by a mossy stone   5
   Half hidden from the eye!
—Fair as a star, when only one
   Is shining in the sky.

She lived unknown, and few could know
   When Lucy ceased to be;   10
But she is in her grave, and, oh,
   The difference to me!
                                         1800

Lucy Gray

   Or, Solitude.

   [*Written at Goslar, in Germany, in 1799. It was founded on
a circumstance told me by my sister, of a little girl, who, not
far from Halifax in Yorkshire, was bewildered in a snow storm.
Her footsteps were tracked by her parents to the middle of a lock
of a canal, and no other vestige of her, backward or forward,*

*could be traced. The body, however, was found in the canal. The
way in which the incident was treated, and the spiritualizing of
the character, might furnish hints for contrasting the imagina-
tive influences, which I have endeavoured to throw over common
life, with Crabbe's matter-of-fact style of handling subjects of the
same kind. This is not spoken to his disparagement, far from
it; but to direct the attention of thoughtful readers into whose
hands these notes may fall, to a comparison that may enlarge
the circle of their sensibilities, and tend to produce in them a
catholic judgment.]*[1]

Oft I had heard of Lucy Gray;
And, when I crossed the wild,
I chanced to see at break of day
The solitary child.

No mate, no comrade Lucy knew;   5
She dwelt on a wide moor,
—The sweetest thing that ever grew
Beside a human door!

You yet may spy the fawn at play,
The hare upon the green;   10
But the sweet face of Lucy Gray
Will never more be seen.

"To-night will be a stormy night—
You to the town must go;
And take a lantern, Child, to light   15
Your mother through the snow."

"That, Father! will I gladly do:
'Tis scarcely afternoon—
The minster-clock has just struck two,
And yonder is the moon!"   20

1. Wordsworth's note.

At this the Father raised his hook,
And snapped a faggot-band;
He plied his work;—and Lucy took
The lantern in her hand.

Not blither is the mountain roe: 25
With many a wanton stroke
Her feet disperse the powdery snow,
That rises up like smoke.

The storm came on before its time:
She wandered up and down;   30
And many a hill did Lucy climb
But never reached the town.

The wretched parents all that night
Went shouting far and wide;
But there was neither sound nor sight   35
To serve them for a guide.

At day-break on a hill they stood
That over-looked the moor;
And thence they saw the bridge of wood,
A furlong from their door.   40

They wept—and, turning homeward, cried,
"In heaven we all shall meet;"
—When in the snow the mother spied
The print of Lucy's feet.

Then downwards from the steep hill's edge   45
They tracked the footmarks small;
And through the broken hawthorn hedge,
And by the long stone-wall;

And then an open field they crossed:
The marks were still the same;   50

They tracked them on, nor ever lost;
And to the bridge they came.

They followed from the snowy bank
Those footmarks, one by one,
Into the middle of the plank;   55
And further there were none!

—Yet some maintain that to this day
She is a living child;
That you may see sweet Lucy Gray
Upon the lonesome wild.   60

O'er rough and smooth she trips along,
And never looks behind;
And sings a solitary song
That whistles in the wind.

1800

Nutting

——————It seems a day
(I speak of one from many singled out)
One of those heavenly days that cannot die;
When, in the eagerness of boyish hope,
I left our cottage-threshold, sallying forth   5
With a huge wallet o'er my shoulder slung,
A nutting-crook in hand; and turned my steps
Tow'rd some far-distant wood, a Figure quaint,
Tricked out in proud disguise of cast-off weeds[1]
Which for that service had been husbanded,   10
By exhortation of my frugal Dame[2]—
Motley accoutrement, of power to smile
At thorns, and brakes, and brambles,—and, in truth,
More ragged than need was! O'er pathless rocks,

1. Clothes.
2. Ann Tyson, with whom Wordsworth lodged while at Hawkshead grammar school.

Through beds of matted fern, and tangled thickets,   15
Forcing my way, I came to one dear nook
Unvisited, where not a broken bough
Drooped with its withered leaves, ungracious sign
Of devastation; but the hazels rose
Tall and erect, with tempting clusters hung,   20
A virgin scene!—A little while I stood,
Breathing with such suppression of the heart
As joy delights in; and, with wise restraint
Voluptuous, fearless of a rival, eyed
The banquet;—or beneath the trees I sate   25
Among the flowers, and with the flowers I played;
A temper known to those, who, after long
And weary expectation, have been blest
With sudden happiness beyond all hope.
Perhaps it was a bower beneath whose leaves   30
The violets of five seasons re-appear
And fade, unseen by any human eye;
Where fairy water-breaks[3] do murmur on
For ever; and I saw the sparkling foam,
And—with my cheek on one of those green stones   35
That, fleeced with moss, under the shady trees,
Lay round me, scattered like a flock of sheep—
I heard the murmur and the murmuring sound,
In that sweet mood when pleasure loves to pay
Tribute to ease; and, of its joy secure,   40
The heart luxuriates with indifferent things,
Wasting its kindliness on stocks and stones,
And on the vacant air. Then up I rose,
And dragged to earth both branch and bough, with crash
And merciless ravage: and the shady nook   45
Of hazels, and the green and mossy bower,
Deformed and sullied, patiently gave up
Their quiet being: and, unless I now
Confound my present feelings with the past,
Ere from the mutilated bower I turned   50

---

3. Places where rocks break a stream's flow.

Exulting, rich beyond the wealth of kings,
I felt a sense of pain when I beheld
The silent trees, and saw the intruding sky.—
Then, dearest Maiden, move along these shades
In gentleness of heart; with gentle hand   55
Touch—for there is a spirit in the woods.

                                        1800

I Wandered Lonely as a Cloud

I wandered lonely as a Cloud
That floats on high o'er Vales and Hills,
When all at once I saw a crowd
A host of dancing Daffodils;
Along the Lake, beneath the trees,   5
Ten thousand dancing in the breeze.

The waves beside them danced, but they
Outdid the sparkling waves in glee:—
A Poet could not but be gay
In such a laughing company: 10
I gaz'd—and gaz'd—but little thought
What wealth the shew to me had brought:

For oft when on my couch I lie
In vacant or in pensive mood,
They flash upon that inward eye   15
Which is the bliss of solitude,
And then my heart with pleasure fills,
And dances with the Daffodils.

                                        1807

The World Is Too Much with Us

The world is too much with us; late and soon,
Getting and spending, we lay waste our powers;
Little we see in Nature that is ours;

We have given our hearts away, a sordid boon!
This Sea that bares her bosom to the moon,　　　　　　　5
The winds that will be howling at all hours,
And are up-gathered now like sleeping flowers,
For this, for everything, we are out of tune;
It moves us not.—Great God! I'd rather be
A Pagan suckled in a creed outworn;　　　　　　　　10
So might I, standing on this pleasant lea,[1]
Have glimpses that would make me less forlorn;
Have sight of Proteus[2] rising from the sea;
Or hear old Triton[3] blow his wreathèd horn.

1807

James Wright
1927–1980

> *In his poetry, Wright often grapples with the tension between two visions of midwestern America: the social forces that can cripple individuals and the natural forces that have a restorative power. Like many poems since the Romantic era, "A Blessing" describes a moment of heightened awareness or perception during which the things of the world seem to harmonize in unusual splendor. (Twilight seems to be the appropriate time for such moments.) What distinguishes Wright's poem is the comparison of the slender pony to a girl: what does this metaphor suggest about the speaker's relationship to the phenomena he perceives?*

A Blessing

Just off the highway to Rochester, Minnesota,
Twilight bounds softly forth on the grass.

---

1. I.e., open meadow.
2. In Greek myth, the "Old Man of the Sea," who rises from the sea at midday and can be forced to read the future by anyone who holds him while he takes many frightening shapes.

3. The son of the sea god, Neptune; the sound of his conch-shell horn calms the waves.

And the eyes of those two Indian ponies
Darken with kindness.
They have come gladly out of the willows   5
To welcome my friend and me.
We step over the barbed wire into the pasture
Where they have been grazing all day, alone.
They ripple tensely, they can hardly contain their happiness
That we have come.   10
They bow shyly as wet swans. They love each other.
There is no loneliness like theirs.
At home once more,
They begin munching the young tufts of spring in the darkness.
I would like to hold the slenderer one in my arms,   15
For she has walked over to me
And nuzzled my left hand.
She is black and white,
Her mane falls wild on her forehead,
And the light breeze moves me to caress her long ear   20
That is delicate as the skin over a girl's wrist.
Suddenly I realize
That if I stepped out of my body I would break
Into blossom.

                                                    1963

Mary Wroth

1587?–1651?

*"My pain, still smother'd in my grieved brest" comes in the middle
of a long sequence called* Pamphilia to Amphilanthus *that was an
appendix to Wroth's prose narrative* The Countesse of Montgom-
eries Urania. *Pamphilia is the central character of that rambling
book, and her pursuit of Amphilanthus provides the central plot.
The book attacks the notion that sexual fidelity is honorable for
women but irrelevant to a man's honor. The poems appended to
the* Urania *were meant to be taken as written by Pamphilia. The
poems before and after this one in the sequence suggest that the pain
in the first line comes from Pamphilia's jealousy.*

My pain, still smother'd in my grieved brest

My pain, still smother'd in my grieved brest
    Seeks for some ease, yet cannot passage find
    To be discharg'd of this unwelcome guest;
    When most I strive, more fast his burdens bind,

Like to a ship, on Goodwines[1] cast by wind,   5
    The more she strives, more deep in sand is pressed
    Till she be lost; so am I, in this kind
    Sunk, and devour'd, and swallow'd by unrest,

Lost, shipwrecked, spoiled, debared of smallest hope,
    Nothing of pleasure left; save thoughts have scope,   10
    Which wander may: Go then, my thoughts, and cry

Hope's perish'd; Love tempest-beaten; Joy lost,
    Killing despair hath all these blessings crossed;
    Yet faith still cries, Love will not falsify.

1621

Sir Thomas Wyatt
1503–1542

    Wyatt introduced the sonnet into English and first modified the Petrarchan or Italian rhyme scheme into the English scheme adopted and popularized by Shakespeare generations later. "My Galley" is a translation of one of Petrarch's sonnets. The speaker, as in most sonnets of the sixteenth and seventeenth centuries, is a male lover pining over his beloved's cold indifference. "They Flee from Me" introduces an interesting comparison between the speaker's lover and a wild animal in the first stanza. Part of this poem's continuing appeal is the range of emotions expressed: try to trace the speaker's vacillating attitudes toward this fickle woman, which are reflected in subtle changes in tone.

---

1. Goodwin Sands, a dangerously shallow stretch of the English Channel.

My Galley

My galley charged[1] with forgetfulness
    Thorough sharp seas in winter nights doth pass
    'Tween rock and rock; and eke mine enemy,[2] alas,
    That is my lord, steereth with cruelness;
And every oar a thought in readiness,   5
    As though that death were light in such a case.
    An endless wind doth tear the sail apace
    Of forced sighs and trusty fearfulness.
A rain of tears, a cloud of dark disdain,
    Hath done the wearied cords[3] great hinderance;   10
    Wreathed with error and eke with ignorance.
The stars be hid[4] that led me to this pain;
    Drowned is reason that should me consort,
    And I remain despairing of the port.

                       1557

They Flee from Me

They flee from me that sometime did me seek
    With naked foot stalking in my chamber.
I have seen them gentle tame and meek
    That now are wild and do not remember
    That sometime they put themselves in danger   5
To take bread at my hand; and now they range
Busily seeking with a continual change.

Thanked be fortune, it hath been otherwise
    Twenty times better; but once in special,
In thin array after a pleasant guise,[1]   10
    When her loose gown from her shoulders did fall,
    And she me caught in her arms long and small;

1. I.e., laden.
2. I.e., love. *Eke*: also.
3. The worn lines of the sail, with a possible pun on the Latin for heart *(cor, cordis)*.

4. I.e., the lady's eyes.
1. In a thin gown, made in a pleasing fashion.

And therewithal sweetly did me kiss,
And softly said, *Dear heart,*[2] *how like you this?*

It was no dream, I lay broad waking.   15
　But all is turned thorough my gentleness
Into a strange fashion of forsaking;
　And I have leave to go of her goodness
　And she also to use newfangleness.
But since that I so kindely[3] am served,   20
I would fain know what she hath deserved.

1557

William Butler Yeats

1865–1939

> *Born into an old Irish family, Yeats cherished "the ambition . . . of living in imitation of Thoreau on Innisfree, a small island in Lough Gill," a lake on Ireland's west coast. In his autobiography, Yeats tells us that once, on the streets of London, he saw in a shopwindow a display with a little spout of water, and he thought of writing "The Lake Isle of Innisfree." "Who Goes with Fergus?" illustrates how much modern poets valued mythology, which they thought could function in modern society the way the Bible functioned before Darwin. The myths created nationalist, even tribal identities. In one of many versions of the story, Fergus traded his kingship over Ulster, which comprises today's Northern Ireland, for a life "at peace hunting in the woods." Most critics think "Adam's Curse" records an actual conversation; if Yeats is the speaker in the poem, he is probably addressing Maud Gonne, a woman he was in love with for many years, sometimes encouraged by her, sometimes discouraged, but never fulfilled. "An Irish Airman" turns on the peculiar place of the Irish fighting in World War I. Air warfare was a novel form of battle in World War I, and it often was characterized in chivalric terms, especially compared to the grueling anonymity of life and death in the trenches. The airman in the poem*

---

2. With a pun on "heart" and "hart" (as deer).

3. I.e., in the way typical of female nature, or "kind"; with kindness (ironic).

was the son of Yeats's friend and patron Lady Augusta Gregory; he actually died in the war. "Easter, 1916" commemorates a nationalist uprising in Ireland on Easter Monday of that year. Yeats was a nationalist himself, but, as a member of the Protestant Ascendancy class, he thought himself superior to most Catholic nationalists, those with whom he exchanges "polite meaningless words" in the poem. The men he names in the poem were executed by the British; Yeats knew them all. "The Second Coming" was written just after World War I, and its apocalyptic images were provoked by the Bolshevik Revolution in Russia. Yeats originally titled "Leda and the Swan" "The Annunciation." The poem's depiction of a god, who appears as a swan, raping a mortal woman, deliberately insulted Catholic readers, who saw in the poem a comment on the Virgin Mary's impregnation. Yeats meant the violent and obscene imagery to defy the censorship laws of the increasingly conservative and Catholic government in Ireland. "Sailing to Byzantium" was published when Yeats was sixty-three years old and felt there was little place for old men like himself in the young country.

The Lake Isle of Innisfree

I will arise and go now, and go to Innisfree,
And a small cabin build there, of clay and wattles made:
Nine bean-rows will I have there, a hive for the honey-bee,
And live alone in the bee-loud glade.

And I shall have some peace there, for peace comes dropping
    slow,   5
Dropping from the veils of the morning to where the cricket
    sings;
There midnight's all a glimmer, and noon a purple glow,
And evening full of the linnet's wings.

I will arise and go now, for always night and day
I hear lake water lapping with low sounds by the shore;   10
While I stand on the roadway, or on the pavements grey,
I hear it in the deep heart's core.

1892

Who Goes with Fergus?

Who will go drive with Fergus now,
And pierce the deep wood's woven shade,
And dance upon the level shore?
Young man, lift up your russet brow,
And lift your tender eyelids, maid,   5
And brood on hopes and fear no more.

And no more turn aside and brood
Upon love's bitter mystery;
For Fergus rules the brazen cars,
And rules the shadows of the wood,   10
And the white breast of the dim sea
And all dishevelled wandering stars.

                              1893

Adam's Curse

We sat together at one summer's end,
That beautiful mild woman, your close friend,
And you and I, and talked of poetry.
I said, 'A line will take us hours maybe;
Yet if it does not seem a moment's thought,   5
Our stitching and unstitching has been naught.
Better go down upon your marrow-bones
And scrub a kitchen pavement, or break stones
Like an old pauper, in all kinds of weather;
For to articulate sweet sounds together   10
Is to work harder than all these, and yet
Be thought an idler by the noisy set
Of bankers, schoolmasters, and clergymen
The martyrs call the world.'

                              And thereupon
That beautiful mild woman for whose sake   15
There's many a one shall find out all heartache
On finding that her voice is sweet and low

Replied, 'To be born woman is to know—
Although they do not talk of it at school—
That we must labour to be beautiful.'   20
I said, 'It's certain there is no fine thing
Since Adam's fall but needs much labouring.
There have been lovers who thought love should be
So much compounded of high courtesy
That they would sigh and quote with learned looks   25
Precedents out of beautiful old books;
Yet now it seems an idle trade enough.'

We sat grown quiet at the name of love;
We saw the last embers of daylight die,
And in the trembling blue-green of the sky   30
A moon, worn as if it had been a shell
Washed by time's waters as they rose and fell
About the stars and broke in days and years.

I had a thought for no one's but your ears:
That you were beautiful, and that I strove   35
To love you in the old high way of love;
That it had all seemed happy, and yet we'd grown
As weary-hearted as that hollow moon.

1904

An Irish Airman Foresees His Death

I know that I shall meet my fate
Somewhere among the clouds above;
Those that I fight I do not hate,
Those that I guard I do not love;
My country is Kiltartan Cross,   5
My countrymen Kiltartan's poor,
No likely end could bring them loss
Or leave them happier than before.
Nor law, nor duty bade me fight,
Nor public men, nor cheering crowds,   10
A lonely impulse of delight

Drove to this tumult in the clouds;
I balanced all, brought all to mind,
The years to come seemed waste of breath,
A waste of breath the years behind   15
In balance with this life, this death.

                    1919

Easter, 1916

I have met them at close of day
Coming with vivid faces
From counter or desk among grey
Eighteenth-century houses.
I have passed with a nod of the head   5
Or polite meaningless words,
Or have lingered awhile and said
Polite meaningless words,
And thought before I had done
Of a mocking tale or a gibe   10
To please a companion
Around the fire at the club,
Being certain that they and I
But lived where motley is worn:
All changed, changed utterly: 15
A terrible beauty is born.

That woman's days were spent
In ignorant good-will,
Her nights in argument
Until her voice grew shrill.   20
What voice more sweet than hers
When, young and beautiful,
She rode to harriers?
This man had kept a school
And rode our wingèd horse;   25
This other his helper and friend
Was coming into his force;
He might have won fame in the end,

So sensitive his nature seemed,
So daring and sweet his thought. 30
This other man I had dreamed
A drunken, vainglorious lout.
He had done most bitter wrong
To some who are near my heart,
Yet I number him in the song; 35
He, too, has resigned his part
In the casual comedy;
He, too, has been changed in his turn,
Transformed utterly:
A terrible beauty is born. 40

Hearts with one purpose alone
Through summer and winter seem
Enchanted to a stone
To trouble the living stream.
The horse that comes from the road, 45
The rider, the birds that range
From cloud to tumbling cloud,
Minute by minute they change;
A shadow of cloud on the stream
Changes minute by minute; 50
A horse-hoof slides on the brim,
And a horse plashes within it;
The long-legged moor-hens dive,
And hens to moor-cocks call;
Minute by minute they live: 55
The stone's in the midst of all.

Too long a sacrifice
Can make a stone of the heart.
O when may it suffice?
That is Heaven's part, our part 60
To murmur name upon name,
As a mother names her child
When sleep at last has come
On limbs that had run wild.

What is it but nightfall?   65
No, no, not night but death;
Was it needless death after all?

For England may keep faith
For all that is done and said.
We know their dream; enough   70
To know they dreamed and are dead;
And what if excess of love
Bewildered them till they died?
I write it out in a verse—
MacDonagh and MacBride   75
And Connolly and Pearse
Now and in time to be,
Wherever green is worn,
Are changed, changed utterly:
A terrible beauty is born.   80

1921

The Second Coming

Turning and turning in the widening gyre
The falcon cannot hear the falconer;[1]
Things fall apart; the centre cannot hold;
Mere anarchy is loosed upon the world,
The blood-dimmed tide is loosed, and everywhere   5
The ceremony of innocence is drowned;
The best lack all conviction, while the worst
Are full of passionate intensity.

---

1. The image of the falcon circling the falconer symbolizes human history; in Yeats's view, the cyclical nature of history can be described by cones. The point of one cone is the birth of Christ, which initiated a two-thousand-year era of individualism that reached its highest moment in the Renaissance and was, by the twentieth century, spinning out of control. The mass politics of democracy and communism were symptoms of this dissolution. At the widest point of this cone, a new era, the point of a new cone, would appear, and history would oscillate in the opposite direction, gradually expanding the influence of an opposite force.

Surely some revelation is at hand;
Surely the Second Coming is at hand: 10
The Second Coming! Hardly are those words out
When a vast image out of *Spiritus Mundi*
Troubles my sight: somewhere in sands of the desert
A shape with lion body and the head of a man,
A gaze blank and pitiless as the sun,   15
Is moving its slow thighs, while all about it
Reel shadows of the indignant desert birds.
The darkness drops again; but now I know
That twenty centuries of stony sleep
Were vexed to nightmare by a rocking cradle,   20
And what rough beast, its hour come round at last,
Slouches towards Bethlehem to be born?

1921

Leda and the Swan[1]

A sudden blow: the great wings beating still
Above the staggering girl, her thighs caressed
By the dark webs, her nape caught in his bill,
He holds her helpless breast upon his breast.

How can those terrified vague fingers push   5
The feathered glory from her loosening thighs?
And how can body, laid in that white rush,
But feel the strange heart beating where it lies?

A shudder in the loins engenders there
The broken wall, the burning roof and tower   10

1. In Greek mythology, Leda, a human woman, was raped by the god Zeus, who appeared in the form of a swan. Leda gave birth to Helen, who eventually married Menelaus, a Greek king. When Paris of Troy kidnapped Helen, the Greeks, led by Menelaus's brother Agamemnon (who was married to Helen's sister, Clytemnestra), banded together to invade Troy and retrieve Helen. The long history of the Trojan War, including Clytemnestra's murdering Agamemnon upon his return, was engendered by this rape. Yeats considered this story to be an analogue of the Christian annunciation, when God, in the form of a dove, impregnated Mary. In Yeats's idiosyncratic theory of history, the birth of Jesus initiated a two-thousand-year epoch that culminated in the mass politics and wars of the twentieth century.

And Agamemnon dead.
                    Being so caught up,
So mastered by the brute blood of the air,
Did she put on his knowledge with his power
Before the indifferent beak could let her drop?

                                                    1924

Sailing to Byzantium[1]

I

That is no country for old men. The young
In one another's arms, birds in the trees
—Those dying generations—at their song,
The salmon-falls, the mackerel-crowded seas,
Fish, flesh, or fowl, commend all summer long   5
Whatever is begotten, born, and dies.
Caught in that sensual music all neglect
Monuments of unaging intellect.

2

An aged man is but a paltry thing,
A tattered coat upon a stick, unless   10
Soul clap its hands and sing, and louder sing
For every tatter in its mortal dress,
Nor is there singing school but studying
Monuments of its own magnificence;
And therefore I have sailed the seas and come   15
To the holy city of Byzantium.

---

1. Byzantium (now Istanbul) was for centuries the capital of the Eastern Roman Empire. Yeats saw in its mosaics the prototype of an artificial, symbolic art that made no attempt at realism. Byzantium became, in his imagination, a country of unchanging, undeveloping artifice, and this permanence he contrasted with the mutability of a young country, like Ireland, which had gained its independence just six years before he wrote this poem.

3

O sages standing in God's holy fire
As in the gold mosaic of a wall,
Come from the holy fire, perne in a gyre,[2]
And be the singing-masters of my soul.   20
Consume my heart away; sick with desire
And fastened to a dying animal
It knows not what it is; and gather me
Into the artifice of eternity.

4

Once out of nature I shall never take   25
My bodily form from any natural thing,
But such a form as Grecian goldsmiths make
Of hammered gold and gold enamelling
To keep a drowsy Emperor awake;
Or set upon a golden bough to sing   30
To lords and ladies of Byzantium
Of what is past, or passing, or to come.

1927

Politics

> *'In our time the destiny of man presents its meanings in political terms.'*
> —Thomas Mann.

How can I, that girl standing there,
My attention fix
On Roman or on Russian
Or on Spanish politics,
Yet here's a travelled man that knows   5

2. The speaker is asking the sages to come down as if out of the golden mosaics painted on the inside of a dome and inspire him. *Perne*: Yeats's coinage, referring to thread pulled from a bobbin; the unwinding thread would appear to make a conical shape. In this comparison, the thread would be the sages, and the point of the cone would be the speaker into whom these sages are descending.

What he talks about,
And there's a politician
That has both read and thought,
And maybe what they say is true
Of war and war's alarms,   10
But O that I were young again
And held her in my arms.

1939

Biographical Sketches

Diane Ackerman (*b. 1948*) Ackerman was born in Illinois and earned her undergraduate degree from Pennsylvania State University. She earned three degrees from Cornell University: an MFA in 1973, an MA in 1976, and a PhD in 1978. Her work has ranged widely, from her confessional and nature poetry, to nonfiction books on the "natural history" of romantic love, the workings of the human brain, gardening, and endangered species. She has won numerous awards; perhaps the most unusual was her semifinalist finish in the Journalist-in-Space Project.

Kim Addonizio (*b. 1954*) Born in San Francisco and long associated with the Bay Area, Addonizio has won several awards, including Guggenheim and National Endowment for the Arts fellowships, two Pushcart Prizes (one for her poems, one for essays), and the John Ciardi Lifetime Achievement Award. Known for her edgy subject matter, Addonizio has published six books of poetry, a few novels, and several edited volumes. Independent of universities, Addonizio conducts poetry workshops in Oakland, California, and she's written two books on the craft: *The Poet's Companion: A Guide to the Pleasures of Writing Poetry* and *Ordinary Genius: A Guide for the Poet Within.*

Paul Allen (*b. 1945*) Allen teaches courses in writing poetry and in writing song lyrics at the College of Charleston in Charleston, South Carolina, where he is Associate Professor of English. His first book of poems, *American Crawl*, received the Vassar Miller Poetry Prize and was nominated for a Pulitzer and a National Book Award. In 2000, Glebe Street Records released Allen's *The Man with the Hardest Belly: Poems & Songs*. Another poetry collection, *The Clean Plate Club*, appeared in 2001.

Matthew Arnold (*1822–1888*) Arnold was a sort of jack-of-all-trades: a preeminent poet of the Victorian era, a pioneer in the field of literary criticism, an educator, a government official, and an influential public figure. Arnold's father was the headmaster of Rugby, a prestigious English prep school, and Arnold grew up knowing many of the leading intellectual and literary men of his day. He was educated at Winchester, Rugby, and Balliol College, Oxford, later serving as fellow of Oriel College, Oxford. In 1851 he married Frances Lucy Wightman, and when the newlyweds visited Dover on their honeymoon, Arnold wrote the earliest drafts of "Dover Beach." Arnold was well-known in his own day as an arbiter of culture, and his theories of literary criticism are still highly influential today.

John Ashbery (*b. 1927*) Ashbery was born in Rochester, New York, and has spent most of his life in the Northeast—graduating from Harvard (A.B. in 1949) and attending Columbia University (MA in 1951) and New York University; working for the *Partisan Review, New York* magazine, and *Newsweek*; and teaching at Brooklyn College and Bard College. He has been considered the vanguard of a new type of poetry, the voice of the cacophonous late twentieth century, and he has influenced many contemporary poets. He has published over thirty books of poetry, beginning in 1953, and numerous other works, including translations.

Margaret Atwood (*b. 1939*) Atwood spent the first eleven years of her life in sparsely populated areas of northern Ontario and Quebec, where her father, an entomologist, spent eight months of each year doing research in the forest. The Atwood family stayed in a cabin heated by a wood stove and lit by kerosene lanterns. One of Atwood's few sources of entertainment was reading, and she soon began to write, too, beginning with poems, plays, comic books, and an unfinished novel about an ant. By sixteen, she had decided that all she wanted to do was write. Atwood received her bachelor's degree from Victoria College at the University of Toronto and her master's degree from Radcliffe College. She also studied at Harvard University. Together with a friend Atwood published her first book of poems on a small flat-bed press and sold copies for fifty cents each. She has received numerous prizes for her poetry as well as for her fiction, including the 2000 Man Booker Prize for her novel *The Blind Assassin*.

W. H. (Wystan Hugh) Auden (*1907–1973*) Born to a medical officer and a nurse, W. H. Auden attended Christ Church College, Oxford, where he distinguished himself more as a poet than as a student. While at Oxford, Auden formed friendships with such writers as Stephen Spender, C. Day Lewis, and Christopher Isherwood. Not only was Auden the principal poet of his generation, but he was also a playwright, librettist, editor, and essayist. He is widely admired for his technical virtuosity, his success with diverse poetic forms and themes, and his encyclopedic intellectual range. Auden moved to New York City's Greenwich Village in 1939 and became an American citizen in 1946. For many years he was actively involved in politics, vigorously opposing fascism. But he shocked audiences on both sides of the Atlantic when he repudiated the political scene by publishing "In Memory of W. B. Yeats" in *The New Republic*. Auden received the Pulitzer Prize for his body of work and served as a chancellor of the Academy of American Poets.

Jimmy Santiago Baca (*b. 1952*) Santiago is part Chicano, part Apache, and grew up in poverty in New Mexico. Convicted of drug crimes, Santiago learned to write poetry in prison, and since his release has conducted workshops with prisoners, ex-cons, and others on the fringe of society, as well as in universities. He has published several books of poetry, such as *A Place to Stand* (2001) and an award-winning, autobiographical verse-novel, *Martin and Meditations on the South Valley* (1987). He has won several awards, most notably the Cornelius P. Turner Award, which recognizes significant achievement in social justice among earners of graduate equivalency diplomas (GEDs). His non-profit organization, Cedar Tree, Inc, teaches iteracy, writing, and language skills to prisoners, at-risk youth, and other underserved communities.

Anna Letitia Barbauld (*1743–1825*) Born Anna Letitia Aiken in Northamptonshire, north of London, Barbauld was a prodigy and received from her father an education that was unusually thorough for women in the eighteenth century, which included Latin and Greek. Her first collection of poems was published in 1773 and was admired by Samuel Johnson and William Wordsworth, and brought her into the world of English letters. She was a Unitarian in religion and, as a public figure, supported radical politics. She married Rochemont Barbauld, taught in his school, and, in order to supply her youngest pupils with proper materials, wrote two significant children's primers, the first of their kind in England. After her husband's death in 1808, she edited an influential fifty-volume series called *The British Novelists*, which helped to legitimize that genre in the eyes of critics. One of her more popular works is comprised of her correspondence with literary figures like Wordsworth and the Irish novelist Maria Edgeworth.

Aphra Behn *(1640[?]–1689)* Behn probably was born Alpha Johnson two years before the English Civil War effectively dethroned Charles I and closed London's theaters. The daughter of a barber, she grew up on the fringes of the aristocracy with which she would align herself in later life, somehow securing an excellent education. After the restoration of the monarchy and the reopening of theaters, she began writing plays. Her first, *A Forc'd Marriage*, was performed in 1670. Much of the poetry she wrote celebrated the Catholic-leaning Tory faction in English politics, and she died one year after the exile of the Tory king, James II. In her lifetime, Behn's fame rivaled that of any male English poet, playwright, and novelist, and upon her death she was given the honor of a tomb in Westminster Abbey.

John Berryman *(1914–1972)* In 1926, Berryman's father shot himself, and Berryman, then a boy of twelve, found the body. In 1936, he graduated from Columbia University, and published a number of critically successful books of poetry in the subsequent years, beginning in 1942. Through most of the 1940s he taught at Princeton, increasing not only his poetic reputation but his reputation as a critic. Berryman taught poetry at the influential Writers' Workshop of the University of Iowa, and among his students were some of the best poets in what came to be considered the "confessional" school of poetry, including Philip Levine, Robert Dana, and W. D. Snodgrass. In 1964, the first volume of his *77 Dream Songs* won the Pulitzer Prize and helped establish Berryman as one of America's finest poets; the second volume, *His Toy, His Dream, His Rest,* won the National Book Award in 1969. His life was plagued by alcoholism and depression, which often impeded the progress of his career (he was dismissed by the University of Iowa for public intoxication); however, the associative style of his *Dream Songs* is sometimes likened to intoxication. After 1955, he taught at the University of Minnesota. He killed himself by jumping from a bridge in Minneapolis.

Elizabeth Bishop (*1911–1979*) Bishop lost both of her parents early in her life. She was shuttled between her father's wealthy Massachusetts family and her mother's rural Nova Scotia family throughout her childhood. Bishop was educated at Vassar College, where she fell in with a group of young, talented writers. In 1935 she met Marianne Moore, whose work deeply impressed Bishop and whose friendship was to become a stabilizing force in her life. *The Partisan Review*'s March 1940 publication of "The Fish" launched Bishop's career, and from then on her work frequently appeared in magazines such as *The New Yorker*. Bishop went on to win virtually every poetry prize in the country. She served as a chancellor of the Academy of American Poets, a member of the American Academy of Arts and Letters, and a consultant in poetry to the Library of Congress in 1949–50. She taught at the University of Washington, Harvard, New York University, and, just prior to her death, the Massachusetts Institute of Technology.

William Blake (*1757–1827*) Though Blake is today considered one of the earliest and greatest figures of English Romanticism, at the time of his death he was a little-known artist and an entirely unknown poet. Having been apprenticed at the age of fourteen, Blake's only formal education was in art, and he was an accomplished painter and engraver. For most of his life he made his living illustrating books and magazines, giving drawing lessons, and engraving designs made by other artists. From childhood, though, he spent most of his spare time reading, and often tried his hand at poetry. By adulthood, he was dissatisfied with the reigning poetic tradition and was testing new forms and techniques. In 1789, the year that the French Revolution began, he published *Songs of Innocence*, a series of poems accompanied by his own illustrations. In 1794 he published a parallel series, *Songs of Experience*. Together, Blake wrote, these two series portray "the two Contrary States of the Human Soul." He was a devout Christian who saw a close relationship between his religion and his art, declaring that "all he knew was in the Bible" and that the "Old and New Testaments are the Great Code of Art."

Anne Bradstreet (*1612* or *1613–1672*) Bradstreet's father, Thomas Dudley, steward of the Earl of Lincoln's estate, took care to see that his daughter received a better education than most young women of her day. At sixteen she married Simon Bradstreet, a recent graduate of Cambridge University and assistant of her father. Bradstreet was soon appointed to assist in preparations of the Massachusetts Bay Company, and so the Bradstreets and Dudleys sailed with Winthrop's fleet to Massachusetts. In leaving

"Old England" for "New England," Anne Bradstreet gave up a life of relative comfort and culture for the wilderness of the New World. When visiting England in 1650, Bradstreet's brother-in-law published a volume of Bradstreet's poetry without her consent. This volume, *The Tenth Muse*, was the first book of poetry written by a resident of the New World and was widely read throughout England. The verses for which she is remembered today were not published until 1678 in a posthumous edition. Bradstreet was an ambitious poet whose work is firmly grounded in English religious, political, and cultural history.

Emily Brontë *(1818–1848)* Brontë and her sisters, Anne and Charlotte, all became successful novelists in England. They grew up in Yorkshire, near the dreary moors of England's north, and as children they created an extensive fantasy world called Gondel; many of Emily's poems are dramatic monologues spoken by characters in this elaborate story. She and her sisters published the financially unsuccessful *Poems by Currer, Ellis, and Acton Bell* in 1846 (Emily's pseudonym was "Ellis"), and then Emily's masterpiece novel, *Wuthering Heights*, appeared in 1847. Initially, that book was poorly received by the critics, and Brontë died of tuberculosis the next year, before she received eventual literary fame as a novelist.

Gwendolyn Brooks *(1912–2000)* Born in Topeka, Kansas, and raised in Chicago, Brooks began writing poetry at the age of seven. After graduating from high school, she attended art school at the South Side Community Art Center. Her main interest, however, was poetry, and she soon demonstrated her talent by winning contests sponsored by *Poetry* magazine and various other organizations. She published her first book of poetry in 1945. Her second book of poems, *Annie Allen*, won Brooks the distinction of being the first African American to be awarded the Pulitzer Prize, which she received in 1950. Brooks's early works concentrate on what Langston Hughes called the "ordinary aspects of black life," but her later poetry deals more with issues of African American consciousness and activism.

Elizabeth Barrett Browning *(1806–1861)* The eldest of twelve children, Barrett Browning was the first in her family to be born in England in over two hundred years, as the Barretts had lived in Jamaica for centuries. Though she lived at home under her father's strict rule, Barrett Browning began writing poetry at an early age, publishing her first volume when she was only thirteen and gaining a considerable following by the time she was in her thirties. Her 1844 collection, *Poems*, caught the eye of Robert Browning, and the two exchanged 574 letters over a period of twenty months.

Her father did not want any of his children to marry, and so Elizabeth was forced to elope with Robert, who was six years her junior. The two settled in Italy, where Barrett Browning bore a son; saw her chronic lung condition improve; and published *Sonnets from the Portuguese*, a sequence of forty-four sonnets that record the stages of her love for Robert Browning. Critics have compared the imagery of the sonnet sequence to that of Shakespeare and the skillful use of form to that of Petrarch.

Robert Browning *(1812–1889)* Born in a suburb of London, Browning spent much of his childhood in his father's extensive library. From early on his aim was to become a poet; he abandoned his schooling in order to dedicate all his energies to the realization of this goal. His parents supported him until he was in his thirties. Browning admired the poetry of Elizabeth Barrett and began to correspond with her in 1844. Two years later they were married. In 1849 they moved to Italy because the warm climate there helped Elizabeth's lung condition. After Elizabeth died in 1861, Browning returned to London and began to establish his literary reputation. Today he is recognized as one of England's most prolific poets.

Robert Burns *(1759–1796)* Burns was born and grew up on a farm in Scotland, in a house ruled by Calvinist parents, though his upbringing instilled in him an unusual religious tolerance and dislike of privilege. Handsome and charming, he had many affairs and had nine children with six different women. He published his first book of poetry, *Poems, Chiefly in the Scottish Dialect*, in 1786, and was instantly recognized as a major talent. His poems were among the first Romantic movement, expressing profound philosophical and moral issues in the guise of the humble and everyday—such as a mouse unearthed by a plow. He tried his hand at farming, then became a tax collector, and spent his later creativity mostly on Scottish songs, such as "Auld Lang Syne." He died of heart disease.

Lord Byron (George Gordon) *(1788–1824)* Byron was born George Gordon, and his short life, lived so fully, became a prototype for other Romantics: the original live-fast, die-young "Byronic" hero. He grew up fatherless and in poverty, until his granduncle died in 1798, leaving the ten-year-old boy heir to a title of nobility and a landed estate. After his schooling, he took the traditional "tour" of the continent but went farther afield than the typical Englishman, traveling to the exotic Middle East. He wrote a slightly veiled verse autobiography of these travels, *Childe Harold's Pilgrimage*, which made him an instant celebrity. His notorious

affairs with many women, including his half-sister, and his radical poli-
tics led to his exile from England. This alienation, coupled, paradoxically,
with the immense celebrity given to superior talent, is one of the chief
features of Byronic hero. On the continent, Byron cultivated friendships
with the poet Percy Shelley and the young novelist Mary Shelley, and a
romantic liaison with Mary's sister. He published many satires, continued
new installments of *Childe Harold*, and worked on the unfinished narra-
tive poem, now recognized as his masterpiece, *Don Juan*. He aided Italian
nationalists in their fight against aristocratic tyranny, and in 1824, he went
to Greece to help that nation win independence from Turkey. He died of
malaria in that cause.

Thomas Campion *(1567–1620)* Campion attended Cambridge and studied
law at Grays Inn, though he never followed that career. He is best known
today as a composer of songs—ayres or airs—that are still performed and
regularly recorded. In his own day, he was, perhaps, best known as a writer
of Latin verse and of "masques," a strange genre of literature that died in
the seventeenth century. They were elaborate productions melding drama,
poetry, music, and stage-setting, often commissioned by aristocrats to cel-
ebrate a particular occasion, such as a wedding.

Nick Carbó (*b. 1964*) Born in the Philippines and adopted by white
parents, Carbo grew up in Manila and immigrated to the United States,
where he graduated from St. Mary's University and earned an MFA from
Sarah Lawrence College. He has become a conduit of Filipino/a–American
literature, having edited two influential volumes of such writers, *Returning
a Borrowed Tongue* (1996) and *Babaylan* (2000). He has published three
books of poetry, including *Secret Asian Man*, which appeared in 2000. He
works in the English department of Florida International University and is
married to the poet Denise Duhamel.

Lewis Carroll (*1832–1898*) Charles Lutwidge Dodgson was the man
behind the pen name of "Lewis Carroll." Dodgson was born in Dares-
bury, Cheshire, England, to an Anglican clergyman who eventually had
eleven children. He was educated at Richmond School, Rugby, and Christ
Church, Oxford. A man of diverse interests, Dodgson was actively engaged
in many fields: mathematics, logic, photography, art, theater, religion,
medicine, and science. In 1855 Dodgson finally attained a college Master-
ship at Oxford, a position that he was to hold until 1881. For some time
he aspired to the priesthood, and he even went so far as to be ordained
as a deacon in 1861. Dodgson was happiest in the company of children

for whom he created puzzles, clever games, and charming letters. He was particularly close to the children of Henry Liddell, dean of Christ Church, and wrote most of his stories for their amusement. Alice Liddell was his favorite, and it is she who stars in *Alice in Wonderland* and *Through the Looking-Glass*.

Geoffrey Chaucer (*1340[?]–1400*) Chaucer lived an active life, fighting in England's wars (he was once captured in France and ransomed by the king), acting as diplomat, and serving in a variety of public offices. He was well traveled, knew both Boccaccio and Petrarch, two of the literary titans of the Italian renaissance, and was well versed in medieval science. His best-known work is *The Canterbury Tales*, a cycle of stories, told in verse, during a pilgrimage to the shrine of St. Thomas à Becket. He wrote before the European invention of printing—all of his work would have been circulated in manuscript and read aloud in gatherings.

Lucille Clifton (*1936–2010*) The descendant of Virginia slaves and free blacks from Dahomey (an African kingdom in what is now Benin), Clifton was born near Buffalo, New York, where her father was a steel worker. Neither parent graduated elementary school, but Clifton attended Howard University on a scholarship funded by the family's church. There and at Fredonia State Teachers College (near Buffalo), she met black intellectuals like Amiri Baraka and Ishmael Reed, who introduced her poems to Langston Hughes. Hughes published a few of her early poems in his *Poetry of the Negro* anthology. In the late 1960s, she began publishing her own books of poetry and also children's books. Clifton taught creative writing at Coppin State College, the University of California at Santa Cruz, St. Mary's College of Maryland, and Columbia University.

Samuel Taylor Coleridge (*1772–1834*) Coleridge was born in the small town of Ottery St. Mary in Devonshire, England, the youngest of ten children. When his father died in 1781, Coleridge was sent to a London charity school for children of the clergy, Christ's Hospital, where he read widely and finished first in his class. Coleridge went on to attend Jesus College, Cambridge, though he was forced to leave without a degree after he fell into debt. After a brief stint in the army and an attempt at lecturing, he married Sara Fricker and tried to settle down. He became friends with Wordsworth and the two men collaborated on a number of literary projects, notably *Lyrical Ballads*. Coleridge spent two years in Malta trying unsuccessfully to recover from painful rheumatism. Upon his return he dissolved his unhappy marriage, which had been strained by his love for another woman. As the years passed, he became more estranged from his family and more addicted to opium to ease his pain. Coleridge was also a literary critic.

Billy Collins (*b. 1941*) Collins lives in New York City and is professor of English at Lehman College of the City University of New York. He has received fellowships from the National Endowment for the Arts and the Guggenheim Foundation, and his work has been published in such venues as *Poetry, American Poetry Review, American Scholar, Harper's, The Paris Review, The Atlantic Monthly*, and *The New Yorker*. Collins's collections include *Picnic, Lightning; The Art of Drowning; Questions about Angels*; and the CD *The Best Cigarette*. He has won numerous awards, among them the Pushcart Prize and the National Poetry Series publication prize.

Countee Cullen (*1903–1946*) Cullen grew up in the Bronx under adoptive parents, prospered in school, and earned a graduate degree from Harvard before returning to New York City and joining the vibrant black arts movement called the Harlem Renaissance. His career flared brightly in the 1920s with the publication of several books of poetry, including *Color* (1925), *Harlem Wine* (1926), *Copper Sun* and *The Ballad of the Brown Girl* (1927), and *The Black Christ and Other Poems* (1929). Briefly, he was married to W. E. B. Du Bois's daughter Yolande. Some evidence suggests that he had a romantic relationship with another teacher, Harold Jackman; certainly they were very close friends. After 1934, he taught English and creative writing at Frederick Douglass Junior High School in New York and wrote for the theater.

E. E. (Edward Estlin) Cummings (*1894–1962*) Cummings was born in Cambridge, Massachusetts, to particularly supportive parents who encouraged him to develop his creative gifts. His father was a former Harvard professor who had become a Unitarian minister, and Cummings received both his BA and his MA from Harvard University. While there, he wrote poetry in the pre-Raphaelite and metaphysical traditions and published it in *The Harvard Advocate*. Cummings joined the Ambulance Corps the day after the United States entered World War I. During the war, he spent three months in a French prison because his outspoken anti-war convictions led the French to accuse him of treason. He transmuted this experience into his first literary success, *The Enormous Room*. After the war he shuttled between New York City's Greenwich Village, Paris, and New Hampshire. He showed little interest in wealth or his growing celebrity.

Carol Ann Davis (*b. 1970*) Davis graduated from Vassar College in 1992 and from the University of Massachusetts, Amherst, in 1996 with an MFA. Her first book of poems, *Psalm*, was published in 2007 by the Tupelo Press. She won a WK Rose fellowship from Vassar in 1999 and in 2007 was awarded a National Endowment for the Humanities fellowship. She teaches creative writing at the College of Charleston in South Carolina.

Natalie Diaz (*b. 1978*) A Mojave and Pima Indian, Diaz has won awards for her fiction and poetry, including the Nimrod/Hardman Pablo Neruda prize. After college, she played professional basketball in five European countries before returning the United States, where she earned an MFA from Old Dominion University. Her first book of poetry, *When My Brother Was an Aztec*, was published by Copper Canyon Press in 2012.

James Dickey (*1923–1997*) Dickey grew up in a comfortable suburb of Atlanta, where he was a better athlete than scholar. At Clemson University, he joined the Air Corps and flew in thirty-eight combat missions in the Pacific during World War II. Upon returning, he graduated from Vanderbilt University, then the center of a Southern renaissance in literature. He taught English in a variety of schools and worked in the advertising industry before his first book of poems was published in 1960. His 1970 novel, *Deliverance*, was made into a popular movie, and it brought Dickey wealth and fame, but this success also initiated his long, debilitating battle with alcoholism. He taught poetry at the University of South Carolina from 1969 until his death.

Emily Dickinson (*1830–1886*) Dickinson's grandfather founded Amherst College, and her father was a state senator and U.S. congressman. Dickinson attended Amherst Academy and spent a year at the Mount Holyoke Female Seminary (now Mount Holyoke College). She spent the rest of her life in her father's Amherst mansion. Visitors were scarce, and Dickinson herself rarely ventured out. Though Dickinson was a prolific poet, her talents were not recognized in her day: only ten of her poems were published in her lifetime. After her death over seventeen hundred poems were discovered bound neatly in booklets. Four years later, Thomas Wentworth Higginson, an editor for the *Atlantic Monthly*, with whom Dickinson had corresponded, smoothed and regularized some of her poems and published them in a book. Editors did not restore her idiosyncratic expressions and punctuation until the twentieth century.

John Donne (*1572–1631*) The first and greatest of a group that came to be known as the "Metaphysical" poets, Donne wrote in a revolutionary style that combined highly intellectual conceits, or metaphors, with complex, compressed phrasing. Born into a Catholic family at a time when Catholics were a persecuted minority, Donne felt his religion was central to his identity and to much of his poetry. He studied at both Oxford and Cambridge Universities but took a degree from neither school because to do so he would have had to subscribe to the Thirty-nine Articles, the tenets of Anglicanism. From Oxford and Cambridge Donne went to Lincoln's Inn, where he studied law. Two years later he relented and joined the Anglican Church, motivated in no small part by the recent death of his brother, who had been imprisoned for his Catholicism. After he secretly married the daughter of an aristocrat, Donne was briefly imprisoned himself. This politically disastrous marriage dashed his worldly hopes and forced him to struggle for years to support a large and growing family. During this time, he wrote on the lawfulness of suicide (*Bianthanatos*). He eventually managed to reestablish himself and by 1615 was sufficiently well known that King James I appointed him dean of St. Paul's Cathedral in London. Most of his published works were sermons; Donne circulated his poetry among learned people, but it was not published until after his death.

Mark Doty (*b. 1953*) Doty has written eight books of poetry and several essays, which have won numerous awards, including two Lambda Awards and the National Book Award for *Fire to Fire: New and Selected Poems* (2008). His third book of poems, *My Alexandria* (1993), which explores issues arising out of the AIDS epidemic, won the National Book Critics Circle Award. In addition to eight books of poetry he's written several memoirs, including the *New York Times* bestseller *Dog Years*. Doty is also keenly interested in painting and wrote a book on seventeenth-century Dutch painting, *Still Life with Oysters and Lemon* (2002). He taught writing for many years at the University of Houston.

Rita Dove (*b. 1952*) Growing up in Akron, Ohio, Dove wrote stories and plays for her classmates to perform. After being named a President's Scholar, Dove went on to attend Miami University in Ohio, study for a year at Tübingen University in Germany as a Fulbright scholar, and receive an MFA in creative writing from the University of Iowa. She was also awarded fellowships from the Guggenheim Foundation and the National Endowment for the Arts. She served as Poet Laureate of the United States between 1993 and 1995, the youngest person ever to do so. In 1987 Dove was awarded the Pulitzer Prize for Poetry. She has taught creative writing at Arizona State University and is currently the Commonwealth Professor of English at the University of Virginia and an associate editor of *Callaloo*, the journal of African American and African arts and letters.

Denise Duhamel (*b. 1961*) The daughter of a baker and a nurse, Duhamel grew up in Rhode Island, earned a BFA from Emerson College and an MFA from Sarah Lawrence College (in 1987). Since 1993 she has published numerous books of poetry and won many awards, including a fellowship from the National Endowment for the Arts. She now teaches at Florida International University. She is married to the Filipino poet Nick Carbó.

Bob Dylan (*b. 1941*) Robert Allen Zimmerman (Dylan's given name) grew up in a middle class family in Hibbing, Minnesota. After graduating from high school, he joined the folk music scene in Minneapolis, immersed himself in the music of Woody Guthrie, and took off on the road, eventually landing in New York, where he installed himself in Greenwich Village. He soon became a folk sensation. He is largely credited with transforming American popular music into a serious, thoughtful, even poetic venue. His early music was closely associated with the social unrest of the 1960s—the civil rights movement, the anti–Vietnam War movement, the student movement—and many young people considered him to be the voice of their generation. In a dramatic and controversial move, he began performing with an electric guitar in 1965, and he has reinvented himself a number of times since.

T. S. (Thomas Stearns) Eliot (*1888–1965*) T. S. Eliot was born in St. Louis, Missouri, into a New England family. His grandfather founded Washington University and the first Unitarian Church in St. Louis. Eliot traveled to New England for college, received his BA and MA from Harvard, but eventually abandoned his doctoral studies in philosophy. He went to England in 1914, read Greek philosophy at Oxford, and published "The Love Song of J. Alfred Prufrock" the next year, with Ezra Pound's help. Eliot became a British citizen in 1927, and, in that same year, he shocked many of his fellow modernists by declaring that he had become a "classicist in literature, royalist in politics, and Anglo-Catholic in religion." Accordingly, his later works explore religious questions in a quieter idiom. Working for the publishing house of Faber & Faber in London, Eliot helped publish a number of young poets and eventually became the director of the firm. His unhappy marriage to Vivienne Haigh-Wood ended in 1933, and he married Valerie Fletcher in 1956. Eliot was awarded the Nobel Prize for Literature in 1948.

Thomas Sayers Ellis (*b. 1963*) Ellis was born and raised in the District of Columbia and earned an MFA from Brown University. He has published two books of poems by Graywolf Press: *The Maverick Room: Poems* (2005) and *Skin Inc.: Identity Repair Poems* (2010). A serious percussionist as well as a photographer, Ellis has performed in an documented D.C.'s Go-Go scene, a genre of live music that combines rhythm and blues, hip hop, and call-and-response interaction with audiences. Ellis teaches writing at Sarah Lawrence College in New York.

Louise Erdrich (*b. 1954*) Erdrich is the daughter of a French Ojibwa mother and a German-American father; the eldest of seven children, she grew up in North Dakota near the Turtle Mountain Reservation. Both of her parents taught at a Bureau of Indian Affairs school in an era when the primary aim of these schools was to acculturate their Native American pupils. Erdrich recalls that while she was growing up her mother read stories out loud and her father regularly recited poetry. She attended public schools until she enrolled at Dartmouth College in 1972 as part of the school's first coeducational class. During her junior year, she published a poem in *Ms.* magazine and won the American Academy of Poets Prize. After graduating from Dartmouth, Erdrich taught poetry and writing to young people through a position at the State Arts Council of North Dakota. Later on, she devoted herself full time to her own writing, working to support herself until she was able to live on what she earned from her poems and novels. Erdrich's novel *The Round House* won the 2012 National Book Award for Fiction.

Martín Espada (*b. 1957*) With a degree in law from Northeastern University, Espada has long represented tenants and championed their rights, an ethic evident in his poetry, essays, and many edited volumes. He enjoys a reputation as the voice of immigrant, Latino, and working-class America. He has won dozens of awards, including fellowships from the Guggenheim Foundation and the National Endowment for the Arts, and a Pushcart Prize. Espada teaches at the University of Masschusetts–Amherst.

Nikky Finney (*b. 1957*) Lynn Carole Finney grew up in South Carolina, graduated from Talladega College, moved the west coast, and pursued photography as a vocation. She majored in African American Studies at

Atlanta University, but continued writing poetry, and her first book, *On Wings Made of Gauze*, was published in 2005. Finney works extensively with two poetry organizations, Affrilachian Poets and the Cave Canem Foundation, which both support black poets. She taught for many years at the University of Kentucky, and her most recent book of poems, *Head Off & Split: Poems* (2011) won the National Book Award.

Carolyn Forché (*b. 1950*) Born in Detroit, Michigan, Forché attended the Justin Morrill College at Michigan State University, where she studied five languages, creative writing, English literature, and international relations. Her first poetry collection, *Gathering the Tribes*, won the Yale Series of Younger Poets Award. In 1977, she traveled to Spain to translate the work of Salvadoran-exiled poet Claribel Alegría and, upon her return, received a John Simon Guggenheim Foundation Fellowship, which enabled her to work as a human rights activist in El Salvador for two years. Her experiences there informed her second book, *The Country Between Us*, which received the Poetry Society of America's Alice Fay di Castagnola Award and was the Lamont Selection of the Academy of American Poets. In March 1994, Forche's third book of poetry, *The Angel of History*, received *The Los Angeles Times* Book Award. Forché has worked as a correspondent in Beirut for National Public Radio's "All Things Considered" and as a human rights liaison in South Africa. She has held three fellowships from the National Endowment for the Arts. Forché teaches in the M.F.A. program in poetry at George Mason University in Virginia.

Robert Frost (*1874–1963*) When Frost was eleven, his father died of tuberculosis and his mother moved the family from San Francisco to New England, where she raised him and his sister on her salary as a schoolteacher. Frost studied classics in high school, and he and his future wife, Elinor Miriam White, were the co-valedictorians of their class. Frost entered and dropped out of both Dartmouth and Harvard. He married White, and while Frost tried to make his name known in literary circles, the young couple taught in a private school Frost's mother had opened. After the death of Frost's first child, his grandfather bought a farm in Derry, New Hampshire, for Frost and his wife, and the growing family lived there for a decade. Still struggling to get his work into print, he journeyed across the Atlantic to meet Ezra Pound, T. S. Eliot, W. B. Yeats, and other literary figures in London. Under Pound's patronage, Frost's work soon appeared in *Poetry* magazine, and his first book followed. In 1961, well over eighty years old, Frost read a poem at John F. Kennedy's inauguration.

Zulfikar Ghose (*b. 1935*) Ghose was born in what is now Pakistan, and moved to Bombay during the turbulent years leading up to the independence and partition of India. A Muslim in a Hindu city, he eventually left Asia for England, where he worked as a journalist for many years and published his first books of poetry and novels. Best known as a novelist, he moved to the United States and began teaching at the University of Texas at Austin in 1969. His first book of poems, *The Loss of India* (1964), established his theme of being alien to both one's home and adopted countries.

Allen Ginsberg (*1926–1998*) Ginsberg's childhood in Paterson, New Jersey, was overshadowed by his mother's severe mental illness. Intent on following his father's advice to become a labor lawyer, Ginsberg enrolled at Columbia University in New York. He soon became friends with fellow students Lucien Carr and Jack Kerouac, as well as locals William S. Burroughs and Neal Cassady. He and his friends experimented with drugs, took cross-country treks, and worked to develop a new poetic vision. Ginsberg eventually graduated from Columbia in 1948 and went to San Francisco, where he did some graduate work, performed odd jobs, and spent eight months in a psychiatric hospital. In 1956 his first book of poems, entitled *Howl and Other Poems*, was published with an introduction by his mentor William Carlos Williams. With the publication of *Howl*, Ginsberg was catapulted to fame as a member of the Beat generation and as a significant poet in his own right.

Thomas Gray (*1716–1771*) Perhaps the most important years of Gray's life were those in which he attended Eton College. There he met two boys, Horace Walpole and Richard West, who would be his lifelong friends. Gray's feelings for them were homosexual, but there is no evidence that the feeling was mutual. Gray went on to Cambridge, where he studied Greek and history and led a fairly secluded life. At Cambridge, Gray shone academically, emerging as one of England's best scholars. When West died of tuberculosis in 1742, Gray began writing poetry, most of which was inspired by his grief for his beloved friend.

Thomas Hardy (*1840–1928*) Hardy was the son of a master mason in Upper Bockhampton and was apprenticed to a local architect at the age of fifteen. He wrote novels in his spare time and managed to publish one in 1871, but continued to make his living as an architect until his thirty-third year, after which time he devoted himself entirely to literature. He spent the next quarter of a century writing novels. After his *Jude the Obscure* was harshly criticized, he abandoned fiction for poetry. Much of his writing is situated in or is about "Wessex," the fictional area of England centered in Dorset. In Hardy's later years, he wrote his autobiography, which he arranged to have published after his death under the name of a friend. Hardy took a pessimistic view of the human condition and held that indifferent forces—not any divine plan—circumscribe human lives. This perspective is evident in both his novels and his poetry. Hardy is buried in Westminster Abbey, though his heart was removed and lies at Stinsford Church near his former residence.

Joy Harjo (*b. 1951*) Born in Tulsa, Oklahoma, Harjo is a member of the Muscogee tribe and a family of painters. She earned a BA from the University of New Mexico in 1976, and an MA from the University of Iowa two years later, where she befriended the writers Leslie Silko and Galway Kinnell. Her second book of poetry, *What Moon Drove Me to This?*, was published in 1979; it was followed by half a dozen more books of poetry and numerous awards, including a fellowship from the National Endowment for the Arts. She plays tenor saxophone in her band, Poetic Justice, in Albuquerque and teaches creative writing at the University of New Mexico.

Robert Hayden (*1913–1980*) Hayden was born Asa Bundy Sheffey in Detroit, Michigan. His childhood was tumultuous, as he was shuttled between the home of his parents and that of a foster family next door. His impaired vision kept him from participating in sports, and so he spent most of his free time reading. With the help of a scholarship, he studied at Detroit City College (now Wayne State University) and at the University of Michigan with W. H. Auden. He taught at Fisk University for over twenty years and at the University of Michigan for more than ten. Hayden produced ten volumes of poetry during his lifetime, though he did not receive acclaim for his work until late in his life. In the 1960s Hayden resisted pressure to express the activist sentiments that were growing stronger in the African American community and thereby alienated himself from a growing African American literary movement. In 1976, he became the first black American to be appointed as Consultant in Poetry to the Library of Congress (later called the Poet Laureate).

Terrance Hayes (*b. 1971*) Born and raised in South Carolina, Hayes attended Coker College, where he studied painting and literature. He earned his MFA from the University of Pittsburgh, has published several books of poetry, and has earned several awards, including Guggenheim and National Endowment for the Arts fellowships. His book, *Lighthead*

(2010), won the National Book Award. He teaches creative writing at the University of Pittsburgh.

Seamus Heaney (*1939–2013*) Heaney was born on a farm in Mossbawn, County Derry, Northern Ireland. He was among the first to take advantage of reforms that allowed Catholics access to a top-notch education in that province of Great Britain, which traditionally discriminated against Catholics in favor of Protestants. Educated and subsequently appointed as a lecturer in English at Queen's University, Belfast, Heaney began to publish work in university magazines under the pseudonym "Incertus." Heaney produced his first volume, *Eleven Poems*, in 1965. After experiencing six years of civil strife in Northern Ireland, Heaney published *North*, his most political book of poems by far. He held teaching positions at the University of California at Berkeley, Carysfort College in Dublin, and Oxford University, and served as the Boylston Professor of Rhetoric and Oratory at Harvard University. He won the Nobel Prize for Literature in 1995.

Felicia Dorothea Hemans (*1793–1835*) Born in Liverpool, England, Felicia Browne spent most of her childhood in Wales, voraciously reading everything in her father's library. She published her first book of poems when she was fifteen, and others soon followed. She married an Irish officer, Alfred Hemans, in 1812, and in six years gave birth to five children. Then she and her husband separated, and she supported her family with her writing. Hemans was extremely popular in her lifetime, and counted Sir Walter Scott and William Wordsworth among her friends. Her poetry fell out of fashion in the twentieth century, but recently readers have again begun to take her work seriously.

George Herbert (*1593–1633*) Herbert grew up in privilege, attended and excelled at Cambridge, but his bright prospects in the court of King James of England ended with the king's death in 1625. In 1630, Herbert became a rector at an obscure church far from London, where he worked on his poetry. Writing in the "metaphysical" style of the age, he crafted his poems carefully, experimenting with the visual shape of his lines. He died of tuberculosis not long after finishing his book, *The Temple: Sacred Poems and Private Ejaculations.*

Robert Herrick (*1591–1674*) Herrick was the seventh child of a Cheapside, London, goldsmith who committed suicide only fifteen months after the poet's birth. He was apprenticed to his goldsmith uncle, Sir William Herrick. Herrick eventually decided to leave business and pursue his education, so he went to St. John's College, Cambridge. There, he earned a BA in 1617 and an MA in 1620 and, perhaps more importantly, became the eldest of the "Sons of Ben," poets who idolized Ben Jonson. He would have liked nothing better than to live a life of leisured study, discussing literature and socializing with Jonson. For a number of reasons, though, he took religious orders and reluctantly moved to Dean Priory, Devonshire. In 1647 the Protectorate government expelled Herrick from his post for his support of Charles I. He fled to London, where in 1648 he published a volume of over fourteen hundred poems with two different titles: *Hesperides* for those on secular subjects and *Noble Numbers* for those on sacred subjects. These poems did not fare well in the harsh Puritan climate and went unnoticed until the nineteenth century. Herrick was eventually restored to his Devonshire post and he lived out his last years there quietly.

Tony Hoagland (*b. 1953*) Hoagland grew up in the South, as his father moved from one military base to another. A somewhat circuitous route through his college years ended with his BA from the University of Iowa. He went on to earn an MFA from the University of Arizona, and he teaches now at the University of Houston. Reputed to be a deliberate reviser of his poems, he has published a new book every five or six years, beginning in 1992 with *Sweet Ruin*. His 2003 *What Narcissism Means to Me*, was a finalist for the National Book Critics Circle Award.

Gerard Manley Hopkins (*1844–1889*) Hopkins was the eldest of eight children of a marine-insurance adjustor (shipwrecks later figured in his poetry, particularly *The Wreck of the Deutschland*). While studying at Balliol College, Oxford, Hopkins was drawn to the religious revival that John Henry Newman was leading there. He followed in Newman's footsteps and, despite his family's opposition, converted from the Anglican to the Roman Catholic Church. He was twenty-two years old at the time. A few years later he joined the Jesuit order, burning all of his early poetry, which he considered "too worldly." From then on he asked the rector to approve the subjects of his poems, most of which were either devotional or occasional. Hopkins kept most of his later poetry to himself, only occasionally including poems in letters to his friends. Consequently, it was not until after his death that his work was published. Near the end of his life he was appointed professor of Greek at University College, Dublin. He died there of typhoid at age forty-four.

A. E. (Alfred Edward) Housman (*1859–1936*) Housman was born in Fockbury, Worcestershire. His father was a solicitor from Lancashire;

his mother was Cornish. He was raised in the High Church part of the Church of England, but converted to paganism at eight, became a deist at thirteen, and switched to outright atheism at twenty-one. Housman did well at school and won a scholarship to St. John's College, Oxford, where he studied classics, ancient history, and philosophy. "Oxford had not much effect on me," he said, "except that there I met my greatest friend." The friend in question was Moses Jackson, who was willing to be Housman's friend, although Housman wanted a more intimate relationship. Housman shocked his friends and teachers at Oxford by failing his final examinations. His biographers often attribute this failure to the psychological turmoil that resulted from his suppressed love for Jackson. Housman next obtained a job in the civil service and pursued his classical studies. In 1908 he was appointed the Chair of Latin at University College, London, and he served as professor of Latin at Cambridge from 1911 until his death. Most of his poetry came in a creative burst that lasted about a year in the mid-1890s. He published his first book, *A Shropshire Lad*, in 1896. Housman aimed to write poetry that was both compact and moving. His work was influenced by Greek and Latin lyric poetry, by the traditional ballad, and by German poet Heinrich Heine.

Langston Hughes (*1902–1967*)   Hughes, born in Joplin, Mississippi, was a major figure of the intellectual and literary movement known as the Harlem Renaissance. His parents separated when he was young and he grew up with his maternal grandmother, residing only intermittently with his mother in Detroit and Cleveland and with his father in Mexico. Hughes was elected Class Poet in high school and went on to attend Columbia University. After a year of college, he dropped out and began to travel and write and publish poetry. His work was included in important African American periodicals like *Opportunity* and *Crisis* and anthologies like *The New Negro* and *Caroling Dusk*. Hughes graduated from Lincoln University in 1929 and began to travel again, working as a correspondent and columnist. When the Great Depression brought the Harlem Renaissance to an abrupt end, he became involved in activist politics, including the American Communist Party. In addition to writing poetry and novels, Hughes also founded theaters and produced plays.

Gary Jackson (*b. 1981*)   Jackson grew up in Topeka, Kansas. In 2008, he earned his MFA from the University of New Mexico, and the following year won a Cave Canem Prize for his 2009 inaugural book of poetry, *Missing You, Metropolis*. Currently, he teaches creative writing at the College of Charleston.

James Weldon Johnson (*1871–1938*) Johnson grew up in Florida, graduated from Atlanta University in 1894, and was one of the first African Americans since Reconstruction to pass the bar exam in Florida. For a career, he pursued education, first as a teacher, then as the principal of a grammar school in Jacksonville, and later in life as a college professor at Fisk University. He served as the executive secretary to the NAACP from 1920 to 1930. A leading figure in the Harlem Renaissance, Johnson wrote songs for musical theater, poems, and essays. Among his more celebrated works is the novel *Autobiography of an Ex-Colored Man* (1912).

Ben Jonson (*1572–1637*) Poet, playwright, actor, scholar, critic, translator, and leader of a literary school, Jonson was born the son of an already deceased clergyman and the stepson of a master bricklayer of Westminster. He won a scholarship to a prestigious London grammar school where he learned from the great scholar William Camden. He had an eventful early career, serving in the army at Flanders, killing an associate in a duel and narrowly escaping the death penalty, and converting to Catholicism. In the middle of all this, Jonson managed to write a number of plays, including *Every Man in His Humor* (in which Shakespeare played the lead role), *Volpone*, *The Alchemist*, and *Bartholomew Fair*. Jonson was a favorite of King James I, who made him England's Poet Laureate and granted him a substantial pension in 1616. In the same year Jonson published *The Works of Benjamin Jonson*, and by doing so made it clear that he considered writing his profession. This gesture broke with the Elizabethan tradition of circulating poems only among the aristocracy until the poet's death, at which point the author's poems were made available to the general public.

John Keats (*1795–1821*) Keats's father was head ostler at a London livery stable and inherited the business after marrying his employer's daughter. Keats was sent to the Reverend John Clarke's private school at Enfield, where he was a noisy, high-spirited boy. His teacher, Charles Cowden Clarke, took Keats under his wing, encouraging his passion for reading, poetry, music, and theater. After both his parents died, his uncle took him out of school and apprenticed him to an apothecary and surgeon. He subsequently studied at Guy's Hospital, London. After qualifying to practice as an apothecary, he abandoned medicine for poetry over his guardian's vehement protests. The decision was influenced by Keats's friendship with Leigh Hunt, then editor of *The Examiner*, and a leading political radical, minor poet, and prolific critic and essayist. Keats was one of Hunt's protégés, and Hunt introduced him to great poets such as Hazlitt, Lamb, and Shelley. In February 1820 Keats coughed up blood and realized that he had caught tuberculosis, which had already claimed the lives of his mother and brother. He died at the age of twenty-five, with his third book just barely off the press.

Jane Kenyon (*1947–1995*)   Born in Ann Arbor and educated at the University of Michigan (where she met her future husband, the poet Donald Hall), Jane Kenyon is known for her spare verse about rural and quotidian life. Kenyon used her experience with depression and appreciation of the natural world to write short lines that turned dogs, ponds, hospitals, and even pillowcases into objects of import. Called both Keatsian and Plath-like, she forged her own place in a simpler syntax. During her sadly brief life (she passed away at 47 from leukemia), Kenyon published four books of poetry—*From Room to Room* (1978), *The Boat of Quiet Hours* (1986), *Let Evening Come* (1990), and *Constance* (1993)—as well as a book of translation, *The Twenty Poems of Anna Akhmatova* (1985). Months before she died, Kenyon was appointed the poet laureate of New Hampshire.

Galway Kinnell (*1927–2014*)   Kinnell was born in Providence, Rhode Island. He earned his BA from Princeton, where he and classmate W. S. Merwin read each other their poems, and earned his MA at Rochester. But the process of writing poetry was for him largely a process of deeducation. He viewed all poetry as an attempt at self-transcendence, and he consequently dramatized the process by which he stepped out of himself and into other things and creatures. Kinnell fused a life of poetry with one of politics: he ran an adult education program in Chicago, lived as a journalist in Iran, and worked in the field registering voters for the Congress of Racial Equality in Louisiana. He also served in the Navy in 1945 and 1946 and taught at over twenty colleges and universities. He earned various awards, including the 1983 Pulitzer Prize, and grants, including those from the Rockefeller Foundation and the National Endowment for the Arts.

Etheridge Knight (*1931–1991*)   Knight was born in Corinth, Mississippi, one of seven children. He lied to join the army when he was sixteen, fought and was wounded in the Korean War. Upon his return to the United States, he fell into using drugs, eventually turning to crime to support his habit. He was incarcerated in Indiana in 1960. While in prison, he met Gwendolyn Brooks, who encouraged him to write. He had always been a poet, using words as "weapons," as he put it, when he was growing up; in prison however, his craft became a discipline. Following Brooks's advice, he discovered his talent; members of the Black Arts movement, such as

Sonia Sanchez, discovered it as well. His *Poems from Prison* was published in 1968. That same year he was released from jail and married Sanchez. The brief marriage was followed by two more wives, as well as a total of five volumes of poetry that were characterized by their respect and tenderness toward the women in his life. He taught at a number of universities, and continued, throughout the 1970s, to battle his addictions. He died of lung cancer at the age of fifty-nine.

Yusef Komunyakaa (*b. 1947*) Yusef Komunyakaa was born in Bogalusa, Louisiana, in 1947, the eldest of five children. He graduated from Bogalusa's Central High School in 1965 and later joined the United States Army to serve in Vietnam. While in Vietnam he began to write, serving as a correspondent and later as managing editor of *The Southern Cross*. For his work with the paper Komunyakaa received the Bronze Star. Upon leaving the army in the early 1970s he enrolled at the University of Colorado. Before graduating with his BA in 1975, he took a creative writing course and discovered that he had a talent for poetry. He went on to take his MA in creative writing at Colorado State University in 1978, eventually leaving Colorado for the University of California, Irvine, where he received his MFA. He has published thirteen books of poems, among them *Neon Vernacular*, a Pulitzer Prize winner, and *Thieves of Paradise*, a National Book Award finalist. Komunyakaa is interested in the influence that jazz music has had on poetry and was, along with Sascha Feinstein, the co-editor of *The Jazz Poetry Anthology*. Komunyakaa is a professor in the Creative Writing Program at Princeton.

Maxine Kumin (*1925–2014*) Born in Philadelphia and educated at Radcliffe College, Kumin settled in the suburbs of Boston to raise a family and write poetry. There, Kumin "workshopped" many of her poems with her close friends Anne Sexton, John Holmes, and George Starbuck. Over the years she published twelve books of poetry, including *Up Country: Poems of New England*, which was awarded the Pulitzer Prize in 1973. She was also the author of five novels, a collection of short stories, more than twenty children's books, several books of essays, and a memoir. Kumin served as a Consultant in Poetry to the Library of Congress as well as Poet Laureate of New Hampshire. She received grants from such prestigious foundations as the National Endowment for the Arts, the National Council on the Arts, and the American Academy of Poets. She taught at many colleges and universities, among them Princeton, Columbia, Tufts, Washington University, Randolph-Macon, and the University of Massachusetts.

Letitia Elizabeth Landon (*1802–1838*) Landon, descended from a landed family that had lost its fortune, was born into a middle-class household in the Chelsea section of London. She attended school there. At the age of eighteen she published her first book of verse, and within a few years had achieved a large measure of fame and notoriety as the mysterious female poet L.E.L. After her father's death in 1824, she supported her mother and brother with the money she earned from writing. She was among the first writers in England to earn a living as a writer. Her life as a single woman earning her own money was sensationalized in the press, with rumors of affairs and illegitimate children. Such speculations increased after her brief marriage to the British governor of Ghana ended with an overdose of prussic acid. The official inquest ruled her death accidental.

Philip Larkin (*1922–1985*) Larkin was born in Coventry, England, and after being deemed unfit for military service, he attended Oxford University during World War II. The misery of his undergraduate years is depicted in *Jill*, the first of his two novels. At Oxford, Larkin belonged to the group of writers that came to be known as "the Movement." Members of this group refused to employ rhetorical excess in their poetry, opting instead to use more even-tempered, conversational idioms. Though his first book of poetry was strongly influenced by W. B. Yeats, his later works were more like those of Thomas Hardy, Wilfred Owen, and W. H. Auden. Larkin believed that to these people, technique mattered less than content; the same might be said of Larkin himself. After taking his Oxford degree, Larkin went to work as a university librarian for a number of universities, though mainly at the University of Hull. When Sir John Betjeman died in 1984, it was widely assumed that Larkin would succeed him as Poet Laureate. However, Larkin died before a successor to Betjeman could be appointed, and so the author of such colorful poems as "This Be the Verse" and "High Windows" never penned a Royal Birthday Ode.

Li-Young Lee (*b. 1957*) Lee's great-grandfather was president of China from 1912 to 1916, and his family was wealthy and well-connected, even after the communist revolution. His father was once Mao Zedong's doctor. In the midst of political upheaval, the family fled to Indonesia, and Lee was born in Jakarta in 1957. Oppression of the Chinese minority in that city set the family on an odyssey that ended in the mid-1960s in a small Pennsylvania town, where Lee's father became pastor of the Presbyterian church. Lee studied at the University of Pittsburgh, the University of Arizona, and the State University of New York at Brockport. He has published *The Rose* and *The City in Which I Love You*, both books of poetry, and *The Winged Seed*, a critically acclaimed memoir.

Robert Lowell (*1917–1977*) Lowell came from a well-established New England family. He took a dim view of his family, though, and published an unattractive portrait of it in one of his later books, *Life Studies*. Lowell's life was turbulent, in great part because he suffered from manic depression. He attended St. Mark's School, then enrolled in Harvard where he studied English literature for two years before abruptly transferring to Kenyon College so that he could study the classics, logic, and philosophy under John Crowe Ransom. He then attended Louisiana State University to work with Robert Penn Warren and Cleanth Brooks. He converted to Catholicism and also became a great pacifist, opposing both World War II and the Vietnam War.

Susan Ludvigson (*b. 1942*) Ludvigson was born in Rice Lake, Wisconsin, and is the author of seven books of poetry and two chapbooks. Her work appears regularly in such magazines and journals as *The Atlantic Monthly*, *The Nation*, *The Ohio Review*, and *Antioch Review*. She has received a writer's Fulbright Fellowship as well as grants and fellowships from the Guggenheim Foundation, the Rockefeller Foundation, the National Endowment for the Arts, and the North and South Carolina arts commissions, as well as other institutions. Ludvigson represented the United States at the First International Women Writers Congress in Paris. She is professor of English and Poet-in-Residence at Winthrop University.

Archibald MacLeish (*1892–1982*) MacLeish grew up in Glencoe, Illinois. He described his father as a "devout, cold, rigorous man of very beautiful speech," and his mother, who had taught at Vassar College before becoming his father's third wife, as having come of a "very passionate people with many mad among them." He attended Hotchkiss School in Connecticut and then earned his BA from Yale and his JD from Harvard. He went to France to serve in World War I. In the years following the war, MacLeish worked as a lawyer in Boston. In 1923, having found that his work distracted him from poetry, he moved to France to participate in the modernist movement and published four books of poetry. He returned to America in 1928 and retraced by foot and mule-back the route that Cortez's conquering army took through Mexico. The literary product of this journey, *Conquistador*, won the Pulitzer Prize for 1932. As World War II approached, he served as Librarian of Congress, Director of the Office of Facts and Figures, and Assistant Secretary of State. In 1949 he returned to Harvard, where he served as Boylston Professor of English Rhetoric until 1962.

Ed Madden (*b. 1963*) Writer, educator, and community activist, Madden grew up on a farm in northeast Arkansas, where he developed his love of nature and all things Elvis. After graduating from a small religious college in Arkansas, Madden attended seminary in Austin, Texas, and graduate school at the University of Texas. Madden is an associate professor of English at the University of South Carolina and the poet in residence at Riverbanks Botanical Gardens in Columbia, South Carolina. He has also been an artist in residence for the South Carolina State Parks system. Madden's first book of poems, *Signals*, won the 2007 South Carolina poem book prize and was published in 2008.

Christopher Marlowe (*1564–1593*) Marlowe was born to a shoemaker in Canterbury, only two months before the birth of William Shakespeare. Marlowe attended Corpus Christi College in Cambridge, holding a sixyear scholarship ordinarily awarded to students preparing for the ministry. At the end of his studies he did not take holy orders, but began to write plays. He won fame at age twenty-three with his tragedy *Tamburlaine*, but lived for only six more years. During this time he managed to write five more plays: a sequel to *Tamburlaine*; *The Massacre at Paris*; two major tragedies, *The Jew of Malta* and *Dr. Faustus*; and a chronicle history play, *Edward II*. Marlowe's productivity was remarkable considering his tumultuous and short life. He was killed with a dagger during an argument over a bill in a tavern when he was only twenty-nine.

Andrew Marvell (*1621–1678*) Marvell was born in Yorkshire, England, and was educated at Cambridge University. He completed his BA in 1638, just a few years before the start of the English Civil War. What he did after his years at Cambridge is uncertain, though it is well known that he supported the Puritan cause during the Civil War. In 1650 he served as the private tutor of the daughter of the Lord-General of the Puritan troops and in 1657 he was appointed to assist Oliver Cromwell's blind Latin secretary, the poet John Milton. Beginning in 1659, Marvell represented his hometown of Hull in Parliament. He survived the Restoration and even managed to save Milton from imprisonment and possible execution.

Claude McKay (*1890–1948*) McKay was born and raised in Jamaica, where, under the tutelage of a white patron, he published two volumes of "dialect" poetry. He came to the United States in 1912 to study at the Tuskegee Institute, then at Kansas State College. By the 1920s he had become a figure in New York's Harlem Renaissance, writing for left-wing journals and publishing poems protesting the vicious and violent racism he witnessed in

America. He published collections of poems and novels, and by the 1930s was living in Morocco, where he influenced the black cultural resurgence in the disintegrating French empire. He returned to the United States in 1940; a committed socialist, he converted to Catholicism and spent his final years employed by the Catholic church in Chicago.

Edna St. Vincent Millay (*1892–1950*) Millay was born in the small coastal town of Rockland, Maine. Her parents divorced when she was a child, and her mother, Cora, supported herself and her family of four by working as a nurse. Millay wrote her first poem at age five and as a child submitted her poetry regularly to various magazines. She attended Vassar College through the generosity of a benefactor who was impressed by her writings. She graduated when she was twenty-five years old, and her first book of poetry was published that same year. Millay then moved to Greenwich Village in New York City, where she fell in with the literary and political rebels who lived there. She seemed to embody all the qualities of the modern woman of the 1920s: she was talented, energetic, independent, and liberated. Of course, she was not completely typical: she was openly bisexual, and even when she did marry, hers was a "sexually open" marriage. In the same year that she married and moved to the Berkshires, Millay was also awarded the Pulitzer Prize.

John Milton (*1608–1674*) Milton was the eldest son of a self-made London businessman. As a child, he exhibited unusual scholastic gifts: he had already learned Latin and Greek and was well on his way to mastering Hebrew and most of the European languages before he entered Cambridge University. After graduation, Milton retired to his father's house, where he read for six years. His father then sent him abroad for a year of travel and study. After returning to England, Milton became embroiled in political controversy. He wrote pamphlets defending everything from free speech to the execution of Charles I. When the monarchy was restored, Milton found himself impoverished and imprisoned. And he had lost his sight. Still, he spent his later years writing the masterpieces for which he is known today: *Paradise Lost*, *Paradise Regained*, and *Samson Agonistes*.

Marianne Moore (*1887–1972*) Moore was born in Kirkwood, Missouri, a suburb of St. Louis. When she was young, her father abandoned her family. Moore was raised in the home of her grandfather, a Presbyterian pastor, until his death, after which Moore's family lived at first with other relatives in Missouri and then on their own in Carlisle, Pennsylvania. She graduated from Bryn Mawr College in 1906, and went on to work as a schoolteacher at the U.S. Indian School in Carlisle. She and her mother moved to New York City in 1918, and Moore began to work at the New York Public Library. In New York she met such influential poets as William Carlos Williams and Wallace Stevens and began to contribute her poetry to *Egoist, Poetry, Others*, and *Dial*, the prestigious literary magazine Moore eventually came to edit. In 1921, Hilda Doolittle published Moore's first book of poetry without her knowledge. Moore was widely recognized for her work: her *Collected Poems* won the Bollingen Prize, the National Book Award, and the Pulitzer Prize. Moore lived with her mother and brother in Brooklyn for most of her life.

Pablo Neruda (*1904–1973*) Neftalí Ricardo Reyes Basoalto (he adopted his pen name when he was sixteen) was not one of those poets who remove themselves from the turbid ebb and flow of public affairs. His second book of poems, *Twenty Love Poems and a Song of Despair*, rocketed him to fame when he was just seventeen. Though he published more poems and fiction, in 1927, for financial reasons, he took a job as a consul for his native Chile in Rangoon, a decision that launched a diplomatic career and eventually brought him to Spain during that nation's Civil War. Witnessing that fight between the fascists and the communists politicized Neruda and began his lifelong commitment to advancing leftist causes. In the early 1940s he was in Mexico and was tangled in the intrigue surrounding the assassination of Leon Trotsky, Joseph Stalin's Russian rival. Back in Chile in 1945, he was elected to the Senate; three years later he went into exile when the government cracked down on communists. Eventually, he returned to Chile and his diplomatic career, but after a right-wing coup in 1973 the ailing Neruda died under murky circumstances. His literary output is gigantic, and most critics think Neruda is one of the three or four most important writers in the Americas in the twentieth century.

Sharon Olds (*b. 1942*) Olds was born in San Francisco and raised, as she puts it, "a hellfire Calvinist." She received her BA from Stanford and her PhD in English from Columbia. Olds recalls standing on the steps of the Columbia University library and vowing to become a poet at all costs. In her poetry Olds deals with such personal topics as her father's alcoholism and abusiveness and her own miscarriage and abortion. She has received grants from the National Endowment for the Arts and the Guggenheim Foundation and has won numerous awards, including the Lamont Poetry Selection and the National Book Critics Circle Award. Her books include *Blood, Tin; Straw; The Gold Cell; The Wellspring; The Father; The Dead & the Living;* and *Satan Says*. Olds lives in New York City and was the New York State Poet Laureate for 1998–2000. She teaches poetry workshops at New York University's Graduate Creative Writing Program and at Goldwater Hospital on Roosevelt Island in New York.

Judith Ortiz Cofer (*b. 1952*) Though raised in New Jersey, Judith Ortiz Cofer was born in a small town in Puerto Rico and often traveled back there throughout her childhood. Following her father's military career, the family moved to Augusta, Georgia when Cofer was fifteen. She went on to earn her BA in English Literature at Augusta College and her MA from Florida Atlantic University. Cofer comes from a long line of female storytellers who inspired her from a young age to tell stories both on and off the page. Her work—she writes not only poetry but also fiction, creative nonfiction, and sometimes a hybrid of all three—reflects her biculturalism, exploring the fissures and fusions between her split cultural backgrounds. Cofer has received fellowships from the National Endowment for the Arts and the Bread Loaf Writers' Conference, and in 2010, she was inducted into the Georgia Writers Hall of Fame. Her many publications include the novel *The Line of the Sun* (1989), the poetry collection *A Love Story Beginning in Spanish* (2005), and *The Latin Deli* (1993), a multi-genre work that was nominated for the Pulitzer Prize.

Wilfred Owen (*1893–1918*) The oldest of four children in a workingclass Shropshire family, Owen left school in 1911 after he failed to win a scholarship to London University. For some time he assisted the vicar of a parish church, but abandoned his position after losing his faith. In 1913, he went to France to teach English at a Berlitz school in Bordeaux. He returned to England in 1915, enlisted in the army, and was immediately sent to the front in France. Two years later he was evacuated to Craglockhart War Hospital for treatment of shell shock. There he met the poets Siegfried Sassoon and Robert Graves. Once he had recovered, he returned again to the front, was caught in a German machine gun attack, and was killed just seven days before the signing of the armistice, at age twenty-five. Owen's poems, poignant and technically refined, portray the horror of trench warfare and satirize the unthinking patriotism of those who cheered the war from their armchairs. His poems were published posthumously after his friend Sassoon brought a collection of Owen's poems back from France.

Marge Piercy (*b. 1936*) Piercy grew up in Detroit, Michigan, in a working-class neighborhood. She won a full scholarship to the University of Michigan; when she received her BA in 1957, she became the first person in her family to graduate from college. She won a fellowship to Northwestern University and earned her MA the next year. Piercy began writing during the movement against the war in Vietnam, and since then she has primarily been concerned with the relationship between the sexes. Believing that she voices the rage of women who are dominated by men, Piercy has said, "I imagine that I speak for a constituency, living and dead." Piercy has given workshops, readings, and lectures at over 350 institutions. She lives in Massachusetts, on Cape Cod.

Sylvia Plath (*1932–1963*) Plath's father, Otto, left Poland for the United States and eventually became a professor at Boston University, where he met his future wife, Aurelia Schoeber. Plath was born in Boston and raised in the suburbs. Her father died when she was eight, and her mother assumed responsibility for the family. As a child, Plath wrote poems and published them in local and national magazines. She went on to graduate *summa cum laude* from Smith College and win a Fulbright scholarship to Newnham College, Cambridge. In 1956 she married the British poet Ted Hughes. They returned to America after Plath completed her studies at Cambridge, living for a time in Northampton, Massachusetts, while Plath taught at Smith, moving back to England soon thereafter. They settled in Devonshire with their two children, Frieda and Nicholas. In 1960 Plath published her first book of poems, *The Colossus*, which was well received. Plath's marriage to Hughes slowly began to deteriorate, and Plath moved to London with her two young children. There, she slipped into a deep depression and committed suicide at the age of thirty. Multiple volumes of Plath's poetry were published posthumously, and her *Collected Poems* won the Pulitzer Prize in 1982. Plath is also the author of a novel, *The Bell Jar*, as well as many short stories.

Li Po (*701–762*) Likely born in central Asia, Li Po (also commonly known as Li Bai) grew up in the Sichuan Province in China during the Tang Dynasty. Always a voracious reader, Li began writing poetry as a young man. He left home in his mid-twenties to travel the Yangtze River Valley and eventually found himself in Chang'an at the court of the emperor, where he held a post writing poetry at the Hanlin Academy. Though widely admired for his art and intellect, Li was eventually sent into exile when some members of court took offense to his poetry. After a few years' interlude in which he settled in the Shandon Province and befriended the poet Tu Fu, Li served under the Prince of Yun during a time of political upheaval. Following an arrest for treason and subsequent pardon, Li chose to return to his wayfaring ways along the Yangtze River Valley, enjoying the pleasures of good food, drink, and poetry. His informal tone and precise imagery influenced a number of twentieth-century poets, among them Ezra Pound, who translated Li's work, and James Wright.

Edgar Allan Poe (*1809–1849*) Poe's mother, Elizabeth Arnold, was an actress and a teenage widow when she married his father, David Poe, an alcoholic actor who soon abandoned his family. Poe was born in Boston, and his mother died not two years afterward. A young merchant named John Allan took Poe in and educated him in England and Virginia. After a quarrel with Allan, Poe went to find his paternal relatives in Baltimore and ended up joining the army. Poe and Allan reconciled, and Allan helped Poe get admitted to West Point. There, he ruined any chance he might have had of becoming Allan's heir by getting expelled for missing classes and roll calls. After leaving West Point he went to live in poverty with his relatives. He soon fell in love with and secretly married his cousin Virginia when she was only thirteen years old. Desperate for income, he took a position at the *Southern Literary Messenger*. There and at other publications, his prospects as a writer and an editor flourished. But drinking and depression eventually ruined his career, and he was unable to resurrect it.

Ezra Pound (*1885–1972*) Pound was born in Hailey, Idaho, but he was raised in Philadelphia. At the age of sixteen Pound enrolled as a "special student" at the University of Pennsylvania to study, as he put it, "whatever he thought important." There he met William Carlos Williams and Hilda Doolittle. He enrolled at Hamilton College in 1903 and took a degree from that institution in 1905, returning to the University of Pennsylvania for his MA in 1906. He moved to Europe in 1908 and ended up spending most of his life there, living in Ireland, England, France, and Italy. In 1912, Pound, along with Hilda Doolittle, Richard Aldington, and F. S. Flint, founded the Imagist group in order to sanction experimentation in verse form. Pound advised and assisted such authors as W. B. Yeats, T. S. Eliot, William Carlos Williams, James Joyce, and Robert Frost. He served as a propagandist for Mussolini during World War II, and when the United States captured him in 1943 he was indicted for treason. In 1945 he was remanded to St. Elizabeth's, an institution for the criminally insane, and he remained there until the indictment was dismissed in 1958. He retired with his daughter and longtime companion to Italy, where he spent the rest of his life.

D. A. Powell (*b. 1963*) D. A. Powell earned his BA and MA from Sonoma State University and his MFA from the Iowa Writers' Workshop. In his attempt to "unlock" the "profound mysteries throughout creation," Powell is simultaneously accessible and original. He often experiments with poetic forms—altering his sentence length, word rhythm, and page formatting—and physical forms, sometimes using toilet paper rolls or candlesticks as his paper. Powell challenges himself to write many of his poems from the point of view of the "other" in an attempt to acknowledge unspoken or unrecorded voices. His first three collections, *Tea* (1998), *Lunch* (2000), and *Cocktails* (2004), are poems of witness to the AIDS epidemic and serve as a kind of trilogy. Powell has been awarded fellowships from the National Endowment for the Arts and the Guggenheim Foundation. His most recent collection, *Useless Landscape, or A Guide for Boys* (2012) won the National Critics Circle Award for Poetry.

John Crowe Ransom (*1888–1974*) Ransom was born in Pulaski, Tennessee. He received a BA from Vanderbilt University in 1909 and as a Rhodes scholar received a BA from Christ Church, Oxford. He served as a lieutenant in World War I and then returned to Vanderbilt to teach. During his lifetime, he published three volumes of critically acclaimed poetry, but, after 1927, he dedicated himself primarily to literary criticism. In 1937 he made a surprise move to Kenyon College, where he founded and edited the *Kenyon Review*. He remained at Kenyon until his retirement in 1959. Ransom guided a group of writers known as the Fugitives who were wary of the social and cultural changes sweeping the South and who sought to preserve a traditional aesthetic ideal rooted in classical values and forms. Many of the Fugitives championed the New Criticism, whose methods of close reading are still taught in many English departments today.

Adrienne Rich (*1929–2012*) Among Rich's recent books are *The School Among the Ruins: Poems 2000–2004* and *Fox: Poems 1998–2000* (Norton). A selection of her essays, *Arts of the Possible: Essays and Conversations*, was published in 2001. A new edition of *What Is Found There: Notebooks on Poetry and Politics*, appeared in 2003. She was a recipient of the Lannan Foundation Lifetime Achievement Award, the Lambda Book Award, the Lenore Marshall/Nation Prize, the Wallace Stevens Award, the Bollingen Prize in Poetry, and the National Book Foundation's 2006 Medal for Distinguished Contribution to American Letters among other honors.

Edwin Arlington Robinson (*1869–1935*) Robinson grew up in the small, bleak town of Gardiner, Maine. It was here that he situated much of his poetry. The third son of a family in decline, he had a difficult childhood and a rather unhappy life. In 1890 he recognized that he was "doomed, or elected, or sentenced for life," as he put it, "to the writing of poetry." Robinson attended Harvard University as a special student, rather than a degree candidate, between 1891 and 1893. His years at Harvard increased his commitment to literature. He published his first book at his own expense in 1896, and his second in 1897. His third book, which he published in 1903, came to the attention of President Theodore Roosevelt, who wrote a magazine article in praise of Robinson and found him a position in the New York Custom House. Between 1910 and 1920 Robinson published the three books that established his literary reputation. During the 1920s he was awarded the Pulitzer Prize three times.

Mary Robinson (*1758–1800*) A precocious youth with a promising career in acting, Robinson married a rogue, whose dissolute life landed them both in debtors' prison, where Robinson wrote and published her first book of poems and gave birth to her first child. Upon release from prison, she started a successful career on the stage, became the scandalous mistress of the Prince of Wales (later King George IV), and, eventually, a popular poet and editor in the Romantic movement. She circulated among liberal intellectuals like William Godwin and Mary Wollstonecraft, and was the friend of Samuel Coleridge. She wrote eight novels and an influential sonnet sequence, *Sappho and Phaon* (1796), which reversed the traditional gender roles of lover and reluctant beloved.

Theodore Roethke (*1908–1963*) Roethke was born in Saginaw, Michigan. At six feet two and over two hundred pounds, Roethke was an imposing figure. But he was not as solid on the inside as he was on the outside: he suffered from alcoholism and frequent breakdowns. He earned his BA and MA from the University of Michigan and then spent a year studying at Harvard. He subsequently taught at several colleges and universities, including the University of Washington, where he taught from 1948 until his death. Roethke wrote little poetry, but took great care with what he did write. His first book, *Open House*, attracted considerable attention upon its publication in 1941. His collected poems appeared under the title *Words for the Wind* in 1959, only four years before his death. He earned a Guggenheim Fellowship, Ford Foundation grants, a Fulbright grant, the Pulitzer Prize, the Bollingen Prize, and two National Book Awards.

Emily Rosko (*b. 1979*) A former Wallace Stegner Writing Fellow and Ruth Lilly Poetry Fellow, Emily Rosko earned her MFA from Cornell University and a PhD in Creative Writing and Literature from the University of Missouri. With a focus on the lyric and the organic, Rosko's poems have been called both rhythmic and raw. For her first book of poetry, *Raw Goods Inventory* (2006), Rosko won the Iowa Poetry Prize. Her most recent book, *Prop Rockery* (2012), for which she was awarded the Akron Poetry Prize, draws much of its poetics from Shakespeare. Rosko calls the poems of her forthcoming collection, *Weather Inventions*, "quieter" in style, and inspired by meteorology in history and myth. She is an assistant professor of English and Creative Writing at the College of Charleston and an editor of the literary magazine *Crazyhorse*.

Christina Rossetti (*1850–1894*) Rosetti was born into an accomplished family of Italian-English artists and intellectuals, which included her famous brother, the painter Dante Gabriel Rossetti. She was devoted to the Anglican church her whole life, even breaking off two engagements because she perceived religious incompatibilities in her suitors. She briefly ran a school with her mother in 1853 but spent most of her life writing and as her mother's companion. Her personality melded intense spirituality, characterized by an instinct of self-denial, and a contrary sensuous passion. In addition to her poems, Rossetti published children's books and devotional literature.

Anne Sexton (*1928–1974*) Sexton married young, eloping with a salesman, Alfred Sexton, in 1948. Unlike most contemporary poets, Sexton never graduated from college—her young adulthood was spent as a housewife. After the 1954 birth of a daughter, she experienced a breakdown due to postpartum depression. During her treatment for bipolar disorder, her therapist encouraged her to write poetry. She took a workshop class from Robert Lowell; befriended other young poets: Maxine Kumin, Sylvia Plath, and W. D. Snodgrass; and was quickly successful in publishing poems in leading magazines, such as *The New Yorker* and *Harper's*. She established herself as a leading practitioner of the confessional style of these writers. Her intimations went well beyond even most confessional poets when she consented to have tapes of her therapy sessions made available to biographers after she died. She killed herself by carbon monoxide poisoning. A subsequent biography, which made use of those tapes, stirred significant debate about patient/doctor confidentiality.

William Shakespeare (*1564–1616*) Shakespeare was born in the English town of Stratford-on-Avon. His father was a tradesman and a prominent citizen who sat on the Town Council for many years and served as bailiff, or mayor, in 1568. His parents had eight children, three of whom died in childhood. Shakespeare attended a Stratford grammar school, and married

Anne Hathaway, the daughter of a local farmer, in November 1582, when he was eighteen and she was twenty-six. Their first child was born in May of the next year, and in early 1585 Anne bore twins. By 1592, Shakespeare had established his reputation in London as an actor and playwright. He was a founding member of the Lord Chamberlain's Men, a highly popular repertory theater company, and wrote approximately two plays a year for the company to perform. When city officials closed theaters to prevent the plague from spreading, Shakespeare wrote poetry, including *Venus and Adonis* and *The Rape of Lucrece*, his first two published works, and his *Sonnets*, which circulated privately until a London printer published them without Shakespeare's consent in 1609. Upon ascending to the throne, James I granted royal patronage to the Lord Chamberlain's Men, which thus became the King's Men. After 1611 Shakespeare seems to have retired from the London theatre scene to Stratford. Six years after his death in 1616, the *First Folio*, the first collected edition of his plays, was published.

Percy Bysshe Shelley (*1792–1822*)　Shelley was born in Sussex; his father was a wealthy baron who later became a member of Parliament. Shelley was educated at Eton and Oxford and was expected to inherit his father's baronetcy and seat in Parliament. Not long after being expelled from Oxford for publishing a pamphlet entitled "The Necessity of Atheism," Shelley eloped with Harriet Westbrook, enraging the elder Shelley so much that he disinherited his son. Shelley and Harriet had two children, but their marriage was unhappy. Within three years Shelley had abandoned his wife and eloped with Mary Wollstonecraft Godwin, the daughter of his mentor, William Godwin. More than two years after Shelley left her, Harriet committed suicide. Her family arranged for Shelley to be found unfit to raise his children by Harriet, and so, after marrying Godwin, Shelley moved with her and their children to Italy. There he wrote some of his most famous works, including *Prometheus Unbound* and "Ode to the West Wind." His life in Italy was plagued by misfortune: already ostracized by his family and friends, he also lost all but one of his children to disease and suffered almost constant financial difficulty. Shelley remained in Italy with his wife until he drowned in a storm at sea.

Sir Philip Sidney (*1554–1586*)　Sidney was born on his family's landed estate, Penshurst, not far from London, and was educated at Oxford. His uncle was a duke, his sister a countess, and his father was Lord Lieutenant of Ireland, essentially the English dictator of that country. Sidney left Oxford for a three-year tour of the Continent, which he used to finish his education, meeting important Renaissance figures in France, Italy,

Germany, Austria, and Poland. He was a soldier, diplomat, and a feature of Queen Elizabeth's court. He wrote a long epic-pastoral prose work, *Arcadia*; the sonnet sequence, *Astrophel and Stella*; and the first treatise on literary art in English, *the Defense of Poesy*. Long a militant advocate of Protestantism, he died fighting Spanish Catholics in the Netherlands.

Stevie Smith (*1902–1971*) Florence Margaret Smith was born in Yorkshire and grew up near London, essentially without her father, who abandoned the family to follow a life at sea. She earned her nickname later in life, when someone remarked that her horse-riding reminded him of a famous jockey, Steve Donaghue. She spent much of her adult life as secretary to Sir Neville Pearson. As a novelist, she wrote semiautobiographical fiction, beginning in 1936; her last novel provided portraits of her close friend, George Orwell. Her first of several books of poems was published in 1937. The publication of her 1957 *Not Waving but Drowning* cemented her reputation as a major poet. She died of a brain tumor.

Tracy K. Smith (*b. 1972*) The youngest of a large family, Tracy K. Smith was born in Falmouth, Massachusetts and raised in Northern California. With an MA from Harvard and MFA from Columbia, Smith proves that intellectualism has a place in accessible contemporary poetry. Whether writing about the cosmos or David Bowie, death or a diet of bread and coffee, she pens poems that are both wide in scope and narrow in focus. Her work has been widely recognized, winning the Cave Canem Prize for her first book of poetry, *The Body's Question* (2003); the James Laughlin Award for her second, *Duende* (2007); and the Pulitzer Prize for her third, *Life on Mars* (2011). *Life on Mars* is a tribute to Smith's father, a scientist who worked on the Hubble Space Telescope and passed away in 2008. In this collection, Smith gazes outward at the universe to uncover dark truths about our own present on Earth. She currently teaches creative writing at Princeton University and lives in Brooklyn with her husband and three children.

Susan B. A. Somers-Willett (*b. 1973*) Somers-Willett earned her undergraduate degree from Duke University, and an MFA and a PhD from the University of Texas at Austin. Her first book of poems, *Roam* (2006), won the Crab Orchard Review Award, and her second book, *Quiver* (2009), was recognized by the Writers' League of Texas. She has collaborated on a multi-media project, "Women of Troy," recording the life of the economic recession on poor women in the working-class city of Troy, New York. Somers-Willett has taught at the University of Illinois–Champagne and

Montclair State University, and has won several writing awards, including a Pushcart Prize and the Robert Frost Foundation Poetry Award.

Edmund Spenser (*1552–1599*) Spenser attended Cambridge as a "poor" student, needing to perform menial tasks to earn his keep, unlike most of his aristocratic fellow students. In his early life he was molded into a militant Protestant, vehemently opposed to Catholicism. In the late 1670s, he published his first major work, *The Shepherd's Calendar*, which he dedicated to Sir Philip Sidney; he had by this time entered Sidney's circle, which was patronized by Robert Dudley, Earl of Leicester. In 1680 he began his career in Ireland, first as secretary for the Lord Lieutenant (the English dictator of that colony), and later, after acquiring land confiscated from Catholics, as a proper gentleman. There he wrote his famous allegorical poem, *The Faerie Queene*, the Elizabethan epic of Protestant nationalism. In 1695 he published *Amoretti and Epithalamion*, which included the sonnet sequence that celebrated his love for and marriage to Elizabeth Boyle. In 1598, an uprising of the Irish destroyed his estate, and, probably weakened by the crisis, he died later that year in London.

Bruce Springsteen (*b. 1949*) Springsteen was born in Freehold, New Jersey. During high school he began playing the guitar and joined a succession of small bands before settling down with the Bruce Springsteen Band. He signed with CBS Records as a solo artist and released his first album, *Greetings from Asbury Park, N.J.*, in 1973. Though the album sold poorly, it received a good deal of praise from critics in the United States and the UK. Soon thereafter he released *The Wild, the Innocent, and the E Street Shuffle*, which also sold poorly. Slowly, word about Springsteen spread, and when *Born to Run* came out in 1975, it shot to the top of the charts. The album received rave reviews, and Springsteen appeared on the covers of *Newsweek* and *Time*. Since then, he has recorded numerous albums and won numerous awards.

William Stafford (*1914–1993*) Stafford was born in Hutchinson, Kansas, to a family that loved to read. He earned two degrees from the University of Kansas, working his way through school by waiting tables. He was drafted in 1940 and, as a conscientious objector, spent World War II in the "alternative service," working in forestry and soil conservation in Arkansas and California. In 1948, Stafford published his master's thesis, a book about conscientious objectors entitled *Down in My Heart*. He went on to earn a PhD from the creative writing program at the University of Iowa, and taught at Lewis and Clark College in Portland, Oregon, from 1948 until his retirement thirty years later. He published his first book of poems at age forty-six. Stafford won numerous awards and honors, including the National Book Award, and served as Consultant in Poetry for the Library of Congress and Poet Laureate of Oregon.

Wallace Stevens (*1879–1955*) Stevens spent three years at Harvard before leaving school to pursue a literary career. But he was determined never to "make a petty struggle for existence." After receiving a law degree from New York Law School, he went to work as an executive at Hartford Accident and Indemnity Company, becoming a vice president in 1934 and working there until his death. Having started to write poetry in 1904, ten years later he began to publish his work in various magazines and to attend literary gatherings in New York City. But he had little interest in the causes artists tended to espouse, and so after his move to Hartford, he abandoned his old literary circles. Stevens's first book, *Harmonium*, came out in 1923. Before his death, he received the Pulitzer Prize, the Bollingen Prize, and the Gold Medal of the Poetry Society of America.

Anne Stevenson (*b. 1933*) Anne Stevenson was born in Cambridge, England but was raised primarily in the United States. She enrolled in the University of Michigan as a student of music but soon turned her attention to poetry, earning her BA and MA in English Literature. Since releasing her first poetry collection, *Living in America* (1965), Stevenson has become a prolific writer, publishing more than a dozen books of poems and several works of prose including biographies, essays, and literary criticism. Her 1989 biography of her similarly transplanted peer Sylvia Plath, *Bitter Fame*, sparked much controversy and, for a time, eclipsed her own poetic achievements. Stevenson went on to become the inaugural winner of the Northern Rock Foundation Writer's Award and later received both the Lannan Lifetime Achievement Award and the Poetry Foundation of America's Neglected Masters Award for her collection *Stone Milk* (2007). For Stevenson as for Plath, poetry is the form through which she can "approach her emotional truth." Despite going deaf several years ago, Stevenson continues to write poems that come to her first as "tunes in the head." She has lived in England most of her adult life and currently resides in Durham. Her sixteenth book of poetry, *Astonishment*, was published in 2012.

Rabindranath Tagore (*1861–1941*) Tagore was born into a Brahmin family, part of the upper caste in Indian culture, that traced its lineage back four hundred years. Though India was ruled by England, Tagore grew up in privilege and wealth. Educated to be a lawyer, by the time he was thirty he was managing his family's vast farms and numerous farmers. Heavily influenced by folk songs and culture, he worked in many media, composing thousands of poems and songs, writing fiction and drama, even drawing and painting. His work was the core of literary nationalism that helped the anti-colonial cause in India. Tagore is, perhaps, the early twentieth-century Indian writer best known in the West, which was both a boon and an impediment. Though his work is widely circulated, typically it has been cast in the colonial stereotype, "primitive," as if the writers on the periphery of European empires were less sophisticated as well as less corrupted by modernity than Western writers.

Alfred, Lord Tennyson (*1809–1892*) Tennyson was born the fourth of twelve children to a family in Somersby, Lincolnshire, England. He was educated at home by his father, a bitter man who had been the heir to a large estate before being disinherited. Drawn to poetry from an early age, Tennyson composed a six-thousand-line epic poem at the age of twelve. The same year that he entered Cambridge University, he and his brother Charles published a volume entitled *Poems by Two Brothers*. At Cambridge, he found himself in a secret society of promising intellectuals who called themselves "The Apostles," and published a second book of poetry. When one of his books was harshly reviewed in 1832, Tennyson was so demoralized that he hid from the public eye until 1842. Then he published a volume called simply *Poems*, which was such a success that Tennyson was soon named England's Poet Laureate and eventually even made a baron. By the middle of the nineteenth century, he was the most popular poet in the English language.

Dylan Thomas (*1914–1953*) Thomas was born in Swansea, Wales, in what he called the "smug darkness of a provincial town." His father, a schoolteacher, encouraged him to enroll at a university, but Thomas began writing poetry early in his life: his style was formed by the time he was seventeen, and he published his highly successful first book, *18 Poems*, when he was twenty. He proceeded to move to London, where, in 1936, he met Caitlin Macnamara, an Irishwoman whose temperament was almost as volatile as his own. The couple married the next year and together had three children. Thomas had a successful, though turbulent, literary career. He published poetry, short stories, and plays.

Natasha Trethewey (*b. 1966*) Very much a poet of the South, Natasha Trethewey was born in Gulfport, Mississippi, and spent her childhood between Atlanta, Georgia, and New Orleans, Louisiana. Trethewey is the daughter of a white Nova Scotian poet and a black Mississipian social worker who married when it was illegal to do so in most of the South. When she was six years old, Trethewey witnessed her parents' divorce; thirteen years later, her mother was murdered by her second husband. Trethewey's work often examines the experience of lower class, mixed-race Americans, as exemplified by her award-winning first book of poetry, *Domestic Work* (2000). Trethewey won the Pulitzer Prize for her 2006 collection *Native Guard*, which ties her own turbulent history with what she terms "cultural memory and historical erasure." Her poems thus often combine the pain of a racially divided past with the pleasure of free verse and traditional forms. Her many accolades include fellowships from the Guggenheim Foundation, the Rockefeller Foundation, and the National Endowment for the Arts. In 2012, Trethewey was one of the youngest writers to be named U.S. Poet Laureate. She is currently a professor of English and Creative Writing at Emory University.

Catherine Tufariello (*b. 1963*)   Tufariello earned her BA from SUNY Buffalo (1985) and an MA (1990) and PhD (1994) from Cornell University. Her third book, *Keeping My Name*, won the 2006 Poets' Prize, and her poems have appeared in *Poetry*, *The Hudson Review*, *The New Penguin Book of Love Poetry*, and *Western Wind*.

Derek Walcott (*b. 1930*)   Walcott was born into a mixed-race family on St. Lucia in the Caribbean, and soon proved to be a prodigy, publishing his first book of poems at sixteen years old. At eighteen, he moved to Trinidad, where he continued his literary rise, writing poetry, writing plays, and founding a theater company. He graduated from the University College of the West Indies in Jamaica in 1953. His 1962 collection of poems, *In a Green Light*, established his reputation as a fine poet, and it was followed by numerous volumes of poetry and plays. He has taught at a variety of American universities, including Harvard, Rutgers, Columbia, and Yale. In 1992 he won the Nobel Prize in Literature.

Alice Walker (*b. 1944*)   Growing up in Georgia, Walker and her family suffered the deprivations imposed by a white supremacist government and society. Her father was a sharecropper. Though her mother was a maid earning $17 a week, her fierce determination helped secure for Walker a good education. Succeeding against very long odds, Walker attended Spellman College and graduated from Sarah Lawrence College in New York in 1965. An influential poet and essayist, her most famous work is the novel, *The Color Purple* (1982), which won both the National Book Award and the Pulitzer Prize.

Her enduring contribution to the Civil Rights movement was to persuade people to fight not just racism but sexism, especially sexism embedded in black culture and within the ranks of activists themselves.

Phillis Wheatley (*1753–1784*) Born in Senegal in 1753, Phillis Wheatley was sold into slavery and transported to North America when she was six years old. She was purchased by a prominent Boston family who recognized her intelligence from a young age and taught her to read and write. With the Wheatleys, Phillis led the life of a privileged slave, but a slave nonetheless. She continued to carry out domestic duties but also learned history, astronomy, and geography and became well versed in the Bible, British literature, and the Greek and Latin classics. Wheatley published her first poetry book, *Poems on Various Subjects, Religious and Moral* (1773), at the age of nineteen, astonishing incredulous whites at home and abroad and making her the first African American woman to be published in modern times. She wrote heroic couplets in the style of Alexander Pope, but with shades of religious iconography, her African heritage, and her experience as a slave woven in. Following her freedom from slavery after the death of her mistress, Wheatley married a free black man who worked as a grocer. The two lived in poverty and their three children died in infancy. Wheatley managed to continue to write and publish poems during those years, though her output was lean and she could not find the support to publish a second volume. She died at a boarding house at age thirty-one. Scholarship about Wheatley has surged in recent years as critics today wrestle with the fact that a young woman of color was both famous and condescended to by her contemporaries.

Walt Whitman (*1819–1892*) Whitman was born on Long Island and moved to Brooklyn, where he quit school at the age of eleven to work in a lawyer's office, then a printer's. He spent most of his youth in the printing business, then in newspapers, as a compositor and a writer. He burst on the literary scene with the first edition of *Leaves of Grass* in 1855. The eminent American writer Ralph Waldo Emerson told him in a letter, "I greet you at the beginning of a great career," and indeed, Whitman's career was launched not without Emerson's help, since his endorsement was printed as a preface to the second edition of *Leaves of Grass* in 1856. During the Civil War, he visited military hospitals and worked in the army's Paymaster Office, and two of his most famous poems commemorated Abraham Lincoln after his assassination. Few American poets have created such a public voice as Whitman, so that the speaker in his poems (for better or for worse) is often taken to be the poet/prophet speaking to his nation.

Richard Wilbur (*b. 1921*) Wilbur was born in New York City and raised in rural New Jersey. He graduated from Amherst College in 1942 and, after serving in World War II, received an MA from Harvard in 1947. He was elected to Harvard's prestigious Society of Fellows and used his three years as a fellow to write verse. After teaching at Harvard, Wellesley, Wesleyan, and Smith, he succeeded Robert Penn Warren and became the second Poet Laureate of the United States. In addition to writing five volumes of poetry, he has translated French literature; written lyrics for the comic opera based on Voltaire's novel, *Candide*; and written two children's books and a collection of prose pieces. Two of his volumes, *New and Collected Poems* and *Things of This World*, won the Pulitzer Prize, and the latter also won the National Book Award. Wilbur has received a number of other prestigious awards, including the Bollingen Prize, two Guggenheim fellowships, and a Ford Foundation award.

William Carlos Williams (*1883–1963*) Williams was born in Rutherford, New Jersey, where he practiced obstetrics and pediatrics for most of his life and where he finally died. Though he studied abroad—in Paris and Leipzig—Williams was the most rooted of the modern American poets. His first book of poems was published in 1909, and he then published two more volumes under Ezra Pound's tutelage. But the publication of *Spring and All* (1923) announced his break with the other modernists: he gave up the erudite, philosophical, and cosmopolitan poetry of writers such as T. S. Eliot and championed a new poetry ignorant of forms, stripped of ideas, and rooted in "local conditions." In addition to his lyric poems, Williams wrote essays and novels and edited a literary magazine. A long poem, *Paterson*, crowned his career. When he died, he was working on the sixth book of that American epic.

William Wordsworth (*1770–1850*) Wordsworth was born and raised in a modest cottage in Cockermouth in West Cumberland, on the northern fringe of England's Lake District. When he was eight, his mother died, and he and his three brothers were sent to school at Hawkshead, near Esthwaite Lake. After studying at St. John's College, Cambridge University, he spent a year in France in order to witness the French Revolution. There he became involved with a French woman of Catholic and Royalist sympathies. Financial difficulties forced him to return to England, and he had to leave behind his lover and their child, with whom he never reunited. Living with his sister Dorothy in Dorsetshire, Wordsworth began to devote himself exclusively to poetry. There he became close to Samuel Taylor Coleridge, with whom he wrote *Lyrical Ballads* in 1798. The two revolutionized English poetry with their use of colloquial diction and simple subjects. By the time Wordsworth was forty he had written most of his great work, including his masterpiece, *The Prelude*. In 1843 Wordsworth was made England's Poet Laureate.

James Wright (*1927–1980*) Wright grew up in Martins Ferry, Ohio, a poor town that the Great Depression only made poorer. Upon graduating from the local high school, he joined the United States Army and served in Japan during the American occupation. In 1948 he left the military and returned to Ohio to attend Kenyon College on the GI Bill. At Kenyon he studied with John Crowe Ransom, and at the University of Washington he and his close friend Richard Hugo studied with Theodore Roethke. He earned an MS and a PhD and won a Fulbright Scholarship to continue his studies at the University of Vienna. He taught at the University of Minnesota, Minneapolis, between 1957 and 1964 and at Hunter College in New York City between 1966 and 1980. His first book, *The Green Wall*, won the Yale Younger Poets competition, and his *Collected Poems* won the 1971 Pulitzer Prize.

Mary Wroth (*1587–1651?*) Wroth, the daughter of the Earl of Leicester, came from a literary family: she was the niece of Sir Philip Sidney and the cousin of Sir Walter Raleigh. Her marriage to Sir Robert Wroth brought her into the circle of King James's court, where she became close friends with the poet Ben Jonson. She acted in at least two of the masques he wrote for the court. Her marriage was unhappy, and her long-term affair with the Earl of Pembroke, with whom she had two children, ended her days at court. In 1621 she published the remarkable book *The Countess of Montgomeries Urania*. It was the first long work of fiction published by a woman in English, and, through the guise of an imagined kingdom of Pamphilia, it gave a woman's perspective on English society. The central female character, for instance, the Queen of Pamphilia, engages in a type of soul-searching not normally expected of women in the English renaissance, and the book's main theme attacked the sexual double standard that required women but not men to be faithful lovers. The book satirized contemporary figures and court intrigues so well that Wroth was obliged to withdraw it from publication. She was banished from court, and her later years are shrouded in oblivion.

Sir Thomas Wyatt (*1503–1542*) Wyatt was born at Allington Castle in Kent and educated at St. John's College, Cambridge. He spent most of his life as courtier and diplomat in the service of King Henry VIII, for whom he acted as Clerk of the King's Jewels and as ambassador to Spain and to the Emperor Charles V. His life was not calm: he was arrested and imprisoned twice, once after quarreling with the Duke of Suffolk and once after officials suspected him of treason. He managed to regain the king's favor and received a pardon after each of these incidents. It is hardly surprising that he should write in praise of a quiet life in the country and make cynical comments about court life after such experiences as these. Though Wyatt intended to publish a collection of his poems, he never did, and most of his verse was collected only after his death.

William Butler Yeats (*1865–1939*) Yeats was born into an artistic family that divided its time between bohemian London and rural Sligo on the west coast of Ireland. He attended high school and art school in Dublin, but soon gave up painting and threw himself into literary work and began publishing poetry. In 1889 he fell in love with Maud Gonne, a nationalist and a beauty, and he later remarked that it was then that "the troubles of [his] life began." In 1903 Gonne married Major John MacBride, and as her politics became more extremist, she and Yeats grew further apart. He married an Englishwoman, Georgie Hyde-Lees, in 1917, and with her had a son and daughter and lived in a Norman tower called Thoor Ballylee near Coole. Yeats avidly pursued two occultist movements, the Theosophical movement and the Golden Dawn. His occultism came to form the basis of his complicated and esoteric symbolism. His poetry was also informed by his politics, and, fittingly enough, many of his poems were first published in newspapers. Yeats founded Ireland's national theater (the Abbey Theatre), joined a paramilitary organization committed to freeing Ireland from England (the Irish Volunteers), and served as a senator in the Irish Free State. Yeats won the Nobel Prize in 1923 and is generally recognized as Ireland's national poet.

Glossary

alliteration the repetition of words with the same consonants within a line of poetry. For example: "In what distant deeps or skies" (Blake, "The Tyger").

allusion a reference within one literary work to another literary work. For example, the following lines allude to the New Testament account of John the Baptist's beheading:

> Though I have seen my head (grown slightly bald) brought in upon a platter,
> I am no prophet—
> > (Eliot, "The Love Song of J. Alfred Prufrock")

anapest a metrical foot with two unstressed syllables followed by a stressed syllable. For example: "of the night."

assonance the repetition of words with the same vowel sounds within a line of poetry. For example: "Has found out thy bed" (Blake, "The Sick Rose").

audience the character within a poem who is listening to the speaker, or the readership for which a poet writes a poem.

ballad a lyric poem that tells a story in quatrains; some but not all ballads use the standard ballad stanza. For example: "Sir Patrick Spens."

ballad stanza a quatrain in which the first and third lines are iambic tetrameter, and the second and fourth lines, which rhyme, are iambic trimeter. For example:

> Because I could not stop for Death—
> He kindly stopped for me—
> The Carriage held but just Ourselves—
> And Immortality.
>
> (Dickinson)

blank verse unrhymed lines of iambic pentameter.

canon a list of literary works approved by some body of evaluators; this process may be formal, as in the books of the Bible, or informal and debatable, as in the canons of Western literature or American literature.

carpe diem literally, "seize the day." It is a philosophy of life that values taking pleasure in the present for fear of not being able to in the future. Usually, the pleasures are sexual. *Carpe diem* is a genre of lyric poems in which the speaker invokes this ethic to seduce his or her audience. For example: Marvell, "To His Coy Mistress."

citation a formal way of directing your readers to a source to which you refer in your own paper. Different disciplines use different conventions for citing those sources; most literary journals use the Modern Language Association (or MLA) style sheet for citations.

close reading careful, attentive reading of a work with an eye not just to what happens, but to the literary elements, like metaphor, meter, assonance, etc., that create meaning in a work.

colloquial informal or regional use of language. For example: Williams, "This Is Just to Say."

connotation the nonliteral associations, often emotional, attached to a word.

convention the use of some motif, situation, character, form, etc. that has become customary within a genre. For example: comparing a woman to a rose is a convention of love poetry.

conventional symbol an object that carries symbolic meaning only within a particular culture. For example: in Blake's "The Lamb," a poem written within the Western, Christian world, the lamb represents Christ.

couplet two consecutive rhymed lines of poetry. Usually a couplet contains a completed thought. For example:

> If this be error and upon me proved,
> I never writ, nor no man ever loved.
>
> (Shakespeare, Sonnet 116)

dactyl a metrical foot with one stressed syllable followed by two unstressed syllables. For example: "willowy."

denotation the literal (or "dictionary") meaning of a word.

diction the type of words a writer or speaker uses. The style of words that educated people often use is called "high," while "low" diction may refer to the language of less-educated people. Diction might be artificial or "poetic." For example, when Keats says, "Oh for a draft of vintage!" he employs a poetic way of saying, "I wish I had a glass of good wine!" Note that diction does not mean "word choice." It is a style of language, not the use of a particular word. Paul Allen's "The Man with the Hardest Belly," for example, uses the diction of a Southern evangelical preacher. But Andrew Marvell's decision to describe his love as "vegetable" is not a matter of diction. "Vegetable," though unusual, does not indicate a manner of speech to which the speaker adheres.

dramatic monologue a lyric poem that sounds like a speech lifted from a play; the speaker is talking to someone in the midst of a scene that might be dramatized on stage. Usually, dramatic monologues tell stories, and often they are ironic. For example: Robert Browning, "My Last Duchess."

elegy a melancholic lyric poem meditating on something, usually a death. For example: Gray, "Elegy Written in a Country Churchyard."

end rhyme rhymes at the end of lines in poetry. For example, couplets share an end rhyme:

> This thou perceiv'st, which makes thy love more strong,
> To love that well which thou must leave are long.
> (Shakespeare, Sonnet 73)

English sonnet [also, **Elizabethan sonnet** or **Shakespearean sonnet**] a lyric poem of fourteen lines divided by its rhyme scheme into three quatrains and a concluding couplet. For example: Shakespeare, Sonnet 73.

enjambment the continuation of the sense and grammatical construction beyond the end of a line of verse. For example:

> But oh! that deep romantic chasm which slanted
> Down the green hill athwart a cedarn cover!
> (Coleridge, "Kubla Khan")

explication an interpretation that closely discusses a poem's figurative and literal meaning, often line by line.

extended metaphor   a metaphoric comparison that extends beyond a single line of poetry. For example: Keats's "On First Looking into Chapman's Homer" metaphorically compares traveling to reading through the sonnet's first eight lines.

feminine rhyme   end rhymes of two syllables with the accent on the second-to-last syllables. For example:

> Then be not coy, but use your time,
>   And, while ye may, go marry;
> For having lost but once your prime,
>   You may forever tarry.
>   (Herrick, "To the Virgins, to Make Much of Time")

"Marry" and "tarry" are feminine rhymes.

figurative language   expressions that communicate beyond their literal meanings and therefore must be interpreted in some other way. For example: metaphor, irony, hyperbole, and symbol.

figurative level   meaning generated by a poem's figurative language.

figure of speech   see **figurative language**.

foot   see **meter**.

free verse   poetry with no metrical pattern or set line lengths and usually no rhymes; its rhythms are often established by grammatical repetitions and parallelisms. For example: Whitman, "When I Heard the Learn'd Astronomer."

genre   a grouping of literary works usually based on similar formal structures; works within a genre will share conventions. For example: the sonnet.

heuristics   strategies and techniques of applying general problem-solving frameworks to a particular problem or question.

hyperbole   a figure of speech in which what is literally said overstates the meaning. For example:

> An hundred years shall go to praise
> Thine eyes, and on thy forehead gaze;
> Two hundred to adore each breast,
> But thirty thousand to the rest . . .
>   (Marvell, "To His Coy Mistress")

iamb   a metrical foot with one unstressed syllable followed by a stressed syllable. For example: "the book."

image   a sensation—visual, tactile, auditory, olfactory, or gustatory— conveyed by language. Anything you see, hear, feel, smell, or taste in a poem is an image.

internal rhyme rhyme between a word within a line and another word at the end of the same line or within another line. For example:

> Look left, look right, the hills are bright . . .
> (Housman, "1887")

irony a figure of speech in which what is literally said is different from (and often the opposite of) what is meant. For example: The last two lines of Piercy's "Barbie doll" read: "Consummation at last. / To every woman a happy ending." The speaker means that this ending is not happy.

Irony may be more complex. For example, the carved words on the pedestal in Shelley's "Ozymandias" that say, "Look on my Works, ye Mighty, and despair!" certainly were meant to be taken at face value. But in their present context, on the pedestal of a ruined statue surrounded by desert, they communicate Ozymandias's impotence rather than his might.

"Irony" is also used to describe poems in which the poet disapproves of or disagrees with the speaker. For example: the speaker in Browning's "My Last Duchess" voices despicable things that Browning means for us to disapprove.

Italian sonnet [also **Petrarchan sonnet**] a lyric poem of fourteen lines divided by its rhyme scheme into an octet and a sestet. For example: Keats, "On First Looking into Chapman's Homer."

literary symbol an object that carries symbolic meaning only within the context of a particular literary work. For example: in Blake's "The Tyger," the tiger represents evil, sin, experience, etc. But these meanings are invented by Blake. In another context, an image of a tiger would suggest none of these meanings.

litotes a figure of speech in which what is literally said understates the meaning.

lyric poem a relatively short poem. Every poem in this volume is a lyric poem.

metaphor a figure of speech that compares one thing to another; the expression will literally make no sense; its meaning can be understood only by applying one term's connotations to the other. For example:

> That time of year thou may'st in me behold
> When yellow leaves, or none, or few, do hang . . .
> (Shakespeare, Sonnet 73)

The age of the speaker is compared to the season of late autumn.

meter the measurement of poetry's rhythms based on stressed and unstressed syllables. The basic unit of meter is a "foot." Each foot consists of two or three syllables. The most common feet and their notations are

iamb: [˘ ´] unstressed, stressed syllables

trochee: [´ ˘] stressed, unstressed syllables

spondee: [´ ´] stressed, stressed syllables

pyrrhic: [˘ ˘] unstressed, unstressed syllables

anapest: [˘ ˘ ´] unstressed, unstressed, stressed syllables

dactyl: [´ ˘ ˘] stressed, unstressed, unstressed syllables

Meter also describes line lengths. For example, a line with

one foot is monometer;
two feet is dimeter;
three feet is trimeter;
four feet is tetrameter;
five feet is pentameter;
six feet is hexameter; and
seven feet is heptameter.

The rhythm of a line can be described by combining these two notations. For example, a five-foot line with mostly iambs is called "iambic pentameter."

motif a recurring feature of a literary work or genre, usually an image, idea, situation, or theme. For example, sexual seduction is a motif of *carpe diem* poems.

natural symbol an object that carries symbolic meaning that is suggested by its own nature and, therefore, is the same in various cultures. For example: the sunrise symbolizes new beginnings.

occasional poem a poem written to commemorate or interpret a particular public event. For example: Hardy's "Convergence of the Twain" was written on the sinking of the *Titanic*.

octave an eight-line stanza.

ode a usually long lyric poem, often irregular in form, on an occasion of public or private reflection in which personal emotion and general meditation are united. For example: Keats's "Ode to a Nightingale" is a personal meditative ode.

off rhyme a rhyme in which the sounds are similar but not exact. For example: "stopped" and "wept," "home" and "come."

onomatopoeia a word or phrase that mimics the thing it literally means. For example: "splash" sounds like an explosion of water.

oxymoron a paradoxical phrase linking two contrary terms. For example: "waking dream" in Keats's "Ode to a Nightingale."

paradox a figure of speech in which the literal meaning seems to contradict itself but really expresses a higher truth. For example:

> Except you enthrall me, never shall be free,
> Nor ever chaste, except you ravish me.
> (Donne, Holy Sonnet 14)

paraphrase a translation of a poem or a part of a poem into the style of everyday, common prose. A critic will paraphrase a passage to be sure he or she understands its literal meaning.

parody a work that makes fun of the conventions of a particular genre, usually by exaggerating them. For example: Collins's "Sonnet" is a parody of the sonnet form.

pastoral a poem that uses shepherds as characters; or the use of pleasant images from the country.

personification a type of metaphor in which some nonhuman object or abstraction is compared to a human being. For example, in this line from Donne's Holy Sonnet 10, Death is compared to a tyrannical ruler: "Death, be not proud, though some have callèd thee / Mighty and dreadful[.]"

Petrarchan sonnet see **Italian sonnet**.

prose poem a short piece of writing in paragraph form rather than in meter, but which in other ways resembles a poem. The subject matter and treatment are like poetry, and the sentences, despite the lack of meter, create a strong sense of rhythm. For example: Forché, "The Colonel."

prosody the study of meter.

quatrain a four-line stanza.

rhetorical situation the fictional scene that encompasses a poem: who the speaker is; who the audience is; the setting surrounding them;

the occasion that has prompted the speaker to speak. Sometimes the rhetorical situation is impossible to define.

rhyme the repetition of sounds. For example: "forever" rhymes with "never."

rhyme scheme a notation used to describe the rhymes of a poem. For example, the rhyme scheme of the following lines is *aabcc:*

> Let us go then, you and I,
> When the evening is spread out against the sky
> Like a patient etherised upon a table;
> Let us go, through certain half-deserted streets,
> The muttering retreats . . .
> (Eliot, "The Love Song of J. Alfred Prufrock")

rhythm the musical quality of a poem usually established by a pattern of stressed and unstressed syllables.

satire a literary work that tries to correct social institutions or human behavior by making fun of them.

scansion a description of a poem's meter that marks feet (/) and stressed (´) and unstressed (˘) syllables. For example, here is a scanned line from Keats's "On First Looking into Chapman's Homer":

> ˘　　´　　˘　　´　　˘　　´　　˘　　´　　˘　　´
>
> And man / y good / ly states / and king / doms seen

sestet a six-line stanza.

sestina a poem of six sestets plus a concluding tercet. The end words of each line in the first stanza are used as end words (in varying order) in the following five stanzas. The concluding tercet uses the end words in the middle and at the end of each line. For example: Bishop, "Sestina."

Shakespearean sonnet see **English sonnet.**

simile a metaphor that introduces its comparison with the word "like" or "as." For example:

> Here and there
> his brown skin hung in strips
> like ancient wallpaper.
> (Bishop, "The Fish")

The skin of the fish is compared to old wallpaper.

sonnet a fourteen-line poem, usually in iambic pentameter. The two main types of sonnets are English and Italian. Often they are written in cycles, or sequences, of many poems, and they typically explore the theme of love.

speaker the person who is uttering the words in a poem. Unless you have evidence to the contrary, you should assume that the speaker is *not* the poet—that the speaker is a fictional persona.

spondee a metrical foot with two consecutive stressed syllables. For example: "bookcase."

stanza a division of lines within a poem. Usually a stanza is indicated by white space on the page; often stanzas are indicated by repeated patterns in a rhyme scheme (each unit that is repeated is a stanza).

subgenre a genre within a genre. For example: the lyric poem is a subgenre of poetry, and the sonnet is a subgenre of the lyric poem.

symbol an object that carries meaning on the literal level and also stands for something else on a figurative level. Sometimes, one object might symbolize another object. When you say, "Give me a hand," the "hand" represents the whole person from whom you are requesting help. More often, a symbolic object will represent an abstraction (or a range of abstractions). For example: the American flag symbolizes (among other things) the United States and those qualities commonly associated with it, such as political freedom and prosperity. To some individuals and cultures the same flag might represent cultural imperialism.

symbolic action that which happens to the symbols in a poem: do they change? are they acted upon? For example: the jar in Stevens's "Anecdote of a Jar" represents, among other possibilities, human civilization. The "action" of the jar is to take dominion over the wilderness; so, *symbolically,* human civilization also takes dominion over the wilderness.

syntax the order of words to form phrases and sentences. Syntax in poetry is often more complex than the syntax we use in our everyday language, and occasionally it violates Standard English. Such violations are called "poetic license." Paraphrase helps to untangle difficult syntax.

tercet a three-line stanza.

theme the abstract subject of a poem; what the poem is about. For example, some themes in Shelley's "Ozymandias" are "mutability," "ambition," "art," and "nature."

thesis statement a sentence or small group of sentences that summarize what a critic is trying to persuade his or her readers to believe about a story. It must be a matter of opinion rather than fact, and it is the main point of a critical essay.

tone the verbal indication of a speaker's (and a poet's) attitude toward the poem's subject. For example, Arnold's "Dover Beach" begins with a light, even hopeful tone, but quickly becomes melancholic.

trochee a metrical foot with a stressed syllable followed by an unstressed syllable. For example: "hover."

universal symbol symbols that seem to carry the same meanings in many cultures. For example: sunrise as a symbol for birth, or the crown as a symbol of monarchy.

villanelle a poem of five tercets and a quatrain using just two rhymes. The first and third line of the first tercet are repeated throughout the other stanzas. For example: Thomas, "Do Not Go Gentle into That Good Night."

*

Permissions Acknowledgments

Diane Ackerman: "School Prayer" from *I Praise My Destroyer: Poems* by Diane Ackerman, copyright © 1998 by Diane Ackerman. Used by permission of Random House, an imprint and division of Random House LLC. All rights reserved. Any third party use of this material, outside of this publication, is prohibited. Interested parties must apply directly to Random House LLC for permission.

Kim Addonizio: "Sonnenizio On a Line From Drayton," from *What Is This Thing Called Love: Poems* by Kim Addonizio. Copyright © 2004 by Kim Addonizio. Used by permission of W. W. Norton & Company, Inc.

Paul Allen: "The Man with the Hardest Belly" from *American Crawl*, University of North Texas Press, 1997. Reprinted by permission of the author.

John Ashbery: "The Painter" (39 lines) from *Some Trees*, by John Ashbery. Copyright © 1956 by John Ashbery. Reprinted by permission of Georges Borchardt, Inc., on behalf of the author.

"At North Farm" from *A Wave* by John Ashbery. Copyright © 1981, 1982, 1983, 1984 by John Ashbery. Reprinted by permission of Georges Borchardt, Inc., on behalf of the author.

Margaret Atwood: "You Fit Into Me" is taken from *Power Politics*, copyright © 1971, 1996 by Margaret Atwood. Reprinted with permission of House of Anansi Press. www.houseofanansi.com.

Robert Lowell: "For The Union Dead" and "Skunk Hour" from *Collected Poems* by Robert Lowell. Copyright © 2003 by Harriet Lowell and Sheridan Lowell. Reprinted by permission of Farrar, Straus and Giroux, LLC.

Susan Ludvigson: "After Love" from *Everything Winged Must be Dreaming* by Susan Ludvigson. Reprinted by permission of LSU Press. Copyright 1993 by Susan Ludvigson.

Archibald MacLeish: "Ars Poetica" from *Collected Poems 1917–1982* by Archibald MacLeish. Copyright © 1985 by The Estate of Archibald MacLeish. Reprinted by permission of Houghton Mifflin Harcourt Publishing Company. All rights reserved.

Ed Madden: "Sunday Morning, Wadmalaw" from *Signals*. © 2008 University of South Carolina. Reprinted by permission of the University of South Carolina Press.

Claude McKay: "America" from *Selected Poems of Claude McKay*. Courtesy of the Literary Estate for the Works of Claude McKay.

Edna St. Vincent Millay: "Love is not all: it is not meat nor drink," "I, being born a woman and distressed," and "What lips my lips have kissed, and where, and why" from *Collected Poems*. Copyright 1923, 1931, 1951, © 1958 by Edna St. Vincent Millay and Norma Millay Ellis. Reprinted with the permission of The Permissions Company, Inc., on behalf of Holly Peppe, Literary Executor, The Millay Society, www.millay.org.

Marianne Moore: "Poetry." Reprinted with the permission of Scribner Publishing Group, a division of Simon & Schuster, Inc., from *The Collected Poems of Marianne Moore* by Marianne Moore. Copyright © 1935 by Marianne Moore, renewed 1963 by Marianne Moore and T. S. Eliot. All rights reserved.

"The Steeple-Jack," copyright 1951, 1970 by Marianne Moore. Copyright renewed © 1979 by Lawrence E. Brinn and Louise Crane, Executors of the Estate of Marianne Moore, from *The Complete Poems of Marianne Moore* by Marianne Moore. Used by permission of Viking Penguin, a division of Penguin Group (USA) LLC.

Pablo Neruda: Republished with permission of University of California Press, from *Selected Odes of Pablo Neruda*, by Pablo Neruda, translated by Margaret Sayers Peden, Copyright © 1990 by the Regents of the University of California; permission conveyed through Copyright Clearance Center, Inc.

Sharon Olds: "The One Girl at the Boys' Party," and "Sex Without Love" from *The Dead & The Living* by Sharon Olds, copyright © 1987 by Sharon Olds. "I Go Back to May 1937" from THE GOLD CELL by

Index